SPEED CLEANING

JEFF CAMPBELL AND THE CLEAN TEAM

**Tips, Tricks & Strategies
to Get Everything Done
in Half the Time or Less**

RODALE

Because the subject is cleaning, and because that subject often involves a mother's duty, I'm often asked about the influence of my own mother, Betty Campbell, on my career choice and interest in cleaning. Actually, I don't remember. I do remember we had a dog back then, and now that I have a couple of them myself, I know how much hair is flying around my house. I've tried to remember seeing dog hairs in my childhood home, but I can't. Whatever she did with them and whatever I picked up from her about this subject, "Thanks, Mom. I'm enjoying myself."

To Dan and Peggy
They deserve great happiness and have earned great success.

To my friends and partners at The Clean Team. Before them, I mistakenly thought that work wasn't any fun. Thanks to them, I look forward to weekdays also.

© 2005 by Jeff Campbell

Published by arrangement with The Bantam Dell Publishing Group, a division of Random House, Inc.

Printed in the United States of America
Rodale Inc. makes every effort to use acid-free ⊗, recycled paper ♻.

Illustrations, page 400, courtesy of The Hoover Company, who reminds us to "Always disconnect the cord from the electric outlet before servicing the [vacuum] cleaner."

Illustrations by Axelle Fortier, Los Angeles, CA

Book design by Gavin Robinson

Library of Congress Cataloging-in-Publication Data

Campbell, Jeff.
    Speed cleaning : tips, tricks, and strategies to get everything done in half the time or less / Jeff Campbell and The Clean Team.
        p.   cm.
    Information in this book was previously published as: Good as new, Speed cleaning, Spring cleaning, Talking dirty, published 1985–1998.
    Includes bibliographical references and index.
    ISBN-13 978–1–59486–274–8 hardcover
    ISBN-10 1–59486–274–5 hardcover
    1. House cleaning.   I. Clean Team (San Francisco, Calif.)   II. Title.
TX324.C368   2005
648'.5—dc22   2005021291
      8   10   9   7   direct mail hardcover

RODALE
LIVE YOUR WHOLE LIFE™

We inspire and enable people to improve their lives and the world around them

For more of our products visit **rodalestore.com** or call 800-848-4735

Contents

Introduction   v

Part 1: Speed Clean

Chapter 1:   Get Motivated to Clean 3

Chapter 2:   The Clean Team Rules 6

Chapter 3:   Tools, Equipment, and Supplies 14

Chapter 4:   Safety 30

Chapter 5:   The Kitchen 33

Chapter 6:   The Bathroom 48

Chapter 7:   Dusting 63

Chapter 8:   Team Cleaning 79

Chapter 9:   An Encouraging Word 84

Part 2: Deep Clean

Chapter 10:   Deep Cleaning 87

Chapter 11:   The Oven .89

Chapter 12:   The Refrigerator 94

Chapter 13:   Carpet Care 96

Chapter 14:   Floor Coverings 135

Chapter 15:   Washing Windows 177

Chapter 16:   Washing Ceilings 202

Chapter 17:   Washing Walls 213

Chapter 18:   Other Types of Cleaning 226

Chapter 19:   Getting the House Ready
for Weekly Cleaning 228

Chapter 20:   Outside Cleaning Services 271

Part 3: Keep It Clean . . . .

Chapter 21:   Death, Taxes, and Maintenance 295

Chapter 22:   Prevention 301

Chapter 23:   Maintenance Rules 305

Chapter 24:   Alphabetical List of Home Items 308

Chapter 25:   Environmental Impacts
of Household Cleaners 414

Appendix A: How to Order Tools, Equipment,
and Supplies 429

Appendix B: References 431

Acknowledgments 434

Index 437

Introduction

Speed Cleaning will teach you how to do housecleaning in the very best way possible and in the most efficient way possible. And not by working harder. Just smarter! The result? You will reclaim that spare time that has vanished from your life.

Speed Cleaning is the first comprehensive solution to the housecleaning chores that each of us cope with and must find time for virtually every week of our lives. It finally pays attention to the fact that almost no one in our culture is actually taught *how* to do this. We seem to assume that if you drop someone in the middle of a dirty house, she (or he) would instinctively know how to go about getting it clean: sort of a cleaning gene at work. However, for those of us who arrived without the magic gene, *Speed Cleaning* provides the very first step-by-step set of instructions on housecleaning. It's a proven method that furnishes even the most profoundly cleaning-impaired the wherewithal to clean in the smartest way possible.

This book also takes very, very seriously the amount of time that housecleaning consumes and the limited amount of time in which we have to do it. It's about time that someone respected all those hours you spend scrubbing, dusting, and vacuuming. Whatever housecleaning skills most of us have were handed down by our mothers or grandmothers, who were able to do the work on a full-time basis. Given how our society has changed—now that so many women in America are working, commuting, and keeping house—those full-time cleaning methods no longer work. Full-time techniques won't fit into a weekend. Besides, not many of us look forward to spending precious weekends cleaning house. It's like going from one job to another.

Speed Cleaning teaches new skills. Learning how to clean (or do anything else) the very best possible way can change how you feel about the activity. As you get better and better at a task, you move closer to the cutting edge of your attention. (Just watch a kid play a computer game.) As you get closer to that edge, it's nearly impossible to dislike what you're doing. When you learn how to shave unnecessary steps, motions, and repetitions, you'll move closer and closer to full attention. You'll become a pure cleaning machine—a Ninja warrior of cleaning, if you wish.

If you already enjoy cleaning, the payoff is that you'll have a thoroughly clean house in as short a period of time as possible. If you *don't* enjoy cleaning, that's still not a problem. You'll get the same clean house and the same extra time for other activities, and you'll dislike it less.

Becoming an expert at what you do makes the activity itself easier. It's much easier to use a computer the 100th time or to change the oil in the lawn tractor the second or third time. When it comes to cleaning, it also turns out to be easier to work clockwise around a room once, cleaning from top to bottom and from back to front as you go, than it is to make fitful stops and starts and countless trips back and forth and up and down.

Being an expert is also a morale booster. It's downright depressing to have a dirty house and not have the time to clean it. An almost universal lament in America has become "I love a clean house, but I just don't have the time." In this situation, you either (a) give up and get depressed or (b) keep trying to catch up, but never do, so you're robbed of any satisfaction for your efforts. *Speed Cleaning* allows you to do the cleaning well and to do it as quickly as humanly possible. *It will give you back your weekends.* You can reclaim time for other things that are fun, relaxing, or otherwise rewarding. And you can enjoy a clean house in the meantime.

Although *Speed Cleaning* methods have stood the test of time, cleaning products change, are invented, and are improved continually. The first thing we learned was that if we were going to earn a living, we had to complete just about every one of those thousands of cleanings efficiently. This means learning how to get the cleaning over with *fast*. Whether money is involved or not, who doesn't want to get their cleaning over with more quickly?

Those cleaning trade secrets became this book. *Speed Cleaning* shows you how to finish weekly or biweekly cleaning in minutes instead of hours. It also teaches you how to complete occasional cleaning tasks with skill and efficiency. We now test products from around the world to be able to offer the best homecare products available, and we've put that information into a catalog. If you would like to receive a free copy, please call us at 800-717-CLEAN (that's 800-717-2532), and we'll be happy to oblige. That telephone number is also a cleaning hotline, so whenever you have a housecleaning question of any kind, call and we'll do our best to answer it.

Don't be alarmed. We're not going to try to sell you cleaning supplies or even suggest that you might be happier if you change the brands you use. As pleased as we are with what we've learned about cleaning products, that wouldn't be fair. The book is about solving cleaning problems for *you*. But in the interest of simplicity, when we refer to a cleaning product, we will specify the name of the product The Clean Team prefers. For example, for a heavy-duty liquid cleaner like Fantastik, Formula 409, or Simple Green, we'll refer to Red Juice. For a glass cleaner like Windex or Glass Plus, we'll refer to Blue Juice. Unless otherwise indicated, when we list consumer products that we don't use on a daily basis, we are just giving examples. We are not expressing an opinion one way or the other as to their merits or demerits because of the wide range of surfaces, dirt, and conditions of exposure in households. (Besides, their legal department is bigger than our legal department.)

The Clean Team tests cleaning products regularly. These days, manufacturers even send us new products to test. We look at more than just how they clean. First, is the product being tested personally safe? We insist that the products we use day after day be user-friendly because we're exposed to them far longer than the average consumer. We look for products that are nontoxic, use as little dye as possible, don't smell awful, don't make it hard to breathe, and don't burn or otherwise irritate our skin or eyes. No matter how effective a product is, if it causes grief to the person who's using it, it isn't going to pass our test. In addition, we select products that do an excellent job at whatever it is they are supposed to do, and do it quickly. Next, they must not degrade the environment. Finally, if we find two or more cleaners to be equally safe, equally effective, and equally fast, then we consider cost. If a product saves times because it outperforms another product, even if it costs more initially, the additional expense is usually slight—especially over the life of the product—and negligible compared with the leisure time added to your life. (If you would like to know more about any of The Clean Team products, see Appendix A. Catalogs are free.)

Also, we rely on products that everyone can purchase. We don't experiment by mixing chemicals, and we don't advise you to start mixing them either. Some people mix chemicals in the belief that they are making a cleaner that is safer for the environment, cheaper, or more effective. These goals usually aren't accomplished, and in the meantime, scads of precious leisure time can be wasted. Products manufactured by reputable companies with advanced-degree chemists and million-dollar labs routinely manage to produce something more effective than what you make in your kitchen sink. In addition, household chemistry can be downright dangerous. The most common hazard comes from mixing chlorine bleach with ammonia. Every year, a few people in the United States die because they mixed the two. (Ammonia releases the toxic gas from the bleach.)

The method you have before you was developed by my company, The Clean Team—San Francisco's preeminent housecleaning service. Since 1979, we've kept records of every visit to thousands of households in San Francisco. We used time-and-motion analysis and an endless comparison of cleaning products and equipment to develop a method that would save every step and every moment possible. The result is a thoroughly tested system of cleaning without a wasted motion. Besides being fast, we're very, very good: Our waiting list has, at times, been 6 months long.

Part of cleaning well involves choosing the right cleaning products and tools. We have listed the products that The Clean Team has found to be the best and the fastest—after testing them in thousands of homes. We've been receiving tens of thousands of letters a year requesting information about where to get these products. The Clean Team Catalog Company was formed to help make available safe, fast, and professional products for the homes of interested nonprofessional cleaners: legions of busy, harried professional working people who want to get the housecleaning over with and move on to the more interesting things life has to offer.

Part 1, "Speed Clean," is a weekly cleaning system for areas that need attention every week or two: a thorough cleaning of the kitchen and bathrooms, including washing the floors in those rooms and dusting and vacuuming throughout the house. The second part, "Deep Clean," covers the jobs that you don't tackle every time you clean but that you shouldn't ignore forever either: jobs like washing windows and waxing floors. And the third part, "Keep It Clean," has our recommendations for keeping what you own in the best condition possible.

Because of our professional experience, we get to be The Boss for the time being. Maybe you'll develop your own system someday or customize ours for your own situation, but for now, we're going to relieve you of the burden of making decisions. No arguments. No discussions. No compromises.

We clean more than 18,000 times a year. Our three-person team can clean an average house in 42 minutes—start to finish! A one-bedroom apartment takes about 18 minutes! Believe it. And now we're going to show you how. Good luck, and have some fun with the time you save. May *Speed Cleaning* change your life.

Part 1: Speed Clean

Chapter 1: Get Motivated to Clean

Recently, my neighbors introduced me to a friend who promptly asked me a question about housecleaning. People ask me such questions fairly often. But I was just starting this book, so I was particularly interested in her question, and I wanted to articulate an especially brilliant reply.

She asked me how to clean light fixtures that were similar to ones I have in my kitchen. The fixtures are heavy, awkward, and made of clear glass. Airborne kitchen grease settles on them, so they look dirty much of the time.

I began to tell her how to wash such fixtures by hand in the sink, the big secret being to use a toothbrush to clean the grooves that trap greasy dirt. She explained, "No, no, no. I couldn't do that!" So I cleverly offered an alternative: "Put them in the dishwasher." Her reply: "No, no. You don't understand. I don't do things like that." It was as if I were proposing an exotic mating ritual.

So I learned, as I started this project, that people often ask cleaning questions in a style that doesn't actually lead to their doing anything. For years, I had been answering cleaning questions and assuming that people were following my advice, not just ruminating over it. So this new insight was somewhat discouraging.

Then there's the case of my friend who asked me how to get rid of hard-water spots in his shower. I told him to use a squeegee, but he interrupted and told me that he knew about squeegees, and he "couldn't bear the thought" of using one. So I started to tell him about how to remove the spots with a tile brush, Tile Juice, and a white pad. He knew all about these too, and he didn't like this solution any better.

And so I next concluded that people sometimes ask cleaning questions as a form of wishful thinking: They think they already know the answer, but they don't like it, and they are casting about for a more palatable one. Hmm.

Other folks appear to ask housecleaning questions to demonstrate their interest and to feel that they are really doing something positive about their housecleaning problems. They also seem to neglect to make actual plans to act on the answer, however. It's akin to buying a wax stripper and then storing it under the kitchen sink for the rest of your natural life. It's as if the activity of inquiring or buying would itself strip the wax off the floor.

If one is to benefit from a housecleaning question, one must accept, nay, even embrace, the fact that the answer inevitably should lead to an activity, usually one of a housecleaning nature, although it's always possible that the answer could be to move, to sell the house, or to run for the hills. But the answer should also lessen stress when it's time to do the cleaning. It should enable you to feel better about your ability to keep the home front civilized, comfortable, and relatively presentable. Feelings of guilt and frustration should be replaced with feelings of accomplishment.

I once wrote an article to be distributed, as part of a kit, to people returning to their homes after a flood. This was a case where the correct answer to a cleaning question was to move out of the home! Questions about cleaning after a fire also tend to yield answers that are very difficult to implement.

Our teachers told us that the only stupid question is the one that isn't asked. And I've been asked thousands and thousands of cleaning questions since The Clean Team first started. Not long ago, an article about The Clean Team appeared in a magazine devoted to country life. At the end of the article, people were invited to call with their cleaning questions. And they sure did—in droves. I discovered that cleaning problems that *don't* involve pigs, cows, horses, goats (and births thereof!), flies, manure, tree sap, grease, barns, and wheat, barley, or oat chaff are much, much easier to answer than ones that do. That was a real eye-opener.

So. Those of you who are having a hard time revving yourself up for action—even after you have the answer to your cleaning question—remember that there are cleaning problems vastly more difficult than your own. I know that's just like my mother telling me to eat my food because people were starving abroad, but, hey, it worked.

When answering questions, we try to give the single best answer. We avoid the easy answer: "Try this, and if it doesn't work, try that, and then the other." But sometimes a single answer doesn't work. For example, one surface may require a different cleaning process from another, and the only way to find out in that particular case is to try various solutions.

We still get questions every day. We call upon nearly 25 years of cleaning experience, along with the valuable information we learn from our readers, friends, and suppliers, to help people solve cleaning problems. We've learned a lot about what people want to know about housecleaning. Your most frequently asked questions are answered in this book. You can fine-tune your housecleaning to save even more time and effort—all so you can reclaim more of your precious free time. So, are you ready to begin?

Chapter 2 The Clean Team Rules

The Clean Team rules are the ones we practice every business day of the year. As a business, we really don't have a choice about saving time, but you do: You can continue wasting time on an activity that you probably detest, or you can learn a systematic method to get it over with fast. (At least you have the luxury of a choice—that's something of a consolation!)

We formalized our rules after we realized that we needed a way to train new Clean Team members in as efficient a way as we worked. Our first attempt at a rational list was made after scouring the library (surprise!) for literature on the principles of time-and-motion economy.

Well, the literature's formal rules were just that—too formal. But we found that if we sat down and transcribed our practical experience directly into a set of rules, we were coming up with almost exactly the same intent as more traditional time-and-motion principles. So here they are—more tried-and-true than they may at first appear because they have been put through the wringer (so to speak) by generations of Clean Teams in legions of homes.

Here are our trade secrets. We observe every one of them. Every day.

Clean Team Rule 1: Make every move count. This is probably the most important rule, so let's elaborate a bit.

Perhaps you know what it's like to clean without a system. Let's say you are working your way around the room with the furniture polish in one hand and a polishing cloth in the other. You run into a nest of fingerprints on the wood-work. You don't want to spray polish on the wall, so you drop what you're doing, walk to the kitchen, and rummage around for a spray cleaner. It's not where it was the last time you saw it. You mutter to yourself and hurl accusations at whoever else lives in the house. You finally find it behind the bag of cat litter. The cat is eyeing you suspiciously. You traipse back across the house to the fingerprints, at which time you realize that you cannot use the polishing cloth with the liquid cleaner. Presuming you can resist the TV on the trip to and from the kitchen to get a paper towel or two or three, you now feel ready to tackle the fingerprints. You spray. You scrub. You inspect. The smudges are still there. Just the upper layer of dirt was excavated. The bottom layer must consist of some challenging substance like raspberry jam. But by now, the poor paper towel is shredding. An expedition back to the kitchen follows. The TV is looking better and better. . . .

Another common approach to cleaning is more systematic, but it still wastes a lot of time. In this strategy, a person goes around the room once per task. Once to pick things up, once to dust, once to do fingerprints. Once to do the upholstery, and so forth. Trouble is, as I'm sure you're aware, every step that you take that is not engaged in that task is wasted and will have to be repeated for the next task. If you ever draw a map of your actual progress around the room, it would be a genuine revelation. And if you don't do it in the right order, you're in trouble too. One of our customers explained her system, in which she first vacuumed (because it seemed most important to her) and then dusted. Not such a good idea if you want the dust to go away.

You get the point. We've all been cleaning like that for years. That was our grandmother's full-time method, and nobody ever taught us any differently. Add to these miseries a bad memory ("Now where did I put that rag?"), a lack of supplies ("Who used the last of the paper towels without replacing them!"), and a million distractions ("The dog ate my homework!"). *That's* where the time evaporates.

But ah! Relief is at hand. Clean Team Rule 1: *Make every move count.* That means working your way around the room once—not backtracking. To accomplish this, you'll have to carry all your tools, equipment, and supplies with you. How much faster (not to mention more pleasant) it would be to have everything you need within reach—without having to take a single step. That's what a cleaning apron does (see page 18). It's worth its weight in chocolate truffles. And it's at the heart of Clean Team Rule 1.

If you observe this rule correctly, you will stop wasting steps that will have to be repeated. Train yourself to detect even a single step that was made without purpose or that will have to be repeated. And then just quit making those extra steps or movements. They waste time. It will become instinctive after a very short while.

No need to be neurotic about it either. It's more a matter of attention than tension. After a while, it actually becomes a pleasure to try to hone down your movements to make every one count. There's a real sense of accomplishment to it. That's how you turn a boring task into one that both elicits alertness and gives some measure of satisfaction. Also a certain well-earned smugness, because you know you're going to be done that much faster. We're serious about cutting your time in half too: We train people all the time. You can even reduce it by substantially more than half if you apply yourself.

This once-around-the-room rule is not unique to cleaning, of course. I once asked a journeyman painter why he kept a 2-inch paintbrush in the paint tray along with the roller. He explained that instead of going around the room once to do the trim and another time to roll out the walls, he worked his way around the room only once. He did the trim with the brush as far as he could safely reach. Next he set the brush in the shallow end of the tray (out of the way of the roller) and rolled out as far as he could safely reach. Then he repositioned the ladder and started the next area of the wall. That simple strategy probably saved him 30 percent of his time. (I wish he'd write a book called Speed Painting!)

It is true that when we say to work your way around the room "once," we are using poetic license just a teensy bit. Obviously, you cannot drag a vacuum cleaner around with you as you dust. Likewise, we haven't yet figured out a way to mop the kitchen floor at the same time that you work your way around the kitchen cleaning the counters, refrigerator, stove, sink, and so forth.

The point is that you do, indeed, have to go around the room more than once: once to clean and once to do the floor. If there were a way to merge them both into one trip, you'd better believe we'd do it.

Clean Team Rule 2: Use the right tools. Housecleaning, as an activity, has the unfortunate distinction of having accumulated more gadgets than tools. Maybe it's because it isn't esteemed enough to merit the distinction of its own tools. Baloney! Anything that takes this much time *needs* its own tools. Any other task that is taken seriously has developed its own equipment, and by now, you must surely know that we take housecleaning seriously.

As we said under Clean Team Rule 1 on page 6, the major tool in saving time is a cleaning apron. That's what is going to make it possible for you to move your other tools, supplies, and equipment around the room with you within arm's reach.

And what are you going to put in this apron? Well, we happen to have a few suggestions. First, you should carry a set of three tools adaptable enough to be useful in all sorts of circumstances and in all sorts of room in the house: a heroic version of a toothbrush, a single-edge razor blade in a holder, and a small scraper or putty knife. We'll describe these items in detail in the next chapter.

The rest of the stuff in the apron will be supplies (e.g., furniture polish) and equipment (e.g., cleaning cloths) needed to get the job done. Also lined pockets for debris or a wet sponge. It's that simple. But it took us 4 to 5 years to get it that simple—after dozens of design changes to make the apron's seven pockets and two loops work just right.

Clean Team Rule 3: Work from top to bottom. Every once in a while, some brave souls announce a breakthrough in cleaning: Centuries of common wisdom are wrong, and you should defy both common sense and gravity by working from bottom to top. Dear folks, some things are eternal. This is one of them. Work from top to bottom.

Ah! But your active mind is racing to find an exception, and it believes it has come up with a real killer—washing walls. Why? Because you have noticed that when you start at the top, dribbles of cleaning solution find their way down the wall and leave clean and annoyingly visible trails behind them. It may indeed look like you're bleaching streaks in the wall, but you're not. The dribbles are just precleaning modest little paths earthward. Nothing to worry about. Wipe them off, clean over them as you work your way down the wall, and they will eventually blend in. (More of this in Chapter 17.)

Clean Team Rule 4: If it isn't dirty, don't clean it. This rule isn't as dumb as it sounds. You'd be amazed at the amount of time that is wasted cleaning surfaces that weren't dirty to begin with. When Clean Team trainees first tackle the front of a refrigerator, for example, their first impulse is to spray the whole thing head to foot with liquid cleaner. Meanwhile, the old pros size it up and spot-clean the fingerprints, polish the chrome, and move on. The result in both cases: a clean door—but with an obvious difference in time. Vertical surfaces are almost never as dirty as horizontal ones, and areas high up in a room, such as upper shelves and molding, are cleaner than lower ones. So all parts of a room don't merit equal zeal or attention.

Clean Team Rule 5: Don't rinse or wipe a surface before it's clean. There you are, scrubbing away at something unspeakable on the kitchen counter and wishing you were done. You decide that surely all the grunge is gone by now, and you take a chance on rinsing. Alas, the grunge remaineth. But you secretly knew it was still there all along, didn't you? You were just trying to wish it away. Nice try, but grunge cannot read your mind. And now you endure the time-consuming task of starting all over again.

The alternative to this little game? Learn to "see through" the dirt you're cleaning until you're really done, so you only have to rinse or wipe once. Actually, you're often "feeling through," not seeing. That is, keep scrubbing until you feel the actual surface below the dirt—a real change in the way the brush touches the surface. And try to disengage your capacity for wishful thinking at the same time, which is more difficult. There's no hurry to wipe off the gooey mess that you're making. Just bide your time until the area you're working on is really clean all the way to the surface. The scrub brush or cloth will feel different as soon as the grunge is really gone. *Then* wipe clean. You will be thrilled with your new self-discipline, but it is one of those quiet little jobs that cannot easily be shared.

Clean Team Rule 6: Don't keep working after it's clean. (Or "Enough! Enough already!") To be sure, this rule is abused far less often than the previous rule. It's just that sometimes we have a need to keep scrubbing in an utterly useless manner. The point is simple: If you're paying attention to what you're doing, you're going to detect when you've hit ground zero more quickly. Then just stop, wipe or rinse clean, and move on. Otherwise, you're cutting into VLT—Valuable Leisure Time.

Clean Team Rule 7: If what you're doing isn't going to work, shift to a more heavy-duty cleaner or tool. Most of the time, we do this instinctively. If you're cleaning the stove top and come upon a little glob that doesn't easily wipe up with a cloth, your impulse would be to take after it with a more heavy-duty tool: your fingernail. We'll offer some better options—such as a toothbrush, scraper, razor blade, or white pad. But the idea is to use as little cleaning power as possible to save the most time. Then shift to the next heaviest tool when necessary.

You're going to get very good at knowing what tool or product to use without having to throw everything in the book at it. You'll be learning to anticipate what to reach for before you start a task so you won't have to shift.

You'll finish fastest by shifting tools or cleaners as early as possible in the cleaning process. Red Juice (explained in the next chapter) is going to work a lot better and faster on fingerprints than is Blue Juice (ditto). A lot of this will be learned by experience, of course, but it is also one of the reasons we wrote *Speed Cleaning*—to pass along some of our experience, so you can be spared all the hard work we went through.

Clean Team Rule 8: Keep your tools in impeccable shape. Store your cleaning supplies coherently and always in the same place—not stashed in some dark cubbyhole where you will have to rummage through everything to find what you're looking for. If you have the room, store your supplies in a closet. If you have to use the area under the sink, consider installing shelves to keep things organized. Cleaning trays with separate compartments can also be a great help. You can reach in and pull out what you need quickly, and you can also have a separate tray for each of the major types of household cleaning: kitchen, bathroom, and dusting. If you're zeroing in on the bathroom, for example, you'd just grab the bathroom tray, and you'd be on your way.

If you let your razor get rusty, it will cause more havoc than cleaning. If you wash your furniture-polishing cloth along with a rag that was just used with abrasive cleaner, your polishing cloth may pick up some of the grit and start scratching your furniture. If you ignore the funny whine your vacuum is making, it just may burn out a motor or break a fan belt to get your attention. If you store your mop in a damp spot, you may have to send it to the Pasteur Institute to subdue the mold population.

Clean Team Rule 9: Repetition makes for smoother moves. No motor skill that we are aware of comes without practice—good old repetition. To make repetition work smoothly, you've got to put your tools back in the same place every time—both in your apron and in the cleaning tray. And you can't afford to leave them lying around in alien places for the dog to carry away. When you reach for your Red Juice, you don't have time to look to see if (a) it is really there, or (b) it is another kind of cleaner. So it's important that the Red Juice is *always* on the same apron loop time after time. Once you get your cleaning routine down, don't mess with it unless you have a compelling reason.

Clean Team Rule 10: Pay attention. One of the mottoes of the Jesuit Order of Catholics is *Age quod agis*—"Do what you are doing." Zen Buddhists call the same idea "mindfulness." If what you're doing is cleaning, then just clean—that's all. Anything that Jesuits and Buddhists independently discover is worth serious scrutiny.

If you work with full attention, you are working at the edge of your full abilities—one of the reasons that video games are so addictive. Working at the edge of your full abilities is fun. In spite of yourself. Besides, you'll get the task over with quicker, and you'll probably do a better job of it. All by not working harder, just smarter—by working at full attention. Pay attention to the work that you're doing right in front of you. Just clean.

Clean Team Rule 11: Keep track of your time; get a little faster every time. It's helpful to feel encouraged about what you're doing, and the only way to do that is to keep track of your progress. A healthy dose of discouragement isn't such a bad idea either, as long as you have some idea of what's contributing to the lack of progress and then take steps to correct it.

Clean Team Rule 12: Use both hands. Why not, if you are so blessed? Using only one is like typing with one hand.

One client called our attention to the fact that not all folks have two hands. We did not mean to be insensitive—it's just that we wanted to point out that you should use all of your available resources and not leave any such capacity idle. If you are blessed with two hands, reach for the polishing cloth with one hand as the other one sprays furniture polish. Clean with one hand while the other one stabilizes an object. One hand can scrub with a brush while the other manages the cleaning cloth to wipe up. The examples are endless.

Clean Team Rule 13: If there's more than one of you, work as a team. Working in a team has lots of advantages. Foremost among them, from our point of view, is that you get done sooner! Besides, maybe someone else helped get the house dirty to begin with.

Disputes over household chores are ranked as one of the most important sources of household disharmony. Andy Rooney once questioned a statistic he had read about cleaning that claimed 63 percent of all households argue about housework. He thought it was more like 100 percent. We agree. Learning to work together on these chores may get you back not just your spare time. Who knows, peace may break out in your home.

And for husbands who have felt frozen out of the household scene, working on a team with the rest of your family can be the way out. We believe many men have strayed away from cleaning because they haven't been taught a step-by-step, systematic approach—as they have for carpentry or mechanics—and they have developed a scorn for it. In that light, it's easier to see how men in our culture developed an aversion to cleaning. But there's no reason for that attitude to continue now. And many wives are also working 40 hours a week and commuting. We're on everybody's side—men or women or children— who want to learn a systematic approach to this work. The floor doesn't know who's mopping it!

That's it. Those are the rules we distilled from more than 25 years spent cleaning houses—nearly 500,000 times. Read them over once or twice, and you'll find them seeping into your way of working. You'll also be discovering them on your own as you develop the satisfaction of working in a way that uses your time and abilities at maximum efficiency. Like any new skill, Speed Cleaning must be learned, practiced, reviewed, and perfected. It's worth it. The payoff is that you will save hours every week. Hours that add up to days that you will spend not cleaning the house.

But you need more than rules. Rules are the why of all this. You also need to know how to put the rules into place. And what to use in order to do it. That's what the following chapters will do. First we'll review the cleaning tools, equipment, products, and supplies that will get you out of the house fastest. Then we'll go step by step through the heavy cleaning tasks that you are likely to encounter in your home.

Chapter 3 Tools, Equipment, and Supplies

As you know, there are a lot of cleaning products on the market. Accordingly, there are a lot of choices to make. How do you know which ones work? Are there any real differences among products? Should you believe the ads? Should you keep using what your mother used 15 years ago?

One of the first things we realized when getting our cleaning business off the ground was that we were going to have to wade through that array of products and make some decisions about which ones worked and which ones didn't. We learned quickly that there were significant differences between products that appeared to be similar. And many are quite expensive, which makes the comparison process one that cannot be taken too lightly.

And we also learned that several products that were as traditional as Mom and apple pie were just too slow. An example in this regard is the sponge. A sponge doesn't scrub, rinse, or even absorb as well as plain old cotton cleaning cloths. As a result, sponges tend to leave streaks, which means extra work and extra time.

Traditional cleaners can also be downright user-hostile. The old standby spray-on cleaners sold in grocery stores are a prime example. Some are just plain nasty when inhaled, especially in close quarters. Maybe the manufacturers (or public relations firms) think people have to hack and wheeze when using a product to believe it really works—who knows? Most also generate unwanted suds that may make you feel good, but they really slow you down because you have to get rid of the suds along with the dirt.

We began our long (in fact, continuing) search for products that are *fast* and that *work* without compromising quality. Using a product day after day, as we do, gave us an intimate knowledge of it that can be gotten in no other way. That's nothing new—just ask a skateboarder about his or her board, and you will probably hear a dissertation on it molecule by molecule. Before we settled on 100 percent cotton restaurant table napkins as cleaning cloths, we used to buy assorted lots of rags. But the teams quickly developed a decided preference for white cotton rags—by trial and error—because they worked so much better. Before going off to work in the morning, the teams used to pick through the pile of rags with the visual acuity of bald eagles to find the white cotton ones. The tiniest bit of polyester or color doomed the cloth to the bottom of the heap. The lesson was learned.

Experience was and is our teacher, and we are passing along the benefits of it to you. Even without the right products, you're still going to save time if you learn our methods. It's just that you won't save as much. And when you get expert at anything, you just can't stand using products that get in your way—whether it's a lousy fishing pole or an ineffective furniture polish.

What follows is an alphabetical list of the products we use. One of them (the cleaning apron) is our own design. Some are plain old garden-variety cleaning products, but they're the best of their kind if you're going to save time. Others are commercial products not sold in grocery stores. And when a retail product really does what it promises to do, we don't hesitate to recommend it. Where a product has a brand name, we're not afraid to tell you. None of their manufacturers solicited our endorsement. We're only reporting what we've learned by trying innumerable products side by side.

For any number of reasons, leisure time for most of us is finite and valuable. Maximizing that time may require trading money for time. Consider the lowly vacuum. Few of us would feel we ought to save money by cleaning with a $5 broom rather than a much more costly vacuum. But what about a professional squeegee for $10 or a wet-dry vacuum for $150? We believe that the same principle applies. If you get back your weekends, it's worth every penny.

We recognize that our method works best when you have access to the same products that we use. (There are two aspects to this system: methods and products.) Accordingly, you can order just about everything we mention—including professional formulas—through our mail-order catalog (see page 429). At the same time, our system isn't so specific that you must use these very products. That wouldn't be fair. So we also present complete descriptions, so you can substitute other products at your discretion.

This chapter has as exhaustive a list as we could make because we had in mind all of the potential cleaning chores. Obviously, if you are not contemplating cleaning the windows, you will have little need for a window squeegee (unless you want to keep one handy for the glass shower door—but that's another story). In most chapters, we list the specific tools, supplies, and equipment that are needed for the job at hand. Certain items appear in almost all lists, such as the cleaning apron and its tools. Others are highly specific to the job.

After you're equipped with the proper products, guard against the entire Speed Cleaning process being slowly sabotaged because of tools wearing out or supplies running low. We're offering you time to spend *not* cleaning. Get and keep the right supplies and tools.

The strict rules you have learned about cleaning also apply to storing your cleaning supplies. Your tools are too important for you to have them scattered around the house where they could be lost, damaged, or not available when they are needed. If you are going to clean your house in 42 minutes, you can't spend 22 minutes gathering your supplies. We'll tell you where each item is stored and who uses it in the kitchen, bathroom, and dusting chapters.

Finally, if you're concerned about the environmental impact of the products you use, read Chapter 25 before making your final choices.

Acrylic floor finish. It may be easier to say "acrylic wax," but it really isn't a wax. It's more like liquid plastic. Accordingly, it is not something you would want to put on wood floors (*that's* what you want liquid wax for). Acrylic finish is suitable for resilient flooring such as sheet vinyl. We use a professional formula, called Acrylic High-Gloss Floor Finish, which is detergent-resistant and can be buffed to a high shine. To maintain it, it should be swept and damp-mopped. The idea is to keep as thin a layer as possible on the floor to avoid yellowing and stripping.

Alcohol. It's not often used for regular housecleaning, but since it's used regularly in maintenance cleaning, especially on electronics equipment, here's a bit more information about it. Household alcohol (aka rubbing alcohol, isopropyl alcohol, and/or denatured alcohol), although okay for cleaning jobs that call for the use of alcohol, is not the best choice because it's only around 70 percent alcohol: 90 percent or 95 percent alcohol has fewer impurities, will leave less residue, and is better for cleaning. Purer alcohol formulations are also available at drugstores for just a little more money. These are all nondrinkable (denatured) varieties of alcohol, but according to audio expert Lewis Downs, vodka is also a very pure alcohol and can be used for cleaning jobs in a pinch. Finally, even though it may not be noticeable to you, alcohol ultimately dries out rubber, so try to avoid rubber parts when cleaning with alcohol, or at least use very small amounts of it on or around rubber. Better yet, purchase a specialized product such as TASCAM RC rubber cleaner.

Ammonia. We use clear ammonia only, never "sudsy" or "detergent." There is no need whatsoever for suds to help convince you that what you're doing is working. They just get in the way. Ammonia is one of the fundamental cleaning agents. Used to maintain floors not suited to cleaner/polisher, it's found in all sorts of cleaners—such as brass polish, wax stripper, and glass cleaner.

Bleach (in a spray bottle). Use primarily to kill mold and mildew in the bathroom. If it's available in your area, we recommend Clorox Fresh Scent because it has a far less disagreeable odor than standard bleach. It's important to keep bleach stored in an opaque bottle. If light gets through to it, it can turn the product black. Also, as you must know, bleach must be treated as though it were radioactive. It will obliterate the color of almost anything—including some types of floor tile. It can even eat through stainless-steel pots if left in place long enough. (Don't ask. That was a memorable experience.)

We use Clorox either full strength or half strength diluted with water, depending on the severity of the mold population and the durability of the surface. Hospitals use bleach diluted even more as a disinfectant, so it is a very effective product. Naturally, you must be diligent not to breathe in its fumes. We usually do a spray-and-run operation in a bathroom, closing the door behind us and keeping a window open. Rinse a surface well after bleach has done its job, so it doesn't go to work on the surface itself or doesn't react with any chemicals subsequently applied to the same surface.

Blue Juice (in a spray bottle). A lighter-duty liquid spray cleaner. It is intended mainly for cleaning mirrors and glass, and it evaporates slightly faster than Red Juice (see page 25) for that reason. We use a professional formula called The Clean Team Blue Juice. Like many similar retail products, it's blue—hence the name. Consumer products include Windex or any similar liquid cleaner. We keep Blue Juice in a spray bottle with a blue top, as you might have guessed. Like Red Juice, it is always kept on the same apron loop.

Brushes. Brushes can increase the effectiveness of cleaning efforts many times over. They often last for years. Use them handheld or on a pole, depending on the job at hand. Here are some of the ones you'll find handy to have around.

Ceiling and wall: Use to remove spider webs and dust in high places.

Dusting: It's really a good paintbrush, with natural bristles and feathered ends, but don't call it that, or it'll disappear. Use on wicker furniture, computer keyboards, lamp shades, picture frames, molding, stereo equipment, light fixtures, the tops of books, car dashboards, etc.

Soft-bristled: Use for wet-cleaning miniblinds, windows, and window screens.

Stiff-bristled: Same idea as a toothbrush, but for bigger jobs. Used to scrub grout lines between glazed and paver tiles, concrete floors, and patio stones. Also for scrubbing floors, greasy bricks, stove hoods, and many other rough surfaces. One aging former member of The Clean Team with arthritic knees and a touchy back swears by this brush: Attached to a long handle with a 360-degree swivel head, it can scrub surfaces without the operator having to bend over or kneel down.

Carryall tray. Permanent storage for cleaning supplies. It makes good sense to keep your supplies organized between uses, so we recommend a carryall tray with steep sides (so things won't fall out) and separate compartments. If you're going to get the job over with in a hurry, you can't afford to root around in the dark under the sink for 20 minutes looking for supplies. It also makes it easy to transport supplies to the site for a major cleaning operation.

Cleaning apron. The first time we cleaned a house, we showed up at the door with grocery bags full of cleaning products. (We've come a long way, baby.) It soon became crystal clear that dozens of trips back and forth to these bags for supplies was not going to cut the mustard. We had to carry around what we needed as we cleaned. After a certain amount of head-scratching, we designed our first cleaning apron.

Nothing makes sense in this system without an apron. It saves more time than all the other products combined. It carries the supplies and tools that allow you to "walk around the room once, and you're done" (see Clean Team Rule 1 on page 6). If you're mad at having to wear one, especially with all this stuff packed into it and dangling from it, go ahead and have your tantrum. Then get over it. *Wear it when cleaning—start to finish.*

When's the last time you saw carpenters work without aprons? Do you think they're going to run up and down their ladders every time they need more nails? Telephone linemen have more stuff hanging off them than a Christmas tree does. Isn't it about time such a basic idea was applied to something that *you're* doing so many days of your life? We sure think so, and we've developed the first commercially available cleaning apron that we're aware of.

Over a period of years, we've fidgeted with the position of every pocket and every loop, how many of each pocket there are going to be, what size they're going to be, and how to keep the loops open so you can hang the handle of the spray bottles with ease. If any of these variables are off, the apron will be uncomfortable and less efficient.

Yeah, yeah. We've heard all the arguments. There were yowls of protest from the teams when we first introduced them: "Men do not wear aprons." (What are carpenters—sissies?) "It feels awkward." (Get over it.) "It gets in the way." (Well, yes, it does, at first. Then it doesn't. Life's like that.) "Things will fall out." (No, they won't, if you stay awake.) "It will scare the cat." (Let the cat outside.) "The neighbors will laugh." (Wave to them as you drive away to the beach while they're still cleaning.)

Just wait. If you give it a fighting chance, you'll soon feel lost without it, and you'll even have temper tantrums if someone messes with it or walks off with it.

The Clean Team uses our own special aprons, featured in the illustration below. You can make your own apron too: Just be sure it has lots of pockets for your tools, loops for your Red and Blue Juice, and will tie securely around your waist. Wear it every time you clean!

We haven't seen or heard about a store-bought apron that works as a substitute. They range from a frilly full-length production to a leather carpenter's apron, with a few styles in between. The apron material shouldn't be stiff enough to interfere with bending over. It must be machine-washable. It must also have loops at both sides that will stay open so you can hang spray cleaners from them smoothly.

A smart way to tie the apron on is to put it on backward, tie it, and turn it around. The Clean Team apron has seven pockets, three of which are dedicated to the toothbrush, razor-blade holder, and scraper. A fourth pocket is used as a temporary storage for debris you encounter while cleaning. This saves extra trips to the trash. Use a gallon-size Ziploc storage bag as a liner and heavy-duty paper clips to keep it in place. If you're working with damp rags or scrub pads, you can also line another pocket with a second plastic bag.

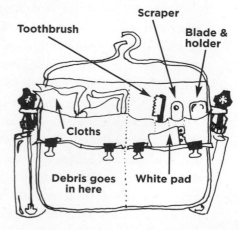

Cleaning cloths. Besides the apron, good cleaning cloths are the next best way to cut your cleaning time down. Somewhere, we've read that contemporary homemakers actually spend *more* time than our grandparents taking care of the house. One of the reasons is that we've become accustomed to modern gadgetry that occasionally is less efficient than its predecessor. The feather duster is one example of a more efficient item that's often been replaced needlessly. Cleaning cloths are another. They're more practical than sponges for several reasons: You can scrub with them, they rinse much faster, they often absorb liquids faster, and they last much longer.

There is only one acceptable type of cleaning cloth: 100 percent cotton. White. Hemmed. Period. No polyester. No colored cloth, especially *red!* Red dye will wipe off onto surfaces in front of your very eyes. (Do you want to hear the horror story about the owner of a Nob Hill mansion who cleaned her white walls with red rags? No, you don't.)

After considerable research with the alternatives, we settled upon white table napkins. They're just the right size, they're hemmed, they're white, and they're usually 100 percent cotton. They're also expensive, but they'll last for *years* under reasonable household use. Or, you may be able to find used table napkins at a local linen service. So in the long run, they're actually cost-effective.

Don't substitute! Retire those old T-shirts, underwear, socks or hosiery, sheets, and most especially newspapers. Trying to use them to clean will make work and waste time. Keep a supply large enough that you will not run out once you've started to clean. When they are too worn for general use, use them on the oven or other heavy-duty jobs and discard them. Notice that we call them "cleaning cloths" so as not to suggest they're in tatters. We use retired cotton napkins that show some signs of wear, but they stop far short of being rags. We wash them in hot water with a liquid detergent and chlorine bleach to sanitize them.

Here are a few simple diagrams on the proper folding of your cleaning cloths. Why are we bothering to delve into something so mundane? For starters, we don't want you to wad up the cloths into nasty piles and mush them into the carryall tray. When you reach for one later on, a whole bunch of them will leap out of the tray. Besides, all you will have is an unruly mass of wrinkles that will need managing before you can proceed. In addition, if you fold them properly and line them up in the carryall tray, you will have an exact idea of how many cloths you have left. And you will be very pleased with yourself.

The next best alternative to table napkins are 100 percent cotton unfolded diapers (with hems, if possible). Salesclerks will give you strained, pitying looks

Fold in half   **Fold again**   **Fold top to bottom**

when you ask for them in stores because throwaway diapers have dominated the market for several years. But if you have trouble locating a retail supply, we understand that the Sears mail-order catalog still carries them. Don't get the prefolded kind.

The third alternative is paper towels. Some people do not appreciate the inconvenience of washing the cleaning cloths, or may prefer paper towels for other reasons. If you want to use them, get the best. No point in saving 40 cents only to have the paper towel shred and leave lint everywhere. Our vote is for Bounty paper towels.

Whatever your choice, we will refer to them as "cleaning cloths" from now on.

Double bucket. The perfect bucket for cleaning windows. You can keep supplies in one side and the washing solution in the other. It can also be put to splendid use on floors by having the washing or stripping solution in one side and the rinsing solution in the other.

Feather duster. We are well aware of the purists who insist that feather dusters only move the dust around and don't get rid of it. We agree wholeheartedly that dust does need to be controlled in the home as much as possible. In some cases, this can mean wiping the dust up with furniture polish and a cloth, or washing baseboards, or vacuuming shelves. However, when maintaining a basically clean home on a regular basis, moving a small amount of dust very quickly from one (higher) level to another (lower) level where most of it is vacuumed away is a decidedly good thing. And a good feather duster happens to do this better than anything else. Get an air purifier if you are kept awake at night wondering what happened to all the dust.

The only feather duster that works is made with real feathers—ostrich down to be exact. Down feathers are full, soft, and almost spiderweb-like at the ends. The feather duster we use is 18 inches long (including the handle). They're expensive, and they're worth it. When you see how they cut your cleaning time in half, you'll appreciate how valuable they are.

Fifty-foot extension cord on a cord caddy. Every time you run out of cord while vacuuming you have to walk back across the house, pull the plug, mutter to yourself, find another plug, walk back to the vacuum, and wonder if you're going to make it to the end of the hall without doing it all over again. Besides being exasperating, this is a glorious waste of time. The solution is simple: a long extension cord that you plug in once only. We use a round cord because it generates fewer knots than a flat cord, and if there are knots, they are easier to unravel. One fine rip-snorter of a knot can take as long to unravel as it takes to vacuum a whole room, so avoid them at all reasonable costs. Instead of allowing the cord to degenerate into a nest in between uses, we wrap it around a portable rack or caddy. And when we get to work, we unravel only as much cord as we expect to use for that job.

Floor cleaner/polisher. We use Brite. The coating that it leaves is water-soluble, so it doesn't build up over time.

Floor scrub brush. You know that annoying feeling when you watch the sponge mop gliiiide over dead raisins or unidentified but nevertheless sticky globs on the floor? And then it just gliiiides over them again . . . and again . . . and again? Or have you noticed how the mop manages merely to shuffle the dirt into the cracks or the grout or the fake grout? What you need is a giant version of the toothbrush. What the toothbrush is to countertops, this brush is to floors. It slides into the end of our mop after the sponge mop is removed, or else it just screws into the end of a standard threaded broom handle. It enables you to power-scrub the floor and cut time to shreds. Whatever brush you use—be it ours or one you already have at home—it should have tough, stubby, thick bristles set in a sturdy base, so you can apply pressure when needed.

Furniture feeder. A suspension of carnauba wax and restorative agents in a solvent base. An application or two of furniture feeder, and you'll swear you just revarnished your neglected possessions. It removes dirt, grime, oil, cooking vapors, and that nasty wax buildup, leaving a warm sheen of fine carnauba wax.

Furniture polishing cloth. You know, those yellow things you see in the stores—but get the untreated ones if you can. Use only for furniture polishing—not with Blue Juice or Red Juice. Don't wash in the same load with cloths that have wiped up powdered cleanser. The cleanser can be absorbed by the polishing cloth and scratch furniture.

Green scrub pad/sponge ("green pad"). This is the heavy artillery in the war on dirt. It will scratch anything that moves or doesn't move if you're not careful. Think of it as green sandpaper attached to a sponge. *Always* use on a wet surface with appropriate pressure. The only consistent use we have for this is for cleaning ovens.

Grout-coloring agent. Used to cover up permanent stains in grout lines. Not a cleaner, it's more like a coat of paint over dirty grout. It cannot replace missing grout, no matter how hard you try. Our product is called Grout Whitener.

Grout sealer. A product used to fill the pores and microscopic cracks in grout, so they won't collect dirt or stains instead. Sealer should be applied on all newly installed grout. Reapply it per the manufacturer's instructions, generally once or twice a year. Besides grout, many finely pitted surfaces benefit from a sealer. Stone, brick, cement, crazed (finely cracked) tile, and other nonglazed tiles are examples. Our product is called Grout Sealer.

HEPA. High-efficiency particulate air filter (often in three stages). A "true" HEPA filter will capture 99.97 percent of particles larger than 0.3 micron. But read the product's specs carefully: HEPA is a term applied somewhat overzealously these days. HEPA filters were originally developed to trap radioactive dust in atomic plants.

Kleenfast pad. Also known as a "doodle bug," this is a swiveling scrub-pad holder that can be used either with a long handle or held by hand. Scrub pads of various coarseness are available, depending on the application—e.g., scrubbing or stripping floors. The swiveling action lets you scrub floors or baseboards at a convenient angle without straining your back.

Liquid floor wax. Unless you have days to spend on the project or a host of servants at your command, paste waxing of wood floors is out of the question. The next best option, in the real world, is to spread as thin a layer as humanly possible of a liquid floor wax. It should be able to be buffed if you so wish. The formula we use is called Fortified Floor Wax.

Miscellaneous. Keep a small emergency kit at hand. Or at least know where the following are: pliers, a Phillips screwdriver, a slotted screwdriver, the telephone number to call in a medical emergency, and a spare fan belt and bag for the vacuum. We presume you already know where the bandages are. Once you are on the job, you can't waste time looking for anything to solve little breakdowns.

Mop. We clean bathroom floors with cleaning cloths, but there's no escaping a mop for kitchen floors or for washing ceilings and walls. We use a serious mop made by Continental Manufacturing Company with a 13-inch sponge mop head, steel handle, and handle-operated wringer. When a piece of equipment is this large, it's got to be able to do multiple functions. (That principle is important enough to turn it into another Clean Team Rule.) In this case, we happened upon a bit of manufacturing genius that enables the mop to swap its sponge-mop head for a scrub brush *or* floor squeegee.

Then there's the "Sh-Mop." A major new design in cleaning is rare, but the Sh-Mop folks have done it. The Sh-Mop uses a flat rubber surface (a full 8 by 15 inches) covered with a removable, reusable, and washable terry-cloth cover. That's 120 square inches of scrubbing power on the floor versus about 25 square inches for a sponge mop, so the Sh-Mop is three to four times faster than even an excellent sponge mop. It also gets the floor cleaner, reaches into corners better, and cleans under the edges of appliances. It can also clean your walls and ceilings in nothing flat, but that's another story. And since the covers are tossed into the wash after use, it's like having a new, sparkling clean mop each time you clean. It comes with a supply of three terry-cloth covers.

No-rinse stripper. Now that you've found such good floor finishes, how are you going to get the old yellow stuff off the floor, you ask? Liquid strippers are notoriously ineffective, as we're sure you will agree if you've ever tried one. But chemistry has taken a few giant strides in this regard in recent years. It had to. Many of the older floor strippers were designed more for waxes in the strict sense than for acrylics or the new "metal interlock" finishes.

But relief is at hand on two fronts: relief from the frustration of having to excavate layer after layer of old finish only to have it seem like each stripping attempt has done no good whatsoever; and relief from the fumes of many ammonia-based strippers.

This particular relief takes the form of another professional-formula wax stripper that is applied with a mop and doesn't even have to be rinsed off. Ours is called Mop-on No-Rinse Acrylic Stripper. If you prefer to use a standard floor stripper, you'll still end up at the same place; you'll just have to hang in there longer and use substantially more elbow grease.

No-wax finish. For "no-wax" floors only. We recently switched to Brite— a retail product from Johnson Wax Co. It cleans and maintains a shine without building up over time, which most other products seem inevitably to do.

One-pint plastic container. (What's left over after you've eaten the expensive ice cream.) Use it in the bathroom to help rinse the hard-to-reach areas of the shower.

Oven cleaner. We haven't found a better product than Easy-Off spray.

Powdered cleanser. We use Comet. Use it to clean inside tubs, sinks, and toilets.

Pumice stick. A chunk of pure lava. It's really remarkable how fast it removes scale, rust, and mineral deposits from porcelain. Just rub gently, and they're gone! Other applications are limited only by the imagination: quickly cleans ovens; removes carbon buildup on grills and iron cookware; removes paint and graffiti from tile, concrete, and masonry walls; removes scale from swimming pools.

Pump-spray furniture polish. We like Old English, and the pump-spray container carries well in the apron.

Pump-up pressure sprayer. This is a device that lets you manually pressurize a spray bottle for easy application of a liquid to a large area. Prevents wear and tear on your hand on big jobs like spraying a carpet.

Rabbit-ear duster. An extension duster that can be bent to mimic the shape or angle of the surface to be dusted.

Razor-blade holder. For even more heavy-duty cleaning and for specialized tasks, it's time to call on a safety razor in a holder. It's great for soap scum on shower doors, paint splatters on glass, and baked-on food on oven windows and surfaces of appliances. This is one of the three tools carried in the apron at all times. The one we use has a three-position blade for added safety.

Red Juice (in a spray bottle). A heavy-duty liquid spray cleaner. This product, along with the cleaning apron, is at the core of time saving in our system. You need a spray cleaner that you can rely on without being caustic to two- and four-footed creatures or harmful to surfaces. Ours is a professional formula called The Clean Team Red Juice. We called it Red Juice because it's tedious to say "Please pass the heavy-duty red liquid spray cleaner." It was shortened to "Gimme some Red Juice" early in The Clean Team's history, and the shorthand stuck. Other retail products include 409, Fantastik, and similar red spray-on liquid cleaners.

Red Juice is the finest heavy-duty cleaner/degreaser we've ever found— and we've tried them all, believe me. It's odorless, biodegradable, and safe to use around food. In its most concentrated form, it's used to degrease diesel engines, so you can imagine what it does to household dirt.

We keep Red Juice in a spray bottle with a red top, so it can be identified in a flash. (When you get expert at all this, you don't even want a second's hesitation when you're looking for a cleaning product.) And we always hang it on the same side of the apron when not in use. We recommend the right side if you're right-handed (and vice versa) because you will use Red Juice more often than Blue Juice—its lighter-duty cousin.

Rubber gloves. Essential for cleaning the oven or for anything that may endanger your skin or that is too gross for words. Use relatively loose-fitting, heavy-duty gloves. The cheap ones rip immediately.

Scraper. Occasionally, you will encounter mysterious globs that are difficult to remove with the toothbrush—like petrified lumps of pancake batter or squished raisins. They can be removed in seconds with a scraper. Also, there are times when the space you're cleaning is too narrow even for the toothbrush—like between the two shower doors. Those are the times to reach for the scraper. We use a 1½-inch-wide steel spatula with a plastic handle. This is one of the three tools carried in the apron at all times.

Spray bottles. We use three refillable color-coded spray bottles: one for Red Juice (red), one for Blue Juice (blue), and one for bleach (white). You need a bottle with a long and durable handle that can hook easily on the apron loops.

The spray bottle should also have a nozzle that can screw off for cleaning. The fastest way to clean a clogged nozzle is to unscrew it and scrub it with the toothbrush under running water. It's not a good idea to poke anything metallic (e.g., a needle) into the orifice because it has a good chance of deforming it and ruining the spray pattern. In many cases, what's thought to be a clogged nozzle is actually a clogged filter screen at the intake end of the tube—provided your spray bottle has one, which it should. Again, the solution is to remove the screen and scrub it under running water.

Squeegee. There's only one way to clean a window fast, and that's with a professional-quality window squeegee. We're not talking about those clumsy things with ¼-inch-thick blades that leave streaks for miles. You're far better off with a quality product that can keep a firm, flat grip on the window surface. You can choose almost any size from 6 to 22 inches, depending on the size of the windows in your house. We use the model manufactured by Ettore.

Squeegee extension pole. If you have windows that are beyond comfortable reach, we recommend a telescoping metal extension pole for the window squeegee. It saves all that time setting up the ladder, climbing up and down, worrying about falling off, and so forth. It also earns its keep as an extension pole for paint rollers and as a handle for the floor scrub brush, push brooms, and anything similar that has a standard threaded socket. We use the model manufactured by Ettore.

Squeegee scrub sleeve. And how do professionals *scrub* windows that are out of reach? The most practical solution is a fuzzy brush that quickly slips over the squeegee blade. With it, you can transport liquid cleaning solution to the window and scrub the surface at the same time. Then it pops off quickly, and you are ready to squeegee the surface clean and dry. Actually, it's so convenient that we also recommend it for windows that are within easy reach. We use the model manufactured by—you guessed it—Ettore.

Squirt bottle. Use it to apply Tile Juice. Any tile cleaner you purchase should already be in a container like this.

Tile brush. We found that the fastest way to spread tile juice around, as well as to scrub tile and grout at the same time, is with a large brush. It will power-scrub those shower stalls, tubs, and sinks in nothing flat. We use a brush originally designed to clean commercial dairies. It has long, stiff synthetic bristles, angled so they dig into difficult corners and remote recesses and rinse very quickly.

Tile Juice (in a squirt bottle). Soap scum and minerals conspire with each other to form a film that is highly resistant to cleaning, as anyone who has cleaned a shower stall or tub can testify. You need a cleaning agent that can break up this unholy alliance, and that's what we call Tile Juice. Most such products consist of one or more acids that dissolve away the alkali soap/mineral conspiracy, and they differ mainly in their dilution. We use an industrial-strength tile cleaner. A variety of retail products are also available in grocery or hardware stores.

Toilet brush. We use brushes with stiff bristles to improve their scrubbing ability. Don't buy the brushes with bristles held in place by a twisted wire. They aren't worth the wire they're twisted in.

Toothbrush. This small brush is indispensable for getting into tight spots and even not-so-tight spots. Brushes scrub many times faster than a sponge, rag, or paper towel, and their bristles can dig into irregular surfaces as well. You'll be amazed how often a spot will not respond to wiping but will come right up when agitated with a brush and a cleaning agent such as Red Juice. Unexcelled for treating carpet spots: Spray on Red Juice, agitate with brush, and blot up residue. Also used around faucet handles, on tile grout, around light switches, in shower-door runners, and so forth. Keep one in the glove compartment of your car. It will get a real workout when the car is washed.

The brush we use has bristles that are considerably thicker and stiffer than a real toothbrush's. It's a simple brush, but it's amazingly effective and took us a heck of a long time to find. This is one of the three tools carried in the apron at all times.

Vacuum cleaner (the "Big Vac"). You don't have to go buy one if you don't have this type already. But next time you buy a vacuum, this is the one to get. It's easy to maneuver, it has a second motor in the beater head, and it quickly separates so the hose can be used for other tasks as the need arises.

We use a canister vacuum with two motors: one for suction and one to turn the brush in the suction head. This style is a hybrid between the traditional *upright* (the one with the big bag), whose main asset was its ability to brush up deeply lodged dirt; and the *standard canister* (the one with a hose), whose main asset was strong suction. The modified canister is an ideal combination of the best of both types.

Most vacuums offer you a choice of cloth or paper bags. After using cloth for a considerable time, we got tired of the fuss and occasional dust storms occasioned by thrashing around with cloth bags. At the same time, we found that paper bags make better suction possible. Cloth bags can clog relatively easily, and when that happens, the suction diminishes sharply. For example, one of our clients had a carpeted floor that was plagued with a recurrent layer of fine brick powder. (The bricks in the building were so old that they were disintegrating.) A recently emptied cloth bag would clog within *moments* of starting to vacuum. The small grains just fill in the holes in the weave of the cloth, and the vacuum is useless. We switched to paper bags and had no further trouble.

Vacuum cleaner (the "Little Vac"). There are times when you'll need more than one vacuum if you are working in a team. And there are some tasks that are accomplished faster with a more maneuverable vacuum. So we also use this smaller, portable canister vacuum. This is especially true if you have hardwood floors anywhere in the house.

Vinegar, white. White vinegar is 5 percent acetic acid—the mildest acid available. It's sometimes suggested as a floor cleaner or as a safer alternative cleaner for removing hard-water deposits in the shower, but it's not particularly effective for either of these jobs because it's so mild. This mildness can be overcome when something with hard-water deposits can be soaked in it. Examples are showerheads or deposits in vases. It's acidic, so don't use it on marble. White vinegar can also be used in a dishwasher to remove stains.

Wax applicator. One of the most important things to do when waxing a floor is to apply as thin and as even a coat as possible. While you're at it, you will probably prefer not to be on your hands and knees (especially if you've just stripped the floor). The solution is one of those cheap, fake lamb's-wool wax applicators at the end of a non-backbreaking pole. When you're done with the pad, clean it, or just throw it away to avoid the possibility of cross-contaminating the wax next time you use it.

Whisk broom. Buy one with plastic bristles. Use it to clean the edges of carpets, especially on stairs, and for generalized brushing chores (e.g., between cushions on the couch).

White scrub pad/sponge ("white pad"). Occasionally, you must abandon brushes for the more concentrated abilities of a white scrubbing pad. White pads are the least abrasive of the several types on the market—green and gray (or black), increasingly in that order, being abrasive. White pads are widely advertised as not being likely to scratch surfaces, which is generally true. But after a while, you will discover (if you haven't already) that anything can scratch anything. Or at least it seems that way. But given moderate pressure and a wet cleaning surface, your chances of scratching something with a white scrub pad are minimal. We use the one made by Scotch-Brite, which has a sponge on the other side. As much as we have reviled sponges, in this case, they do serve a purpose by retaining a bit of liquid that's helpful in the scrubbing process. Used when a cleaning cloth isn't strong enough.

Chapter 4 Safety

We don't want to throw cold water on your efforts to master faster cleaning techniques, but it would be silly for us not to pass on some of the safety lessons we have learned along the way. You'll be concentrating, you'll be trying to pick up speed, and you'll be learning new practices and procedures—all of which can set the stage for an accident. Having said all that, you should know that cleaning is still a very safe activity. It's just nice to keep it that way—that's all.

Don't back up without knowing who or what's behind you. Get in the habit of looking over your shoulder while you're standing still—then back up. Accidents happen when you start backing up before you check. So make it second nature to look before you move—a little like checking to see if you have your door keys before you close the front door of your house behind you.

Don't bend over in front of a door. If it can swing toward you, someone could open it and knock you on the head with it. If it can swing away from you, it doesn't mean it's safe. Someone could still walk through the doorway and run into you. If you must bend over in the vicinity of a door, stand off to one side. Or keep your hand on the doorknob, or block it with your foot, so the door won't open, or just lock it.

Be especially careful when you're looking up as you're working. For example, when foraging for spiderwebs on the ceiling. It's easy to get absorbed with what you're doing and walk smack-dab into something or someone. As in the case of backing up, stand still while you're cleaning, and check where you're going before you take the next step. After a while you'll develop "eyes" not only in the back of your head but in your shins too (and qualify for a cameo role in *Star Trek* perhaps).

If you drop something made of glass, get out of the way. Neither a $5 fishbowl nor a $500 vase are worth getting cut by shards of glass. The first impulse is to grab at the falling object, but that can prove to be disastrous. Let it go.

Be careful when reaching under sofa and chair cushions with your hands. The nerve endings in your fingers make it amazingly painful to discover pins, thumbtacks, and razor blades by touch. Likewise, be careful when you reach into your apron trash pocket with your hand. It's best not to store dangerous objects there, such as broken glass, pins, etc. Go right to a trash can with them, or wrap them in other debris (such as a piece of paper) before depositing them in the apron pocket.

Don't play Spider-Man when washing windows. Clean windows are not worth getting yourself killed for. Do not hang out of windows while supporting your weight with one hand. While working on ladders, do not reach beyond the center of gravity, and do not step on the upper two ladder rungs.

When cleaning tubs that have a buildup of soap scum, remember that this soap is going to be set loose when you wash the tub or shower walls. As soap (unlike detergent) consists largely of fats, it is going to be slippery. So use sensible precautions to prevent slipping in the tub: Stand outside when you can. Keep your tennis shoes on if you must step inside, and step on a layer of rags when possible to give you better footing.

Is there anyone in the world who has not been told to avoid mixing ammonia and chlorine bleach? It's simple chemistry: Ammonia releases chlorine gas from the liquid bleach, and chlorine gas is deadly.

There are sneaky ways of mixing the two chemicals that you might not be aware of. Perhaps someone else had used ammonia on a surface and didn't rinse it off well enough. If you come along afterward and apply bleach, you may be in trouble. At the first sign of a really nasty chlorine smell, get fresh air fast. A smart idea is simply not to use ammonia in the bathroom at all. Most of the time, bleach and other cleaning products take care of the demands of bathroom cleaning, so there's no compelling reason even to take a chance of mixing ammonia and bleach. Another good reason to keep ammonia out of the bathroom is that many automatic bowl-cleaning products contain chlorine, and it would be easy to mix the two without realizing the hazard.

Be very careful when spraying liquid cleaners in a confined area. We're sure you've noticed by now that more than one retail product on grocery shelves is murder on your lungs. Ammonia can also be a serious problem if you inhale its fumes for a prolonged period. Keep a window open when using any strong-smelling cleaner, and turn on the fan. Take a fresh-air break every now and again. You're not being a wuss.

Wear rubber gloves at the slightest provocation. Your skin is worth it. If you find yourself debating about whether you should or not, it's already time to put them on.

Hang pictures and mirrors with decent heavy-duty hangers, nails, or screws. It's amazing how many people hang such things with thumbtacks or pushpins, in flagrant defiance of gravity. There are many more sensible things to challenge than gravity. It's right up there with death and taxes. This really does have to do with cleaning because you will have to clean these hanging items every once in a while without them falling off the wall.

Don't clean when you're angry. Go punch a pillow (it really does work) or do a few pushups or take a few deep breaths—whatever you need to do. When you break something while cleaning, it's remarkable how often you will find that you were angry at the time. ("Next time that shameless hussy shows up in her fake furs and press-on nails I'll . . ." CRASH!) Objects just seem to fly out of hands when you're thinking nasty thoughts about shameless hussies or your boss or the IRS or the transcendent unfairness of life in general.

Chapter 5 The Kitchen

This chapter is designed to teach you how to clean any kitchen quickly, easily, and efficiently. Stock your carryall tray with the following items.

Materials

- 1 can of powdered cleanser
- 1 spray bottle of Blue Juice
- 1 spray bottle of Red Juice
- 1 white scrub pad/sponge combination (white pad)
- 1 green scrub pad/sponge combination (green pad)
- 1 pad of #000 steel wool
- 1 feather duster
- 1 whisk broom
- 1 oven cleaner
- 1 pair of rubber gloves
- 1 bottle of floor cleaner/polisher (or ammonia)
- 10 cleaning cloths (folded)
- 3 terry-cloth Sh-Mop covers

Stock your cleaning apron with these items.

- 1 scraper
- 1 toothbrush

1 razor-blade holder with a sharp blade
2 plastic bags (as liners) with clips

Hand-carry the following item.
1 Sh-Mop or your choice of mop

The Starting Point

Lean your Sh-Mop just inside the door. Put your carryall tray on the counter-top just to the right of the sink. The strategy for cleaning this room is to work around the room clockwise, cleaning as you go—never backtracking, carrying all the tools and cleansers necessary in your apron.

This room is cleaned with lots of "pick up and replace" motions. For example, pick up your feather duster, use it, replace it; pick up the Red Juice, spray and wipe, replace it; pick up your toothbrush, etc. And when we say "spray and wipe," we mean that you'll be using a cleaning cloth and the Red or Blue Juice. These motions will become smooth and effortless with practice. We've picked your starting place for you: where you put your tray.

Our kitchen:

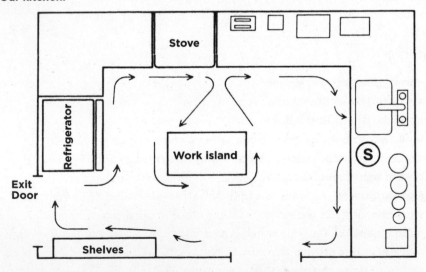

We've drawn the floor pan for a sample kitchen and shown your trajectory through the room. "S" is where you start, and your path is indicated with arrows. It's a good idea to draw your own kitchen floor plan after you've read this chapter. It will help you visualize your proposed cleaning trip around your kitchen and especially will help you to decide when to clean something in the middle of the room (like a worktable, for example).

Getting Dressed

Tie your apron around your waist tightly. Check to be sure that the toothbrush and other tools are in their proper pockets. Hang the Blue and Red Juice by their handles on your apron loops on the appropriate side. By "appropriate," we mean that if you put the Blue Juice on the left side, then *always* put it on the left side. This is so you can quickly reach for your Red or Blue Juice without stopping to see which is which. It saves time. The tops of the spray bottles have an annoying tendency to come loose at the worst possible moments, spilling the contents everywhere. Avoid this potential catastrophe by automatically tightening the tops when you first pick them up. Stick your feather duster in your back pocket. Put a whisk broom in your other back pocket. Use it to brush dirt out of vents and corners, and away from walls and appliances that the vacuum doesn't reach. Estimate the number of cleaning cloths you'll need, and transfer them from the tray to your apron. At first, just guess by grabbing 8 to 10 cloths; as time goes on, you'll know how many you use. You're ready to move on.

Setting Up

Put any trash containers just outside the door or in the doorway, making sure they are out of the way (as much as possible) of the person who will be vacuuming. (Follow these directions even if you're working alone, since it is work you will do later, and you want these items out of your way now.) Also, lay any throw rugs outside the door *flat* on the floor or carpet. That's *flat*: F-L-A-T. Flat. No corners tucked underneath. No rumpled mess. You're expecting the vacuumer to do the rug, so you'd better not make him or her stop to flatten it if you want to avoid a brawl in the hallway. Similarly, the person collecting the trash is not going to take the time to rummage around the kitchen on your behalf. That's your job as the Kitchen Person. If you save someone else on the team a step, you're saving yourself a step, and you're all going to the movies that much sooner. That's the idea.

Cupboards and Counters and Fingerprints

You are now going to start cleaning your way around our sample kitchen, *moving to the right, working from high to low* as you go. Above the counter are cupboards, and, since they are the highest, start with them. Usually all you have to clean are the fingerprints near the handles. Fingerprints need Red Juice, so grab your spray bottle from your apron loop, and spray the prints lightly. Replace the spray bottle on your apron loop as you wipe the area dry with your other hand.

You will generally be using two cloths. Carry the drier cloth over your shoulder, so it's easy to reach. When that cloth gets too damp for streakless cleaning (chrome fixtures, glass, etc.) but is still usable for general wiping, keep it in the apron pocket between uses, and sling a new dry cloth from your apron supply over your shoulder.

Cleaning fingerprints is a task where we are careful to apply Clean Team Rule 4 (on page 9): "If it isn't dirty, don't clean it." If all you need to do is remove a fingerprint or two from an otherwise clean cabinet door, just spray the prints and wipe dry. Takes about 5 seconds. Don't haphazardly spray a large area of the cabinet door (which takes longer) and then have to wipe this larger area dry (which takes longer still). You've forgotten that all you wanted was that fingerprint, and now you're cleaning the entire door. Stay focused on what you're doing, which is only the 5-second job of a quick spray-and-wipe of a few fingerprints.

The places that often *don't* need cleaning are the vertical surfaces of the kitchen (the fronts of the cabinets, for example). The horizontal surfaces like the flat top of the counter will need cleaning every time. We have Newton to thank for this principle, plus his falling apple, gravity, and such. We are not proposing an excuse to be lazy or to skip things that need to be cleaned. Rather, the idea is to learn to be fast and efficient and aware of what you are doing. That includes *not* cleaning clean areas. After the fingerprints on the cabinet door, wipe the wall between the cabinets only if it has splatters. Otherwise, it's not dirty, so don't clean it.

Spray and wipe the countertop area in front of you. (Pick up your carryall tray, spray and wipe the counter underneath it, and replace the tray.) Work from back to front, moving items to clean beneath and behind them. The "items" we're talking about are the sugar, flour, and tea canisters, the toaster, the food processor, and so forth. The spice rack may get moved to dust *behind* it, but that's all. Dealing with those individual containers is not light housecleaning, so just hit at the spice containers with your feather duster and save cleaning each spice bottle until some night when you feel like doing it in front of the TV. Besides, the easiest way to clean a spice rack is to throw out all the old spices.

When moving items on the counter, move them straight forward just far enough for you to wipe the counter behind them. Before you move these items back into place, now is the time to dust or wipe them. Dust them if that is all they need since that is the faster operation. Now move them back and continue on down to the drawers below.

Be sure to dust or wipe the tops of the drawer fronts as you come to them. Always check drawer handles and knobs for fingerprints (same rule as above, for cabinet doors).

The drawer knobs or the cabinet handles are often easier to clean by using your toothbrush in the tight areas rather than by trying to fit your cleaning cloth into a small or awkward place. The toothbrush is in your apron and is perfect for corners and other areas difficult to clean with a cloth alone. Use the tooth-brush and your Red Juice, and then wipe dry. After you've cleaned them with the toothbrush, a quick wipe with a cloth will suffice for many future cleanings.

As you work your way around the kitchen, you will do a lot of spraying and wiping, spraying and wiping. Usually you can do this with the spray bottle in one hand and a cloth in the other.

When cloths get too wet or soiled, put them in the plastic-lined pocket. Or throw them to your tray if you're a good shot. But be careful: Cloths soaked with Red Juice or almost any other cleaner may leave spots on the floor.

Get in the habit of always putting the spray bottles back in your apron loops, *not on the countertop.* We know it seems faster to leave them on the countertop, but it isn't. This may seem awkward at first, but do it—it's faster, and it saves time.

Countertop Problems

So here you are, cleaning the counter with malice toward none and a song in your heart. Then you discover remnants of: (a) Saturday night's failed soufflé, (b) Sunday morning's blueberry pancake batter, and (c) other as-sorted stone artifacts that were once food. You are not amused. You took neither Chemistry nor Advanced Blasting Techniques in college. More to the point, you discover that when you spray and wipe these globs once, little or nothing happens. What to do?

First of all, when you come to a little nightmare on the countertop, you have to resort to tools with greater cleaning power. Use your cleaning cloth most of the time since it normally will clean the countertop as it wipes up the Red Juice. When you encounter pockets of resistance like dried-on food, just move up to the tool of next magnitude—your white pad.

The white pad should be in your apron in a pocket lined with a plastic bag. When finished, always replace it in the same lined pocket. It doesn't matter that it gets dirty and begs to be rinsed, because you use it just to loosen dirt and not to remove it. Unless you just can't stand it anymore, don't rinse it until you get to the sink. Do try to get used to its being full of gunk.

Spray with Red Juice and agitate with the white pad until a mess of Red Juice and reconstituted 5-day-old vegetable soup appears. This is the mess you need to learn to "see through" (Clean Team Rule 5, on page 10). To do this, you have to learn how to tell how the counter feels when you've cleaned through the goop to the surface without rinsing or wiping to take a look. If you have difficulty judging when you have scrubbed down to the actual bare surface (without wiping), try spraying a little Red Juice on a clean counter area next to the dirty area you are cleaning. By first rubbing your white pad on the clean area and then the dirty area, you quickly learn to tell the difference by touch alone.

Another example of switching to a higher-horsepower tool is when you encounter food dried so hard that even a white pad takes forever to work. Let's say drips of pancake batter have dried to malicious little bits of stone stuck to the counter. When you tried your white pad, you found that you were rubbing one micron or so off the top of the dried pancake batter every swipe. You were using up MGT—Movie-Going Time—again. When you first encounter the problem, better to put your cloth away, grab your scraper, and scrape the batter loose in a second or two. Replace the scraper and continue along your way. Be careful not to scratch the surface: Spray the surface first and keep the blade at a low angle. Remember, increase the force or strength of the tool only as necessary (Clean Team Rule 7, on page 10).

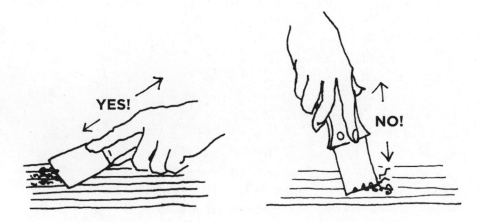

Picture Glass, Window Glass, and Mirrors

You need your Blue Juice and a dry cloth to clean these items, and since you are carrying them with you in your apron, there is no need to go back to the tray. To clean, spray lightly and evenly with Blue Juice, and wipe with a dry cloth until the glass is dry. If you don't wipe it completely dry, you will leave streaks—and if you don't use a very dry cloth, you are wasting time since it will take you longer to wipe the glass dry. When we say spray lightly, we mean it. Glass or a mirror cleaned with a quick light spray of Blue Juice gets just as clean as when you overspray! So don't. Replace the Blue Juice sprayer after each use—back where it was on your apron loop.

Cobwebs and Doors

As you continue around the kitchen moving to the right, working from high to low, look all the way to the ceiling each time you advance to check for cobwebs. Spiders like corners. When you see a cobweb, grab your feather duster from your back pocket, mow down the cobweb, replace the duster, and proceed. If you can't reach the cobweb, use the detached vacuum wand as an extension for the feather duster.

You're now ready to pass a doorway in our sample kitchen. Another place to check for cobwebs as you pass by is the top of the door frame. Did you also check for fingerprints where people (especially very little people) seem to grab the door frame as they pass through? Good.

Open Shelves

Next are some shelves used to store cookbooks, pots and pans, and other kitchen stuff. Hit at the leading edges of these shelves with your feather duster only. (An alternative method is to clean thoroughly *one* shelf each time you clean the kitchen.) To clean a shelf, move all items to the right side and clean the left side, then move everything to the left side and repeat. Finally, redistribute the items as they were. Or, if there are too many things on the shelf, move just enough items to the floor or counter, so there is space to move the remaining items. When moving items to the floor or counter, move them the least distance possible.

Refrigerator—Outside

Wipe the top first. Once you are cleaning this room on a regular basis, you may be able just to feather-dust the top, which takes only a second or two.

If the top of the refrigerator is used as a storage area, then just dust around all the items up there, and treat it like the shelf we just described.

Clean the fingerprints from the outside of the fridge—and there are always some! Don't spray and wipe the entire refrigerator unless it needs it. Clean around the hinges and the nameplate of the refrigerator—your toothbrush is the best tool. Open the refrigerator door to wipe and clean the rubber gasket. If it is dirty, make sure to use your toothbrush here also. Once you get many areas like this clean, you won't have to do them again for a long time: e.g., the refrigerator hinges, nameplate, rubber gasket, and cabinet and drawer handles.

Wipe the refrigerator air vent (down near the floor) while the door is open—or if it is just dusty, use your feather duster or whisk broom. While the door is open, wipe fingerprints on top and on the side of the door near the handle. Also, clean off the line left by the gasket on the inside door lining. Check for easy or obvious little wipes that are needed on the visible areas of the interior shelves. Don't get carried away—it could take forever. (Instructions for a thorough cleaning of the inside of the refrigerator are in Chapter 12.)

The Stove Top

After you've cleaned the area above the stove—the hood usually needs to be sprayed and wiped—start at the back and work forward. Clean the vent filters by running them through the dishwasher occasionally. If they're gross or dilapidated, replace them. There are two main types of stove tops. Here is how to clean them.

Gas Ranges

These are easier to clean than electric ranges. Clean one side and then the other. First take the grates from the gas burners on the left side, and set them on top of the grates on the right. Now spray and wipe the left side as necessary. You'll usually need your white pad here to get at the burned-on crud. If your pad won't work, use your scraper where possible, but the stove's curved edges often make this difficult.

If you are still unable to get the stove top clean, turn to your tray (next to the sink) and get your powdered cleanser. Use a tiny bit with your white pad. You will be using so little cleanser that you shouldn't even sprinkle it on the stove top. Instead, dab a bit from the top of the cleanser container with the wet edge of the white pad. If there is no cleanser on the top for you to use, then sprinkle a *small* amount on the stove top, and dab with your white pad to pick up a little bit. As a last resort, use steel wool instead of the white pad. But take care not to scratch the surface.

After you have cleaned the left side, wipe (if needed) and replace the left grates, and then move the grates on the right side to the *counter* immediately to the right of the stove. Now clean the middle of the stove top and the right side, and replace the right grates. The grates themselves can be cleaned when necessary by putting them in the dishwasher.

Electric Ranges

Usually there is a chrome or aluminum ring around the burners that needs attention. Normally, you can clean around these rings (the edge of the ring where it meets the stove top) by spraying with Red Juice and using your toothbrush around each ring. Before you wipe, use your white pad to clean the metal itself. Now wipe dry with your cleaning cloth. As usual, work from back to front and from left to right. If necessary, use steel wool to clean the metal rings.

If you can't get the stove top clean without moving the metal rings, then go ahead and lift up that particular ring (only that one), and spray and agitate with your white pad and wipe. If there is an accumulation under the burner that must be removed (*don't* if it's not much), then pull the burner up, remove the drip tray, and dump loose debris into your plastic-lined apron pocket. Use Red Juice and the white pad or steel wool to quickly clean, then wipe and replace. Don't try to make this drip tray look like new: If it's hopeless, it's smarter to throw it away and replace it once or twice or 12 times a year—possibly with one of those nifty Teflon-coated pans. But they do get reasonably clean in the dishwasher, and you can use powdered cleanser to remove residual grime.

The Stove Front

Now that the top is clean, start down the front of the stove. The first little roadblock here is the row of burner control knobs. They can be cleaned by spraying with Red Juice and using your toothbrush on them and around their edges.

If you can't get this area clean without removing the controls, *first clean and wipe the knobs themselves while in place.* Then pull each one straight out, wipe it clean, and set it on the counter to the right of the stove in the same relative position it was in while on the stove. While the knobs are off, clean the area of the stove front you couldn't clean while the knobs were in place. Use Red Juice and white pad on this area, and wipe it dry before replacing the knobs. This chore shouldn't have to be done often (unless the chef of the household is inclined toward hysterical flinging).

Open the oven door to get the oven side of the window. It can be cleaned with your razor blade. Be sure to spray the window first with Red Juice: It's easier to clean, and it's also more difficult to scratch the glass when it's wet. This window should be cleaned even if you're not cleaning the inside of the oven. (Oven cleaning is the subject of Chapter 11.)

Wipe the rest of the front of the stove as necessary. Don't automatically clean the entire front of the stove. Remember that horizontal surfaces get dirty faster than vertical ones. Once again: If it isn't dirty, don't clean it.

The Middle of the Room

Now is the time we chose to turn around and do the work island in the middle of the sample kitchen. Not much to do here. Just spray and wipe the work space. The important thing is not to overlook it. Be sure to draw anything similar on your own floor plan and show by arrows when you are going to clean it.

Toaster, Toaster Oven, Can Opener, and Microwave

Return to the last bit of counter area to clean these items. You can make your 10-year-old appliance look like new by removing that burnt-on "brown" stuff with your razor (*gently*) and a white pad. Unplug the toaster and be brave. Wet the toaster liberally with Red Juice before you use the razor, or you will scratch it. Just like the scraper, keep the razor at a low angle. Clean the rest of the toaster with Red Juice and your white pad, and use your toothbrush around the handles. Wipe the chrome dry and streakless (as you would glass). Clean the toaster oven similarly with Red Juice, and use your toothbrush in those areas you are learning that your cloth won't reach. Also, use your razor blade on the (wet) inside glass of the toaster-oven door. Clean the can opener with Red Juice, and use your toothbrush around the cutting wheels and gears as necessary. If any parts are removable, pop them into the dishwasher. The microwave is easy. Spray and wipe inside and out.

The Sink

You will finish the trip around the kitchen by ending up in front of the sink. If there are dishes in the sink, there shouldn't be. That is not *weekly* cleaning. It is a *daily* cleaning. The dishes should be put in the dishwasher or otherwise dealt with before you start this weekly cleaning.

Clean above the rim of the sink with Red Juice (not cleanser) and a cloth—all except in the bowl of the sink itself. Every time you clean, use your toothbrush around the faucets and where the sink meets the counter. It makes a vast difference, and it takes only a few seconds.

Now use the powdered cleanser in the bowl of the sink. (Use powdered cleanser *below the rim only,* or you'll spend too much time rinsing.) Conveniently enough, the cleanser is in your carryall tray right next to the sink on the counter—where you left it when you started your trip around the kitchen. Wet the inside of the sink. Sprinkle cleanser lightly on the bottom of the sink, put the cleanser back, and then use your white pad to agitate the cleanser around the bottom and sides of the sink. Use your toothbrush to clean the little groove around the drain or garbage-disposal opening.

Rinse the sink thoroughly to remove the cleanser. Use your fingers to feel the sink bottom to be sure all the cleanser is removed. This is especially important since you may be using the sink as a bucket for some ammonia and water (see page 44), and some residual bleach from the cleanser could react with the ammonia. So rinse well. Now dry the faucet spigot and handles with a very dry cloth, so they will shine nicely.

Put the Red and Blue Juice and the feather duster into your carryall tray. Take either ammonia or floor cleanser/polisher (see page 45) and put it in your apron pocket. Set the tray just outside the kitchen door (out of the path of the vacuuming).

A Little Reminder

Remember, don't "come back" to anything. Make sure everything has been attended to the first time around. If you have to go back to clean something you missed, you are doing something wrong, and you are wasting valuable time better spent elsewhere.

The Floor

First step is to sweep or vacuum the floor with the Little Vac and its large brush attachment. Vacuum into the room so the cord or exhaust is not dragging or blowing debris. Pick up large items that may clog the vacuum—like dog or cat food, dried lettuce leaves, carrot slices, nylon stockings, sleeping hamsters, etc. Pay particular attention to corners and to the grout on tile floors. Use a broom if no vacuum is available. (It can actually be faster, unless there are lots of dust balls around.)

The next step depends on what type of floor you have. Use Method 1 (ammonia and water) if your floors are "no-wax" vinyl, hardwood floors coated with polyurethane, or tile floors (glazed, unglazed, or quarry). Use Method 2 (floor cleaner/polisher) if your floors are "wax" or "no-wax" vinyl or linoleum. (You may have noticed that "no-wax" vinyl floors made both lists. Use Method 1 or 2 on no-wax floors or alternate between them.)

Grab the Sh-Mop from the doorway where you left it when you started the kitchen. Take two or three clean terry-cloth Sh-Mop covers from your tray and put them in your apron. Put the bottle of ammonia or floor cleaner/polisher in your apron pocket, depending on whether you're using Method 1 or 2 below.

Method 1: Ammonia and Water

Close the sink drain and run an inch or so of warm water into the sink. Then add a small amount of ammonia (approximately 3 tablespoons, depending on how dirty the floor is). Dip a Sh-Mop cover in this solution. Wring it out but leave it almost dripping wet, and place the cover over the Sh-Mop head. Start in the corner farthest away from the exit door, and clean an area of the floor. When the terry-cloth cover is too dry or dirty to continue, put the soiled cover into your lined apron pocket, and dip a clean one in the ammonia solution in the sink. Repeat as necessary. As with other surfaces, different degrees of cleaning are called for: The dirtier areas of the floor in front of the stove, refrigerator, and sink require harder scrubbing than less-traveled areas. As you're mopping, be prepared to use your scraper to loosen mystery globs on the floor. Use the white pad to remove smears and heel marks.

Since you don't rinse the soiled terry-cloth covers in the sink, the water in there stays perfectly clean. This means that a bucket is unnecessary, even for the most fastidious of cleaners.

When you pass the sink for the last time, let the water drain, rinse the sink, and dry the chrome if necessary. Mop your way out of the kitchen. Put the soiled terry-cloth covers in the wash with the dirty cleaning cloths.

Method 2: Floor Cleaner/Polisher

Close the sink drain and add just an inch or so of warm water. Dip a Sh-Mop cover into the water, and wring it out a bit, but leave the cover almost dripping wet. (Or run a little warm water over it from the tap.) Put the cover on the Sh-Mop, and go to the corner of the room farther from the exit door. Apply a thin line of cleaner/polisher about 4 feet long directly to the floor. Don't apply closer than 2 feet to any wall or cabinet. Spread this line of cleaner/polisher as evenly as possible over an area of floor approximately 4 feet by 6 feet, using enough pressure to clean as you go. Your purpose is to use the Sh-Mop to pick up the dirt while leaving a little cleaner/polisher for the modest shine.

When using your scraper on blobs that the Sh-Mop doesn't remove, loosen them (once again at a low angle) and then either mop them up or pick them up and deposit them in your apron pocket. Sprinkle a little more water on the terry-cloth cover as needed. Use the cover until it is too heavily soiled. Then put it into your lined apron pocket, moisten a fresh cover, and continue.

When you pass the sink for the last time, let the water out, dry any water spots on the chrome, and clean your way out of the kitchen. Put soiled terry-cloth covers into the wash with your cleaning cloths. Don't let them dry out before washing because most cleaner/polishers dry as hard as old paint. If it's going to be a while before you wash them, rinse the cleaner/polisher from the covers now.

If you have one of the shiny floors that tend to show streaks (marble, wood, smooth vinyl, for example), you can eliminate the streaks by drying the floor quickly with your Sh-Mop. Do this with a clean and *dry* terry-cloth cover. Because the Sh-Mop has such a large surface area, it takes just a minute. And it works amazingly well—just as if you dried it with a towel on your hands and knees!

YOU'RE FINISHED!

If you're working alone, it's time to start the bathroom. If you're working in a team or two, report to your partner if he/she has finished the bathroom and begun dusting. If you have finished the kitchen first, then *you* start the dusting and give your partner a secondary assignment for when your partner finishes the bathroom. (See Chapter 8.) If you're working in a team of three, go see the team leader.

Below is a summary of the kitchen procedures. You are most welcome to tape a photocopy of it at eye level in the kitchen to help you on your first adventure or two with Speed Cleaning your kitchen.

Kitchen Summary

(1) Lean Sh-Mop just inside door. Put tray on counter to right of sink. Hang spray bottles on apron loops. Put duster and whisk broom in back pockets and cloths in apron. Put trash cans and rugs outside. Spray/wipe around room to the right and top to bottom. When too wet or dirty, store cloths in plastic apron pocket or throw them into tray.

(2) COUNTER: Move items forward to wipe counter behind them. Dust/wipe items and replace. Use Red Juice and cloth, white pad, or scraper on counter. **Note**: Fill in Steps 3 to 6 for your own floor plan.

( ) REFRIGERATOR: Red-Juice outside. Open door: Clean door gasket and air vent.

( ) STOVE TOP: Clean hood, then work from back to front with Red Juice and cloth, white pad, scraper, cleanser, or steel wool.

—Gas: Set left grates on right grates. Clean left side and wipe and replace left grates. Set right grates on counter. Clean middle and right of stove top, then replace right grates.

—Electric: Try cleaning with toothbrush around burner with ring in place. If that fails, remove burner/ring assembly, dump debris into lined apron pocket, clean, and replace.

( ) STOVE FRONT: Try using toothbrush and Red Juice without removing knobs. If that fails, clean knobs in place, remove and wipe them, set them on counter, clean stove behind them, and then replace.

( ) MIDDLE OF ROOM: Small appliances

(7) SINK: Red-Juice rim. Use toothbrush around base of faucet. Sprinkle cleanser into bowl only and scrub with white pad. Rinse sink. Replace spray bottles and feather duster in tray. Set ammonia or Brite by sink. Set tray outside door.

(8) FLOOR: Vacuum with Little Vac or sweep. Fill sink with 1 inch warm water.

—Method 1: Add 3 tablespoons ammonia. Dip Sh-Mop cover in solution. Wring but leave almost dripping. Put it on mop head. Start in far corner, changing covers as needed. Use scraper or white pad on problem spots.

—Method 2: Dip Sh-Mop cover in water. Wring but leave almost dripping. Put it on mop head. Start in far corner, spreading 4-foot line of Brite for each 20 to 25 square feet. Change covers as needed.

Last time at sink, drain and rinse sink, polish faucet, and Sh-Mop your way to the exit. Put soiled covers in wash.

Chapter 6 The Bathroom

Here is *your* bathroom. Looks a mess. Towels—some wet, some dry—in heaps everywhere. Mold growing in crevices. Toothpaste smeared on the mirror. Crud on the grout. Looks like a weekend job? The equivalent of three trips to the beach? Not at all! Eventually you'll be out of here in just 15 minutes or less. Stock your carryall tray with the following items (see page 108).

Materials

1 can of powdered cleanser (with a plastic 1-pint container inverted over the top)
1 white scrub pad/sponge combination (white pad)
1 spray bottle of Blue Juice
1 spray bottle of Red Juice
1 toilet brush
1 tile brush
10 cleaning cloths (folded)
1 feather duster
1 whisk broom
1 spray bottle of bleach diluted one to four with water
1 squirt bottle of Tile Juice

Stock your cleaning apron with these items.

1 scraper

1 toothbrush

1 razor-blade holder with a sharp blade

2 plastic bags (as liners) with clips

The Starting Point

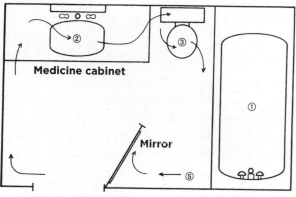

Our bathroom:

Medicine cabinet

Mirror

Walk into the bathroom. Do not be afraid. Face the tub. Put your tray down on the floor at the right end of the bathtub. The strategy for cleaning this room is to pick a starting point and proceed around the room clockwise, cleaning as you go—never backtracking, carrying all the tools and cleaners necessary with you in your apron and pockets. We've picked your starting point for you: where you put the tray.

Above, we've drawn the plan for a sample bathroom and shown your trajectory through the room. "S" is where you start, with arrows indicating the proper path to take. As with the kitchen, it's a good idea to draw the floor plan for your own bathroom.

Getting Dressed

Tie your apron around your waist tightly. Check to be sure the toothbrush and other tools are in their proper pockets. Hang the Blue and Red Juices by their handles on your apron loops on the appropriate side: If you put the Blue Juice on the left side, then always put it on the left side. This is so you can quickly reach for your Red or Blue Juice without stopping to see which is which. It saves time. (Remember, the tops of the spray bottles have an annoying tendency to come loose at the worst possible moments, spilling

Different Bathroom Floor Plans

If there is a shower stall only and no tub, then treat the shower stall as you would the tub. In other words, set your tray by the right side of the shower when you first enter the bathroom.

If there is a tub separate from a shower stall, start by setting your tray down as we just taught you. Then clean the tub, the shower stall, the sink (inside), and the toilet (inside). Finally, clean around the room as previously discussed.

the contents everywhere. Avoid this by automatically tightening the tops when you first pick them up.)

Don't put your feather duster or whisk broom in your back pockets or put cleaning cloths in your apron yet. In the bathroom, you'll be making two trips around the room instead of one: the first to do the wet work (the shower, tub, sink, and toilet) and the second to do the rest of the room.

Alert readers will notice that asking you to make two trips seems to be a violation of Clean Team Rule 1 (on page 6). It is. Without going into a lengthy explanation, we're asking you to work like this in the bathroom (a) to avoid splashing previously cleaned areas, and (b) because you will be using brushes you normally don't carry with you. Don't think about it too much: Just take our word for it.

Setting Up

Put any trash containers just outside the door (or in the doorway). Lay any throw rugs outside the door *flat* on the floor: no corners tucked under-neath. No rumpled mess. You're expecting the vacuumer (who may very well be you) to do the rug later, so make it as easy as possible.

The Shower and Tub

Set any items that are around the edge of the tub out on the floor. Whenever you move items like this, move them the shortest distance pos-sible and keep them in the same relative position they were in. For example, if there is a shampoo container or a rubber ducky, move it straight toward you and set it in on the floor in front of the tub. There are two reasons for doing it this way: (a) It is faster, and (b) When it comes time to replace the items, you automatically know where they were. If there's a bar of soap, put it upside down on a folded cleaning cloth on the floor. (You're keeping the soft side up, so soap isn't smeared all over.) Now that we've covered how to move a bottle of shampoo, a bar of soap, and a rubber ducky, let's move on.

Shower Walls

First, clean the shower walls around the tub—at least the areas that get wet when the shower is on. Wet the walls using the shower wand. Then use Tile Juice and the tile brush. (You have two brushes—one for the toilet and the other for the tub/shower and sink.) Although these are not in your apron, they are in your tray. And your tray (thanks to your observation of Clean Team Rule 1 on page 6) is right at your feet. The Tile Juice is in a plastic squeeze bottle that squirts instead of sprays, so you don't have to inhale the fumes.

Most people's arms are long enough to reach into the tub enclosure to clean—and remember the brush adds more length too. So we recommend that you stand outside the tub to clean. An effective cleaner like Tile Juice liberates an extremely slippery layer of soap onto the tub floor. If you decide to step into the tub or shower to clean, at least make sure you are wearing non-slip rubber-soled shoes. And lay down a couple of cleaning cloths to stand on to make the surface less slippery. When you step out, step onto dry cloths, so you don't slip or track Tile Juice plus gunk into the room.

Don't squirt Tile Juice in the areas that are already clean. (The higher part of the shower wall doesn't normally get wet during a shower and therefore doesn't need cleaning very often.)

Start by squirting some Tile Juice on the wall of the shower that is farthest from the drain, and use your brush to spread it around evenly. Don't scrub. Continue around the shower, squirting Tile Juice and spreading it around with circular movements of the brush. Just distribute the juice with the brush until you've covered the area of the shower wall that needs cleaning. Tile Juice works mainly by chemical action, so scrubbing is a waste of time at this point. It's got to sit there for a couple of minutes to loosen the soap scum and hard-water deposits. With the possible exception of the burned-on goop on the inside of an oven, there is nothing more resistant to cleaning than the hard-water and soap scum deposits you encounter in an ordinary shower—so let the Tile Juice work for you.

If there are shower doors, continue applying Tile Juice on the inside of the doors after you've finished coating the walls. Replace the Tile Juice in your tray. Now start scrubbing the shower wall where you first applied the Tile Juice. The brush works much better than your white pad here because it digs into the grout between the tiles as well as the tiles themselves. Scrub in circles from top to bottom. Clean the plumbing fixtures as you come to them, using the tile brush (and toothbrush) as needed.

You'll be making a bubbly mess on the wall. Relax. It's just Tile Juice agitated by your scrubbing action, mixed with the soap and hard-water deposits you are cleaning off. "See through" this mess (Clean Team Rule 5 on page 10), so you can tell when it's clean underneath and can quit cleaning one area and move on. You do this by learning to tell the difference between how your brush feels when it is cutting through the scum versus when it is down to the clean bare surface. One way to learn this difference is to scrub a clean tile high on the wall and then scrub a dirty one. Notice the difference in friction between the two areas as you scrub. Or use your fingers on the clean versus dirty areas to be able to feel the difference.

When you come to the soap dish, clean it with your toothbrush: First scrape off the soap that has collected in the dish with the *handle* end of your toothbrush. Now brush out the remaining soap with the bristle end. Use Red Juice only if necessary. Final rinsing comes when you rinse the tub/shower area.

Shower Doors and Runners

After you have scrubbed the tile wall, continue around to the inside of the shower door. Switch to the white pad for the shower doors, because it's more effective on this surface than the tile brush. (But only a white pad— never a green pad, which can scratch the glass.) If you have a shower curtain, skip ahead. (Don't try to clean it by hand: Throw it in the wash with a towel or throw it away.)

If the shower doors overlap, and you can't clean the area where they overlap by moving the doors, then spray some Red Juice on your white pad, wrap the pad around your scraper, and slide it into the gap between the doors. (If the white pad is too thick, use a cloth instead.) Now move the scraper up and down to clean this area. Be careful as you work that the scraper doesn't get exposed because it could scratch the glass. Next, remove the scraper and wrap a dry cloth around it for a final wipe. The reason you use Red Juice here instead of Tile Juice is that it's a difficult area to rinse, and Red Juice doesn't require the rinsing that Tile Juice does.

If there is anything like paint or those 1960s daisy stickers on the shower door that can't be removed with the Tile Juice and white pad, use your razor blade. Be sure that the blade is sharp and use it properly (at a low angle), and

you won't scratch the glass. And be careful not to nick the rubber gasket around the glass door.

It's still not time to rinse.

Next, take care of the shower door tracks (runners). Usually you can clean them with your toothbrush and Red Juice. If this doesn't work, use your scraper wrapped with a cloth. Move it back and forth inside the runner to clean it. Or fold your white pad in half, push it into the runner, and move it back and forth. Again, *don't rinse yet.* There will probably be a lot of junk in the tracks, and the temptation to rinse repeatedly will be strong. Cleaning the shower runners is one of those jobs that's a mess the first time, so don't expect it to be perfect yet. It becomes less of a chore each time you do it, eventually needing only a quick wipe.

The Tub

Next is the tub—leaving the shower runners, the shower doors, and the shower walls clean but covered with Tile Juice and whatever ungodly mess you have loosened up—all *unrinsed.* We haven't forgotten.

Wet the sides and bottom of the tub if they need it. Get the powdered cleanser out of the tray, and sprinkle it in the tub. Don't apply it anywhere but *in* the tub—not on the shower walls or faucets or shower head—just in the tub. Use the cleanser appropriately. If the tub isn't very dirty, don't use very much. While you are learning, resist your impulse to bombard the tub. Be conservative, since most powdered cleansers are abrasives and wear out porcelain. Also, it can take as much time to rinse it away as it does to scrub the whole tub. If you have a nonporcelain tub, use a specialty product instead of powdered cleanser.

Use your tile brush to scrub the tub, starting at the end away from the drain. Use the same "see through" method so that you know when the porcelain under the foam and powder is clean. As necessary, use your toothbrush at the top of the tub where the tile meets the tub. This is often Mold Heaven (or Hell). It comes off rather easily if you can get at it with your toothbrush. The problem arises when it is found growing in the tiny cracks in the grout and can't be removed with your toothbrush. Remove what you can. Later, you can use bleach on the rest, but not until you are just about to leave the bathroom, since chlorine bleach is obnoxious, and you don't want to breathe it if you can help it.

Rinsing the Shower and Tub

Now everything inside the tub/shower areas is a clean but foamy mess, and you are ready to rinse. Put your *unrinsed* tile brush in the sink, and leave it there while you rinse the tub/shower area.

Turn on the shower to rinse. Use cold water, so you don't fog up everything. If you are lucky enough to have a detachable shower head on a hose, rinsing is a pleasure. We happen to think that rinsing is a good enough reason to buy one—let alone being able to wash the dog with it.

Completely rinse the walls and doors before you rinse the tub. Rinse the shower walls from front (starting above the drain end) to back and from top to bottom. If there are areas that you can't reach with the shower spray, first try using your hand to deflect the spray to the area you need to rinse. If you still can't get it all rinsed, then use the plastic container that was over the top of the cleanser to catch water and throw it to those last nasty unrinsed spots.

After the walls are rinsed clean, rinse the tub—this time back to front toward the drain. *Use your fingers* to feel the bottom of the tub to know when all the cleanser is rinsed out. Don't depend on sight alone, because it is impossible to see a little leftover cleanser in a wet tub. The reverse, of course, is also true: If you leave a tiny bit of cleanser in the tub and wait for it to dry, it makes a powdery film that you can see halfway down the block.

After you have rinsed the tub, and there is no leftover cleanser or Tile Juice, turn off the water. Don't replace the items from around the tub yet, because if there's any mold left, you will spray it with bleach in a few minutes. But now is the time to wipe the chrome dry and shiny in the tub/shower area.

The Sink—Inside

Reach into the sink where you had set your tile brush. Wet the bowl of the sink. Since the brush is still full of cleanser from the tub, use it as is to clean the sink. Be careful to keep the cleanser only *inside the bowl* of the sink, because it is difficult to rinse away. *Never* let powdered cleanser get onto an area that is hard to rinse—especially the top ledge of the sink around the faucets.

When the sink is clean, rinse out your tile brush in the sink, and put it away in your tray. Rinse out the sink. You haven't touched the sink rim or faucet yet because you will do that on the second trip around the room. Grab the toilet brush and cleanser from your tray.

The Toilet—Inside

Sprinkle cleanser in and around the sides of the toilet bowl. Wet the toilet brush by dipping it in the toilet and sprinkle some cleanser on it. Start high in the bowl, on the inside upper rim. Move the brush in a circular motion, and clean as deep into the bowl as you can. The water will quickly become cloudy, so be sure to start at the top and methodically work your way around and down the bowl. Don't forget under the rim! All kinds of gremlins live there.

As you wash the toilet bowl, you are also washing and rinsing the toilet brush free of the cleanser you originally sprinkled on it. Shake excess water into the bowl and replace the brush. Flush the toilet. That's out of the way!

The Second Trip

Now it's time to clean around the room. Stick your feather duster and whisk broom into your back pockets. Estimate the number of cleaning cloths you'll need, and transfer them from the tray to your apron. At first, try grabbing six to eight cloths. As time goes on, you'll know how many to use. You're ready to move on to the easy part.

You will generally use two cloths. Carry the drier cloth over your shoulder so it's easy to reach. When that cloth gets too damp for streakless cleaning (mirrors, chrome fixtures, glass shelves, etc.) but is still usable for general wiping, keep it in the apron pocket between uses, and sling a new dry cloth from your apron supply over your shoulder. Throw your old cloth to the floor near your tray. If there's any danger of damage to the floor, put (or toss) the soiled cloths in your tray, or you may ruin the carpet.

Mirrors

Start at the right of the tray, cleaning your way around the room, moving to the right and working from high to low. Be sure to close the door as you go by. There is often a mirror on the inside of the door, and it needs to be cleaned. You need your Blue Juice and a dry cloth to do this, and since you are carrying these items with you in your apron, there is no need to go back to the tray.

To clean a mirror, spray it *lightly* and evenly with Blue Juice, and keep wiping with a dry cloth until the glass is dry. People who have trouble with streaks leave the mirror slightly damp. If you wipe completely dry, you'll eliminate streaks. Replace the Blue Juice sprayer after each use—back where it was on your apron loop.

Fingerprints

The door also may have fingerprints on it that need a quick spray-and-wipe. Fingerprints need Red Juice, so reach for it, spray the prints, replace the bottle, and wipe the area dry.

Here's a task where we are careful to apply Clean Team Rule 4 (page 9): "If it isn't dirty, don't clean it." If all you need to do is remove a fingerprint or two from an otherwise clean door, just spray the prints and wipe dry. Takes about 2 seconds. Don't haphazardly spray a large area of the door (which takes longer) and then have to wipe this larger area dry (which takes longer still).

The places that often *don't* need cleaning are the vertical surfaces of the bathroom (the front of the toilet tank or the outside of the tub, for example). However, the horizontal surfaces (shelves or the top of the toilet tank, for example) will need cleaning every time.

Cobwebs

Train yourself to look all the way to the ceiling to check for cobwebs each time you advance. Spiders seem to especially like corners. When you see a cobweb, grab your feather duster, and proceed. If you can't reach the cobweb, use one or two of the vacuum tubes as an extension wand for the feather duster.

Towels

Towel racks often need your attention—especially where the towel rack is attached to the wall. This is a place to use your toothbrush. A quick swipe with the toothbrush can clean such places much faster and better than your cleaning cloth alone.

Also clean the corners of the towel racks using your toothbrush and Red Juice, and then wipe dry. After you've cleaned them with the toothbrush, a quick wipe with a cloth will suffice for many future cleanings. Fold and re-hang towels after you've finished with the rack.

The Medicine Cabinet

Wipe the very top with a cloth, and then clean the mirror. If it has an outside shelf (usually with a supply of bathroom things on top of it—deodorant, toothpaste, perfume, etc.), move all the items to one side, and spray and wipe the cleared area. (If the shelf is too crowded to merge the two halves, move the items to a nearby countertop.) Now pick up each item and wipe the second side, and finally redistribute the items as they were. Don't open and clean the inside of the cabinet itself, because that's not part of weekly cleaning.

Below the mirror, you'll probably find the toothbrush holder. Clean it with a quick spray-and-wipe. To clean the holes in the holder, put a corner of your cleaning cloth through each hole, and pull up and down a couple of times.

The Sink—Outside Only

When you come to the sink, use the Red Juice to clean around the faucets and the rest of the outside area of the sink—all but the inside of the sink it-self (it's already clean, remember?). *Don't use powdered cleanser!* Use the toothbrush around the base of the faucets each time. Use your white pad and Red Juice around the rest of the outside of the sink. Then wipe as usual. Use a dry cloth for a final wipe and shine of the chrome sink fixtures. Don't dry the whole sink, just the chrome.

Debris

Check below the sink and around the cabinet for fingerprints. Continue around the bath to the right, working from top to bottom. Pay particular at-tention to plants (dust them and then remember to put the feather duster back in your rear pocket), windowsills, pictures, moldings, etc. Don't miss the light fixture in the middle of the room. As you encounter loose trash, dump the debris into the plastic-lined pocket of your apron. (Don't walk to the trash can.)

The Toilet—Outside

When you come to the toilet itself, start at the top of the tank and work
down using Red Juice and a cloth. Once again, Clean Team Rule 4 (page 9)
applies: "If it isn't dirty, don't clean it." If the front of the toilet tank isn't
dirty, don't take the time to "clean" phantom dirt. Don't forget to wipe the
flushing handle as you go by.

When you get to the seat and lid, put them both in the "up" position and
follow this sequence carefully. After you've done it a couple of times, you'll
find that the explanation is much more complicated than the doing.

1. **Spray the underside of the seat, and lower it.**

2. **Spray the top of the seat. Don't wipe yet.**

3. **Spray the underside of the lid, and lower it.**

4. **Spray the top of the lid. Also spray the hinges and the small flat area
   of porcelain on the far side of them.**

Hang your Red Juice on your apron loop, and wipe in the reverse order
that you sprayed. That means you start with the small porcelain area and
hinges. Now start using your toothbrush where needed. The first target is
around those hinges. Then wipe the porcelain, the hinges, and the top of the
lid dry. Raise the lid.

Use your toothbrush around the rubber bumpers and hinges (again). Wipe
clean and dry. Be careful about splattering the clean porcelain. Wipe the top
of the seat and raise it. Use the toothbrush again where needed and wipe dry.
You're done with the lid and seat.

Now spray the top porcelain rim of the bowl. Tilt the seat and lid half forward with one hand and with the other retouch the hinge area of porcelain
(catching any splatters). Push the lid and seat back fully upright and wipe the
rim clean.

Clean all the way down the outside to the floor, using the toothbrush on
areas such as where the toilet meets the floor and around those annoying little
plastic caps. (The inside of the toilet is clean, so don't touch it at all.) If there
is mold left at the base of the toilet after you've cleaned this area, leave it and
spray it with bleach later. You may very well want to dedicate a toothbrush
exclusively for use in this delicate part of the bathroom ecosystem.

The Floor around the Toilet

Even though you haven't started to clean the floor yet, we prefer to be on our hands and knees, eyeball to eyeball with the toilet, only once. So clean the (uncarpeted) floor around the base of the toilet while you're there. Spray the floor around the entire base of the toilet with Red Juice, and wipe it clean and dry. Remember that you are throwing the cloths into the far corner of the room (or into your tray) as they get too soiled or wet. Also remember not to throw soiled cloths on carpets or wood floors—they might stain. If you have a carpeted bathroom, carry a whisk broom in your spare back pocket to brush the areas of carpet that the vacuum can't reach.

Shower Doors—Outside

Just before you finish your trip back to where you left your tray (on the floor at the right end of the tub), you will pass the shower doors. Clean the *outside* only with Blue Juice. Often all you need to clean are the fingerprints around the handle. The outside of the tub occasionally needs a quick swipe. You're just about done!

The Floor

Take several fairly clean and dry cloths to do the floor. Go to the far corner and (on your hands and knees) start spraying and wiping with Red Juice as you back out of the room. The proper technique is to spray an area about 2 feet square lightly and evenly so that hairs and dust don't fly around. Then wipe up with your loosely folded cloths in a deliberate, methodical side-to-side movement (sort of a flattened "S" pattern). As you pick up hair and debris, carefully fold the cloth to trap the debris you've collected so far and continue. When one cloth is too dirty or full, use another cloth. You don't have to dry the floor, but wipe it and turn your cloths often to avoid making streaks.

When you come to the rubber ducky and bar of soap on the floor, you can put them back around the tub, provided there isn't mold left around the tub or shower. If there is, you'll treat it with bleach in a minute, so hold off replacing the ducky and soap until the treatment is finished.

After you've cleaned your way to the door, you can bundle the dirty cloths into a "ragamuffin," so you won't leave a trail of cleaning cloths and debris on the way to the washing machine later. To make a ragamuffin, spread one cloth on the floor and put the other cloths in the middle. Then tie opposite corners of the flat cloth together two at a time. Presto! A ragamuffin. And you're done with the floor.

Bleach

Now is the time to apply bleach to any remaining mold still clinging for dear life in the bathroom. First, make sure the window is open. Bleach destroys just about everything, so treat it like strontium 90. Hold a cloth under the spray nozzle to catch any drips. Set the spray adjustment of your bottle to "stream" instead of "spray," so you minimize the amount of bleach in the air that you might inhale. Apply it as a liquid dribble directly on moldy areas. Wipe off any bleach that gets on the chrome fixtures immediately. Bleach dripping off chrome turns the tub's porcelain black. The discoloring isn't always permanent, but it can be awfully discouraging. When through, drape the same cloth over the spray nozzle to catch any drips as you take your tray through the house. One drip on a carpet will make a little white spot that

Bathroom Summary

(1) Put tray on floor at right end of tub. Put trash cans and rugs outside room. Load up apron, but don't carry duster or whisk broom yet. Make two trips around room: the first for Steps 2 to 6 and the other for the rest.

(2) SHOWER: Set loose items like soap on a cloth on the floor. Wet shower walls. Spread (don't scrub) Tile Juice evenly with the brush starting with the wall farthest from the drain and ending with inside doors. Replace Tile Juice in tray. Start with first wall and scrub all surfaces with tile brush from top to bottom. Clean door tracks with Red Juice and toothbrush or white pad.

(3) TUB: Wet tub and sprinkle lightly with cleanser. Scrub with tile brush, starting away from drain. Put unrinsed brush in sink.

(4) RINSE: Rinse walls top to bottom, starting near drain. Rinse tub starting away from drain. Shine chrome.

(5) SINK (INSIDE): Use tile brush on bowl. Rinse it and brush and return brush to tray.

(6) TOILET: Clean inside toilet bowl with cleanser and toilet brush. Flush toilet and rinse brush. Put feather duster and whisk broom into

lasts forever! Keep the top of the bleach spray bottle covered with a cloth at all times except when you're using it. Also aim the nozzle toward the center of the tray. Changes in room temperature can make bleach ooze out. So can pressure from other objects in your tray. The first time you dribble bleach on your carpet, you'll realize we were not being too fussy, but it will be too late.

Escape

Replace the covered bleach bottle in your tray, and set the tray outside the bathroom. It's not a good idea to leave bleach on surfaces for more than 5 minutes. Come back to the bathroom to rinse away the bleach. This will also give you an opportunity to admire your work.

After rinsing the bleach, replace the rubber ducky and all the other items you had removed from the shower and tub. If it needs it, redry the chrome quickly to put the finishing touch on the bathroom.

Don't move the trash or the carpet that you previously set outside. They will be taken care of after the carpet is vacuumed, and it's time to empty the trash.

---

back pockets. Add six to eight cloths to apron pocket. Start second trip around room.

Note: Fill in Steps 7 through 9 for your own floor plan.

( ) MISCELLANEOUS: Clean the mirror, bathroom door, towel rods, and medicine cabinet.

( ) SINK (OUTSIDE): Spray/wipe faucet, rim, and front of sink. Shine faucet with dry cloth.

( ) TOILET (OUTSIDE): Spray/wipe tank. Raise lid and seat. Spray underneath the seat and lower it. Spray top of seat. Spray underneath the lid and lower it. Spray top of lid and behind it near hinges. Wipe in reverse order. Spray/wipe rest of toilet and floor near base. Continue your way around rest of room.

(10) FLOOR: Spray/wipe floor with Red Juice and cloths, making large "S"-shaped movements from side to side as you work toward door.

(11) BLEACH: Dribble bleach on areas that are still moldy after cleaning. Immediately wipe off bleach that dribbles onto metal surfaces. Rinse off remaining bleach with cold water in 5 minutes. Dry plumbing fixtures if wet. Replace soap and other items.

(YOU'RE FINISHED!)

Spare Bathrooms

If there is a second bathroom that is used daily, go clean it now in exactly the same way. If there is a spare bathroom not often used, clean it according to the "If It Isn't Dirty, Don't Clean It" rule, and use only as much energy as needed. Don't automatically clean the mirrors if they're not dirty. Don't spray the door for fingerprints if none exist. Dust items that you might normally wipe. If the tub/shower hasn't been used, just wipe it quickly with a damp cloth, or spray and wipe with Blue Juice to remove dust. If you do this, it will be just as clean as the one that is used more often, but it will take you only a couple of minutes.

squiggle squiggle squiggle

Chapter 7 Dusting

The Duster's job is to start cleaning the house except for the kitchen and bathroom. This work is drier than the work in the kitchen and bathroom: less spraying and wiping. There are several rooms involved, but they go faster, and there are no floors to wash—except wiping up an occasional drip of something. If you're going to work in a team, the Duster is also the team leader. But we'll get to that in Chapter 8. Stock your carryall tray with the following items.

Materials

 1 spray bottle of Blue Juice
 1 spray bottle of Red Juice
 10 cleaning cloths
 vacuum attachments
 1 feather duster
 1 whisk broom
 1 50-foot extension cord (on a cord caddy)
 1 bottle of furniture polish
 1 polishing cloth
 1 emergency kit:
   1 multipurpose screwdriver
   1 pair of pliers

1 spare vacuum belt

1 spare vacuum bag

Stock your cleaning apron with these items:

1 scraper

1 toothbrush

1 razor-blade holder with a sharp blade

1 plastic bag (as a liner) with clips

Strategy

The strategy here is similar to the one for the kitchen and bathroom. Start in one place and then work your way through the rooms without back-tracking, using The Clean Team rules.

As before, work from high to low. For the Duster, this instruction takes on additional importance: Dust follows a relentless gravitational path downward, diverted only temporarily by air currents. Unless you have a healthy respect for this physical reality, you will find yourself redoing your work constantly. You will have an understandable human impulse first to dust what's right in front of you or what's interesting or what's easy to reach. Instead, train yourself to look *upward* toward molding, tops of picture frames, and light fixtures first, always checking for cobwebs.

Finish each area as you pass by. Do all the dusting, polishing, wiping, brushing, wet-cleaning, and tidying you need to do in an area as you pass through it. Change tools and cleaning supplies as needed: If you are dusting happily along with your feather duster and happen upon raspberry jam smeared on the top of the TV set, *quick!* pop the feather duster into your back pocket with one hand as you reach for the Red Juice with the other. Spray with one hand as the other wipes the jam with the cloth. Then replace the cloth with one hand as the other hand reaches for the feather duster, and you are on your way again. A true blitz—a sign that you are mastering what you are doing. For pity's and time's sake, don't go around the room once to dust, once to polish, once to tidy things, etc.

Whether or not you are working with others, part of your strategy is to reduce the workload of the Vacuumer. (The Vacuumer will normally be someone else if you are working with another person.) Throughout this chapter, we'll suggest ways you can shorten vacuuming time by doing what would have been some of the Vacuumer's work as you dust your way through the house.

Pay attention. Be alert to smarter ways of doing what you're doing. When you shave off a minute or two each time you clean—not by rushing, but by smarter cleaning—that's what it's all about.

The Floor Plan

Since your home or apartment is unique, and since there are so many possible floor plans, we are going to discuss a typical one. Then after you've read this chapter, you'll draw a floor plan of your own home and chart your way through it. So before you even pick up your feather duster, you'll know where you're going to start, where you're going next, and where you'll finish.

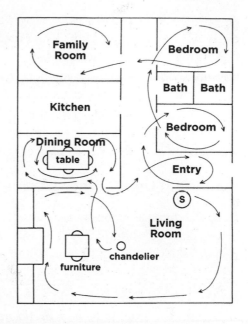

First, though, we'll work our way through the rooms a Duster is likely to encounter—in this case, in our sample home. As we go, we'll explain cleaning methods and techniques to be used in each room and on the furniture, fixtures, and other items. Since there are so many possible arrangements, we do not suppose we're covering them all. We believe, however, that by learning our techniques for these typical rooms, you'll know how to approach items not specifically mentioned here or items arranged in a different order in your home. We know this because it is much more important that you follow *the rules of cleaning* we're teaching rather than learn "hints" about specific items. You use the same technique on a $5,000 Baccarat crystal centerpiece as on a 50-cent garage-sale vase. You may breathe a little differently, but you clean them the same way.

Our sample living room, dining room, entryway, and hall have rugs on a hardwood floor. The bedrooms have wall-to-wall carpeting.

Getting Dressed

Put your apron on and load it from your tray, putting Red Juice on one side and Blue Juice on the other. Put the furniture polish and polishing cloth in your apron. Put your feather duster in one back pocket and the whisk broom in the other. Take six to eight cleaning cloths and put them in the apron. (Next time you clean, you'll know better how many cloths to grab.)

Managing Cleaning Cloths

As you start to spray and wipe your way around the room, carry the drier
cleaning cloth over your shoulder, so it's easy to reach. When that cloth gets
too damp for streakless cleaning (mirrors, picture glass, etc.) but is still usable
for wiping, rotate it to the apron pocket, and sling a new dry cloth from
your apron over your shoulder. Use the damp cloth for wetter cleaning jobs
such as fingerprints, spots on the floor, and windowsills, for example. When
that cloth in turn gets too damp or dirty and is no longer usable even for
wiping, store it in the bottom of your lower right apron pocket.

Managing the Feather Duster

Approach most situations with your feather duster in one hand and the
other hand free. Shift quickly to heavier-duty cleaning options as the situation demands, and gradually you'll notice you're beginning to do so

Dust for Days

*"I pride myself at being a pretty good cleaner, but I can't stay
ahead of dust! What am I doing wrong?"*

Maybe nothing. Some areas and some homes are inherently
dustier than others. Here are a few suggestions, though.

1. Even with regular dusting with a feather duster, an occasional
   thorough dusting with the brush attachment of the vacuum is
   necessary. Use it on all the things you normally dust, such as
   molding, windowsills, miniblinds, tables, pictures, and knickknacks. Also use it behind the couch, the TV, and other areas you
   normally don't vacuum. Change to the furniture attachment, and
   vacuum the furniture and drapes.

2. Make sure your vacuum isn't spewing the dust back into the
   room. Change the bag before it is completely full, make sure the
   fittings and hose are snug, and check to be certain the exhaust
   isn't clogged. Most vacuums have exhaust filters; if yours does,
   change it according to the manufacturer's recommendation.

3. Have the carpets professionally cleaned—especially if the dust
   seems to be the same color as the carpet!

smoothly and to anticipate your next move.

If you use proper technique with the feather duster, you will move most dust quickly from wherever it was to the floor, where it will be vacuumed away. (Top to bottom—Clean Team Rule 3, on page 9.) Poor technique will throw a lot of dust into the air and contribute to the poor reputation unjustly suffered by feather dusters.

Most dusting motions are fast, steady motions over the surface being dusted—a picture frame, for example. At the end of the dusting motion (i.e., at the end of the picture frame), bring the duster to a dead stop. *Don't let the feathers flip into the air at the end of a stroke, thereby throwing all the dust into the air, where it will stay until you've finished cleaning and then settle back on all the furniture you've just finished cleaning.*

By coming to a dead stop at the end of each stroke, you will give the dust a chance to cling to the feathers. To remove the accumulated dust from the feathers, tap the feather duster smartly against your ankle, close to the floor,

4. Change the filters in your heating and air conditioning systems. Upgrade to improved filters if possible. Or purchase an upgraded type of filtration for your heating, ventilating, and air conditioning system.

5. Prevent dust at its source with doormats in front of every exterior door.

6. Install a portable room air purifier (HEPA rated, if allergies are also involved). A purifier can make a big difference. Install it between the probable source of dust (e.g., the front door) and the living area of the room.

7. Eliminate sneaky sources of dust like boxes of pop-up tissues.

8. New carpets can shed a huge amount of fibers at first, so vacuum more often after one has been installed.

9. Caulk around windows and doors or even replace them in extreme cases.

every once in a while. The object is to get the dust to settle on the floor where it will await vacuuming.

The Starting Point

Set your tray on the floor next to the door of the first room you're going to clean. On our floor plan (page 65), the starting point is shown by an "S" in a circle. For our purposes, you're going to start by cleaning the living room.

The Living Room

Cobwebs

Clean Team Rule 3 (page 9) says to work from top to bottom, so the first thing to do is to look up and check for cobwebs. Use your feather duster to remove them. If they're out of reach, stick your feather duster in the end of one or two lengths of vacuum wand. Then do a quick tour of the whole room, because it's too time-consuming to put down and pick up this makeshift apparatus more than once. Kill all spiders. Or catch them and let them loose outside if you're a pacifist or if they beg for mercy.

Fingerprints

Dust door panels or trim with the feather duster. Clean fingerprints around the doorknob with Red Juice (spray and wipe). Then, with Red Juice and cloth still in hand, clean the light switch next to the door. Move to the right along the wall, dusting everything from cobwebs on the ceiling to dust on the baseboards with long "wiping" motions of the feather duster. Remember to stop dead at the end of each swipe. Shift to wet cleaning (Red Juice, Blue Juice, or polish) only if you need to—as Clean Team Rule 7 on page 7 says.

Mirrors and Pictures

Picture glass typically needs wet cleaning only a few times a year. To test for cleanliness, run your *clean* and *dry* fingers lightly over the glass. Any graininess or stickiness means clean it. If it needs it, wet-clean by spraying Blue Juice lightly and evenly and then wiping dry. Wipe it really *dry,* not just until it looks dry. The difference equals a streak: Glass begins to *look* clean as you're wiping it even though it's still slightly wet with Blue Juice. Wipe until it's completely dry. Trust us.

Cobwebs

"What is the best way to remove cobwebs?"

Sometimes one learns more about a subject than one really cares to know. For example, at one time, I innocently supposed that all I needed to remove cobwebs was a feather duster. But professional experience has shown me that so many kinds of cobwebs dwell in so many places that no one tool or method will work unfailingly in every circumstance. There are . . .

1. Cobwebs on ceilings

2. Cobwebs in or on intricate collectibles, plants, chandeliers, etc.

3. Cobwebs in windows and corners

4. Cobwebs in vents

5. Cobwebs in kitchens, or sticky ones anywhere

6. Cobwebs in the garage, basement, eaves, attic, etc.

Feather dusters of various sizes will work in some situations. Small flexible feathers work well for delicate items, plants, chandeliers, and so forth. Longer, more rigid feathers are best for cobwebs in vents, corners, and windows. But you'll need a brush to remove sticky cobwebs and maybe even Red Juice to remove ones stuck to a wall. If your house has high or rough ceilings, beams, or other areas from which cobwebs are hard to remove, a ceiling and wall brush on an extension pole is the answer. An old-fashioned straw broom is just the thing to vanquish an accumulation of many years of cobwebs from the garage or attic or basement. By the way, we're convinced that some spiders spin stickier webs than others and that one or more species must be invisible.

Wipe in broad movements, taking care to wipe the corners well. Don't wipe in small circles or random excursions. Also, stabilize the frame with one hand—*firmly,* don't be halfhearted—while you wipe with the other. If you don't stabilize it, it may fall or leave scratches on the wall from the frame jiggling as you clean it.

The woods are full of people who can do a slow and mediocre job of cleaning glass. Our goals are higher, and one of the things that makes the greatest difference is checking your work. If you look head on into the glass, you will see a reflection of your own sweet face, but you may miss 80 percent of the dirt on the surface. Check it from as narrow an angle as you can.

Once you have cleaned a picture frame or mirror, it probably won't need a thorough wet-cleaning again for weeks or even months. Dust it every week or so on the top of the frame and occasionally even the glass itself.

Wall Marks

As you dust, check the walls for marks and fingerprints. Use Red Juice on wall marks of all kinds. Before you move to the next section of the wall, look all the way to the floor (especially when there is a wood or tile floor) to check for little dried-up spills that should be wiped away.

End Tables—Surface

Clean *above* the end table first. With wiping motions of the feather duster, dust the lamp shade, bulb, lamp, and then the objects on the table. The surface of an end table is rarely touched, so there is no need to use furniture polish every week. Just use your furniture-polish cloth without extra polish. By "polish" we mean either wax or oil—an important distinction to make, it turns out, because the two do not get along well on the surface of furniture. If you've been using an oil polish ("lemon oil," "red oil," etc.) continue using it. Otherwise use the Old English from your apron pocket—a type of liquid wax that we find very easy to use.

End Tables—Objects

When cleaning an object-laden table, just work from top to bottom again. Use your feather duster first (on lamps and objects on the table), then a cleaning cloth (on objects that need more cleaning), and then the polishing cloth (on the table itself).

Use caution. Cleaning and moving small items on shelves and tables is the scene of most accidents for Dusters. A few guidelines will avoid most accidents: Most important, pay attention to what's in front of you. Use both hands to move anything top-heavy or irreplaceable, or anything composed of more than one piece (e.g., a hurricane-lamp base with a glass lantern on top). It's almost never wise to move something on a pedestal by pushing the pedestal.

Steady the top piece with one hand, and grab the pedestal with the other. You usually get to make only one mistake with such things. And keep a wary eye out for heavy objects: *Do not,* oh *do not,* slide them across the surface of furniture. Scratches will follow in their path without fail or mercy.

Dust Rings

Our end table is on a wood floor, so use your feather duster to wipe the floor around the legs and underneath it to save time for the Vacuumer. By dusting these areas where the vacuum would leave rings or where the vacuum can't reach, you are speeding up that job, since the Vacuumer won't have to stop to do it. If furniture is on a carpet, use the whisk broom instead of the feather duster for this job.

Couches

Fabrics vary greatly in characteristics that affect cleaning strategy. If you're lucky, your furniture will need only a quick swipe with the whisk broom. At the other extreme are fabrics that hair will cling to until you pluck it off like a surgeon. In the middle are a great number of fabrics that will cooperate reasonably and respond to your whisk broom. Every so often, even the most agreeable of fabrics could use a good vacuuming, however, to remove accumulated dust. The frequency of vacuuming depends on how dusty your environment is and how sloppy you are. If you like to eat crackers while sitting on your couch or if the cat sleeps there, you will overwhelm the capacities of the whisk broom and will have to call in the vacuum regularly. But not now. *First finish* dusting and polishing.

Back to our sample couch, however, which has pet hair and cookie crumbs on it. Clean from the top down, using your whisk broom. You will be tempted to start with the cushions, as they are easiest to deal with. Resist. First, starting with the left side of the couch, whisk the crumbs and hair from the top, back, and sides. (Careful not to make work for yourself by whisking debris onto the clean end table.) Whisk down and toward the cushion.

Should you clean under the cushions? Ah, the eternal question asked by reluctant cleaners! The answer lies under those very cushions. Lift up a cushion or two and peek. You will know instantly. If it needs a thorough cleaning underneath, set the left cushion on the one next to it to get it out of the way while you whisk out that area. Then move to the next section and (starting once again at the top of the couch) repeat the process. If the area under the cushions only needs a touch-up, just tilt the cushion up for a quick swipe with the whisk broom. Leave the tops of the cushion for the Vacuumer, who can do them much faster.

To signal the Vacuumer that the cushion tops *only* are to be vacuumed, leave a cushion overlapping the next one. The large vacuum has a beater brush that is safe for most fabrics. You simply lift the beater brush up to the couch cushions and vacuum away. No further vacuuming is necessary as long as you have removed the hair and crumbs from the rest of the couch. Keep in mind that you want to do everything possible to make vacuuming easier. These steps greatly reduce vacuuming time.

Be careful. Vacuuming fabric with the beater brush can catch certain loose fabrics, can catch tassels or strings, can damage certain delicate fabrics, or may accelerate the wear and tear of your couch. If you prefer to avoid any risk, use the small vacuum.

If the amount of pet hair on the couch demands that the *entire* couch be vacuumed, then don't whisk it at all. It can be vacuumed with the small vacuum after the dusting. The signal to remind yourself or a partner to vacuum the *entire* couch is to stand one cushion straight up.

To signal the Vacuumer to clean *under* the couch, move one corner of the couch forward. If the couch is the sort that sits flush to the floor, it doesn't need to be moved often, since it's almost impossible for dirt to get under it.

Plants

Continuing top to bottom and left to right, you come upon a large potted plant in the corner. Dust the plant with the feather duster top to bottom. On broad-leaf plants, support a leaf with one open hand while you dust with the other, so the stem doesn't snap. Pick up the dead leaves, which often clog the vacuum, and put them in the apron trash pocket. Our sample plant is close to the wall and too heavy to move easily, so, with a cleaning cloth, dust the hardwood floor around and behind it where the vacuum can't reach—once again, saving the Vacuumer time.

Drapes and Window Frames

Next is a wall with windows. With your feather duster, dust the top of the drapes and curtain rods for cobwebs. Working from top to bottom, dust all the window frames. Don't use a feather duster on wet windows unless you want to ruin your day. (A wet feather duster is a pitiful sight.) Often in the winter, you'll have to wipe with a cloth because the frames are wet. Then dust the windowsill.

Leather Chairs

Particles of dust, sand, and grit work their way into leather and wreak havoc with the finish and stitching. The whisk broom is excellent for dusting leather furniture, especially if the upholstery is tufted and has buttons or piping. And use your toothbrush if the cracks and crevices are dirty: Keep both in hand, because with the whisk broom, you can brush away particles the toothbrush dredges up. (Brush/swipe, brush/swipe, brush/swipe. . . .)

Bookshelves

Next is the fireplace wall with bookshelves on each side. Dust the top of the books if there is room, and dust the exposed edges of the shelves with long wiping motions of the feather duster. Remember to shake the dust out of the feather duster at regular intervals near floor level by whacking it against your ankle.

Dust very ornate objects (e.g., candlesticks) with small squiggly motions of the feather duster so the feathers get into all the little places.

Do not dust the hearth, because you will get soot on your feather duster and ruin it. Leave it for the small vacuum. If the room had wall-to-wall carpeting, you would wipe the hearth with a cloth, so the Vacuumer wouldn't have to bring in the small vacuum just for the hearth. (See the first part of Chapter 13 on vacuuming.)

Middle of the Room

You've worked your way to the entrance to the dining room. Before leaving the living room, dust the molding on the small section of wall between the door to the entry hall and the door to the dining room. Move to the center of the room and dust the chandelier with the feather duster (squiggly motions).

Polishing the Table

On the carpet in front of the fireplace is a card table with four chairs that have been well used. Moving around the table, first pull each of the chairs away from the table and dust each one in turn. Do this with your polishing cloth in one hand and a feather duster in the other. Use the polishing cloth on the tops and arms of the chairs and the feather duster on the frame and slats. Leave the chairs away from the table to make it easier for the Vacuumer to maneuver.

To polish a small tabletop, spray on polish in a thin and even coat. Begin to wipe immediately, because polish left in place even for a minute or so begins to eat into the finish. (If that starts to happen, spray on more and wipe like mad.) *Wipe in the direction of the wood grain.* This is more shrewd than superstitious: Streaks left by imperfect polishing will be camouflaged by blending in with the wood grain if you rub in that direction. Wipe with your polishing cloth folded into an area as large as your hand—not mushed into a ball—so you make maximum use of each swipe. (*Saves time.*) As you rub, the polish will spread out evenly and begin to dry. When it is almost finished drying, flip the cloth onto its back— which should be kept *dry*—and buff the finish to a shine. Make big sweeping movements to save time. When the table exceeds your arm length, spray half at a time. (The table, that is, not your arm.) Don't press down hard as you buff: It's harder work, and you can scratch the surface even with polish. Finally, check for streaks and missed spots, and deal with them with the driest part of the cloth.

The Dining Room

Enter the dining room from the living room, and begin dusting above the doorway, working from top to bottom as always. In the first corner is a plant: Use your feather duster as you did earlier.

Mirror-Top Buffet

Across the back wall is a mirror-top buffet with liquor bottles on top. Move the bottles to the right side, and spray and wipe the vacated area. Use a Blue Juice–sprayed cloth to clean the bottles as you replace them. If you encounter cigarette butts or other debris, remember to deposit them in your apron trash pocket. *Do not* walk around looking for a trash can! Clean the other side of the mirror top and continue. Our buffet sits on the hardwood floor on short legs. The vacuum can get underneath, but use the feather duster around the legs to prevent dust rings.

Dining-Room Table

Polish the dining-room table each time unless it hasn't been used at all. It saves the most time to polish half of the table, dust the chairs closest to you, polish the other half of the table, and then finish the chairs. The point is to minimize retracing your steps. A good brushing is all most chair seats need.

Don't forget to dust the chair rungs or the legs themselves if they curve outward near the tip. While you're down there, check to see if either the pedestal or crossbeams of the table need dusting too.

Hallways

Enter the hall and dust in the same way, beginning above the door and working from top to bottom around the entry. Our table is unused and requires only the feather duster for the objects and the polishing cloth for the table. Use the feather duster around the legs of the table again.

Go farther into the hall and continue in the same top-to-bottom manner but alternately dust and wipe sections of *both walls* as you move down the hall. Don't do one side and then the other; you waste time retracing your route.

The Bedrooms

Enter the first bedroom off the hall. Begin in the same manner, above the door, moving to the right. Pull the foot of the bed away from the wall to

Dust Mites

"I saw a picture of a dust mite, and it's freaking me out. These mites seem to be everywhere, according to the article I read. I don't want those ugly things in my house! What should I do?"

The first thing I suggest is that you relax. Just because we are only now discovering dust mites doesn't mean that they are a new menace. They have probably been around since the dinosaurs. They were certainly present in your mother's and grandmother's homes, yet your family survived them intact.

How important they are to you really depends on whether anyone in your home is allergic to them. The allergen usually isn't so much the dust mite itself as dust mite "dust," composed mainly of assorted dust-mite body parts and feces. If nobody is allergic, there's nothing to be concerned about. Keep the little critters to a minimum with routine housecleaning, perhaps paying particular attention to laundering the bedding regularly as well as vacuuming mattresses and upholstered furniture with care. If you or family members do have allergies, seek advice from an allergist.

indicate that the Vacuumer should clean under it this time. As the Duster, you are in charge of knowing which chores are to be rotated—and which rotation is to be done this time. An example is vacuuming under the bed, which may not need to be done every week but can't be ignored forever either. The same applies to heavy furniture (like the couch) and some high molding and other difficult areas to vacuum.

Desk

The desk in our sample room is so close to the corner that the head of the vacuum won't fit, so use the whisk broom to dust and fluff that section of carpet next to the desk. (Remember, this is a wall-to-wall carpet.) This will keep the carpet pile from looking dusty. You can vacuum this spot every few months when you move the desk to vacuum behind it. Also, set any trash cans as close to the doorway as you can without interrupting your trip around the room.

Telephone

Only rarely can a phone be just dusted, as it is one of the most frequently used objects in the house. Clean it with the already wet furniture polishing cloth. It's a mess to spray the phone directly, as there are all sorts of nooks and crannies. Only if the phone is extraordinarily dirty should you spray it directly with furniture polish and use your toothbrush to dislodge dirt from crevices. Unravel a tangled cord by unplugging one end and uncoiling it. To avoid leaving fingerprints, polish the body of the phone first and then the handset. Likewise, replace the handset not with your bare hand but with the polishing cloth wrapped around it. (It takes time for the polish to dry on such nonporous surfaces, during which time objects fall prey to fingerprints.)

Miniblinds

On the window are dusty miniblinds. Lower them to their full length, and turn the slats to the closed position so the blinds curve away from you. By grasping the string that runs through them, pull them away from the window, so you can reach behind them with your feather duster. Dust them using long *downward only* strokes at a slow speed so the feather duster can do more dust-catching than dust-storming. Remember, stop the feather duster dead still at the end of each stroke. Remove the dust collected after each

Things Often Overlooked by Distracted Dusters

- Areas around electric cords that trap circulating dust

- Backs of chairs

- Baseboards

- Bottom shelves of anything, but especially end tables and coffee tables

- Bulbs in table lamps and inside surfaces of shades

- Chandelier chains

- Crossbeams underneath tables

- Curved feet of chairs and tables

- Drapes near the top

- Hanging light fixtures, especially the bulbs

- Heater and exhaust vents

- Louvered shutters

- Plants (dust broadleaf ones just like anything else)

- Telephones

- Tops of bookshelves

- Tops of drawers and drawer pulls

- TV picture tubes

- Windowsills and molding on windowpanes

stroke by tapping the duster against your ankle near the floor. Now turn the slats forward so the blinds curve *toward* you. Dust the front in the same long, slow *downward* motions.

The Family Room

This room is often full and well used. This makes it doubly important that you follow the Speed Cleaning method exactly.

TV, VCR/DVD Player, and Stereo

The TV is cleaned by using a feather duster on the back and Blue Juice on the body and screen. Use your feather duster on the VCR or DVD player. To remove fingerprints, spray Red Juice on your cloth and wipe them off. Make sure you don't get Red (or any other kind of) Juice anywhere near videotapes or the inner machinery of the VCR or DVD player. Also use your feather duster on the stereo, being careful not to snag the tone arm or needle and thereby destroy the cartridge you just paid a day's salary for. Use your already damp furniture polish cloth to remove fingerprints from the plastic dust cover. Or spray it directly if it's very dusty to protect against scratching the soft plastic.

YOU'RE FINISHED!

It's not quite time for your nap yet—but it's getting close. All that remains is the vacuuming!

Chapter 8 Team Cleaning

You may be lucky enough to have one or two others to work with. If so, someone needs to delegate the tasks and have a good overall view of the work as it progresses. That person is the Team Leader. The primary responsibility of the Team Leader is to see that all team members finish cleaning at the exact same time.

Finally, Some Decisions to Make

To finish together requires some decision making on your part. Like, where do you start cleaning, so you'll finish together? When the Bathroom Person finishes his/her primary job, what's next? The same for the Kitchen Person.

The Longest Job

The key to finishing together is to identify the longest job and get it started at the right time. The longest job is the one that takes the longest time *and* that no one can help with. This is often the vacuuming.

When this longest job should be started is crucial. Get the longest job started early so it isn't still going on when the rest of the team is finished.

The top graph on page 80 shows time wasted by starting the longest job (vacuuming) at the wrong time. The Bathroom Person ended up vacuuming while the other two stood idle. If the Duster had dusted only 10 minutes, started the vacuuming, and then finished dusting, the whole team would have finished together. (See the bottom graph.) They also would finish the entire housecleaning 18 minutes faster apiece—that's nearly 1 full hour less total cleaning time per week!

The First Time

The first time you clean your home, you should start dusting in the living room. If you later find you're unable to avoid having the team end up in the same room toward the end of the cleaning job, then change your starting point to the master bedroom.

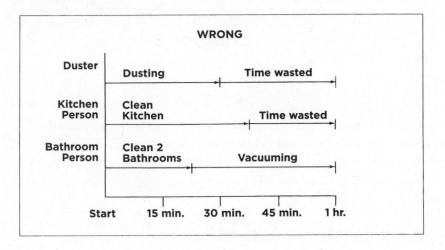

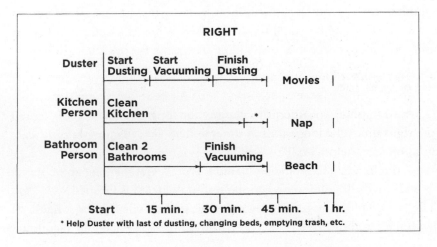

When the Other Team Members Finish Their First Job

As Team Leader, you should ask *whoever* finished first (usually the Bathroom Person) to start vacuuming in the rooms you have already dusted. He should start where you did and follow your same path.

When the Kitchen Person finishes, have her make the beds with you (assuming you make beds when you clean). *Don't* make a bed alone because two people can make a bed four times faster than one person. Then have the Kitchen Person start vacuuming the hardwood floors (using the Little Vac), also starting in the living room and following your same path through the house. The Kitchen Person can also use the Little Vac on any furniture as signaled by you. Next, she gathers up the trash by going from room to room and emptying smaller containers into the largest one, so only one trip is made outside to the garbage can.

Important Points: Back to Basics

We hope all this doesn't sound difficult, because doing it is very easy.

1. If the longest job isn't finished when the rest of the jobs are, then start the longest job sooner the next time you clean.

2. If you all end up in the same room at the end, then dust that room sooner or vacuum it sooner or empty the trash from it sooner.

3. If the dusting job is taking too long, then have a second team member do some of the dusting.

4. If you aren't finishing together even after getting the longest job started earlier, save all the short jobs for last—emptying trash, making bed(s), putting throw rugs back in place, finishing touches, and checking each other's work (nicely, nicely).

5. If you still have problems finishing together, sit down and talk about it. Don't feel that just because you're Team Leader you are alone in a boat adrift. Try suggestions that come from the other team members.

Team Cleaning in a Team of Three or More

Most of what we discussed in this chapter applies to a team of three. The jobs are a Kitchen Person, a Bathroom Person, and the Duster. Teams of four or more are so inefficient (unless you have a huge house) that you may want to rotate people off each time you clean.

Team Cleaning in a Team of Two

In a team of two, one person starts as the Bathroom Person and the other as the Kitchen Person. The Team Leader is the one who finishes the initial assignment first—normally the bathroom. The Team Leader then changes the bathroom tray into a duster tray and starts dusting. The Kitchen Person starts vacuuming with the Big Vac after finishing the kitchen. Make adjustments so that each time the two of you clean, you come closer and closer to finishing at the same time. It is much simpler for two people to finish at the same time than three, since there are fewer possibilities for how to divide up the work.

Teenagers

How do you get teenagers to help clean the bathroom, the kitchen, or any other room of the house?

Learning how to clean is an essential part of the skills required to get along in life. After all, cleaning skills can ease your toil, save time, and result in a more enjoyable living space for the rest of a lifetime. Also, even though your children may not realize it right now (or admit it if they do!), most people find a task more enjoyable once they know how to do it properly and are skillful at it—no matter what the skill is.

In order for teenagers to warm to the prospect of doing their share of cleaning, you might have a fighting chance if they realize they're getting it over with in absolutely the least time possible (this also shows you're respecting their time and interests). As you are no doubt keenly aware, teenagers are in a developmental stage when absolute rules become less and less effective. Adults relate to one another far more often with contracts (agreements) than with rules. So if you can approach your teenagers on more of a contractual basis, you might get a better response—something in the order of "We have a contract: I'll give you an allowance in exchange for meeting certain conditions." You're looking for what's called a meeting of the minds. Oh, you will undoubtedly also need a reward.

Note: Similar tactics also work for adults. For example, if someone just plain doesn't like cleaning and is avoiding it, learning how to do it really helps! A big reason people dislike a task is because they're not exactly sure how to go about it. Learn Speed Cleaning, be done with the cleaning and the guilt, and move on.

Team Cleaning in a Team of One

This is the most efficient way possible. No decisions, no negotiations—just follow the Speed Cleaning method and yet get faster every time you do it.

Working all the time and doing all the chores is dangerous. In her book *The Second Shift: Working Parents and the Revolution of Home,* sociologist Arlie Hochschild calls a woman who tries to do everything the superwoman. It's not possible to do it all. There's just not enough time. There are other prices to pay. Divorce is one of them.

My opinion is that if both spouses are working, a division of labor at home, not biased by gender-specific job definitions, is imperative. It may be that one spouse does all the housework but the other spouse does the shopping and transporting of the kids, for example. Talk to your husband, and negotiate a fairer division of labor at home. If your kids are old enough, or as they get older, recruit them to help also. After all, they contribute most to getting the house dirty. They should help clean it.

Note: Put aside historic gender-specific traditions about who should do what, and develop as fair a division of labor as you can sort out together.

Recording Your Improvement

You might want to chart your weekly housecleaning times, so you can see how dramatically your time improves. Use it to motivate the members of your team during this critical learning period. Post it where it is easily seen, reviewed, and ultimately admired.

Chapter 9 An Encouraging Word

Did you ever despair of learning to tie your shoe, ride a bike, or swim? Can you remember how difficult it was to do something that is now mindless in its simplicity?

Did you ever learn touch-typing? If you did, you know that it took you longer to use touch-typing than your old hunt-and-peck method when you were first learning. You had to break comfortable, old (inefficient) habits and replace them with unfamiliar, uncomfortable, and new (but very efficient) habits.

Also, if you used your old hunt-and-peck method of typing all day long every day, you would never, ever get much faster than 30 words a minute—even with all that practice. However, if you practiced your new touch-type method daily, you would improve your speed constantly. One hundred words per minute is not an unheard-of speed. That's more than three times faster than a method that once seemed just fine to you.

Housecleaning isn't going to go away, so practice. Practice and be fast, and then do something much more fun or satisfying with all the time you saved.

Part 2: Deep Clean

Chapter 10 Deep Cleaning

You've probably already figured out that this is a book about housecleaning written for people who would rather be doing just about anything else. The Clean Team's unique system of cleaning relies on principles of time-and-motion economy to reduce cleaning time by half or more. Our concern is saving time during weekly cleaning—the tasks most of us regard as routine cleaning (e.g., dusting, vacuuming, and cleaning sinks and toilets).

Part 1, Speed Clean, contained the first systematic approach to cleaning an entire household ever presented in print. But it also had a special emphasis: to get it over with as soon as possible—not to linger, fuss, dawdle, or dwell over it. You see, we were really writing just as much about personal freedom as we were about cleaning: how to free yourself from one of daily life's great drudgeries—housecleaning.

Many of us, burdened with the time pressures of working, commuting, and trying to hold a household together, barely seem to have time to butter the toast in the morning, let alone strip the floors. Presuming you can find the time, *how do you start? And will there be anything left of the weekend if you do?* This book offers relief on both accounts.

Part 2 addresses two major types of housecleaning.

1. Spring cleaning. Tasks that need to be done once or twice a year—stripping and waxing floors, cleaning windows, walls, rugs, etc.

We will show you how to do major housecleaning tasks the smart and fast way on your first attempt. And how to do them right, so you won't have to repeat them for the longest possible time. Our method also makes the jobs less frustrating and more rewarding.

2. Heavy (catch-up) cleaning. Tasks that you have to do to be able to start routine cleaning. These include tasks you don't do every time you clean but that you can't ignore forever.

It is for all those who, despite their best intentions, are always falling behind or just never get started. Not that we blame you. We all know what's lurking behind the refrigerator and under the sofa cushions, but we also know it's not going to go away by itself. Many households need a thorough cleaning before a rational person would even attempt weekly or maintenance cleaning. There's little point in cleaning just the top layer of crud over and over; the unexcavated layers are still there.

We are going to teach you one very good way to do each job. It's not that there aren't other alternatives. We just aren't going to mention them. Our steadfast aim is to show you how to get cleaning over with so you have time to go to that evening class, or watch the football game, or take the kids to the park, or whatever else it is in your life that needs some time to flourish. We could gather everything there is to know about window washing, for example, into one surprisingly large book. It would take you all weekend to read it, let alone put it into practice. That's not what we're up to. We will give you as few decisions to make as possible about cleaning methods and products.

The flip side of this issue would be not *enough* information to do the job. We've read books on cleaning that just raise issues and never get around to telling you *what to do* or *how to do it*. After reading them, we still don't know exactly where to start or what materials to use or where to find the materials.

It would be wrong to be smug about all this. We just didn't have a choice, that's all. If we didn't develop a way of cleaning houses fast, we would be doing it for fun, not profit. The profit margin for residential cleaning is just too small to waste a minute's time. Every move has to count, and we also had to find the right products that wouldn't slow us down *or* make us redo our work. It was hard, and we learned some expensive lessons along the way. But *with this book,* you can learn from our experience much faster.

Chapter 11 The Oven

How often you do this chore depends on how often you use the oven. It's a messy and overnight job.

The first thing to notice when contemplating cleaning the oven is whether it is a self-cleaning species. If it is, follow the manufacturer's directions, not ours, and be thankful.

As long as your oven interior is a smooth baked-enamel finish (95 percent chance), you will find this chore yucky but manageable. If you have an oven whose interior feels like fine sandpaper, you have a problem, since the oven cleaner is very difficult to remove after the cleaning process. Give up.

Spray your oven the night before you are going to clean it. You'll need oven cleaner and rubber gloves. (Most of the grocery-store brands do a passable job. We settled on Easy-Off as our first choice.) Before spraying the oven, remove the racks, placing them on top of the stove *the same way you took them out* (so you don't waste time later trying to figure out which is the top and how they go back in). Also remove anything else that should be removed, such as heating coils that pull out or unplug. Even if your whole interior oven comes apart for removal and cleaning, leave it together and clean it our way instead.

Put old cleaning cloths, paper towels, or newspapers on the floor to catch any drips and overspray. Spray the interior of the oven and the door as well. Often, the racks don't need cleaning. Skip them whenever you can, because

---

"Self-Cleaning" Ovens

"How do you clean self-cleaning ovens?"

This really is a good question, but I can't help thinking of questions like "What time is midnight Mass?" or "Who's buried in Grant's tomb?" Self-cleaning or no, ovens always seem to be in some state of dirtiness. And some of us are nervous about the high heat and odor created by self-cleaning ovens—or the power bill that follows—and prefer not to use the self-cleaning cycle. In any event, you must follow the manufacturer's directions to the letter. Don't try to clean them with oven cleaners like Easy-Off, Dow, Mr. Muscle, and so forth. For spots the automatic cleaning cycle misses (such as the edges of the door), use Red Juice and a white pad or green pad. To clean a spattered oven window quickly, use Red Juice and a razor in a holder. Be protective of the oven once it's clean. Use aluminum foil if there's any chance a dish will overflow during baking. Wipe up little spills ASAP. Clean baked-on blackened spots without cleaning the whole oven by spraying with Red Juice and coaxing them off with a pumice stick.

---

they are difficult and time-consuming. If you are *not* cleaning them, leave them on top of the stove until you are done with the oven. If you are cleaning the racks, replace them after you have sprayed the inside of the oven and *then* spray them too. Spray the oven thoroughly: A little too much is better than not enough. If you overdo it, however, oven cleaner will drip onto the floor and make even more of a mess. Avoid the interior light and thermostat when spraying. Be sure to spray the door but not the door edges.

If you are going to clean the broiler too (wow!), then spray it now also. Just spray the broiler tray itself. Don't spray the holder grooves or underneath the broiler. Those areas don't have the cooked-on stuff and can be cleaned with Red Juice and your green pad. (Faster and eminently less messy.)

Put the racks back in if you haven't already, close the door, put away the oven cleaner, and go to bed. Don't heat the oven. Sweet dreams, for tomorrow you'll be up to your elbows in gook.

Next day—if you are also doing the weekly cleaning of the kitchen—clean the oven before you start the regular cleaning sequence. *Don't heat the oven.* Set the trash can by the stove for now, and place a roll of paper towels or old, disposable rags (ones that are no longer good enough to use as regular cleaning cloths) next to it. Also, take the scraper from your apron, and put it on the cloths in front of the stove. You'll be using it repeatedly, and your gloves will be covered with oven cleaner. This way, you'll keep the oven cleaner off your apron.

Start by *putting on the gloves!* First, clean the inside of the oven door with your green pad. Use your razor on the glass door. Wipe the oven cleaner from the door. Then spray the same area with Red Juice, and wipe it clean and dry. Clean the racks next, starting with the highest one. Use the green pad. Pull it out into the locked position to make cleaning easier. As you finish a rack, pull it out and set it in the sink. Rinse well with tap water. Be careful not to scratch the sink. (Use a cloth or two to put under the edges of the rack when rinsing.) After all the oven cleaner is removed, just let the racks drain and dry in the sink while you return to clean the next one down. As you clean them, pay special attention to the leading edges (the ones that you see when the rack is in the oven).

After the racks, clean the inside of the oven starting with the inside top. Systematically agitate with your green pad over the entire top of the oven until all the baked-on residue is loose. But don't remove it yet. Move on to the right side, then the rear, and then the left side before you finish with the bottom. On areas where there are baked-on "lumps" (usually on the bottom only), use your scraper first (remember, it's on the floor in front of the oven). The idea

Stainless Steel Stove Hood

"I have a stove with a stainless steel hood. I can't seem to remove splattered grease from this area. What should I do?"

Cooked-on grease calls for a grease cutter, so grab your Red Juice. Since the hood is stainless steel, we advise using a white pad because even #0000 steel wool can scratch the finish of stainless steel. Scrub with a toothbrush as needed in corners.

Keep this area from becoming a problem so quickly by keeping the filter clean and by wiping the hood inside and out when you do your weekly cleaning. (See page 248 for filter-cleaning instructions.)

Note: We didn't refer you to a specialized stainless steel cleaner because one isn't necessary. However, stainless steel cleaners add a sheen that many find appealing.

Cleaning

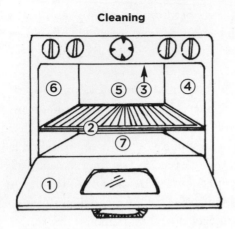

is to knock off most of what you're removing with the scraper first and then get what little remains with the green pad. Saves a lot of time.

Here the concept of "seeing through" the mess of what you're cleaning has particular meaning. Even if the oven were clean, you couldn't see through the oven cleaner. And unless you're much more compulsive than we are, your oven is not clean. You can quickly learn the difference between how your green pad feels when the oven surface is clean and how it feels on a dirty surface that needs additional scrubbing.

This "see-through" process is also especially important here because removing the oven cleaner is a big chore. If you've missed crud and have to re-spray and reclean, you may be tempted to give up cooking rather than go through it again.

Even after you've used the scraper to remove lumps, be prepared to grab for it quickly when you encounter something that your green pad doesn't easily remove.

As you may well have noticed, your green pad became a slimy, gooey, even yucky mess about half a second after you started this delightful chore. Resist the impulse to go to the sink and rinse the pad out. It will return to a slimy mess half a second after you return. It actually works just as well dirty for a long time. And, of course, the whole procedure is much faster if you don't make several trips to the sink to rinse.

When the pad is full of gunk and oven cleaner, it is harder to hold because it gets slippery. Try to overcome this by folding the pad in half or gripping it differently or squeezing it out onto the oven bottom—anything to avoid having to rinse it. When you just can't grip it any longer, go rinse. Also, if the oven is very dirty (especially when you're cleaning the bottom), your pad will lose its effectiveness when it gets thoroughly clogged with debris. When that happens, it's also time to go rinse. (Sounds like something your dentist would say.)

After you have gone over the entire oven this way, rinse out the green pad and scraper, and put them in your apron. Start wiping the inside of the oven using paper towels or old rags. Wipe it out just the reverse of the way you just scrubbed it. Start with the bottom, then the left side, the rear, the right side, and finally the top. Wipe the entire oven out once, rather thoroughly—discarding the towels or rags into the trash can next to you. Now spray the entire inside of the oven with Red Juice and wipe clean and dry to get rid of the residual oven cleaner.

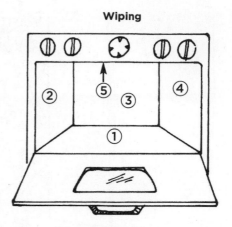

Wiping

If the broiler was previously sprayed, now is the time to finish it. (Don't you really want to do this some other day?) Clean it in the sink with your green pad. Use your scraper if necessary—and it usually is. Protect the sink by putting cloths under the broiler. Rinse it clean, wipe it, and replace it.

Fold up the cloths (or paper towels), pick up the newspapers and discard into the trash, take a deep breath, and start cleaning the kitchen. It's a good idea to turn the oven to 400°F for 15 minutes while you start cleaning the kitchen. This cooks any oven cleaner you may have missed to a nice visible white powder that you can easily see to remove after the oven cools off. Also, if the oven is going to stink or smoke a bit, it's a good idea to get that little episode over with now instead of when you have company over for dinner.

You have cleaned an oven! Amazing how much better it looks—and you get all the credit! You may be tempted to go outside and stop strangers to bring them in and show them your clean oven. Resist: They may track in dirt.

Chapter 12 The Refrigerator

This is not a weekly cleaning. However, if you are going to clean the refrigerator when you do your regular cleaning of the kitchen, do it first—before anything else. If the freezer is to be cleaned, it should have been turned off earlier so that it is defrosted and ready to clean. You can help yourself further with this chore by choosing a time to clean it when it's as empty of food as it gets (according to your weekly shopping schedule). Also, before starting, throw out anything that deserves it.

The freezer is easy to clean once the ice is loose. Put any loose ice and ice-cube trays in the sink and proceed to clean. If possible, don't remove anything else. Rather, move items toward the right, spray the left with Red Juice, and wipe. (If a little Red Juice gets on the frozen-food containers, it won't hurt a thing.) Now move items from the right to the left and repeat. You may have to do that in three moves or more. If the freezer is completely full, remove only as much as you have to. When you move items to make room for cleaning, move them onto a shelf in the refrigerator.

Inside the refrigerator itself, start with the top shelf. These interior shelves don't usually need to be emptied. Items on the shelves should not be removed—just moved to the right. Then clean them with Red Juice and white pad, followed by a cleaning cloth to wipe dry. If the shelves are too full to

Sticker Residue

"How do I get stickers off the front of my refrigerator? I want to sell it, but the remnants of two (both now defunct!) Chinese restaurants' stick-on advertisements seem rather permanent."

I know what you mean. Pasting the stickers seemed like such a good idea at the time. The removal process starts by getting a fingernail or plastic spatula under an edge of the sticker, so you can pull off the top layer and expose the glue underneath. Then use a solvent, such as Gunk Remover or lighter fluid. Apply with a paper towel, and use another one to rub the dissolved glue off.

move things to the side, then remove only enough so that you can move the rest from side to side. When you remove items from a shelf, set them on a convenient countertop or on the floor just in front of the refrigerator in the order in which they were removed. After cleaning, replace the items in reverse order.

Do the next lower shelf and the next until you are finished. Drawers and bins should be removed from the refrigerator because you need to clean them inside and out. Plus, it will remind you to clean the nasty area under the bottom drawers. Crud and water both accumulate here.

Generally, you can clean the door shelves by removing a few items, cleaning that space, and then sliding over a few more things and cleaning under them, etc. Pick up and wipe the bottom of each item as you put it back, so it doesn't leave a spot on the clean surface.

When you are finished with the inside of the refrigerator, don't clean the outside yet. Go back and start to clean the kitchen as you normally would. If you are working as part of a team, it often makes sense to have another team member do the inside of the refrigerator as you begin to clean the rest of the kitchen. The reason is that the kitchen can turn into the largest job, and you want the team to finish at the same time. (See Chapter 8.)

Chapter 13 Carpet Care

Vacuums: There Are Two to Use

In a fair world, you are part of a team and therefore need two vacuums, since the opportunity to save even more time justifies the expense. In an unfair world, you have to get by with one vacuum. Let's assume it's fair for now and ignore the accumulating evidence to the contrary.

Their Uses

Use the bigger, canister vacuum ("BigVac") on carpets, rugs, and some upholstery. Use the smaller, portable vacuum ("Little Vac") on hardwood floors, the kitchen floor, and all types of upholstery. If you don't have two vacuums, don't worry when we tell you to use the Little Vac for one task or another. You can use the BigVac with different attachments just about as easily.

Vacuum Amps

How many amps does a good vacuum cleaner have?

Contrary to what I was told by a devoted employee of a vacuum manufacturer, amps are not a good measure of a vacuum cleaner's performance. The amp rating tells you how strong the motor is, not necessarily how strong the suction power is.

Suction power is actually measured by "inches of water lift." Water lift measures, under test conditions, how high a vacuum can pull water up a tube. So my new and improved advice is to ask about the water-lift measurement of the vacuum. It should be listed in the vacuum's specifications. A good vacuum should be rated at 75 inches or more.

The Clean Team has gone through quite a few vacuums since 1979, and we've tried every major brand. The ideal vacuum should . . .

- **Be the canister type.**

- **Have 75 inches (or more) of water lift.**

- **Be comfortable to hold and to use.**

- **Have a long cord and a place to store the cord between uses.**

- **Have an on/off switch that's easy to reach (preferably with your foot).**

- **Be able to vacuum under most furniture.**

- **Not tip over when yanked by the hose.**

- **Have a hose that never twists during use.**

- **Have a handle for easy lifting.**

- **Be light enough to make lifting less of a strain on your back.**

- **Have a paper dust bag with enough holding capacity to last for several weeks plus a pleated filter that traps particles as small as 0.5 micron.**

Of course, I've never found the ideal vacuum. I don't believe one exists. This being the rather unfortunate case, get as many of these features as possible. The relative importance of the features depends on your own preferences. We've settled on a Swedish model we call the Big Vac.

On the basis of The Clean Team's experience, I *wouldn't* purchase these.

- **A Kirby. It is too klunky, too heavy, too difficult to change bags, and has an array of attachments that will *never* get used.**

- **A Rainbow. The trouble of getting the water in and out and the high price aren't compensated for by better performance. Its carpet and upholstery cleaner attachments are leaky and difficult to use.**

- *Any* vacuum sold door to door. The reason it's so expensive isn't that it's better; it's that the salesperson earns a commission on each sale.

- *Any* vacuum that costs much more than $400—or $500 if very special features (e.g., a HEPA filter) are included. We've paid $1,500 for a vacuum that works essentially the same as $300 models.

How to Vacuum with the Big Vac

The most important point in vacuuming is to follow Clean Team Rule 1 (page 6). Therefore, you plug the vacuum in once and then vacuum the entire house without ever replugging it. This little gem of an idea will save you 20 percent or more vacuuming time by itself. You'll never backtrack (sound familiar?) to first unplug and then go looking in the next room for another plug—which is often behind the TV or couch or in some other infuriating spot.

To accomplish this feat, we use a 50-foot extension cord. Fifty feet should do it unless your home is very large. The cord is stored on a cord caddy that keeps it from tangling and tying itself into knots.

The ideal outlet is also as close to your starting point as possible while still allowing you to vacuum the entire house without replugging. This also means that most of the cord will be *behind* you as you vacuum, which is faster than working toward the cord. Take the time to keep the cord behind you and untangled.

Take the vacuum and extension cord (on its caddy) to your starting point. Unwrap the vacuum cord and connect it to the extension cord only after tying them together in a simple knot. This is important because it will keep them from pulling apart the first time you give the cord a little tug. Next, unwrap most of the extension cord in a neat circular pile that won't turn into a giant knot later. Unwrap and lay the last section of cord in a straight line to the electrical outlet you selected. The cord in front of you is in a straight line and is much easier to maneuver out of your way, since you can move it from side to side a few inches with the beater head of the vacuum without bending to pick it up.

The above applies to wall-to-wall carpeting without modification. If you have any exposed hardwood flooring, put the extension-cord pile on the hardwood floor nearest to where you will start vacuuming the rug. Otherwise you'd have to pick the pile up to start vacuuming.

Floors

Start vacuuming in the room where
the Duster started, and work toward
the right. Vacuum systematically, so
you don't overlook an area or do it
more than once. Usually you can do a
living room in three fairly equal parts.
Use furniture in the room as land-
marks to divide up the room, so you
don't overlap or skip areas. Vacuum
with one hand, keeping the other
hand available to move furniture or
other items out of your way.

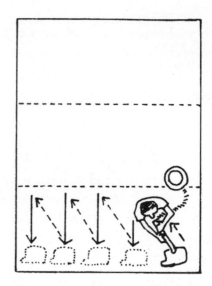

   Typical vacuuming is a forward and
backward motion. Go forward one full
length of the vacuum hose each time. Move sideways one full width of the
vacuum head with each backward motion. Keep the canister part of the
vacuum to your left as you vacuum the room to your right. Be very careful as
you pull the canister, because if an accident can happen, it will. (If you're using
an upright vacuum, move forward one long step and then backward one and
a half steps, because your backward steps are shorter.)

   If some areas to be vacuumed are well traveled and need extra attention,
vacuum more slowly or repeat each push and pull of the vacuum. If an area is
little used, speed up and don't go over it twice.

Furniture

The Duster has left you signals to save time. A cushion overlapping the one
next to it tells you to vacuum the tops of the cushions only. Just move your
beater bar from the floor to the cushion and vacuum away. This will not
harm most fabrics. But don't use the beater on very loose-fitting fabric,
and be careful of tassels or loose strings. (Use the Little Vac instead.) A
turned-up cushion tells you to vacuum the entire couch. You use the Little
Vac to do this, so leave the upturned cushion alone since that will be done
later. If your vacuum doesn't have a motorized beater head, don't use it to
vacuum cushions or furniture. In other words, don't use a nonmotorized
floor attachment, because it will transfer all sorts of fuzz from the floor to
the furniture.

The signal to vacuum under a piece of furniture is when it is moved out at an angle from its normal position. The vacuumer puts the furniture back in its original position afterward.

Moving the Furniture

The rule is to move the item as short a distance as possible: Tip a chair back, for example, instead of transporting it. If you're helping by moving furniture as someone else vacuums, lift the furniture straight up, let your partner vacuum the area, and then replace it. If you're vacuuming on your own, you will have learned not to leave trays, mops, the Little Vac, trash, etc., in your direct path. Move one end of a table an inch or two to vacuum where the legs were, and then replace.

Is a Beater Head Necessary?

"You recommend a beater head for a vacuum, but I find it awkward. I like the other features of a canister vacuum, but much prefer using it without *the beater head. What's your advice?"*

We used to recommend a beater head with a second motor because it "beats" the carpeting to loosen debris and because the beater brush sweeps pet hairs, string, lint, and other surface dirt up into the vacuum. However, vacuums have stronger suction now than they did when we first started using them almost 20 years ago. (They also have better filtration and other advances too.) With such improved suction, in many cases, a beater head is *not* necessary. It all depends on what's in your home and what's being tracked into it. For example, the following situations have less of a demand for a beater head.

1. The carpeting is low or medium pile.

2. You have area rugs on top of hard floors.

3. You have a front and a backyard.

4. You live in a condominium or apartment.

5. Your pets usually don't play in the dirt.

Only if you're working in a team, it's a good idea for you *not* to replace chairs and other displaced furniture. Better to carry on vacuuming, and let someone else (or you) replace items at the end of cleaning. Vacuuming is often the longest job, and every step possible should be taken to avoid stopping once you've started. For example, when you reach a spot where the vacuum head doesn't fit, and an Act of Congress is required to get it to fit—like moving a heavy plant, or a desk, etc.—then this area should already have been cleaned with a whisk broom, feather duster, or dust cloth.

Stairs

Start at the top and vacuum your way down. If you have a canister vacuum, set it six or eight stairs down from the top. When you've vacuumed down to it, move it down six or eight more steps. Use the whisk broom from your back pocket to clean out edges and corners of the stairs as needed. It's easy and fast. Whisk several steps and then vacuum several steps and repeat. Vacuum with back-and-forth motions of the beater head—not side-to-side. Do be careful as you vacuum backward down the stairs because we don't want to lose you.

Throw Rugs

Stand on one end of the throw rug to keep it in place. Don't use back-and-forth motions. Always vacuum away from where you're standing, lift up the beater head at the end of a stroke, and start again to the right. (Move forward on a long run and repeat the process, if necessary, until you reach the other end.) Then come back to the starting point, where you have been standing originally, and do that area from the other direction—again pushing away from you and lifting the vacuum head at the end of a push.

When finished, wrap the cord around the vacuum and the extension cord around the cord caddy.

How to Vacuum with the Little Vac

Unless the Little Vac gets a lot of use (hardwood floors, for example), use it without a 50-foot extension cord. The Little Vac has several attachments. The attachment you choose depends on whether it's being used to vacuum the kitchen floor, the hardwood floors, or furniture.

When vacuuming noncarpeted floors, point the vacuum exhaust away from the area you have yet to vacuum, so you don't stir up dust. Also, pay special attention to areas where there are electrical cords on the floor. The cords trap a lot of dust and debris, so slow down and vacuum carefully.

When vacuuming furniture, follow The Clean Team rules: Start on the left side at the top, and work your way down and to the right.

Expand Your Vacuuming Horizons Outdoors and Save More Time with Better Results

Use your vacuum to clean the front porch at the same time you're doing your regular housecleaning. Just open the front door as you pass by and, using the same floor attachment, vacuum any mats that are there, plus the porch itself. Continue vacuuming on to the sidewalk if it's feasible and if your vacuum will reach. Vacuuming is faster than a broom and does a much better job. In fact, anytime you pass an outside door, open it and vacuum the outside area at hand. At the same time, you can use the vacuum wand alone (or with the brush attachment) to vacuum cobwebs from the porch light fixture, mailbox, furniture, railings, and so forth.

When you come to the door that leads to the deck, do the same thing. If it's a sliding door, first use the vacuum nozzle alone or with the brush attachment to remove debris from the runners, and then proceed to the deck. No matter what flooring material is used on your deck, it will be cleaner when you vacuum it compared with sweeping it. It's quite satisfying to vacuum away leaves, dust, sand, bugs, and what-all that accumulates near these doors and that often finds its way into your just-cleaned house. Also vacuum patio or lawn furniture and anything else you find that needs vacuuming—including the dog or cat if they will stand for it. Keeps them from shedding unnecessarily in the house. If you need an extension cord to reach all of the deck, get one. It's well worth it. Obviously, you won't be able to do much vacuuming outside in a snowstorm, but when possible, learn to make outdoor vacuuming a part of your cleaning routine.

Also use the vacuum in the garage. Sweeping it takes longer, creates dust just by the act of sweeping, and doesn't remove as much dust and debris as a vacuum. The vacuum does it better—without creating more dust!

There are vacuuming chores that need to be done only once a year or so. For example, I've purchased extra vacuum wands and a longer hose, so I can also vacuum the eves of the house. They get covered with spiders and webs.

I get a slightly perverse pleasure from vacuuming them all away! You can also vacuum outside windowsills at the same time.

Please don't worry about using more dust bags. Compared with the time you save and compared with the better job of removing dust, dirt, and debris—some of which would have ended up in your home—the cost of an occasional extra dust bag is well worth it.

Vacuuming Pet Hair

Which vacuum does the best job of picking up dog and cat hair?

It's truly amazing how much hair can come off even one dog or one cat. Most vacuums will pick up shed pet hair—as long as it's just lounging around on a hard-surface floor. The key factor is not so much the vacuum as the location of the hair. It's usually the fabric of the carpet or furniture or clothing that determines how difficult it will be to remove the hair. I realize that you often have no choice in such matters, but there is a window of opportunity when you purchase these goods. If you're a dog or cat person, consider pet-hair removal when you're shopping for new furniture. I've had great success with leather instead of fabric. Also consider color: Don't get white carpeting if you have a black Lab.

When you can't change the carpet or furniture, the vacuum—and its attachments—becomes even more important. A canister vacuum with above-average suction—75 inches or more of water lift—is recommended. (See page 97.) In addition, if you have plush carpeting or pets with long hair, a beater head is best for removing pet hair. Otherwise a well-designed floor attachment will remove hair satisfactorily. Besides getting under more furniture, a canister's hose separates to allow quick spot removal of pet hair or other debris as needed.

The most important attachment for removal of pet hair from upholstery is the one often called the furniture attachment. Look for one whose design uses soft rubber—either a solid piece of rubber or smaller "fingers" of rubber—to rub against pet hairs and pull them out of the furniture's fabric. Wash the rubber when it gets dirty to maintain its effectiveness.

If a vacuum isn't handy, and there are a few pet hairs on furniture, spray your hand with a bit of *Blue Juice* or water and "wipe" the hairs with your hand. The hairs will gather together into a ball that can be easily picked up and discarded.

Probably the single most important thing you can do to combat pet hair is prevention. A neighbor of mine has two indoor cats, yet you will be hard pressed to find more than a couple of hairs in the entire apartment. The secret? The cats get a thorough brushing every day. I try to do the same with my two dogs—only outdoors. When I do, hair in the house is reduced by 90 percent or more. There are vacuum attachments designed to use directly on the animal. Many pets enjoy it—as long as they aren't frightened by the noise.

Note: Limiting your pets to one sleeping spot can help concentrate the hairs and help with flea control at least in one area of the house—that is, until someone opens the front door and hair scatters everywhere.

Time for Carpet *Cleaning*

You have a choice between several very different carpet-cleaning systems. As a quick review, and to make sure you have a chance to consider all the realistic options, here's a brief summary of all five major carpet-cleaning systems in current use. They include ones you can do yourself as well as ones that professionals use. Needless to say, we have an opinion about them, and our recommendations follow.

Extraction

Widely and erroneously known as "steam cleaning," this is the method used by most professionals and is the method associated with most consumer rental equipment. It involves the injection of detergent and water (hot, warm, or cool—but definitely not steam) into the carpet under pressure, followed by the almost simultaneously wet-vacuuming (extraction) of the dirty solution. One variation of this method also involves agitation of the carpet with a brush located immediately after the hot-water nozzle and before the vacuum intake.

Advantages: All things considered, this is the single method that cleans the deepest. The equipment is the easiest to find.

Disadvantages: A significant amount of water can penetrate to the carpet backing and pad and remain there after extraction. If the carpet is badly soiled, this method requires agitation with a brush or rotary floor machine. Heavy units with a built-in brush can be awkward and backbreaking. The carpet requires a long time to dry. Hot water can set some stains permanently—for example, blood and sugar-based stains—so precleaning such stains is mandatory.

Rotary

This method uses a single-disc rotary floor machine. A rotary nylon brush directly scrubs cleaner into the carpet from a tank on the machine. The dirty solution is removed with a wet vacuum.

Advantages: Cleans deeply by agitating the carpet fibers. If rotary and extraction methods are both used, the combination is the most effective approach for heavy soil.

Disadvantages: Requires skill to avoid overwetting. Two machines are required: a floor machine and a wet vac. The carpet must be done in 4-foot by 4-foot areas or else the wet vac will not extract sufficient material. This method is almost always used in conjunction with the extractor method because of the inefficiency of the wet vac.

Foam

A machine applies cleaner in the form of foam that is scrubbed into the carpet with soft nylon reel brushes. The residue is removed with a wet vacuum. Some units have a wet vacuum built in, so the foam is removed almost immediately. Afterward, a thorough dry-vacuuming is recommended.

Advantages: Foam prevents water from soaking deeply into the carpet. The carpet dries relatively quickly.

Disadvantages: Not effective on heavy soiling. Residual cleaner can build up and cause resoiling. Spillage or overwetting can result in water damage. The equipment can be hard to find. The brushes can damage delicate fibers.

Dry Powder

This is a relatively new method in which dry absorbent material impregnated with dry-cleaning solvents and detergents is sprinkled onto the carpet and scrubbed into it with soft nylon reel or rotary brushes. The powder holds dirt in suspension and is dry-vacuumed away.

Advantages: Absolutely no danger of water damage. Carpet can be walked on immediately. Powder can be used as an absorbent immediately after a spill.

Disadvantages: Not effective on heavy soiling. The powder is difficult to vacuum out completely and can remain in the carpet and resoil it. The brushes used to work it into the carpet can damage delicate fibers.

Bonnet

A cotton or rayon absorbent pad (a "bonnet") is used with a single-disc rotary floor machine. Liquid carpet cleaner is applied with a sprayer or through the machine's tank in advance of the machine.

Advantages: The carpet does not get deeply wet, so there is little risk of water damage, and it can be walked on almost immediately. There is relatively little danger of residual cleaner causing resoiling.

Disadvantages: Not effective on heavy soil. The rotary motion can damage delicate fibers.

First, Deep-Clean the Carpet

Given this wide range of choices, what can be recommended for home use? Each method has its pros and cons. All require renting equipment and buying specialized supplies. The answer depends on how dirty the carpet is. If your carpet needs deep-down cleaning, we recommend that you hire a professional to get the job done right the first time. Ask what method the company proposes to use. We recommend that you do business with one that uses either of the two effective deep-cleaning methods: extraction or rotary followed by extraction.

If you want to deep-clean the carpet yourself, chances are that the available rental machine will be some form of an extraction device. Be careful not to soak the carpet and to dry it thoroughly afterward. You should recover 70 to 90 percent of the water going into the carpet. There is always a risk of damage: Moisture remaining in the carpet and/or its backing can seriously damage the carpet fibers, promote the growth of mildew, stretch and/or shrink the carpet, or damage the hardwood or subfloor underneath.

Maintenance Cleaning Using the Bonnet Method

Once the carpet is deep-cleaned (or if it's relatively new or already clean), here's a method of keeping it that way. Using this method, a carpet shouldn't have to be deep-cleaned again for months or years. That statement is absolute nonsense if you have a rugby team hanging out at your place, of course. (Every home has its own unique recleaning schedule!) But what we suggest is that you deep-clean the carpet only as needed—ideally only once—and that you institute an ongoing system of lighter-duty maintenance cleaning, so your carpet will stay relatively clean all the time.

What's the best method for maintenance cleaning? It boils down to a choice between the bonnet and the dry-powder methods. If your carpets will tolerate absolutely no water, or if you cannot wait at all for the carpet to dry, then your only choice is the dry-powder method. But our first choice is the bonnet method. Its drying time is extremely brief—perhaps only 20 minutes, which is a good time to relax a bit. And you won't have to contend with residual powder in the carpet, as in the dry-powder method. Leftover solvent-laden powder continues to absorb dirt, and if you don't get it completely out of the carpet you'll begin to see respotting eventually.

The bonnet method cleans the top of the carpet—where most of the dirt will be accumulating anyway. The cleaner is lightly sprayed on top of the carpet, which makes it difficult to force dirt deeper into the carpet pile. It's then absorbed almost immediately by the absorbent bonnet, which is sort of a giant terry-cloth towel. You use a floor machine that works by spinning the bonnet on the carpet while the weight of the machine holds the bonnet flat against the carpet, where it can absorb the cleaner and dirt very efficiently. If you think about it, the method is really a reliable spot-cleaning method on a large scale. Instead of using a cleaning cloth and spotting solution, you are using a bonnet and liquid carpet cleaner. Safe, reliable, and effective.

Finding the Equipment

The bonnet method requires a floor machine and a supply of bonnets. The floor machine is the same type used to strip wax from resilient floors (see the section on stripping floors in Chapter 14), so you might be able to get double your money's worth by renting it for both purposes over a marathon weekend. You should be able to find it at any full-service rental outlet. It's true that you will have to lug home a machine to do this job, but the equipment is no more bulky than a traditional extraction carpet machine.

Be sure the floor machine you rent is 17 inches or less in diameter. Larger than that is too big for home use. Insist that the salesperson give you a demonstration or good instructions on how to operate and control it. The machine is easy to handle only after you know how. Otherwise, it will seem too difficult, and it can easily result in torn (or very tired) muscles and/or damage to your baseboards or furniture.

The bonnets are not expensive and can be washed and reused over and over, but they will be more difficult to locate than the floor machine. You can try a local janitorial supply house, or order them from our catalog. They come in sizes corresponding to the diameter of the floor machine's disk, so first call the rental store and find out what size floor machine they have. Then order that size bonnet. Using a 17-inch machine, you'll need one or two bonnets for a 10-foot by 10-foot room with a moderately soiled carpet.

Materials

1 17-inch or smaller single-disk floor machine
1 to 2 bonnets per room (the same diameter as the floor-machine disk)
1 bottle of carpet cleaner (most nonfoaming carpet cleaners, especially
   Red Juice, will work well)
1 pump-up pressure sprayer (or spray bottle)
1 measuring cup
1 cleaning apron
5 cleaning cloths
1 spray bottle of Red Juice
1 toothbrush
1 vacuum cleaner (the "Big Vac")

Preparation

Remove all the furniture that you must. One of the rationalizations we think you use to put off cleaning the carpet so long is that you don't want to move all that furniture. So don't. Move only those pieces that can get dirt under them. Like the coffee table, but not the couch. Like the dining-room table and chairs, but not the TV. Like the end tables, but not the china cabinet. See how much easier this is getting?

While dirt can't get under the couch too easily, it can—and does—accumulate right up to the edge of it. So slide the couch back 2 inches. That way, you can get the last bit of dirt that was there, but you avoid lifting it. Some pieces of furniture don't even need to be moved at all—like a console television. Usually you don't need to move the bed—but if you do, just move it a few inches one way and then a few more back the other way. Put aluminum foil or plastic wrap under the legs of any furniture on damp areas of the carpet.

You know by now not to try to move any of these heavy things by yourself. You also don't want to drag heavy furniture across the carpet unless you are fond of ripples in the carpet, which will cause more grief than the entire carpet-cleaning process.

But do move everything out of the way that you are going to ultimately have to move. Now, before you start cleaning. Include the little things like the magazine holder, potted plants, the stack of newspapers, and so forth. Clear the decks.

Thoroughly vacuum all the carpeting you are going to clean. Use a vacuum with a reel-type brush and beater bar to do a deep cleaning.

Mixing the Carpet Cleaner

Mix the carpet-cleaning solution directly in the pump-up pressure sprayer. As usual, follow the manufacturer's directions. Wear your cleaning apron, so you can carry the sprayer in a pocket or on an apron loop when not in use. Your apron is also handy for carrying a few cleaning cloths for any spills as well as a toothbrush if you need to give some extra attention to a spot.

Traffic Areas, Spots, and Stains

You must make two trips around the room for two different jobs. The *first* trip is to pretreat any spots or stains by lightly spraying them first with the carpet-cleaning solution. Also pretreat the dirtier traffic areas: for example, the entrance areas, the area in front of the couch, or the paths from the kitchen to just about everywhere else. Use your toothbrush to agitate any spots or stains that look like they may not come up easily. If there are a whole bunch of little horrors, you may want to treat them with the methods described for spot-cleaning carpets, later in this chapter, before you start cleaning the entire carpet.

Applying Carpet Cleaner

On the *second* trip, lightly spray the whole carpet to be cleaned. This includes respraying the traffic areas and spots you had already pretreated.

Spray and clean one room at a time. Start in the left corner farthest from the exit door. Spray the cleaner evenly and thoroughly in 3-foot strips, moving all the way from one side of the room to the other with each strip. Hold the sprayer nozzle 2 feet or so from the surface. Don't spray under furniture if the floor machine won't fit there unless you want to hand-clean those areas. If so, you can use a cleaning cloth to absorb the cleaner and dirt. Don't spray areas that aren't dirty. Examples are corners or other areas where there is little or no traffic.

It's a little difficult to be sure that you've completely sprayed an area. To help keep track, pick or create a landmark in the room each time you make a new pass. For example, spot where you are in relation to the TV or another piece of furniture each time you start a new 3-foot strip. Or put down a cleaning cloth to mark your spot. When you've covered the entire carpet, you're ready to use the floor machine.

If the carpet is only lightly soiled, you can start scrubbing with the bonnet immediately after applying the cleaner. For moderately soiled carpet, wait 5 minutes. If heavily soiled, wait 10.

Steering It

The secret to using a floor machine is to control its movement and direction by very slightly raising or lowering the handle. These *subtle* changes cause the rotating brush to have a little more traction on the front or back of the brush, which in turn causes the machine to move to the right or the left. Your first (often somewhat hysterical) impulse is to try to change direction of the machine by brute force, which even a very strong person can barely do. Using muscle power alone won't stop the machine in time if it wants to go somewhere (for example, through the glass coffee table). If the machine all of a sudden seems to have a mind of its own and is heading straight for mayhem, let go of the handle. The machine will stop because it's equipped with a safety trigger. Thank goodness. Reminds me of a wonderful story about learning to water-ski and forgetting to let go of the rope after falling, but that's another subject.

Once you try (and remember) the simple up-and-down steering tactic, the machine is easy enough to operate. It doesn't require particular strength, just attention, so just about anyone should be able to tackle this job.

For the sake of your back, find a comfortable level at which to hold the floor-machine handle (usually just below the waist). If you hold it too high, someone may have to massage your shoulders afterward. If you hold it too low, your lower back will let you know promptly.

The best way to manage the long power cord and to keep it out of your way is to put it over one shoulder while the machine is in operation. Also, run the cord out the exit door and into an electrical outlet that isn't in the room in which you're working. Wear an old shirt or blouse because the cord is apt to be dirty. And wear nonslip tennis shoes for traction.

Dirty Traffic Areas

If you have light carpeting throughout your house, it shows dirt much more easily than you might have thought when it was installed. That's "a" problem, but it's not "the" problem, which is that the carpeting gets dirty only in traffic areas. Sometimes the worst is not even at the front door—it's the first few feet into the bedroom or the first few feet into the guest bathroom. It's irksome to pay for a professional carpet cleaning when only two small areas are dirty.

But there is an alternative. Lightly spray Red Juice on an area of 2 square feet or so (after testing it on a hidden patch of carpet). Don't overspray. You want an even mist of Red Juice—kind of like morning dew. Then rub that area with a dry but crumpled-up cleaning cloth. Just hold it in your fist, and rub it back and forth across the misted area. Turn it often. The cloth will pick up the moisture from the carpet, along with the surface dirt that was annoying you. Change cleaning cloths often, and repeat the process until you've cleaned the dirty area. Toss them into the laundry when you're done. Treat yourself to something fun with the money you've saved!

Note: We live in an area with red soil that gets on everything and drives everyone crazy. A woman I know took a handful of the dirt with her when she went shopping for new carpeting. She exactly matched her carpet to the dirt. It worked brilliantly.

The Starting Point

Move the floor machine to the corner of the room where you started spraying the carpet cleaner. To install a bonnet, tilt the machine back and center the bonnet on the rotary brush. Press the bonnet into place and restore the machine to its normal upright position. The bonnet is held in place by the weight of the machine on top of it. Keep a supply of spare bonnets close by. Until you know more about how this process works on your carpets, be sure to check the bonnet frequently to see how soiled it has become. You can check less often once you know how long each side of the bonnet lasts. Turn it over as soon as it's too dirty to absorb more solution. Replace it with a new one when both sides are soiled. Of course, once the bonnet is saturated with dirt and cleaning solution, it loses its ability to clean any further.

The Strategy

The strategy is simple enough. Work your way to the right across the room. Then back up a little less than the diameter of the floor machine, and start working back to the left—overlapping the original pass slightly. If you've sprayed areas the machine will not reach, do them by hand using a cleaning cloth. (Stop the machine to do these areas as you come to them.) Rub the cleaning cloth back and forth a few times over the sprayed carpet to absorb the dirt and cleaning solution.

Reach for your toothbrush and Red Juice if there are small spots that need working. Be careful not to damage the carpet fiber with the toothbrush. A gentle agitation is all that's needed. The Red Juice will help on most spots that are still holding out. Blot it up afterward with another cleaning cloth.

As you progress, try to manage the cord so you don't run over it with the floor machine. It doesn't appreciate it any more than you would.

When you finish cleaning the carpet, pop the bonnets into the washing machine and set it to "stun." Load the floor machine back into the car, and return it to the rental store while the carpet dries, unless you have a saintly rental store that picks up and delivers. If you're ambitious and have taken your vitamins for the day, you might want to use the same floor machine to strip the wax from the kitchen floor. Or you may just want to put your feet up and admire your sparkling clean carpet.

The Finishing Touch

When the carpet is completely dry, vacuum it thoroughly once more. It should take as little as 20 minutes to dry using the bonnet method. But if you're in a cold climate, or if you applied too much cleaner, or if you need to hasten drying time, here's how.

Drying Out the Carpet

After any carpet-cleaning method that uses water, if the carpet feels wet to the touch, you may want to speed the drying process—either to make it usable more quickly or to minimize the possibility of mildew. One very effective way of drying out the carpet relies on the fact that warm air can carry much more moisture than cold air. Heat the room thoroughly to bring the water out of the carpet and into the room air. Then open all the windows and doors and replace the moist warm air with dry cool air. Close the room up again and repeat this cycle a few times until the carpet feels dry to the touch and there is no wet or soapy smell in the room. You'll be amazed how quickly this procedure will dry out the carpet. A rotating room fan can also help speed the process along.

As soon as the carpet is dry and the vacuuming is finished, you can move the furniture back in and start using the room again. If you maintain your carpet with this method as often as needed (maybe once or twice a year), you will always have a great-looking carpet and will rarely have to do a deep extraction cleaning. Besides, you will get so good at using the floor machine that the whole process will get easier and easier. Congratulations.

Maintenance and Prevention between Cleanings

Step 1

The single most important thing you can do to keep your carpet clean is to vacuum it regularly. It seems to us that one reason people resist such a straightforward task as vacuuming is because it's too much trouble to "drag the vacuum out" of wherever it's kept between uses. If that's your excuse, store the vacuum somewhere else. You could even leave it out most of the time—in a corner or somewhere out of the way. Maybe then you would use it daily (if you have kids and pets, for example) or every few days (if not). Stuff it back into the closet when company comes—but only if you promise to bring it back out when they leave.

The other excuse we hear is that the vacuum is too heavy. If that is the case, please replace it as quickly as you can afford to with one that you can manage. A lot of the older uprights actually aren't too heavy. It's just that their suction makes them grab onto the surface in a way that can make them awkward to move. Now there are even rechargeable, cordless electric vacuums that are very light and easy to use. And *fast!* Maybe you could check into purchasing one of these even before you replace the vacuum that you don't use. (It takes soooooooooo very long to wear out something you never use.) Lightweight portables may still have to be supplemented by a deeper-cleaning standard vacuum, but if you're not vacuuming at all, they're certainly better than what you're doing now.

Step 2

The second maintenance step is to clean up spills (you know, those things that turn into spots and stains) as they occur. Very few spills are all that horrendous if you take care of them *immediately*. Red Juice is an extraordinarily broad-based cleaner and will do an excellent job on a wide range of carpet offenses. Keep a bottle handy, together with a toothbrush and cleaning cloths or a roll of paper towels. See the section on spot-cleaning carpets that begins on the opposite page, especially the section on how to remove these accidents before they become stains.

Step 3

Use mats, runners, or throw rugs to protect the house in general and your carpets in particular. Most of the dirt that ends up in your house came in through the doors—up to 85 percent of it, according to some authorities. You can reduce your housecleaning burden tremendously by using mats to catch most of that dirt in its concentrated form before it is disbursed throughout the house.

The correct placement of the mats is both inside and outside the exterior doors of your home. The larger the mat, the better: More dirt will be wiped off. Ideally, each mat would cover four or five steps on both sides of the door, although this is bigger than most of us have room for. We recommend that the mat outside the door be the typical rubber-backed mat that you are used to seeing in store entrances. But don't use a rubber-backed mat inside the house on a vinyl or asphalt floor because it may discolor the floor.

Don't forget that the other thing you want the mat to catch (besides dirt) is water. Get a mat or carpet of a material that will absorb the water, not repel it. Inside the house, we prefer a carpet mat that can be thrown in the washing machine.

Don't let the mats themselves get saturated with dirt, or they won't do any good at all—rather like trying to catch dripping water in a pot that is overflowing with each new drop. Maintain the mats by shaking or vacuuming them daily (or nearly so). It makes sense to have two sets, so you can put out a clean, dry set when one set gets wet or is being washed. Also, now that you're going to have such nice clean carpets using the bonnet cleaning method, use a nice-looking throw rug on an area of carpet that is worn—even if it isn't at a door. This improves the appearance of the whole room and enhances the overall result of your other cleaning efforts.

One note of caution: Occasionally, we see homes with a patch of carpet remnant used as a mat directly on the carpet beneath without an intervening rubber or jute pad. As it comes from the same roll of carpet, it may seem to be a reasonable practice. Unfortunately, the backing of carpeting is much more abrasive than the fibers themselves. If the backing is placed directly on the surface of a carpet without a protective pad, every footstep will wear away a bit of the lower carpet as though it were being sandpapered. A protective pad is mandatory and very inexpensive. And nobody should have to tell you to put a nonslip pad under a throw rug if it's used on a hardwood or other slippery floor.

As with most maintenance, these ideas will cost some money to implement, and they take a little time to perform on a regular basis. The payoff is that they reduce the overall time you spend cleaning the house—so you might actually have some leisure time left over on weekends for a change. And you'll have a nicer home to live in and enjoy that will avoid the violent swings between *very clean* and *very dirty* that are so frustrating and, ultimately, time-consuming.

Spot-Cleaning Carpets

Spots in fabrics are outside the scope of this book, but you'll certainly be running into a few carpet spots or stains as you make your way through housecleaning. "Stain" and "spot" are often used interchangeably, but a consensus exists that a stain is the more permanent of the two. "Stain" is the term your dry cleaner will use, for example, when you bring in what you thought was an innocent little spot: "*This?* You want me to clean *this?* Oh, no, that's a *stain.*"

We will be optimistic and refer to most messes on the carpet as spots. If they remain despite your best efforts, at least you'll know exactly what to call them. First, we'll discuss how to treat spots. Then we'll move on to stains.

In this section, we'll answer questions about some common carpet accidents plus other carpet-related problems. For the most part, we're talking about *fresh* accidents: The spot hasn't dried, which would have made it immensely more difficult or impossible to remove. If you treat such spills while they're fresh, nearly all stains can be avoided. You may notice that our answers are often similar. That's because the solution is generally the same: Get whatever it is back out of the carpet! For dried stains or for stains we don't mention, there are good books available on the subject (e.g., *How to Remove Spots and Stains* by Professor

Herb Barndt). If you want to have a go at dried stains, rehydrate (remoisten) the area slightly, and then proceed as if it were a fresh spot. Considering the value of a carpet, if your efforts are unsuccessful or if you're unsure of how to proceed, don't hesitate to call in a professional carpet-cleaning company right away.

Treating Spots

Needless to say, one of the best ways to prevent a spot from evolving into a stain is to act on the spot immediately, before it has time to go through whatever unwelcome chemical transformations it has in mind. The first thing to do is to blot up as much of the material as possible with a supply of clean, dry cloths. Next apply a modest amount of cool water, and blot up the spill with cleaning cloths. If the spot might also stain your cleaning cloths, you might prefer to use paper towels. White Bounty Microwave towels are the best we've found to date.

Work from the edge inward, turning the cloth often. Don't rub back and forth, or you may drive the spill into the fiber. Instead, *twist* the cloth as you blot. This twisting motion will work the material to the surface more effectively than rubbing back and forth.

Next, spray the area with Red Juice, agitate with the toothbrush if needed, and blot up. After you've blotted up all the moisture you can, place several dry cloths or paper towels over the area. Weight them down with books for a few hours to keep pressure on the area and to help absorb remaining moisture and soil. Red Juice turns out to be one of the best all-around spot removers that we've ever seen—in many cases working when specialty spotting products have failed. We've seen it lift coffee spots right out of carpets after the spots had been neglected for weeks! It can work miracles on all carpet fibers except those whose dyes are not colorfast (which are rare these days). You might want to test an area now, so you'll be able to act immediately if an emergency arises.

If you have a wet-dry vacuum, this is the remedy recommended by the bible of the carpet industry, *The How-To Handbook of Carpets*. This use, plus its back-saving contribution to floor cleaning, makes a wet-dry vac pay for itself many times over. If you have one, start by wet-vacuuming the spot. Next, apply cool water with a cleaning cloth or sponge and revacuum. Continue these two steps, and you may find the spot completely gone. You can also treat the spot with Red Juice, agitate with the toothbrush, flush with water, and then wet-vac again. Finish by placing several weighted-down dry cloths or paper towels over the area, as in the manual method.

If you can't interrupt what you're doing to treat a spot sufficiently—let's say you're in the middle of a dinner for the ambassador—many carpet-cleaning professionals recommend that you sprinkle an absorbent powder on the spot when it's still wet. Traditional absorbents are cornstarch, corn meal, talcum powder, and carpet dry-cleaning powder (e.g, Host). Trouble is, getting the absorbent out of the carpet can be a problem too, especially if you have a dark rug. If you have a dry-cleaning powder, that's the absorbent of first choice.

One of the most frequent spills on carpets is red wine. You will often hear that the best antidote is to douse the spot with white wine. It does appear to work, through a chemical reaction, but you risk saturating the carpet backing with the resulting concoction and doing far more serious damage. You're better off using conventional spot-treatment techniques. (See page 126 for wine-specific recommendations.)

By necessity, we're going to offer two tactics for treating spots that have had a chance to set: *fast* and *fussy*. Naturally, we recommend that you try the fast approach first. Failing that, you'll have to resort to a particular treatment for that type of stain.

Fast Treatment

Materials

1 spray bottle of Red Juice
1 spray bottle of plain water
1 toothbrush
1 scraper
5 to 10 cotton cleaning cloths or a roll of paper towels
1 carryall tray

Preparation

With any luck at all, the majority of stains afflicting your carpet can be banished with Red Juice, the toothbrush, and cotton cloths. Red Juice is a cleaner with a deliberately wide range of effectiveness, and its formula is not dangerous to any type of fiber that we've yet to discover after several years of field experience. Having said that, it is still prudent to check *any* cleaner on an inconspicuous area of the carpet. We know it's aggravating to read that warning over and over (sort of like those annoying tags on furniture that say never to remove them). Unfortunately, there is little other choice unless you are fond of gambling. You should only have to do this test once per carpet per cleaner. Sorry.

The carpet should be vacuumed before attempting to treat a spot. It's rare to be able to solve the problem with vacuuming alone, but removing as much of the material as possible will help your efforts along. Who knows, you may be lucky enough to find that the "stain" is really just a deposit of fine powder.

Treating the Spot

Approach the spot. Do not be afraid. You are bigger than it is. (We hope.) Treatment is best done on hands and knees to spare your back. If your knees need sparing too, and if you have a hoard of spots on the rug, you might consider knee pads. They look odd, but your knees won't care.

Okay, okay, this is one case where the cleaning apron can be less effective than the carryall tray. You'll be on your hands and knees, and it can be difficult to remove and replace the cleaning tools in and out of the apron without stopping to straighten up. Best to keep them in the tray in between uses along with the Red Juice, cleaning cloths, and other supplies. If you're cleaning many spots in close proximity, just keep pushing the tray in front of you on the carpet as you make your way along.

The fast approach to a generic spot is to spray it full blast with Red Juice, agitate reasonably gently with the toothbrush, and then blot up with the cleaning cloths or paper towels. Don't be bashful with the Red Juice. In fact, it's best to set the nozzle more toward "stun" than to the fine setting. On the other hand, don't soak through to the carpet backing. If the stain turns out to be a solid mass of something unfortunate, you may have to break it up with the scraper before proceeding any further with the toothbrush.

Remember that blotting has a little trick to it. Just as when you are treating an immediate spill, you don't want to rub the stain back into the carpet after you've dislodged the dirt with Red Juice and the toothbrush. So twist the cloth as you blot. Again, turn the cloth over and replace it with a clean one as often as needed, so you are always blotting with a clean and dry area of the cloth. As the cleaning cloths become too wet or dirty to use, throw them into the cleaning tray. It's all in the wrist.

Carpet treatment requires one extra step as a precaution against restaining. If even a modest amount of cleaning agent remains in the carpet, it can hold on to new dirt more so than adjoining areas. Hence the puzzling phenomenon of treated areas getting worse after they're treated.

To head this regrettable event off at the pass, you need to flush any cleaner from the carpet after you've finished blotting. The safest means is plain water applied with a spray bottle followed by more blotting. Don't soak the carpet; just use enough water to flush out any remaining cleaning agent.

Small damp areas (a few inches) can be blotted dry. Larger areas should be covered with dry cleaning cloths weighted down with books for a few hours to remove additional moisture and soil from the carpet.

The proper finishing touch is to brush the nap of the carpet in the area you just cleaned and neutralized. When they dry, fibers will adopt the shape and direction in which you left them wet, so why ask for trouble? Just take a moment to reset the nap by brushing lightly against the grain of the carpet. When it dries, you shouldn't be able to notice the difference between the area you treated and the surrounding areas. And it won't restain either. If you have a long shag rug, you can buy a specialized nap brush to reset the nap. Ask at a janitorial specialty store.

Fussy Treatment

By now, it's definitely time to call them stains instead of spots, presuming that they have remained in place long enough to pose a serious threat to removal. The number of potential carpet stains is limitless. And if you review the literature, you'll find a bewildering number of different (and often contradictory) recommendations. To simplify matters to a reasonable degree, we have gathered stains into three major categories. Once you understand what type of stain you're dealing with, the treatments are reasonably uniform per type. One thing all these treatments have in common is that they require pretesting.

Type 1: Solvent Stains

All the stains in this category are dissolved by dry-cleaning-type solvents and *not* by water. They are what would be commonly called oily or greasy stains. They usually appear as dark stains on the carpet, and they usually trap dirt more and more over time.

Here are some examples.

Airplane glue	Lacquer
Asphalt	Oil
Ballpoint-pen ink	Petroleum jelly
Butter	Rubber cement
Cosmetics	Shoe polish
Fat	Tar
Furniture polish	Varnish
Glue, household	Wax
Grease	

Removing these stains requires a solvent. Technically, water is a solvent—it dissolves things like sugar—but when most people use the term, they are referring to the more common understanding of a solvent as a heavy-duty agent. In particular, there are two classifications of solvent that merit our attention (based on Professor Herb Brandt's terminology).

Oil–Based Solvents	**Combination Solvents**
Carbona	Magic
Lacquer thinner	Shout
Lighter fluid	Spray 'n Wash
Professional dry-cleaning fluid	

Oil-based solvents dissolve a stain, mix with it, and then evaporate—leaving a powdery residue behind or none at all. They are potentially very powerful agents, so they must be used with due respect and after the usual pretesting in that same inconspicuous spot we keep talking about. Depending on the makeup of your carpet, some solvents can be harmful to the fabric or to the backing, so several other precautions apply: (1) Do not use on a wet stain. Oil-based solvents and water don't get along. (2) Make sure the room is well ventilated. The fumes don't get along with your liver. (3) Don't saturate the carpet with the solvent. You don't want to soak the backing of the carpet with it. (4) Always wear gloves when working with oil-based solvents.

Among the oil-based solvents listed, our strong preference is for lacquer thinner—a mixture of acetone and several other strong solvents. It's relatively cheap and can be amazingly effective on grease, oil, wax, and gum. It dissolves without leaving a residue. Actually, it is one of the most powerful cleaning agents commonly available—provided it doesn't dissolve the surface you're cleaning. It is safe for most carpet fibers (test first, of course), but it will dissolve many plastics and painted surfaces. Don't pour into a Styrofoam cup while you're working with it because it will eat right through the bottom. It will also dissolve the plastic bristles of some brushes.

Lighter fluid is another superb oil-based solvent that has many applications. It is far less destructive to a surface than is lacquer thinner, but it will leave an oil stain on porous surfaces like flat-finished walls or wallpaper, and it is therefore ill advised for those applications. It is an absolute pleasure to use on the residue of gummy labels (e.g., price tags) and adhesive tape. Readers who have been cleaning for a few years will recall that kerosene used to be one of the main household cleaners. Its effectiveness is very similar to lighter fluid.

Carbona is a quality retail dry-cleaning fluid that has many of the cleaning abilities of lacquer thinner but again is less destructive to many surfaces. If you are on friendly terms with your local dry cleaner, you might persuade him or her to sell you a small supply of professional dry-cleaning fluid.

Here come the warnings: These and other oil-based solvents are highly flammable. Do not use them near an open flame (e.g., a pilot light of an appliance like a water heater.) Store them prudently between uses. Do not use them on an antique or fine Oriental rug because its dyes may not stand up to the treatment.

Combination solvents are a recent development that mix a solvent and glycerin, soap, and/or water. They evaporate so slowly that it's only theoretical, so they must be rinsed after the stain is treated—which requires an extra step or two and extra time. They are more conservative treatments than the oil solvents, but they do not generate obnoxious fumes.

To treat stains with a combination solvent, the safest way to proceed is to apply the solvent to a cleaning cloth—not the carpet itself. Just place it over the stain, and apply pressure without rubbing. Check the cloth. If some of the material is transferring to the cloth, you're in business. Blot toward the middle of the stain, rotating to new and clean areas of the cloth wet with the solvent. When the stain appears to be gone, place a stack of five to six dry cleaning cloths over the stain, and put a weight on top to absorb the solvent. Remove the cloths after a few hours. This is a fine use for your otherwise worn-out cleaning cloths. If you are using your regular cleaning cloths, make sure you launder them before using them for other cleaning tasks.

The above procedure is deliberately cautious. If the stain does not respond, you may want to up the ante by agitating the stain with the toothbrush. Use reasonable caution, and work toward the center of the stain, so you don't spread it. After you've loosened the stain with the brush, blot up with clean cloths. After you get to know how much your carpet will tolerate, you may be able to shift to using the toothbrush right away. As always when using the toothbrush on a carpet, reset the nap by brushing lightly after treating the spot.

If you've used an oil-based solvent and a powdery residue remains, it should come right up with a vacuum cleaner. If you've used a combination solvent, you've got to remove the solvent/stain mixture after treatment. Blot it up as best you can with clean cloths, and follow with a Red Juice treatment and blot. Finally, flush and then blot with cool water.

Shoe Polish

How do you remove shoe polish stains from carpeting? If any solid bits of shoe polish remain, don't try to pick them up or to remove them with a spatula or scraper. This will only spread them or rub them in. Get the vacuum, and put the end of the hose over the bits and suck them away cleanly. The next step is to dissolve the remaining polish with a solvent like Gunk Remover or lighter fluid. Before you try any solvent directly on the shoe polish, test in an inconspicuous place to make sure the solvent doesn't damage the carpet fibers. The tricky part is to get the dissolved polish back out of the carpet. Apply a small amount of solvent to the spot, and immediately blot with a cleaning cloth. Don't rub. Blot. Repeat as needed. Agitate gently with a toothbrush if necessary. When there seems to be nothing left, we like to spray with Red Juice one last time and blot again to remove any traces of solvent and polish. As a last step, brush the wet carpet fibers to match surrounding nap.

Grease

A hot and very greasy hamburger patty can fall onto your carpet and then get stepped on full force by a 195-pound teenager. It does happen. This stain is a combination of grease and blood. Red Juice is a degreaser and as such would be effective. Spray the stain with Red Juice, gently agitate with a toothbrush, and then blot thoroughly with a cleaning cloth. It's a good idea to fold the cloth and put it over the stain, and then stand on the cloth for a few seconds. Do this several times: spray, agitate, blot, spray, and so on. After you have blotted for the last time, place additional dry cloths, a few newspapers, and then several heavy books over the stain. Leave them there overnight. This last step is important and unfortunately is sometimes skipped because it looks as if the stain has been completely removed. However, as the carpet dries, moisture evaporating from the carpet fibers "pulls" more stain material up from deep in the carpet. This will cause the stain to reappear, much to your horror, the next day. Avoid that by repeated wetting and blotting *and* by placing weighted absorbent material over the stain overnight. If there are residual bloodstains, use an ammonia solution as on page 124.

Tape Residue

To get tape off your carpet, a solvent is required to remove the gummy residue. De-Zov-All, lighter fluid, lacquer thinner, or nail-polish remover are all potential candidates. Some laundry pretreatments will also work. Use the same techniques as used for removing shoe polish above.

Type 2: Water-Based Stains

All the stains in this category are dissolved by water or a water-based solution. Alas, there are many subcategories. Although oil-based solvents are powerful agents, they are of little or no use on stains in this category.

Digestive Stains

Removal of these stains requires that they be broken down with digestive enzymes. Here are some examples.

Animal glue	Gelatin
Blood	Gravy
Body fluids	Ice cream
Bugs, squished	Milk
Cream	Pet urine
Eggs	Vomit
Feces	

You can choose from a variety of digestive enzymes.

Amylase	Papain
Axion	Pepsin
Biz	Spit

Bet I know which one caught your attention. Yes, good old spit (saliva if you are a formal person) is a collection of some dandy digestive enzymes. More than one restorer has taken a priceless oil painting into the workshop and dabbed at a noble visage with a cotton swab moistened with . . . spit! Works wonders. Look how well it cleans eyeglasses. But your carpet stain probably needs more than dabbing with a cotton swab, so you're more likely to use Axion or Biz. The other enzymes can be even more effective, but they require a trip to a good drugstore.

Enzymes are applied as a paste. If you have a wet-dry vac, first flush the area with warm water and extract it with the vacuum. If not, apply a little warm water to help speed the enzymes along. But don't soak the carpet. Wear rubber gloves, because you wouldn't want the paste to start digesting your hands along with the stain. (Just kidding—sort of.) Mix equal parts of water and enzyme to make a paste. Work it into the stain with your gloved fingers. Leave the paste in place for half an hour. If it dries out before then, add a little bit of warm water. It's best to keep the area warm to promote activity by the enzymes. If possible, apply hot towels over the mixture for up to 20 minutes.

To remove the paste, flush with warm water. Extract the water with the wet vac if you have one. If not, blot it up with a healthy supply of clean cloths. Reset the nap with the toothbrush. If the area still feels damp, place a weighted pile of four to six dry cloths on top of the area.

Blood

You can remove bloodstains from the carpet. Especially in the case of blood, you have a much better chance when the stain is fresh, so this is no time to stop and mix yourself a drink, much as you may be inclined. Instead, thoroughly blot the bloodstained area with a cleaning cloth or towel. Blotting (not rubbing) helps avoid spreading the stain. Keep at this until you can't remove any more blood. Lightly rewet several times with Red Juice or cool water to dilute the remaining blood, and reblot. If the blood was partially dried, or if there is any stain remaining at this point, rewet with a moderate ammonia solution, and gently agitate with a toothbrush. Blot, rewet, and reblot. Finally, cover with several layers of cleaning cloths, several layers of newspapers, and books to provide some weight to encourage complete absorption.

Note: Any remaining bloodstains usually respond well to hydrogen peroxide. Use the milder solution sold for antiseptic purposes, without diluting it further, but you must pretest because hydrogen peroxide is a type of bleach. Rewet, blot, and cover with cleaning cloths and books as above.

Feces

Remove as much of the feces as you can before you start any other cleaning efforts. The best tools are a spatula and a piece of cardboard. Use the spatula to get under the mess, and use the cardboard to stop the spatula at the edge of the mess, so you don't spread it. Empty the spatula onto newspapers. Take your time with the spatula, and remove as much as you possibly can before you start the next step.

Spray with Red Juice and wipe with paper towels. At first, spray and wipe and respray and rewipe to remove solids instead of rubbing them further into the carpet. When most of the solids are removed, spray with Red Juice, gently agitate with a toothbrush, and blot until the spot is gone. Finally, cover the area with cleaning cloths, then newspapers, then books for weight, and allow to sit overnight. Residual stains or odors can be treated with an enzyme cleaner, as for pet urine.

Note: If the feces are completely dry, lift them off either with a paper towel or with the spatula. Then use the vacuum—either with the crevice tool or the hose with no attachment—to break loose dry particles sticking to the carpet. It will remove practically all of them. Then start with the Red Juice and toothbrush.

Pet Urine

The secret to the successful removal of urine stains is an abundant supply of both patience and paper towels. A common mistake is to grab a few paper towels, blot up the urine, and call it a day. It looks so much better that we're inclined to think we're finished. Oh, but we're not. There's still more than enough urine left behind to reappear as a stain, and an odor will not be far behind.

Blotting up the urine is only the first step. Until the problem is solved, never run out of paper towels. When your pet has a mishap, use a handful of paper towels to blot up as much moisture as you can. Do this several times. Use plenty of paper towels, and stand on them to blot up as much as possible. The next step, which may seem a bit odd since you've just removed most of the liquid from the carpet, is to spray the area with Red Juice—enough to rewet the area with a heavy mist—and blot it up again with fresh paper towels. Urine still remains in the carpet, and the only way to get it out is to dilute the stain and blot it out. Rewet and blot it at least twice. As a last step, place fresh paper towels over the spot, cover them with several layers of newspaper, add a few books for weight, and leave overnight.

If the urine has dried before you discover it, rehydrate the area by spraying with water, and blot with paper towels to remove as much of the urine as you can. Do this several times. Now use a specialized stain- and odor-removing enzyme cleaner like Pet "OOPS" Remover on the spot. Enzyme products combat stains caused by organic sources: blood, urine, feces, food, grass, and so forth. Protein molecules in the enzyme solution eat the organic ingredients of the stain and then expire (presumably painlessly, but certainly quietly) when their food source—urine in this case—is exhausted. For this reason, some enzyme solutions must be mixed fresh to become activated and, once mixed, are good only for a day or two before the protein molecules die of old age, or hunger, or whatever. Enzyme treatments are not instantaneous and may even have to be repeated once or twice, but they work amazingly well, and they are quite safe—both to you and to the surface involved.

Tannin Stains

These are usually tan or brown in color, odorless, and difficult to remove. They include the following.

Alcoholic beverages	**Leaves**
Beer	**Soft drinks**
Coffee	**Tea**
Fruit juice	**Tobacco**
Grass	**Wine**
Inks (certain types)	

Tannin stains are difficult to treat. You'll need to make a potion. Wear gloves while preparing it. The formula recommended by *The How-To Handbook of Carpets* is shown on the opposite page.

Red Wine Spills

Long ago, when I was still a team leader on The Clean Team, I was vacuuming a wealthy customer's home. The cord became stuck, so I yanked on it (something I tell team members *never* to do). As fate would have it, the cord tangled in the legs of a small table holding a crystal decanter of well-aged ruby port. When I yanked the vacuum cord, it upset the table, and the decanter promptly obeyed the laws of gravity. All this happened very quietly because the customer had very thick, very plush, very *white* wool carpeting.

Tannin-Removal Potion

1 oz (2 Tbsp) oxalic acid
½ oz (1 Tbsp) glacial acetic acid or white vinegar
4 oz (8 Tbsp) glycerin
Butyl (not rubbing) alcohol

Mix the oxalic acid and glacial acetic acid or white vinegar. Add the glycerin and stir. Continue stirring while adding enough butyl alcohol to make the mixture clear. Oxalic acid (it's toxic, so be careful with it!) can be found at a hardware store in the paint section, as it is widely used as a rust remover. It might be labeled "wood bleach." The other ingredients may require a trip to the drugstore unless someone in the house is a chemist. Glycerin—a mild solvent—is used to soften the stain.

Apply this potion and leave it in place *for a few minutes only.* Wear gloves, of course, and blot up the potion/stain mess with the clean cloths. Flush with water and reblot or extract with the wet vac. The cleaning cloths are ready for the laundry.

Both the sound of that wine (ever so muffled) and the sight of that wine (a sickening blood-red) are forever etched into my memory. It quickly ran through my mind what it might cost to replace the carpeting, and that was enough to move me to immediate action.

Here's what I've learned about such spills: Immediately blot up as much of the wine as possible. Use cleaning cloths or towels. Don't waste time looking for old towels. Use your best ones if that's all that's handy. Keep using fresh cloths or towels. After you've blotted up as much as you can, spray the area with Red or Blue Juice or even plain water to remoisten (not resoak) the area, and blot again. As needed, gently use a toothbrush or turn the cloth as you blot to help loosen the last remains of the stain. Remoisten and reblot two or three times until what you're blotting up is colorless or the faint color of Red or Blue Juice, but definitely not the color of wine. Stand on the cloths the last couple of times you blot to apply extra pressure. When finished, place additional layers of clean cloths over the damp area, cover them with several layers of newspapers, and then weigh them down with a few books. Leave overnight. After you remove the books, gently brush or vacuum the nap to match the rest of the carpet.

When I was at that customer's home, I could leave the books only until we'd finished the rest of the cleaning and vacuuming. But that was enough. Even though I had to confess what had happened (after all, the wine was missing), a stain never appeared.

Note: A good wet-dry vacuum will pick up 80 to 90 percent of the wine if you use it properly. Then switch to cleaning cloths or towels and proceed as above.

Some of the things you read about carpet stains probably work, but some can make things worse, like adding so much liquid to the spill that it soaks the pad or even the floor under the carpet. It might be okay to apply salt or talcum or a similar absorbent to soak up the wine, but you won't know if it worked or not until it dries. Besides, you're more likely to run out of those items than towels. We prefer to take 10 minutes or so to solve the problem immediately and be done with it.

Metallic Stains

Caused by the deposit of one or more metals, these stains appear as a powdery smear. The color is the clue to what type of stain it is: A green stain is from copper or brass, while a brown stain is from iron rust.

Treatment of the stain will depend on the type of metal. Iron-rust stains call for oxalic acid. Start with a solution of 2 tablespoons per cup of warm water. If your carpet can stand it, you may have to increase the concentration. Apply the solution with a toothbrush.

Copper and brass stains call for white vinegar. Use it full strength. For any kind of metal stains, of course, you will have pretested an area. Follow by treatment with Red Juice or a spotting solution and the usual blotting or extraction techniques.

Dye or Pigment Stains

Stains caused by agents that were intended to stain in the first place are formidable adversaries. Other substances, such as medicines, have similar effects. Here are some examples.

Colored paper	**Medicines**
Furniture dyes	**Watercolors**
Iodine (call a professional)	**Wet inks**

Try full-strength white vinegar followed by Red Juice or a spotter. If the spot remains, try a solution of 1 part clean ammonia to 4 parts water. Agitate, blot, or extract as usual. Don't get your hopes up. You'll probably be making a call to a professional.

Emulsifiable Wet Stains

These are stiff, crusty stains that will usually respond to detergent cleaners. Components of the stain can be emulsified or suspended in the cleaning agent.

This is the "if all else fails, call it this" category. These stains should respond to Red Juice or to a specialty rug-spotting detergent product. Remove all dry material with a vacuum or your scraper first. Then spray with Red Juice, agitate with the toothbrush, and blot up. Follow with a water flush and final blotting.

Type 3: Combination Stains

This type of stain is a mixture of both the solvent and water-based stains. For example, coffee with cream and sugar has both types of stains. First, treat it as a solvent stain and then as a water-based stain.

Chewing Gum

What discussion of carpet stains would be complete without mention of Carpet Public Enemy No. 1—chewing gum? Most of us have heard of the standard solution: Rub the offending wad with ice, and then it's supposed to pop right off. Trouble is, that hardly ever works. It takes forever, and your fingers turn blue. Professionals use a blast of freon or carbon dioxide—eminently colder and faster, but potentially hazardous in the hands of the untrained.

According to our local carpet-cleaning authority, Frank Gromm, the freezing method only really works when the wad of gum is resting on the surface of the carpet. Once it gets smushed into the carpet fibers, freezing it isn't going to do much good at all.

In most cases, the gum is pressed into the carpet too deeply to bother with ice. Try lacquer thinner patiently. It will dissolve the gum, but you'll have to work at it awhile. Wet an old cleaning cloth or piece of terry-cloth towel with lacquer thinner, and work at the gum toward the center of the blotch. Follow with a Red Juice treatment.

Mildew

If you have a family room or rec room on the lower level of your house, below ground level, it probably smells musty down there. You've maybe even noticed brownish-black mildew stains in a couple of areas of your carpet.

This is one of those problems that we probably can't solve, but we can at least help you avoid creating the same situation again in the future. Mildew in the carpet destroys the carpet and the backing by eating natural materials such as wool, jute, or cotton. What's left of these food sources are fibers with very little strength. When moved, the carpet may fall apart. Even if you leave it in place, the stains are nearly always permanent. Sorry. But here's what to do to prevent it from happening again:

1. When you replace the carpeting, select both a carpet and a carpet pad that are 100 percent synthetic. (Mildew eats only natural materials.)

2. Before installation, if the floor is concrete, make sure it is properly sealed. It probably isn't, and moisture seeping up through the concrete will encourage mildew growth. Consult a professional at a paint store for advice on a sealer.

3. If moisture is still a problem, install a dehumidifier.

Much also depends upon the disposition of the gum. Here is our advice:

1. If the gum is sitting on the surface of the carpet. Stalk up to it, grab it with your bare hands, and yank. It just might come loose, if you've led a charmed and virtuous life. If not, the freeze-and-whack technique is next on the agenda. The idea is to chill the gum to the point that it becomes brittle. Many of the mishaps involved with an ice cube probably stem from not taking the time to lower the temperature enough so the gum gets brittle in its full thickness. If your fingers turn blue, use ice tongs to hold the cube.

Note: A commercial aerosol freezing agent will increase your chances of success immeasurably. It's available at janitorial supply stores and some carpet stores.

You're not quite ready to whack yet. When you bring down the spoon, it may shatter the glob into little bits of gum that scatter everywhere. Position a piece of paper or cardboard over the gum with a hole cut out of the middle, or have a vacuum cleaner standing by with the crevice attachment to nab little bits before they warm up and reattach themselves wherever they fall.

Once the gum is thoroughly brittle, you can do the traditional whack with the back of a big spoon, or you can try to gingerly pry off the gum with a spatula. In either case, traces of gum will probably hold on for dear life, so finish up with a swipe or two using a cloth dipped in a solvent like Gunk Remover, lighter fluid, or lacquer thinner. (Pretest, pretest, pretest.) Then feel the area with your hand. If it feels sticky in the slightest way (no cheating!), you're not finished. Resume swiping. When it's finally clean to the touch, give the area a final spray with Red Juice and blot dry. A nice finishing touch is to reset the nap of the carpet by brushing lightly with the toothbrush. Remember to provide plenty of ventilation, to wear gloves, and that this is a potent, highly flammable solvent.

If freeze-and-whack didn't work, cut under the gum with a pair of scissors to remove it.

2. If the gum is smushed into the body of the carpet. Cut out part of it, if you can do so without shortening the carpet fibers so much that it will be noticeable afterward. Use Gunk Remover or other solvent to dissolve the gum and a cleaning cloth to blot it up. According to Frank Gromm, even stubborn cases will eventually capitulate to lacquer thinner if you're patient. Keep working toward the middle of the gum, so you don't spread it even farther. A spatula will usually help your efforts along.

And we hope the person who did the chewing in the first place will have the pleasure of trying to remove the gum—or at least of watching you so he can remove the wad the next time.

Burned Spots

If the burn is severe enough, of course, a professional has to be called in to repair the carpet. Minor burns can be treated by vacuuming first with the crevice tool to generate high suction. But in order to *fix* a burned spot on a carpet, you have to get rid of the burned edges of the carpet fibers. There are two ways to do this. In the order in which you should try them: (1) Use a piece of fine sandpaper to sand off the burned ends. (2) Cut them away with a straight-edge razor in a holder, if you can do so without cutting your finger, or use scissors if you can't be trusted with the razor blade. Use a pair of tweezers to hold up each burned carpet fiber and then cut as close to the burn as you can.

Once you've done this, either you have slightly shorter fibers that no one will ever notice, or the fibers are so short that the carpet backing is visible. If the latter is the case, one solution is to cut some fibers from a remnant or a hidden area of the carpet (e.g., under a piece of furniture or in the corner of a closet). Glue the transplanted fibers into the area where fibers were cut out. (Anything from Elmer's or another clear-drying glue all the way to the amazing 5-minute epoxies will do.) It's possible that you may have to do this again someday in the future, but in the meantime, the problem disappears.

Note: If the burn goes down to the carpet backing, or if you're unsure of all this, call a professional before you do anything. It's likely that she will have a brilliant (albeit more expensive) idea, like installing a patch or doing a carpet equivalent of a face-lift.

Bleach on Carpet

If, at some point, you've managed to leave a trail of drops of bleach all the way from one room to another, take heart. It can happen to anyone. The bad news is that bleach permanently removes color. It's G-O-N-E gone. The good news is that you'll probably be able to replace the color so well that you'll scarcely notice. Well, *you* may notice, but nobody else will.

As for the source of the replacement colors, you have several choices. Probably the best is an artist's felt-tip pen. A good artist's supply store will have an amazing assortment of several hundred colors available. Three brand names are Prismacolor, AdMarker, and Chartpak. The hardest part is trying to decide which color(s) to select. If you have a carpet remnant, bring it to the store. Watercolor paints also work and help you avoid a trip to a store if you have them at hand, but they are somewhat more time consuming.

To restore the color, the strategy is to err on the side of a color lighter than the surrounding unbleached carpet. Also, it's best to dab on the colors in small dots. Your eye can be tricked by a few dots of color more easily than by a solid blob, so "less is better" definitely applies in this case. You'll probably find that a combination of two or three colors will fool your eye better than a single one. This is especially true if the carpet is a blend of colors itself. Whatever method you choose, go easy. Practice on a remnant if you can locate one. On the real thing, start with the most inconspicuous spot, even though your impulses will be to tackle the most obvious one first.

Bear in mind that unless you use permanent aniline-dye marking pens, these repairs are profoundly temporary. They will fade in sunlight—maybe even moonlight—and will go away when you shampoo the carpet. Think of it as carpet cosmetics.

Note: If this whole project gives you the jitters, call in a professional in a heartbeat.

Passing the Buck

As complex as the previous pages may sound, we really just barely scratched the surface of the subject. Red Juice is such a good cleaner that you probably won't have to invoke one of the more labor-intensive treatments just reviewed. If you had to, and if it didn't work, you have a choice about your next step.

Plan A

Consult the literature for more detailed information about your particular stain. There are several excellent sources.

Brandt, Herb. *How to Remove Spots and Stains.* New York: Putnam, 1987. A lucid, scholarly, and eminently helpful book. Covers amazing stains like hoisin sauce and coleslaw. The best book on the subject to date.

Miscellaneous Do-Nots

- Do not use rubbing alcohol to treat stains. It contains water and other ingredients and may cause problems. Go to the drugstore for butyl alcohol if alcohol is called for.

- Do not use lacquer thinner or acetone on acetate or triacetate carpets. They will turn to froth right in front of you.

- Do not apply heat to a fruit, blood, or sugar stain. In general, if you don't know what a stain is, don't apply heat.

- Do not use acids on blood. They may set the stain permanently.

Moore, Alma Chestnut. *How to Clean Everything.* New York: Simon & Schuster, 1952. A classic in the field, with many subsequent editions.

The U.S. Government Printing Office also has a variety of publications on treatments of stains.

Plan B

Call in a professional. Professionals have access to the latest chemical advances in specific stain treatments, which are being made with encouraging frequency these days. You should call in a professional early in your response to a stain if you have a delicate, valuable, or antique rug.

Chapter 14 Floors

Before you can make a sensible decision about the type of treatment for your floors, you'll need to know what type of floor covering you are dealing with. In the sections that follow, we will first give a short primer on each of the major type of residential floor coverings. (Sorry, no Astroturf.) The descriptions are especially intended for those of you who have moved into a house and are not sure of the type of floor covering installed previously. Please bear with us if the terminology is not exactly the same as a flooring contractor or salesperson might use, because terms for products in this field are changing constantly. Following the description, we indicate our recommendations for a sealer (if any) and floor finish.

Which Floor Finish?

First, let's clarify the difference between *floor finish* and *floor coating*. The floor finish is the top protective layer. It's usually a liquid acrylic (e.g., The Clean Team High-Gloss Acrylic Floor Finish, Future, etc.) or paste or liquid wax (e.g., Johnson's paste wax or The Clean Team Fortified Floor Wax). The floor coating is more permanent and lies directly under any floor finish. Examples are polyurethane and varnish; polyurethane coatings usually require no floor finish. (See the illustration on page 152.)

It's either the finish or the coating that you actually clean—not the wood it-self. If you know what the finish is, the usual advice is to continue with the same treatment. So if you know what the coating is, you can get down to business.

The most common coating for the past 40 years or so has been polyurethane, a liquid plastic that dries to a beautiful and ferociously durable finish. Your family and guests and dogs and any other critters that occupy your home can practi-cally skate on it with minimal damage. Other potential floor coatings, especially in older homes, are varnish, shellac, or a stain and wax finish called Swedish finish. It's also possible that the floor has no coating on it at all.

There is no easy test to verify what type of coating is on the floor, but you should try to find out. Either (1) locate the builder and ask, or call in an ex-pert (see "Floor Refinishing" in the yellow pages) and find out once and for all, or (2) err on the side of caution, and follow the directions for polyurethane floors on the opposite page.

Whatever the coating, take into account its condition. Does it protect the wood completely, or is it damaged or missing in some areas? Cracks between floorboards, scratches that cut through the coating, and/or well-worn areas in high-traffic zones mean that the wood itself is exposed. This is where it's par-ticularly easy for water to get between and under the wood and cause the hardwood floor or even the subfloor to warp.

If the coating is broken through to the floor itself in areas, use very little cleaning solution—or even none at all—and just vacuum or dust-mop these areas instead. Damaged or worn floors ultimately must be sanded and refin-ished or replaced.

Floor Finishes

All that being said, there are two main categories of floor finishes: paste and liquid (emulsion) finishes. Paste wax should be used only on wood, linole-um, and cork floors. Because applying and polishing paste wax is so time-consuming, we assume you won't be using them, and we'll have nothing more to say about those products.

An emulsion is just a stable mixture of liquids—in this case, water plus wax, or water plus plasticizers. If you see a reference to an emulsion on a product label, it means it is a water-based finish that can be spread easily with an applicator.

Emulsion finishes, in turn, are divided into waxes and polymers. The most prized of the waxes is carnauba because of its hardness. The waxes are reserved chiefly for wood floors and can be buffed to increase the gloss. The one we use is a commercial emulsion formula called Fortified Floor Wax.

Polymers are finishes that most closely resemble plastics or resins. Just about the only type of polymer you will hear about is an acrylic finish. Our Acrylic High-Gloss Floor Finish has a new commercial formula with a metal cross-link finish that is very hard and durable but that nevertheless can be stripped very easily. It can also be buffed to a higher gloss, unlike most acrylics. Other products include Future, Trewax, and Bruce.

In the sections that follow, when we use the term *wax*, we will be referring to a liquid (emulsion) wax. The only type of polymer mentioned will be *acrylic*. And if we are referring to either type, we will use the general term *floor finish*.

Floor Coatings

Polyurethane

Wood floors are probably the most expensive item in a home that you have much control over. Since they are so important to the appearance of your home, it's essential that you know how to maintain and protect this valuable asset. (By the way, we're using *polyurethane, urethane,* and *Varathane* as synonymous terms.)

Maintain the shine of wood floor coatings with regular sweeping, vacuuming, and washing with a mild, no-rinse, no-residue floor cleaner (again, we like clear ammonia) but not by applying wax or acrylic floor finish.

Polyurethane floor coatings are quite durable and would maintain their appearance for years were dirt and grime not ground into them by foot traffic. That's why regular, as opposed to sporadic, maintenance is so important. Eventually (exactly how eventual depends on how well the floors are maintained), the floors will show signs of wear and start to lose their shine. The proper response to this is to apply additional coats of polyurethane. As long as no wax, acrylic, or silicone has been applied to the coating, adding coats of polyurethane is a relatively easy job that you can tackle yourself if you're so inclined. It involves slightly abrading the old finish either by hand or by renting a rotary floor machine to superclean it. Then you can apply a new coat or two of polyurethane with an applicator pad.

But if wax, acrylic, or silicone (present in some floor cleaners) has been applied, there is no way to remove these products well enough to allow additional coats of polyurethane to adhere properly. Instead the floor must be sanded back down to the bare wood. This is a *big* job. You'll practically have to move out of house and home. *Everything* you own will be covered with sawdust. We repeat: *If you have polyurethane-coated floors, do not apply wax or acrylic floor finish.*

Varnish

Varnish was used long before polyurethane, and though it is a beautiful finish, it is not as durable. Traditionally, a paste wax (such as Johnson's paste wax) or a liquid floor wax (such as our Fortified Floor Wax) has been applied on top of varnish to improve durability and to add shine. Apply additional thin coats of either wax as needed. Keep the floors free of dirt and grime with frequent vacuuming, dust-mopping, and an occasional damp-mopping. Years ago, varnish-coated wood floors were not installed in kitchens or bathrooms. If you have finished wood floors in either room, they're practically guaranteed to be polyurethane.

Proper maintenance will drastically increase the length of time between future coats of wax. Add as few coats of wax as possible, because the time may come when you'll have to remove them.

Note: Conventional wisdom is that if a hardwood floor has a heavy wax buildup, then (1) the floor is old, because wax hasn't been in general use on wood floors since the introduction of Varathane and other plastic coatings, and (2) because it's old, it probably has other problems, such as worn areas, stains, and scratches. Accordingly, most people completely refinish wood floors under the circumstances rather than strip them.

Resilient Floors

"Resilient" means the ability of a material to resist shock or impact without permanent damage. A resilient floor is able to recover its thickness after a compressive force such as a heel has been applied to its surface. Resilient floors come in two forms: *sheets* up to 12 feet and *tiles* either 9 inches (asphalt) or 12 inches square.

Common types of residential resilient floors are vinyl (by far the most popular), polyurethane, and rubber. The lack of seams in sheet flooring makes it a practical choice for bathrooms, kitchens, laundry rooms, and entryways where water is likely to be spilled. Tiles are easy to install, but they must be laid snugly against each other to avoid gaps that can collect grunge and leak water to the subfloor. Paste waxes should *not* be used on any resilient floors except genuine linoleum. Acrylics are the preferred finish for all resilient floors except linoleum.

The following are the major classifications of resilient floors.

Vinyl sheet, inlaid. Particles of vinyl are compressed at high temperature into a thin, very hard layer, which is bonded to a backing material. The color runs all the way through the layer of vinyl. The vinyl is resistant to grease and oil, water, acids, detergents, and many solvents. It comes in "wax" or "no-wax" varieties. A sealer and acrylic finish are recommended for the "wax" type of this floor covering.

Vinyl sheet, rotogravure. If a resilient (spongy) layer is sandwiched between the vinyl and its backing, vinyl flooring becomes cushioned. A clear layer on top resists the wear. It is quieter to walk on than inlaid vinyl and comes in "wax" or "no-wax" varieties. Make sure the kind you purchase has a high-quality backing because a thin backing may allow nail heads to deform and surface eventually. A sealer and acrylic finish are recommended if you have the "wax" variety.

Linoleum sheet. Linoleum is a mixture of ground wood and cork, oxidized linseed oil, turpentine, resins, and pigments, all applied to a burlap or felt backing. Linoleum is no longer manufactured in the United States. Our linoleum is imported from Europe. Popular in the '30s and '40s, linoleum is enjoying renewed popularity recently due to its durability. However, it does require a floor finish because it is susceptible to stains. No-wax floors do not need a floor finish. Unless you have an older and unremodeled house, chances are slim that what's on your floor is linoleum. It may also be found as a countertop in older houses. It should have been sealed with a wood sealer and waxed with a liquid buffable floor wax designed for wood floors—not an acrylic finish. Armstrong has recently introduced a line of linoleum floor care products.

Polyurethane sheet. This is a tough surface that requires little maintenance. Seal and finish it with an acrylic.

Vinyl composition tile. This is a blend of vinyl and other dense materials. It is slightly more vulnerable to household chemical attack than is solid vinyl tile but has good resistance to grease and oil. Seal and finish it with an acrylic.

Vinyl tile. The surface is similar to inlaid vinyl sheet. Seal and finish it with an acrylic.

Rubber tile and sheet. This is made from synthetic and/or real rubber. It is durable, quiet, and waterproof but potentially horrendous to clean if textured. As it does not resist grease and oil, it's of questionable use in kitchens.

It deteriorates in the presence of sunlight, so it cannot be installed in a porch or near an exterior window. Authorities do not recommend a sealer, but some specify two coats of acrylic.

Asphalt tile. This does not resist grease, fats, and oils because it is made from similar substances. Vinegar and fruit juice may soften and stain it if allowed to remain in contact for long. Obviously, it is not recommended for the kitchen. Liquid waxes, cleaners, or paste waxes with solvents must not be used or this floor will be damaged. As it can be similar in appearance to vinyl flooring, how can you tell the difference? The Cleaning Management Institute's test is to take a cloth, and rub a small amount of lighter fluid or turpentine on a dark area of the floor. If the cloth picks up the dark color, the floor is asphalt. If not, it's probably vinyl. Seal and finish asphalt tile with an acrylic.

Cork tile. This is made from the bark of the cork oak tree. The cork is ground up and then fused under heat and pressure. Because it is the most comfortable and quiet of resilient floors, it's appropriate for hallways, libraries, and other rooms where peace is desired. But it performs badly if subjected to grease or oils or moisture and must be sealed and waxed immediately after installation. Seal it with a wood sealer. Wax it with a finish suitable for a wood floor—either a liquid buffable floor wax or a paste wax (the latter if you have lots of time).

Because we recommend that resilient floors be treated differently depending on where they are in your house, these floors are listed below by room.

Kitchen Floors

The great majority of contemporary kitchens have resilient floors of vinyl ("wax" or "no-wax"), asphalt, or vinyl-composition material. If your floor isn't made of something else easily identifiable—such as ceramic tile, quarry tile, wood, or marble—then it is almost certain to be one of the above. We recommend finishing all of these resilient kitchen floors (with the exception of no-wax floors—see below) with Acrylic High-Gloss Floor Finish. It is called a metal cross-link high-gloss acrylic. That's a mouthful, but it's worth the trouble. Its metal cross-link formula was one of the major breakthroughs in floor-maintenance chemistry in the past several years. It has an extremely durable finish that reduces the number of times you will have to refinish and, much more important, to strip the finish off again. Yet its chemical structure allows it to break its molecular bonds in response to floor strippers without putting up the fuss that most older waxes do. When you combine a metal cross-link finish with a no-rinse stripper, you have a state-of-the-art combination.

We also recommend that you seal all resilient kitchen floors before finishing them the first time (except the no-wax floors—see below). Also seal after the first time you strip the floor if you don't know if it had been sealed before. This is not a waste of your time even if it had, in fact, already been sealed. Applying an extra coat of sealer means you can usually get by with one less coat of finish. Besides, the sealer is typically cheaper than the finish, coat for coat. The type we use is a penetrating sealer (as opposed to a surface sealer) than can be used on all resilient floors except linoleum and cork. Those floors and wood floors call for a specialized wood sealer.

No-Wax Kitchen Floors

Well, there are two obvious choices with no-wax floors: (1) take their name literally and don't finish them, and (2) finish (protect) the floors anyway. We used to recommend, as did most others in this industry, that you treat no-wax floors with acrylic finish. This was because no-wax floors also need the protection that acrylics provide against normal wear and tear. But no-wax floors have improved in their durability in recent years, so you have a small decision to make at this point.

So, do you finish no-wax floors or not?

No, as long as you're faithful about a regular maintenance schedule of sweeping or vacuuming, damp-mopping, and occasional washing. Needless to say, this choice is the faster of the two alternatives.

Yes, if you know in your heart of hearts that you aren't all that great about keeping the floor free of the grit and grime that will inevitably wear that nice, bright, new-looking floor finish into something less than that. Besides, does it still come as a surprise to you that "no-wax" floors may need finishing? After all, irons have settings for "permanent press" fabrics. Think about it.

A quality vinyl floor, even with average maintenance, will last for years and years. Sadly, the converse is true: Some inexpensive ones never look great—even with the addition of wax. Once you start waxing, it's a never-ending process of reapplying more wax, stripping it, and then waxing again. It's incalculably easier to protect the floor through routine maintenance. However, you may think that the floor needs or deserves the protection of an additional finish because of the amount of dirt that's tracked into your home or because you don't mop or vacuum as often as you'd prefer. If so, go right ahead and wax away. Treat it like a regular vinyl floor, and use a liquid finish such as The Clean Team's High-Gloss Acrylic Floor Finish. The technique is described on page 168.

Whether you finish them or not, it's not necessary to seal these floors. A sealer will not provide any more protection than that built into the floor covering already.

Bathroom Floors

It doesn't matter what type of resilient flooring is in the bathroom. Don't finish it. A bathroom floor is exposed to too much moisture to be able to maintain a finish without extraordinary effort. Just keep it maintained during your normal cleaning routine. You may, however, apply a sealer if you prefer and if your floor type allows for one. We recommend doing so only when the floor is new and if you are advised to do so by the manufacturer.

Laundry Rooms and Family Rooms

Follow the instructions for kitchen floors.

Skid Marks

"My son likes to do wheelies with his wheelchair in the kitchen. How do I remove the tire skid marks from my vinyl floors?"

A thin oil solvent, like plain lighter fluid or Gunk Remover, is a good starting point. Wipe on the solvent with an old cleaning cloth or a paper towel. A white pad or steel wool will boost the effectiveness of the solvent impressively. Even an eraser (by itself) will work sometimes.

If one of these procedures works up to a point but misses a portion of the tire marks, the wheels may have made indentations or grooves in the floor. In this case, switch to a toothbrush (plus solvent) to remove the deeper marks.

Discouraging thoughts: Wheel rims may have damaged the floor in a way that prevents the marks from being completely removed. Also, solvents do a great job of removing any floor wax along with the tire marks, so you will probably have to rewax the area.

Entryways and Foyers

Treat as you would a standard kitchen floor. Even more important, make sure you have proper mats in these areas. Don't use rubber-backed mats on vinyl, vinyl composition, or asphalt flooring, because they may discolor the surface.

Vinyl Floors with Nooks and Crannies

If you have a vinyl floor with lots of nooks and crannies, like fake grout lines, for example, that look dirty even after you've cleaned the floor, two possibilities come to mind.

1. **Mops tend to glide over the top of dirt trapped in the textured areas and grout lines of floors. To dislodge this dirt, occasionally you'll have to clean the floor with a brush that can reach down into these hard-to-get-at nooks, crannies, and grout lines. Use clear ammonia and water as a cleaning solution. If the odor of ammonia offends you, use pH-neutral Sh-Clean. A wet vacuum comes in handy to remove the dirty liquid afterward. Remember, this is an occasional job. Mop regularly and use the brush only when the dirt in the grout lines builds up again.**

2. **Dirt could be encased in a coat of acrylic. (Oh, lucky you.) You can see the dirt through the acrylic, but your cleaner can't get at it. Alas, the solution in this case is to strip the acrylic from the floor and reapply a new acrylic finish.**

Ceramic and Quarry Tile Floors

The various types of ceramic tiles have in common that they are all baked clay. The finish may be *glazed* (gloss, satin, matte, or flat) and no sealer is required; or *unglazed* (no surface finish, usually earth tones), and it should be sealed. Quarry tile is a natural clay or stone product.

Glazed ceramic tiles themselves are impervious to most varieties of dirt. It's the grout that causes most of the cleaning problems. Whether or not the tile itself is sealed, we recommend that you seal the grout to make it easier to clean and more resistant to stains. Use a specialized grout sealer obtainable at a tile shop, a good hardware store, or through our catalog. Don't use steel wool on grouted tile floors: The steel-wool pads may shed tiny bits of steel that will get caught in the rough grout and rust. (For more information on sealing grout, see Chapter 22.)

The only time sealer is recommended for glazed tile is when the tile itself is very old, and the glaze has been worn off. In that case, the tile becomes porous and very difficult to maintain. (One of the worst cleaning nightmares is a floor made of thousands of small six-sided white tiles. Most of these floors are very old and exceedingly porous.) Seal such floors with a terrazzo sealer (two coats), but don't finish them. You may have to reseal the floor from time to time as the sealer is worn away.

Don't apply waxes or acrylics to the floors listed below. They are quite hard and don't need the protection of a finish coat. Also, omitting the finish coat will result in a less slippery floor—and these tiles do not need any encouragement in that direction.

Glazed tile. This comes in any of the four finishes (gloss, satin, matte, or flat) and smooth or textured surfaces. It includes small mosaic tiles sold in premounted sheets. Sealing is not required except for the grout lines, as mentioned above.

Patio tile. This tile is rough in texture, irregular in shape, and thicker than quarry or paver tiles. It must be sealed.

Paver tiles. These are large, usually unglazed, earth-tone tiles that must be sealed.

Quarry tile. This tile is rough in texture, usually unglazed red clay. Reddish terra-cotta tile (Italian for "baked earth") is just one color of quarry tile. If unglazed, use a terrazzo sealer followed by one or two optional coats of acrylic if a higher gloss is desired.

Note: If you are the person purchasing tile of any ilk for your home, please do yourself an enormous favor and inquire (persistently, if necessary) about maintenance and maintenance products needed.

Masonry Floors

Flagstone floors. Seal these with penetrating masonry sealer, available from a tile shop or our catalog as long as it's pH neutral. Finish with acrylic.

Manufactured stone. These brick or concrete floors are extremely porous and irregular, so they will require several coats of both the sealer (two or more) and the finish coat (start with two). Finish them with an acrylic.

Marble. If you have marble floors in your house (villa?), you are probably in no doubt whatsoever that they are marble. You also probably have chilly feet if you walk around the house barefoot.

Marble floors require a specialized sealer obtainable from a janitorial supplier, a marble dealer, or The Clean Team Catalog. It may also be called a terrazzo sealer because the products are interchangeable. Avoid using steel wool on marble floors because tiny particles of steel left behind may rust. Marble floors, counters, walls, etc. are very vulnerable to any type of acid: orange juice, lemon juice, wine, vinegar, and so forth. If you have an acid spill, wipe immediately or else the marble will be etched and have to be resurfaced. If it is a serious spill, sprinkle baking soda on the area to neutralize the acid. Don't finish marble floors, but you may want to buff them for a higher gloss.

    Slate. Colors of slate include grays, greens, and blues. Slate floors will darken if sealed, so it is *not* often recommended unless you are willing to gamble with the several tons of stone installed as your floor. But you may want to finish them with an acrylic. Make sure that the finish does not make the slate slippery.

    Terrazzo. *Terrazzo* is Italian for "terrace." It is made by embedding small pieces of marble in cement. The Portland cement matrix is vulnerable to spillage, so it should not be placed in kitchens or bathrooms or other areas subject to water damage. In houses, this type of floor is found mainly in outside steps and porches. As terrazzo floors are mostly marble, treat them the same way that you would treat a marble floor.

Cleaning Marble Floors

For starters, a specialized marble cleaner isn't necessary. Almost any reputable floor cleaner will do. We like the floor cleaner Sh-Clean. As usual, though, it's a good idea to test your choice before you start slopping it all over the place. Very highly polished marble floors show off their scratches like glass. As with any floor, it's the grit and grime caught between the floor itself and shoes that cause scratches. Scratches can be avoided only with regular care.

    Marble's other weakness is acid, so don't clean with a vinegar-and-water solution, for example. Even the mild acids in citrus drinks, wine, or colas can etch marble, so wipe up and rinse such spills ASAP.

    Note: When we suggest that you don't need a specialized marble floor cleaner (or lamp shade duster, or wicker chair cleaner, or whatever), it doesn't mean that you can't—or shouldn't—run right out and purchase a specialty cleaner or that you won't be perfectly thrilled with the results. Our approach is that it's simpler to purchase, store, and follow the directions of only one product for many cleaning jobs rather than have a different cleaner for each.

Terra-Cotta Clay Pavers

"The Mexican tiles on my kitchen floor have some kind of mystery finish applied. Spots have appeared where the finish has been scratched off. I have tried acrylic stripper, but it didn't work. I have also applied acrylic wax, but it doesn't cover the spots or make the floor uniform. I guess I have to remove the finish and start fresh."

Maybe not. The floor was probably sealed, and many sealers are semipermanent. They're more like paint than wax. Once they dry, they can't be removed using methods designed for removing other floor sealers. So the best solution is to reapply the sealer over the entire floor after you've stripped off any existing wax.

Talk to the manufacturer or installer to find out what sealer was used. If you're unsuccessful, we'll assume a semipermanent sealer was used on the tile because acrylic stripper had no effect. Most tile stores sell this type of sealer, so you can add coat(s) to cover the areas where the sealer has been scratched off.

If these efforts don't work, you'll have to use a professional stripping solution to remove the sealer. This type of stripper involves heavy-duty solvents, so you're well advised to hire a professional stripper (hmm . . . this could be fun) to do the work for you.

Shining Marble Floors

The most common method of shining is to buff with a rotary floor machine. (If you don't have one sitting in your closet, it can be rented from an equipment rental store.) There are marble polishes designed for small floors, such as foyers, that can be buffed by hand. The Premium Marble Polish we use can be buffed by either method. I would call a professional for larger floors because of the amount of heavy labor involved. Marble floors start off shiny. You can keep them that way with careful maintenance.

Note: Acrylic floor finishes are usually a disaster for marble floors.

Concrete Floors

To improve the appearance of concrete floors, start by sweeping or vacuuming followed by a good scrubbing with a moderate ammonia solution plus a brush or a mop. Add ammonia if more cleaning power is needed. Then rinse thoroughly. A wet vacuum makes this part of the job immensely easier. To improve the appearance of a well-finished smooth concrete floor, apply two or three thin coats of floor sealer next. Then apply either an acrylic floor finish or a traditional paste wax. Concrete is porous enough that several coats of either finish are required. There are many jazzy new polyurethane tints designed especially for concrete. Painting after cleaning is also an option, but you're better off using a specialized paint. Talk to a paint supplier.

Wood Floors

Wood floors come in a variety of styles—stripwood, parquet, and plank being the most common. But for cleaning purposes, the primary consideration is the finish, not the style of installation.

Varathane (plastic) finishes. These days, most wood floors in the home are finished with Varathane, polyurethane, or a similar plastic-like protective coating. If you have such floors—and this includes most install-it-yourself wood floors in the form of 12-inch by 12-inch squares—do *not* seal or finish them. Here's why: The whole idea of plastic-like finishes was to spare you the necessity of all that work. They are superb treatments for wood floors and can last for a decade or more.

It's relatively easy to strip the finish back off no-wax floors, which you may have to do to ensure additional protection of the finish. No such luck with wood floors; stripping them is difficult and hazardous both to the floor and to your lungs (because of the intensity of solvent strippers). Besides, you can add another coat of Varathane in a few years to bring the shine back if necessary. You would have to replace a no-wax floor to accomplish the equivalent effect.

Varnish. Wood floors finished with varnish should be protected with both a sealer and a wax.

The sealer should be a penetrating sealer made for wood floors. Use either a paste wax (if you have all weekend) or a liquid buffable wax designed for wood floors like the Fortified Floor Wax we use. This product has carnauba wax suspended in a liquid vehicle. The carnauba wax provides its extra-hard protective finish that we've all heard about since we were kids. Because it's a liquid, it can be applied with a wax applicator on a long handle, in vivid contrast to paste wax, which is applied on your hands and knees or with a floor machine. Needless to say, a quality liquid wax formulated for wood floors is our first choice.

Water Stain on Floor

"I bought my husband a ficus plant for his birthday and dutifully slid a saucer under it to protect the zillion-dollar new hardwood floor we just had installed. Well, I moved it the other day and discovered, to my horror, that a huge ring has appeared beneath it. My husband hasn't spotted it yet. I need an answer, and I need it now."

You sure do. As the expression goes, time is of the essence. Sounds as if you used a terra-cotta saucer, which, as you know by now, does a dandy job of transmitting moisture from the plant to the floor. You'd better replace it with a plastic, glass, or other impermeable saucer ASAP, but you have more pressing matters to attend to.

Edward S. Korczak of the National Wood Flooring Association has probably come to your rescue. He recommends applying Zud plus enough water to make a paste or poultice (the consistency of toothpaste). Smear a quarter-inch layer of paste on the ring, let it dry to a powder, utter a few incantations, and vacuum the powder away when it is thoroughly dry. Pretest a dime-size area first. Unless you've led a charmed life, you will have to repeat this procedure. Maybe you should suggest to your startled husband that it's a good time to go on a weekend fishing trip or bowling tour with his buddies.

Cleaning Wood Floors

Only the kitchen and bathroom floors need regular washing. In other rooms, just wipe up spills as they happen, dust-mop, and vacuum. As you might suspect, the greatest danger when you wash wood floors comes from the water rather than the cleaning agent. Be sparing with the amount of water you use—especially if the floor coating is damaged at all. (Even if you can't see damage, there are often small cracks in the coating, especially between the floorboards, that can allow water to seep down to where it can cause serious mischief.) Don't put water or cleaning solution directly on the floor. Don't use a "dripping wet" mop. Wring it out so that it is only "almost dripping wet" and work in one small section at a time. Sh-Clean or dilute clear ammonia solution are two of the safest cleaners available. As discussed previously, the water is probably more dangerous than the cleaning agent to a wood floor.

Decisions before Stripping Floors

There are a few decisions to make before you strip wax from your floors, such as whether you should hire someone to do it, rent equipment to help you do it, or do it yourself by hand. But first, let's be sure we all agree what stripping wax off floors means and which specific floors we are talking about.

Wax

By "wax," we mean almost anything that has built up on your floors, no matter what the product is called. Some floor finishes are closer to liquid Saran Wrap than to real wax. "Miracle Floor Finish" this or "Super-Hard Long-Lasting" that are both varieties of what we're talking about. Even if the word *wax* isn't used in the name or printed on the product label, it still needs stripping if it's yellowed or unmanageable or unsightly.

Types of Floors

We are not going to spend much time with you figuring out what your floors are made of. We assume you just want the buildup off the floor and to

Cleaning Waxed Floors

A mild cleaner is necessary, so you won't dull the wax finish. Almost any reputable floor-cleaning product will do. Because they save time, we like liquid floor cleaners that don't require rinsing. That eliminates Spic and Span, for example. Clear ammonia is a no-rinse type of cleaner and has long been a favorite of ours. But be careful. Too strong a solution of ammonia will damage the existing wax coat. Ammonia in sufficient proportions is actually a superb wax stripper! It's a balancing act: Use an ammonia solution that's strong enough to dislodge the dirt but weak enough to avoid demolishing the finish. Test a couple of different dilutions to find one that works for your floor's particular combination of wax and dirt. If you want to avoid the balancing act, Sh-Clean is a good choice. Dirt dulls wax quickly, so keep the floors free of dirt and grime with regular attention, using a good dust mop, a vacuum, or a damp mop between floor cleanings.

get on with the weekend. The procedures described here for stripping floors apply almost exclusively to resilient floors such as vinyl sheet, vinyl tile, vinyl-asbestos, and so forth. The great majority of kitchen and bathroom floors fall into this category.

Precautions

Almost all contemporary floors will stand up reasonably well to the potentially harsh stripping process. You *cannot* use this stripping procedure on wood or cork floors.

The fastest and safest stripping method for any floor is to use as little water as possible. Using less water also means that it will take less time to remove the water from the floor after you're done. It also minimizes possible damage to the floor—especially from leakage through the floor covering to the subfloor below. Even on nonporous, well-maintained floors, water can seep through cuts or other damaged areas, through seams between sheets of flooring, between tiles, along the walls, or in the corners. Buckling, delamination (separation of the flooring from the subfloor), and mold or dry rot can all be the result.

If you have a no-wax floor or a very shiny resilient floor, some scrub brushes can scratch the floor surface. Be sure to check before you really bear down on the floor with your brush, especially right in the middle (most visible) area. So test it in an inconspicuous space. If you can produce scratches with a brush, you'd better not use it. Use a Sh-Mop or sponge mop as much as possible. Resort to a white pad or a white floor pad (in either case, always when the floor is wet) if the mop is not strong enough.

Test Areas

Speaking of tests, you should also do a pretest of the stripper in a small, inconspicuous area of your floor (e.g., inside a closet or pantry) before you start sloshing it all over the place. A test area 6 inches square is just fine. The test will ease any fears about possible damage to the floors. You will also quickly discover if the stripper solution even works. Nice to know before you start work, because some of them don't!

Maybe you're unsure about whether your floors even need stripping. One very simple test is to apply stripper to a small area and see if the floor looks better. Usually the buildup is quite apparent. The floors will look uneven and yellowish or discolored. Unfortunately, it's not so easy to remove or ignore, especially when the in-laws are coming to visit.

Linoleum Floors

Most floors are safe for stripping, but there is one major exception. Stripped, older linoleum flooring (in either sheet or tile varieties) will often soften, and its colors will bleed. It appears to be melting—and it is! To test for this potential disaster, apply stripper to an out-of-the-way test area (6 inches by 6 inches is big enough), and remove the wax from this area. Rinse and dry. If you cannot achieve a satisfactory shine on the test area after applying a new coat or two of sealer and wax, stop what you're doing. You must not strip this floor. You'll just have to keep your floor clean and rewax it until you replace the floor or move out.

Bathroom Floors

If you have wax buildup on your bathroom floors, you shouldn't. Bathroom floors should not have been waxed. Bathroom floors are wet too often and washed too often for waxing to be a good idea. Once you've stripped the wax off this time, don't reapply any. Just keep the floor clean during regular weekly or biweekly cleaning, and you'll be pleased with your decision not to rewax.

Hardwood Floors

Here are the symptoms of wax buildup on hardwood floors: Floors are different in overall color (usually lighter in traffic areas); they have a blotchy surface and color (usually yellowish) in nontraffic areas; and bits of wax can be dug out with your fingernail. Even if you have all the symptoms, you must *not* strip wax from hardwood floors using any process that involves water. Water makes the grain of wood expand, potentially ruining the texture and causing edges to buckle. It's not possible to use water to remove wax without too great a risk of permanent damage to the floors. Try cleaning or buffing the floors to help their appearance instead. The only other alternatives are dry-cleaning stripping methods that require professional assistance, or sanding and refinishing the floors.

Even though you probably shouldn't try to strip this type of floor yourself, you don't have to live with it forever. Your choices are to refinish the floor or to call in a professional to strip the wax with a water-free solvent process using heavy-duty chemicals. If you're still intent on trying it yourself, check at a local janitorial supply store for a waterless stripper. We don't recommend it.

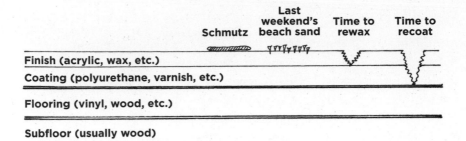

	Schmutz	Last weekend's beach sand	Time to rewax	Time to recoat
Finish (acrylic, wax, etc.)				
Coating (polyurethane, varnish, etc.)				
Flooring (vinyl, wood, etc.)				
Subfloor (usually wood)				

Hiring Someone to Strip the Floor

This is a job that you may want to hire someone else to do. The job can be a difficult and time-consuming one if there is much of a buildup. Also, wax is far easier to remove with professional equipment not found in most households: an electric floor machine to scrub down through the layers of wax and a wet-dry vacuum to pick up the spent stripper and wax *fast*.

Your decision should be based on how expensive it would be to have someone else do it versus how difficult the job will be for you. Perhaps most important, what are your alternatives for the weekend? If the wax buildup is truly demoralizing, you may want to have someone else do it this one time only, and then rewax it yourself. (See page 174.) This will be the only time you'll ever have to spend money to hire someone else to strip the floor because it will never build up like this again if you follow our methods. If you do decide to hire someone, don't be surprised if you're charged by the hour and not by the job. It's often impossible to estimate how long a stripping job will take, especially if you don't know how many layers are on the floor. It's truly disheartening to spend all afternoon stripping a floor, only to find a subterranean layer just as tenacious as the first. And another . . . and another . . . and another . . .

Replacing the Floor Instead

This is absolutely the proper time to consider replacing the floor if it's close to being worn out or if you don't like it that much anyway. How much smarter to make this decision prior to stripping a badly built-up floor! You may be surprised how reasonable the cost of a new floor can be, especially the new seamless and grout-less floors.

Stripping No-Wax Floors

You can strip and rewax a no-wax floor, as long as there's a serious enough buildup of wax or acrylic. It's difficult to tell sometimes, because dirt on the floor can look like wax in need of stripping. Scrub an area well to be sure. If it comes clean, then it doesn't have to be stripped. It just needs a good cleaning.

As to how often you should strip and rewax a vinyl kitchen floor, it's more of a judgment call than a calendar event. It depends on (1) the amount of foot (including paw) traffic; (2) how often you regularly wash and vacuum or sweep the floor (have you noticed how often that word *regularly* keeps popping up in these answers about floor care?); (3) the age of the floor (new floors hold their shine longer than old ones); (4) how many coats of acrylic floor finish are already on the floor; and (5) your fondness for shiny floors. When it doesn't look satisfactory to you even after washing or applying more acrylic finish, it's time to strip off the old coats and start anew.

Choosing the Stripper

It's wise to use the stripper made by the same manufacturer as the wax you intend to strip off because the stripper is formulated specifically to break down that wax. Otherwise, use a professional stripper such as the one we use, which requires no rinsing.

Preparing the Floor

It's a waste of time to wash the floor before you strip it. But do vacuum or sweep it first (if it needs it) to remove grit and debris that could later scratch the floor when it gets caught between the mop and the floor.

Before you start on the floor, take the time to move anything that will be in your way. If possible, move objects to countertops. If not, move them out of the room. If you have a freestanding piece of furniture in an area that needs stripping, you must move it out of the room. Now is also the time to move little items like dog and cat dishes. Don't wait until your hands are wet and slippery, and you can't get a good grip on anything. *Clear the decks.*

Method 1: By Hand

Materials

Wax stripper
1 double bucket or two single buckets
1 Sh-Mop
1 white floor pad, handle, and extra pads, or several white scrub
  pads/sponges
1 scrub brush or scrub brush on a long handle
½ package of coarse (#2) steel wool
1 plastic dustpan
1 spray bottle of Red Juice
10 cleaning cloths
1 cleaning apron
1 toothbrush
1 scraper
1 cleaning tray
1 pair of rubber gloves
1 floor squeegee

Getting Dressed

Buckle your apron snugly around your waist and pull the strap to tighten it.
Be sure the scraper and toothbrush are in their respective pockets. Take four
or five cleaning cloths, and put them in an apron pocket. Also take a white
pad and a steel wool pad, and put them in a plastic-lined apron pocket.
Hang the Red Juice on its proper apron loop. Take the stripper and the
bucket to the sink to mix the proper concentration of stripper.

The Starting Point

Follow label instructions for diluting the stripper. Don't use full strength
unless instructed to do so. Be sure to do a small, inconspicuous test area the
first time you do this job or when you change brands of stripper. Put the
stripper and (usually warm) water solution in one side of the double bucket.
Put the squeegee, dustpan, and scrub-brush attachment in the empty side of
the bucket. Grab your mop and white floor pad, and move to the left-hand
corner farthest from the exit doorway.

The Strategy

The secrets of stripping the floor quickly are to work section by section and always to have a coat of stripper softening the wax in a section *in advance* of the section you are scrubbing. The idea here is to let the chemicals in the stripper loosen up the wax buildup so *you* don't have to. Apply a coat of stripper to Section 1 and Section 2. (See the illustration below.) Then scrub and remove the wax from Section 1. Before you start scrubbing Section 2, apply more stripper in Section 3. The Section 3 stripper will be softening wax while you scrub Section 2, and so forth. That's the general idea. Now let's get more specific.

Change the pattern of the sections as necessary to avoid having to walk in stripper or on already finished sections as you approach the exit. When you get to the last section, park the equipment outside the doorway on newspapers or rags to protect the adjacent floor.

Applying the Stripper Solution

Starting in the left-hand corner farthest from the exit, use the Sh-Mop liberally to wet a section approximately 2 feet deep by 4 feet wide. (Don't follow any label instruction that says 3 feet by 3 feet because you won't be able to reach a problem spot that needs hand-scrubbing on the far side of such a deep square.) Don't make a flood that may loosen the floor covering, but at the same time don't be stingy with the stripper solution—especially in the corners and along the baseboards and other areas where you can see heavy wax. The idea is to get the floor wet enough that it won't dry out before you're finished. You'll quickly learn how much is needed.

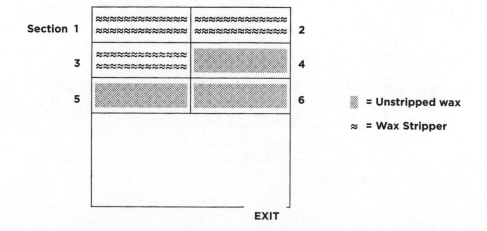

Stripping Test

When stripping a floor, the "inconspicuous test" isn't complete when you strip a small area of the floor to test the effectiveness of the stripper. Unless you're not planning on rewaxing, you must complete your test by sealing this area and then applying a couple of very thin coats of wax (acrylic, etc.). You don't want to strip the floor *before* you discover that when you rewax, the floor doesn't retain a shine!

As soon as the stripper comes in contact with the wax, it starts its chemical attack to soften it. Instead of wasting time waiting while this chemical action takes place, move to the right and wet another 2-foot by 4-foot section. Notice if there is any wax on the baseboards, and remember to wet them also when you first apply stripper.

The Scrub Brush

Next, you'll need a scrub brush or its equivalent to scrub the wax loose. If you're using a Sh-Mop, you can just exchange the mop head for a scrub brush. An extra pole for the brush costs only a few dollars and allows you to avoid having to switch tools back and forth on the same mop handle. If you find that you can apply the stripper satisfactorily with the brush, then you can eliminate the Sh-Mop altogether and just use the brush for both application and scrubbing.

The scrub brush should be right there in the dry side of the double bucket, or you can use a white floor pad on a long handle to scrub with. The other choice is to work on your hands and knees with a handheld brush or white pad. So now, starting in Section 1, use whatever tool you have chosen to finish loosening up the wax.

Scrapers, Steel Wool, and Scrub Pads

Use your scraper on heavily built-up areas—like along the wall and in the corners. Use it carefully, always on a wet floor, and at a low angle. The toothbrush also works well in corners and other tight spots.

You can also very carefully use the corner of the scraper to remove wax from dents in the tile. (Remember when you dropped the iron point-first into the floor, just missing your foot?)

It can be tricky avoiding making scratches when using the scraper. Less troublesome are white pads, steel wool, or floor pads. Because these items don't cost much, we like to have them all available to select which one works best for the particular wax and floor. You'll soon choose your favorites and re-place them only when they're worn out. Start with a scrub brush or floor pad. Then move up to steel wool or a scraper if necessary. (Clean Team Rule 7, on page 10: Shift to a heavier-duty tool.) Careful: Steel wool should not be used on marble or grouted tile floors because tiny bits of steel may become lodged in floor crevices and rust.

Don't drive yourself crazy if a section doesn't respond after a reasonable ef-fort. You may be dealing with layer upon layer of wax. If a section is really stubborn, stop messing with it mechanically. Rather, remove the wax residue, reapply some stripper to the area, and move on. (Don't worry, we won't forget about it.)

Adjusting the Size of the Cleaning Sections

It is important that you not let the floors dry before you've finished scrub-bing. But it wastes time to put on more water than you need because you'll have to remove the excess. So if the floor is getting dry before you finish a section, use a little more stripper solution and/or reduce the size of each section to 2 feet by 3 feet next time. Conversely, if you're having no prob-lems with a section getting dry before you finish it, then you might increase the size to 2 feet by 5 feet. The idea is to make the section as large as you can and yet still be able to finish before the stripper gets dry. This speeds up the job and reduces the time you'll need to finish with this mess.

Baseboards

Previous waxers have often inadvertently waxed the baseboards an inch or two up from the floor. If that's the case, you must remove that accumulation also (and don't reapply it!). Use your white floor pad, white pad, and/or steel wool here.

Don't forget to wipe this wet wax residue off the baseboards with a cleaning cloth after you remove the residue from each section of the floor next to the baseboard because if it redries, it is as tenacious as it was before you started.

Dirty Again Too Quickly

"I stripped my floor with an Armstrong product and then I used your Clean Team Sealer and High-Gloss Acrylic Floor Finish. It looked great for a month, and then it started looking like it had a filmy buildup again. What can I do?"

I believe your floor is showing the effects of incorrect mopping. Not enough of the dirt is being removed during mopping, and the remaining dirt is being smeared together to form a film on the floor. It's not visible right away, but over time, it becomes apparent. If one is daydreaming about Caribbean cruises or romantic Hawaiian sunsets while mopping, occasionally this happens. Not to worry; here's what to do when mopping: (1) Go over each area as many times as necessary to clean it, not just to get it wet. (2) Make more trips back to the sink to rinse dirt off the mop. (3) Give extra attention to high-traffic areas such as in front of the sink, refrigerator, and stove. When you do, the filmy buildup will disappear. With only a bit of practice, you can resume vicarious vacations as you mop.

Note: Using too rich a cleaning solution can make the floor sticky. We've noticed this regularly with a particular oil soap. Be sure to follow the recommended dilution ratios.

Removing the Wax

Once you've loosened the wax—at least most of it—in a 2-foot by 4-foot section, the next step is to remove the fine mess you've made out of water, stripper, partially liquefied wax, grease, dirt, and whatever else was on your floor. Use a squeegee and a plastic dustpan. You can use your prized window-washing squeegee for this task if you plan on replacing the rubber blade with a new one when you finish. Otherwise, use a specialized heavy-duty floor squeegee.

Use the squeegee to pull the waxy mess toward you, to the right, and into the dustpan. Then dump the contents of the dustpan into the empty half of the double bucket. This keeps the stripper solution clean, so it lasts longer. Furthermore, you won't have to run back and forth to the sink to pour out the muck you'd get if you mixed the wax residue with the fresh stripper solution. Alternatively, use two separate buckets (one for stripper and one for the gunk).

If the wax residue on the floor is so watery that the squeegee and dustpan aren't effective, use a large hand sponge or a sponge mop and add clean rinse water to the empty half of the bucket. Squeeze the residue from the sponge into the rinse water, and also use it to rinse the sponge.

When the stripper is removed (using either the squeegee and dustpan or the sponge), apply stripper to the next 2-foot by 4-foot section (Section 3). In most cases, locate it next to Section 2. (See the illustration on page 160.) Do this *before* you scrub Section 2—where the wax by now is mostly softened.

Back to Those Problem Spots Again

Let's say you had to leave behind problem spots in Section 1 that still had some stubborn unstripped wax, and they are now soaking in stripping solution again. Your strategy will be a bit different than if there were no such pockets of resistance. To minimize the number of times you traipse back and forth through wet stripper, it may be best to go to the opposite side of the room for the next section in which to apply stripper. (See the illustration on page 160.) So now presoak Section 3 with stripper. Let the earlier problem spots continue to soak until you are done scrubbing and squeegeeing Section 2. Then go back and finish them before going any farther. Use your scraper or the steel wool if the floor pad isn't strong enough (Clean Team Rule 7, on page 10). This strategy works best in a large room. If it's small, do the best you can to stay out of your own way. If you are having persistent problems removing all the wax, use the stripper full strength (undiluted with water).

Removing the Last of the Stripper

You'll save the most time if you use a no-rinse stripper. If you use a stripper that requires rinsing, be sure to thoroughly rinse the floor after you've finished stripping it because any remaining stripper will react with the wax you're about to apply. This is a time-consuming extra step, of course, requiring extra trips back and forth to the sink that could have been avoided.

When using a no-rinse stripper, be certain to remove all the stripper solution. This isn't all that hard to do. Squeegee carefully and move the little bit of stripper solution that's left over each time into the next section you haven't scrubbed yet. For example, squeegee all the spent solution you can from Section 1 into the dustpan, and pour it into the bucket. Then squeegee into Section 2 the remaining little bit of stripper solution that isn't easy to pick up. This way, you'll

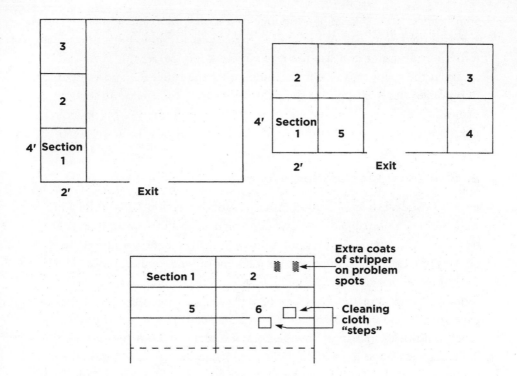

only have to fuss with the last trace of solution once (in the very last section you do). Then use a sponge or cleaning cloth to pick it up.

When you run out of stripper solution and/or finish the floor, dump both sides of the double bucket into a toilet. Make sure it's all rinsed from the sides and then flushed. Flush once or twice more. Also, rinse out both sides of the bucket, so you don't end up with wax buildup there too!

Review

Remember, the secret to stripping the floor as quickly and painlessly as possible is always to have stripper soaking the section ahead of where you are currently working, so it loosens the wax before you get there. The same principle holds true for the problem spots. When they resist your efforts on the first attempt, don't spin your wheels (let alone work up a sweat and waste time). Rather, squeegee the whole section, apply more stripper solution on the problem spots, and move on to the next section. Scrub the next section and return to the previous problem spots before you continue moving on. If they still don't come around after scrubbing a second time, repeat the process by rewetting with stripper and returning once more.

What's Next?

Unless you have decided not to rewax, you should be prepared to apply the wax as soon as the floor dries, or no later than the next morning. (See page 168.) The floor is now nice and clean, and you wouldn't want to wait for it to get dirty before you wax it. To speed drying time, you can aim a room fan across the floor. The air moving over the surface speeds drying time significantly. Heating the room helps too, of course.

Method 2: Using a Floor Machine and Wet-Dry Vac

You may want to be kind to yourself and rent a floor machine and a wet-dry vacuum to assist you in stripping a floor. We heartily recommend this method if you have a large room to strip or if the wax buildup is severe. The floor machine can do double duty as a carpet cleaner (see Chapter 13), and the wet-dry vac will save an amazing amount of time and wear and tear on your back. Both of them are available at most equipment-rental stores.

A floor machine can be difficult for some people to manage. Unless you're someone who is not intimidated by such mechanical challenges, don't even try it. In any event, practice with the machine before you leave the rental store. When considering whether or not to rent machinery, also weigh the time involved to drive to and from the rental place (*twice*) and the extra cost in relation to the size of your floor.

If you do rent the equipment, get both machines (or, better yet, buy your own wet-dry vacuum and just rent the floor machine). There's nothing stopping you, of course, from combining features of Methods 1 and 2. For example, if you don't want to tangle with the floor machine, you might want to scrub with a brush by hand but pick up the stripper solution with a wet-dry vac. Or you could power-scrub with the floor machine but then you will need to pick up the stripper solution with a floor squeegee and dustpan.

Check the list on the following page for the equipment you'll need if you've decided to strip the floor with the aid of a floor machine and a wet-dry vacuum.

Materials

Wax stripper

1 double bucket or two single
   buckets

1 Sh-Mop

3 white scrub pads/sponges

½ package coarse (#2) steel
   wool

1 spray bottle of Red Juice

10 cleaning cloths

1 cleaning apron

1 toothbrush

1 scraper

1 cleaning tray

1 pair of rubber gloves

1 wet-dry vacuum

1 floor machine: 17-inch
   diameter or smaller, plus
   stripping pads

Floor Machine

The floor machine suitable for use at home is one that has a single rotating disk powered by a motor that sits directly above it. The disk is a brush with firm nylon bristles, but they're not for use directly on the floor. Rather, the bristles hold in place plastic pads of varying roughness that do the stripping, scrubbing, and polishing that the machine is capable of.

For our purposes, the floor machine works by scrubbing the wax off the floor with a high-speed rotating stripping pad (usually red or black) that is pressed firmly against the floor by the weight of the machine itself. The stripping pad is the same diameter as the brush and is made of a modern abrasive substance much like the white scrubbing pad we use. Pads come with the floor machine when you rent it. Be sure to explain to the salesperson what you are using the machine for, so he can determine what type of pad you need. (Different pads are used for polishing, applying wax, etc.)

Like the white pad, the stripping pad wears out after some use, so be sure to bring enough of them home so you won't run out halfway through the job. It's no fun to have to make a *third* trip to the rental store to get one more stripping pad! We suggest that you take a few more than the store personnel recommend and, of course, return the unused ones for credit when you return the floor machine.

Rent a machine whose disk is 17 inches or less in diameter. Insist that the salesperson give you a demonstration or good instructions on how to operate and control it. The machine is easy to handle only *after* you know how. Otherwise, it will seem impossible to manage, and it can easily result in torn (or very tired) muscles and/or damage to your baseboards or furniture. For instructions on how to properly operate the floor machine, see Chapter 13.

Getting Dressed

Tie your apron snugly around your waist. Be sure the scraper and tooth-brush are in their respective pockets. Take four or five cleaning cloths, and put them in an apron pocket. Also take a white pad and a steel-wool pad, and put them in a plastic-lined apron pocket. Hang the Red Juice on its proper apron loop. Take the stripper and the bucket to the sink to mix the proper concentration of stripper.

Getting Started

Follow label instructions for diluting the stripper. Don't use full strength unless instructed to do so. Be sure to do a small, inconspicuous test area the first time you do this job or when you change brands of stripper. As mentioned before, a test includes both stripping a small inconspicuous area, plus applying both sealer and wax to the area to be sure the result is satisfactory. Put the stripper and (usually warm) water solution in one side of the double bucket. Move to the left-hand corner farthest from the exit doorway.

With the Sh-Mop, apply the stripper solution to two adjacent sections approximately 3 feet by 6 feet. Keep two such sections covered with stripper at all times. The first is the one you're scrubbing with the floor machine. The second has the stripper, presoftening the wax for easier removal when you get to it with the floor machine. Apply enough solution to this second section, so it doesn't dry out before you get to it. If you do have this problem, then reduce the size of each section to 3 foot by 4 foot. On the other hand, if you're having no problem managing the 3-foot by 6-foot sections, go ahead and make them a bit larger. The fewer and larger the sections, the faster the job will go. Keep moving the bucket, so it is positioned where you'll need it next *and* where it will be out of your way.

Depending on the shape of your room, there are several ways to proceed. Here are two examples: (1) For square rooms, start in the far left corner and work to the right. When you come to a corner, go back to the left wall, move out 3 feet, and work back toward the right. (2) For narrow rooms or rooms with an exit in the middle, it may be faster to alternate from one end of the room to the other. (See the illustration on the following page.)

Corners and Baseboards

You must clean the corners by hand because the floor machine's circular brushes won't reach into them. Carry a white scrub pad or steel wool (except for marble and grouted floors) in your apron pocket for the corners and other places you'll need to get at by hand. The same is true with baseboards if previous waxers have splashed them with wax. If so, be sure to coat the baseboards with stripper when you are applying it to the floor. Be liberal with the stripper in the corners and anywhere else the buildup is heaviest.

Maneuver the machine carefully along the walls. It will splash wax and stripper onto the baseboards (in addition to the stripper you have already applied there). Use a cleaning cloth to wipe the baseboards to remove the wax that was there and any stripper the machine has deposited. The time to wipe the baseboards is when you use the wet-dry vac (or squeegee) to remove the mess on the floor. Wipe them while they're within reach. If you wipe the baseboards too soon, you'll get them dirty again when you bring the floor machine close to that area. If you do fling wax debris onto a surface that you've already cleaned, use a little Red Juice and a cleaning cloth to reclean that area. If you wait too long, you already know what will happen—fossilized floor wax.

This is an important step because if the baseboards redry, the wax and dirt from the floor will be just as hard to remove from them as they were from the floor—except that it is even uglier on the baseboards because it's now lumpy and dirty and disgusting. If the stripper mixture manages to become dry and hard by the time you get to it, dip a white pad into the stripper solution and try again. The stripper will soften the gunk and make it easy to wipe clean.

Wet-Dry Vacuum

The wet-dry vacuum (sometimes called a shop vacuum) is easy to operate and maneuver. It's a logical and reasonable item to purchase for many homes. In addition to stripping and cleaning floors, it can be used for wet-cleaning carpets and upholstery and vacuuming the garage or patio or porch. It's a lifesaver for the occasional household flood (acts of nature or otherwise). But don't buy the cheapest model, because it won't pick up enough water to be helpful.

Picking Up the Mess

During floor stripping, the time to use the wet vac is after you've finished scrubbing each 3-foot by 6-foot section with the floor machine. Let's take a square room as an example. (See the illustration below.) Scrub Section 1 with the floor machine, and leave it at the closest corner of Section 2. Use the wet vac to remove all traces of the stripper solution from Section 1.

When you've vacuumed up all traces of stripper in Section 1, park the wet vac behind your bucket. Apply stripper to Section 3. Then strip Section 2, and so forth until done. The idea is to relocate equipment to a spot as close as possible to the area in which you will use it next—without putting it in your own way.

Stubborn Spots

Don't be afraid to add more stripper to Section 1 if you find that it's not thoroughly stripped of wax. In fact, that's the correct way to get the job

Section 1	Section 2 x Floor Machine	The floor machine is INSIDE section 2.
Section 3	x Wet Vac	
	x Mop & Bucket	The mop and bucket are OUTSIDE future Section 4.

Exit

over as quickly as possible. When a section doesn't come clean after your first effort, don't scrub it again just yet. Rather, apply more stripper where needed to continue the chemical battle and then move on to scrub the next section. Then, after you've finished scrubbing that section, apply stripper to the next section, and return the machine to the problem spots in the original section for another go at them. But finish the problem spots before you get so far away that you have to drag the machine over places you have already stripped and wet-vacuumed dry. Refer to the previous illustration; if you have problem spots in Section 1, reapply stripper to them and move on to Section 2. After you finish Section 2, just be sure to return to Section 1 to finish up there before you move on to scrub Section 3.

Reach for one of your hand-scrubbing tools (steel wool, or white pad, or scraper, or toothbrush) as needed when you're wet-vacuuming and discover you've missed a few small spots. That way you won't have to bring back the floor machine unnecessarily. Your bucket is nearby for additional stripper if you need it, but usually you can do it with just the pad because the wax is already softened.

What's Next?

You should be prepared to go ahead and seal and/or wax the room now because the floor is nice and clean. Who knows how long it will stay that way? If it does get dirty, you will just have to wash it again before you apply wax.

Waxing and Sealing Floors

The first decision to be made is whether your particular floor should be waxed or not. Hand in hand is the decision of whether or not to seal it. And you'll need to know what products to use. If you're familiar with your floor and have already made these decisions, we're ready to get right to it. If you have questions about what type of covering your floor has and whether or not it needs waxing and/or sealing, first check "Floor Coatings" on page 137.

Although we recognize that some floor coverings require waxes and others require acrylics, for the sake of brevity, we'll refer to all finishes as "waxes" in this section. Likewise, as the procedures are the same for applying sealer or wax, we'll refer to sealers as "waxes" also. If your particular floor requires a sealer, apply it before the wax, of course, but in exactly the same way.

Fairies in High Heels?

"I try my best to keep my kitchen floors free of black heel marks, but they keep appearing. It's almost as if little fairies in black-heeled pumps come in the night and dance on my floor. What's the solution?"

Do they leave pixie dust too? Proceed with caution, because fairies have a wicked sense of humor.

If you're lucky, a simple gum eraser may remove the heel marks. It's personally and environmentally safe and practically free. If it works, leave a couple in a kitchen drawer just for that purpose.

It's just as likely, however, that you'll need a solvent. Gunk Remover and lighter fluid work well. Apply either to a paper towel or old cleaning cloth, and wipe off the spot. Spray the same area with Red Juice, and wipe it with a cleaning cloth to remove all traces of the solvent. Or wash the floor with a detergent floor cleaner when you're finished. Some floors allow marks to come up easily with Red Juice and a white pad. You may have to rewax the area you've worked on, and thus the dancing fairies will have had their revenge.

Condition of the Floor

Now that the hard job of stripping the floor is out of the way (it *is* out of the way, right?), and as stripping leaves the floor nice and clean, you can now proceed directly to the easier part—applying the wax. Otherwise, make sure the floor is absolutely clean before you wax it. So if it needs it, wash it thoroughly before applying wax. Use clear ammonia (3 to 4 tablespoons) or Sh-Clean and water on all your floors—including Varathane-finished wood floors (but *not* bare or waxed wood floors). Although these are no-rinse products, rinse the floor only before waxing. The reason for the rinse is that alkalis or other harsh agents in liquid cleaners can react poorly with the floor wax. One of the unfortunate results is "flashing," or irregular spots of dull wax. Because residual alkalis can make it impossible to get a high shine, rinse with care, so your finished work will look as nice as possible after all your effort.

Now the floor is sparkling clean from your stripping or cleaning job. If it isn't, every little piece of fuzz, every single hair, every crumb of every cracker left on the floor will be enshrined in the wax for you to see every time you enter the room until it's time to strip and rewax again. So be sure the floor is clean.

Despite all the advertising hoopla, we have found that how you prepare the floor and how you apply the product are more important than the product itself. Correct preparation and application allow you to get the maximum benefits from the floor finish—in degree of protection, appearance, and duration of coverage. Besides a great-looking floor, you'll also create a lot of free time that you would otherwise have wasted by doing the floor improperly or inefficiently and by having to repeat the whole process in 3 months instead of in 6 to 12.

Materials

Stock your cleaning tray with the following items.

10 cleaning cloths
1 spray bottle of Red Juice
1 white scrub pad/sponge combination ("white pad")
2 pads of #0000 steel wool
1 pair of rubber gloves
Sealer—depends on type of floor (see "Floors" on page 135)
Floor finish—depends on type of floor (see "Floors" on page 135)

Stock your cleaning apron with these items.

1 toothbrush
1 scraper
2 plastic bags (as liners) with clips

Hand-carry the following items.

1 fake lamb's-wool wax applicator with a long handle

This section of the chapter is designed to teach you step-by-step techniques to get waxing over with in as short a time as possible and to free you from repeating the process for a very long time.

The Starting Point

Set your cleaning tray just outside the doorway through which you will eventually exit. Take your apron and tie it around your waist snugly. Check to be sure that the toothbrush and scraper are in their proper pockets. Hang the Red Juice on the side of your apron on which you usually carry it. Put four or five cleaning cloths in an apron pocket. Stuff the white pad and a steel-wool pad into a plastic-lined pocket. Hand-carry the wax applicator and the wax to the far left corner of the room away from the door you'll eventually exit through.

Setting Up

One of the things that makes this job so much easier to experienced professionals is that they take the time to *first* move anything that may eventually be in the way. Move any furniture that you can completely out of the room—not just across the room, where it will be out of the way only half of the time. Likewise, remove the smaller things—like the little trash can in the corner that you would other- wise trip over sooner or later,

spilling half the wax and tipping the garbage into the wet wax. Take the time to tie up the drapes or curtains if they will hang in the path of the wax appli- cator. Do it now, not when you are right in the middle of the job and have to stop everything to find a string or coat hanger. This little preventive step may seem annoying, but the alternative is to end up with wax on your curtains forever more. Close the door to nearby rooms if dust is going to blow in from them. Oh, and put the dog and cat out. You're on your own with your kids.

Now you can move around the room unimpeded instead of tripping over things, wrestling with the curtains, having the dog chase the cat through the wax, or tripping and spilling wax. Why ask for trouble?

Convenience and safety aren't the only reasons professionals move every- thing out of the way. It's also the fastest way to get this job done. They will have the time to do another job. You will have the time to finish this job and still go on a picnic while it dries.

Strategy

The most important strategy to observe while applying wax is to spread the wax perfectly evenly in as *thin* a layer as humanly possible. A thin layer will

Sealing Floors

"I've heard that floor sealers help level a floor. Should I use a floor sealer to smooth over a textured floor?"

No. Sealers contain levelers that fill in only microscopic imperfections in the floor. Sealers don't level floors in the sense of filling up visible nooks and crannies in textured floors or grout lines, even though they may make a noticeable overall difference in the level of shine achieved in a textured floor. But a sealer such as Floor Sealer can make a *big* difference in the ultimate shininess of smooth floors. It can also improve the general appearance of the floor and help protect it. If you apply acrylic to a floor, we recommend that you precede it with several coats of sealer. Apply it with the same fake-wool applicator, and with the same two or three very even, very thin coats. Follow with only one or two coats of acrylic.

give you the most beautiful appearance, the maximum protection and duration, and the easiest removal later if necessary. Two or three very thin coats look much better than one thick coat no matter how carefully the thick coat is applied. Too heavy a coat will make a floor dull, will increase the ability of the wax to trap dirt, and may alter the apparent color of the floor. A very thick coat may harden on the top but stay soft underneath permanently, which causes all sorts of maintenance problems and can make the floor sticky.

Using the Wax Applicator

First of all, use a professional wax applicator. The one we use costs less than $15. Your knees are worth at least that much—or more. Each. Wet the applicator pad with water and wring it as dry as you can, then install it on the applicator base.

Starting in the left corner farthest from the exit, pour a small amount (about ½ cup) of wax directly onto the floor. Don't pour it all in one spot. Instead, squirt the wax in 3-foot lines from one end of the area to the other and back again. This makes a kind of long skinny oblong. Use the wax applicator to spread the wax over an area of the floor about 3 feet by 3 feet.

The best way to evenly distribute the wax is to make back-and-forth motions with the wax applicator from one end of the 3-foot by 3-foot square to the other and then back again. You don't have to step forward and back to do this—just a couple of side steps to get from one end to the other. If you do it this way, it's almost impossible to end up with puddles or thick areas of wax or missed spots. Just don't put too much wax on the floor to begin with. Remember, the ideal is one molecule thick, not ¼ inch!

Do be alert as you move your applicator back and forth not to miss small spots. They will stand out later as prominently as the spots you miss on your car when washing it.

If you don't follow our directions, one of the results may be bubbles in the wax generated by the wax applicator. The way to avoid this is to spread the wax out without going back and forth over the same area repeatedly with the wax applicator. Don't *scrub* with the applicator. It's not a mop. Your goal is just to smooth out the liquid over the surface. Two back-and-forth motions with the applicator should do.

Pouring the wax in small quantities does seem to slow you down, but the results are so much better that it's eminently worth the effort. You are only going to apply this finish once or twice a year, but you will have to look at it a few thousand times a year, so it makes sense to be very exacting during this application stage.

All the usual rules and exhortations apply for protecting your back. If you have a back problem, I'm sure you're well aware of it. Use the applicator while standing as erectly as possible. Bend your legs, not your back.

Working Your Way around the Room

After you complete the first 3-foot by 3-foot area, move to the right and re-peat the process. If you are proceeding properly, the previous area will still be damp, and the wax from the new and old areas will blend together easily. But be attentive when you join two such areas together as it is easy to miss a little bit of floor here. Progress from area to area across the room to the right. Just step back and start across the room in the other direction when you finish your first row. Repeat the process until you've done the entire floor. Remember, the method is the same whether you are applying sealer or wax.

Dirt in the Wax Applicator

If your wax applicator gets dirty, it shouldn't. Your floor should be so clean that the applicator looks wet only, not particularly dirty. If it does get dirty, stop and rinse it clean before proceeding. Repeat if necessary because once it gets dirty, it will start applying some of that dirt back onto the floor mixed in with the wax.

Little Mystery Globs

If, while you're applying wax, you come across mystery matter still on the floor, grab a tool and remove it before proceeding. Use your scraper on larger masses and the toothbrush, white pad, or steel-wool pad (except on marble or grouted floors) on smaller bits of previously missed matter. Deposit the remains in the plastic-lined debris pocket of the apron, so it doesn't end up immortalized in the wax. If necessary, use a little Red Juice to help pick up the more stubborn pockets of resistance. But be sure to wipe any such areas completely dry before you apply any wax because there's no telling how Red Juice or any other cleaner will react with the wax. Use a cleaning cloth from your apron to do this.

How Many Coats?

If you're applying both a sealer and a wax, we recommend two coats of each. It doesn't take long to let the first coat of sealer dry completely—everywhere in the room—before applying another thin coat. One coat of sealer may look great, but go ahead with the second coat to maximize protection and appearance. The goal is not to have to do this again for a long, long time.

As with the sealer, even if one coat of wax looks just fine, go ahead and apply the second coat. You want the layers of wax to absorb the wear and tear without breaking through to the sealer. Again, be sure to let each coat dry completely before starting the next one. As long as you apply the wax in very thin coats, it should dry quite quickly. If your floor isn't dry within 20 minutes, you are probably applying it too thickly.

Avoiding Wax Buildup

You can really do yourself a favor by applying wax correctly in the first place, so you don't create removal problems for yourself later on. The main reason for wax buildup (other than applying it too often and too thick) is applying wax to areas where it doesn't get worn off by foot traffic. You may have noticed when you were stripping the floor that the worst wax buildup was near the walls and in the corners—where there is little foot

Wax Traffic Areas Only

"Can I get away with rewaxing only the part of the floor that gets heavy traffic? I know I'll feel guilty if I do."

Rewaxing only the traffic areas is absolutely the correct way to do it. So you can skip the guilt. When you apply wax or acrylic to the floor, it will stay there until the end of the world, or until it is worn off by foot traffic, or you strip it off. It doesn't evaporate or disappear by any other means. Accordingly, whenever you add additional coats of wax to areas where no one walks, you're adding layer after layer of unnecessary wax to the floor. All that wax is unnecessary because the original wax is still there, and it's all going to have to be stripped off sooner or later—which is a big job. So rewax the entire floor only the first time after stripping it. Don't rewax close to walls or other low-traffic areas on top of previous coats of wax.

traffic. There was little or no wax to strip off from the more traveled areas of the room, where the wax is continually worn off by foot traffic. Because it is almost impossible to walk closer to the wall than 6 inches, any wax applied there will never get worn off. It will remain there unscathed indefinitely.

Here's a rule to avoid wax buildup during application: Apply both coats of sealer and the first coat of wax all the way to the baseboard or wall. But do not apply the second coat of wax any closer than *6 inches* from the baseboard or wall. Also do not apply successive coats—even months later—any closer than 6 inches from the baseboard. This wax-free zone also includes any other places that don't get heavy traffic—like small strips of floor between appliances, or a large corner area that gets little traffic, or under a work island, and so forth. You should be able to recall which areas of your room aren't walked on much if you are the one who had the pleasure of stripping the wax off the floor. The places where the wax buildup was the worst are the same ones to avoid applying a second coat of wax. Even if you didn't strip your floor, take the time to think it over. Don't ignore this rule and routinely apply wax to the entire floor. Not only does overwaxing cause removal problems later on, but also it starts to make the floor look worse and worse.

Cleanup

When you are finished with the final coat of wax, clean the lamb's-wool pad. Washing it is a bit like trying to get all the paint out of a paint roller. Rinse it very well with water to prevent it from hardening as it dries. After it dries completely, store it in a sealed plastic or paper bag to prevent it from accumulating debris in storage. If you wait until the wax dries before you try to clean it, you may find it impossible to do.

Be patient and let the floor dry thoroughly before you try to replace the furniture and other items that you originally moved out of the way. To avoid temptation, it helps to have made plans to be out of the house (treat yourself to something) to let the floor completely dry. It's a shame to move furniture and other items back into the room only to discover that part of the floor wasn't quite dry. You don't want to have to try to figure out how to fix an area—or to have to ignore it and have your footprints immortalized in the wax. This point is really a version of Clean Team Rule 5 (on page 10)— "Don't rinse before it's clean."

Congratulations! If you've followed the directions faithfully, you have just sealed and waxed your floor like a pro. Your floor will look better than it has since it was installed, and it will give you satisfaction a long time before you'll have to rewax.

Rewaxing

As we said, don't apply wax close to walls, corners, or nontraffic areas after the first coat, no matter how long it has been between coats. Wash and rinse the floor well, and apply wax only to the traffic areas of the floor. It doesn't matter that the new and old areas temporarily appear different when you're applying the wax, or that it's so easy to apply the wax right up to the baseboards. Don't do it! The visible difference between the dry strip you didn't wax and the wet wax will quickly disappear. Your floor will look better over a longer period of time, and your total maintenance time will be reduced significantly.

Frequency of rewaxing depends on the traffic in your home, the type and color of the floor, and the sort of abuse it is put through. Try to wax less often than you think is necessary. But your floor really tells you when it's time. It will start to look dull, and washing it doesn't really help. Generally speaking, after you've washed the floor regularly for 3 to 6 months (or washed it six to eight times), it will start to look as if it needs a new coat of wax. Kitchens will need another coat more often than laundry rooms, entryways more often than family rooms, and so forth. And all of these rooms more often than the bathroom because you're never going to wax in there.

Maintenance

You know that if no one ever walked on a floor, it would never need to be rewaxed. Armed with this bit of profundity, it's easy to understand that to reduce overall maintenance of the floor, you must reduce the damage done to the floor finish by foot traffic.

It's more important to sweep or vacuum the floor regularly than it is to wash it—even if it's the kitchen floor. Dirt particles on the floor are driven into the finish (or into the floor itself), which means the beginning of the end for the wax. Or dirt particles are ground between the floor finish and the soles of shoes, which has about the same general effect as using a mild sandpaper

---

"How Can I Extend the Life of My Floors?"

Doormats dramatically reduce the amount of dirt brought into your home, the same dirt and grime that are the primary cause of wear on your floors. Reduce the volume of imported dirt by up to 85 percent by placing mats both inside and outside all entry doors in your home. Install mats that are at least 2 feet by 3 feet and even larger if you can stand it. Coco mats and other grass mats are ineffective because they shed and because it's fiendishly difficult to get accumulated dirt and grit out of them. Use real mats with carpeting over rubber, not carpet remnants whose abrasive backing can scratch floors or create worn spots on the carpet underneath. Remnants also look dirty all the time and very seldom have clean unraveled edges or edges that will stay flat.

Once you have the mats in place, *vacuum or sweep them regularly*—at least as often as you do the surrounding floors—so they don't become saturated with dirt and lose their effectiveness. Mats—plus regular vacuuming, sweeping, dust mopping, and wet mopping—will mean your floors will last so much longer that you'll get tired of them before they wear out. Better yet, it means that your house will retain its value and will look better during that time.

on the floor. The resulting little scratches cumulatively ruin the finish. Also, pick up or clean up anything that is spilled or dropped as soon as you can—not sometime in the future.

Sweeping or vacuuming daily would be ideal, especially if kids, pets, and heavy use prevail in your house. But even with less intense use, do so every few days. In Chapter 13, we tried to convince you to leave the vacuum out to make it more easily available for use. Running the vacuum over the major traffic areas of the carpets and floors every day should take less than 10 minutes in most homes. (Time yourself! It just seems longer.) Don't move the furniture or otherwise make it difficult for yourself. Just vacuum. Your floor finish will last much longer before it needs another coat of wax, and your floors will look better: no "dust bunnies" flying here and there, no pet hairs "everywhere." It's relaxing and so much more enjoyable to be in your home when you keep on top of the maintenance of it, instead of having that awful feeling that it's out of control. A few minutes a day. Try it.

Wash the kitchen floor with a very dilute solution of clear ammonia and water or Sh-Clean and water every couple of weeks. (We presume you don't have unsealed or waxed wood floors in the kitchen.) Do the family room once a month or so, and the entry once a week. This assumes that you're also vacuuming the floors as advised. Needless to say, the less you vacuum, the more you must wash.

Wet versus Damp Mopping

"When I hear the word mop, I guess I know what it means. I get confused, though, when it calls for wet mopping versus damp mopping. What's the diff?"

Wet mopping is synonymous with *mopping*. It means cleaning floors with some type of floor cleaner and water, and it's usually the technique of choice for kitchen and bathroom floors. *Damp mopping* is a term reserved for wiping dust from otherwise clean floors with a barely damp mop or cloth and no floor cleaner. Usually this task is reserved for wood floors or floors that aren't exposed to much traffic or grease or other spills. Examples are the floors around the edge of a rug or bedroom floors.

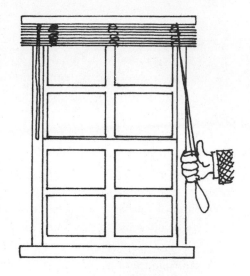

Chapter 15 Washing Windows

If you want to improve the appearance of an entire room in one fell swoop, *wash the windows*. Few things affect how you feel about a room more than the quality of light coming in through the windows. After they're clean, it's amazing how much happier you'll feel about the room and even life in general. And once you learn how, it's also easy to do.

Excuses, Excuses

Cleaning windows has gotten a bad rap for a number of undeserving—and a few deserving—reasons. We suspect that many people don't like to do windows because they don't know how. It's hard work the way most people go about it. It makes your hands and arms hurt. It makes you sweat. It makes you break things. It makes you swear and think about kicking something. And after all that grief, the streaks are often still there. Chances are you're just doing it wrong. Or maybe you've never even tried it. You've heard all the I-don't-do-windows jokes. There must be a reason for them, right? Well, maybe the reasons are wrong.

A Better Way

The good news is that it's not at all as hard as it looks. What you need most is to throw away your old newspapers and to discard exotic schemes for window cleaning that you may have learned. In their place, learn how to use a squeegee, and you'll be done with window cleaning in half the time or less. And it won't be as tiring. And the windows will be cleaner. And there won't be shreds of newspaper all over the house and newsprint all over your hands.

Ever notice that you've never seen a professional window washer use vinegar and newspapers or Blue Juice in a spray bottle and a cloth? That's because *none* of them do. They use squeegees because squeegees work better. If you've ever stopped to watch pros at work, you've noticed how easy they make it look and how fast they finish one window and move on to the next. They aren't hot and sweaty. They can look downright comfortable. They look that way and accomplish so much because they've learned to use a squeegee. Do yourself the same favor. It's not that difficult. Besides, squeegees are cheaper in the long run.

Quick, relatively painless window washing depends on a squeegee. Squeegees are not in widespread use in homes, and that is a shame because of all the time they could save. One of the reasons for their disuse may be the awful quality of many of the squeegees in circulation. Those thick clumsy squeegees that are usually sold for use in cars are nearly worthless if you want a streak-free window.

You'll need a high-quality professional squeegee to get the job done right. We'll tell you how to select one and how to use it like a pro. Once you get the hang of it, you'll see how amazingly fast cleaning with a squeegee can be. Who knows? You may even begin to *enjoy* cleaning windows!

By now, you must realize we're being pretty insistent about learning to use a squeegee. It's easier and faster, so why not? Trying to dry a windowpane by rubbing every square inch of it with messy newspapers or nonabsorbent, linty rags is hard work. *That's* what makes your arms hurt. *That's* what causes you to expend so much energy that you start to sweat. *That's* what causes accidents trying to stretch to reach the last few inches of a window (rather than using a simple squeegee on a pole). And *that's* a slow way to do something you don't even like doing.

Materials

1 squeegee with 1 or more channels
1 double bucket (or a standard one)
1 window scrubber (if top of window is out of reach)

10 cotton cleaning cloths
Dish soap or clear ammonia
1 wide paintbrush
1 variable extension pole (up to 30 feet if necessary)
1 pair of rubber gloves (optional)

Stock your Speed Clean apron with these items.

1 razor-blade holder with sharp blade
1 toothbrush
2 plastic bags as liners with clips

Two of these items deserve a bit of an explanation.

Squeegee. The choice of the size of the squeegee is important. Obviously you don't want one wider than your windows. But you don't want a tiny one either, because you'd be making too many swipes. The size of the squeegee depends on the size of your windows.

There are three parts to a professional squeegee: (1) a handle (preferably one that swivels), (2) a replaceable rubber blade with a very smooth edge, and (3) an interchangeable rigid channel to support the blade.

We said earlier that you need a professional squeegee. One of the advantages of the professional model is that once you purchase the squeegee handle, several channels of different lengths are an inexpensive option. (A channel is the metal strip that holds the rubber blade.) You don't have to buy several different squeegees. You just slide one channel off and slide a different one on as needed. The one we use (an Ettore, manufactured by Steccone

Products Co.) has a quick-release button that allows one channel to be switched with another in a matter of seconds. The squeegee handle pivots to allow you to reach and clean windows at angles never before possible. This lets you wash windows easily despite having furniture or shrubs in the way.

If you have nothing but picture windows, get the widest squeegee you can handle comfortably: We recommend

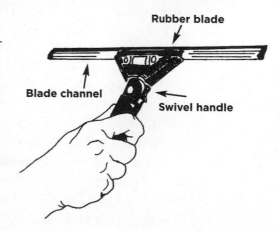

Rubber blade

Blade channel

Swivel handle

French Panes

"My house has many, many tiny windows—French panes. I don't use a squeegee on them, right?"

As long as the panes are at least 6 inches in height *or* width, get a squeegee with a 6-inch blade, and you'll be able to clean them faster than you ever thought possible. Wash several windows at a time, and then squeegee them. It's much faster than spraying them with glass cleaner and wiping each one dry.

18 inches. With little panes (like the ones in French doors), you obviously need a small one (about two-thirds the width of the pane). If you have medium-size windows, you're better off with a 14-inch channel. If you have a mixture of window sizes, the ideal solution may be two or more channels of different lengths.

The squeegee blade inside the channel is a thin strip of rubber with a very exacting edge—something like a heavy windshield wiper. However, just like windshield wipers, they can wear out because the edge becomes rounded with use and loses its effectiveness. The edge can also get nicked by hitting something when cleaning or if it's abused between uses.

A little nick that you might not even notice leaves a streak of water with every stroke of the blade. Luckily the replacement rubber blades are very cheap, so have a couple of extras on hand that fit the various channels you use (or just get several the size of your longest channel, and trim them as needed). One nick leaving a streak with every stroke of the squeegee is downright discouraging. This is one reason why all those grocery-store squeegees are so unsatisfactory: The blades are soon nicked and damaged, but since they are not replaceable, you have to throw the whole squeegee away and buy a new one just to get a new edge. This is also why these cheaper models really aren't.

Window scrubber. This looks sort of like a second squeegee but with a lamb's-wool cover. It's used to apply cleaning solution to the window and scrub it at the same time. Use a sponge or a cleaning cloth if you can reach to the top of the windows in your home. However, neither work anywhere near as fast as a scrub sleeve. And if you have to use an extension pole, they don't work at all without tying them to the squeegee.

Getting Dressed

Tie the cleaning apron snugly around your waist. The apron is designed to keep you from driving yourself crazy running back and forth for items. It will hold the spare and retired cleaning cloths, razor blade, and debris you encounter. It will also hold a small squeegee. Put the paintbrush in your back pocket.

Preparing the Windowsills

If the interior windowsills are dusty, vacuum them first to avoid making mud. If the exterior sills are dusty, hose them down first to avoid muddy streaks running down the side of your home. You can't hose these streaks off after washing the windows for fear of splashing water and ruining your window-washing job. It's usually a good idea to dust or hose down both the interior and exterior sills. The alternative, if the dust is only slight, is to use the paintbrush that you are carrying in your back pocket. You can brush them off just prior to washing them. Include the frame, sill, and glass surface itself, if necessary.

The Cleaning Solution

We're going to give you a choice here between two very effective window cleaners.

Dish soap. Use a small amount of dish soap. Start with a short squirt in half a bucket of water.

Clear, nondetergent ammonia. Read the label carefully. Buy only clear, nondetergent, nonsudsing ammonia because suds are a real nuisance when washing windows—so much so that some professional window washers use just plain water. So use just a little: 2 tablespoons per full bucket or 1 tablespoon per half bucket.

Both Cascade and ammonia are alkali cleaners, and they will work excellently with about 95 percent of windows. But if the peculiarities of the dirt on your window do not respond well to either one of these, chances are that the dirt itself is alkali. You can outwit it by shifting to an acidic cleaner—plain white vinegar—about ¼ cup per full bucket. Don't use cider vinegar or red-wine vinegar, or you'll smell like a salad the rest of the day.

Fill a bucket (or one side of a double bucket) about half full with cool water. The water should *not* be hot because hot water evaporates too quickly on the window surface. On a cold day, when your hands are apt to turn blue, of course you would want the water to be on the warmish end of the scale. Wearing rubber gloves helps a lot when the weather is cold.

How much cleaning solution? Just enough to squeak by (sorry). Start with the amounts just mentioned. If your windows are appalling, replace the cleaning solution more often rather than increasing the concentration of cleaner. Only if you find the solution isn't working should you add more soap or ammonia.

Big Decision 1: Which Side to Do First

Wash the easiest side of the window first—that is, the side that has the easiest access. By cleaning the difficult side last, if you see a smudge, you'll know that it must be on the accessible side of the glass. If one side is in your nice warm dining room, and the other side is exposed to winds howling across the East River, you would be well advised to start in your nice warm dining room. The idea is to have to venture out there only once.

In general, it's easier to wash all the windows from the inside if you can. There is usually shrubbery or some other obstacle in the way of the outside surfaces. Unless it's easy for you to clean there, stay inside when you can. (Read about your type of window below.)

Choosing a Starting Point

Warm sunshine makes washing windows difficult because the heat of the sun evaporates the cleaning solution faster than you can squeegee it back off. The remaining solution turns into streaks, new dirt formations, or an unsightly film. When planning your strategy, arrange to start where the windows are shaded. An even better idea is to do the project on a cloudy day.

Final Details

Approach the windows armed with your equipment and a serene disposition.

Drape a cleaning cloth over one shoulder. Have the razor handy in the apron pocket and the brush in your pants pocket. Two or three spare cleaning cloths should be kept in another apron pocket. The window scrubber can be kept in the dry half of a double bucket between uses.

Put the bucket down to the left of the first window, if you can. Since there are all sorts of obstacles near and in front of windows, we don't care whether you start on the left or right as long as you have a reason for it. Putting the bucket all the way to the right or the left locates it in a place where you are not likely to step into it. Lean the extension pole, if any, against the frame of the window you're starting with—again, ideally in a place where you will not bump into it and make a spectacle of yourself.

In between uses, the best place for medium or large squeegees is inside the dry side of a double bucket. If you're using a conventional bucket, store it upside down on top of the bucket. Don't fill the bucket too full of cleaning solution, or the squeegee handle will get wet. You don't want to splash water or start a clammy dribble down your arm. The handle will stay dry if it is suspended in this manner.

The first time you clean your windows using this method, move anything out of the way that's even close to being a disaster-waiting-to-happen. Move the lamp back a few more feet. Move the table in front of the window *completely* out of the way. Put the curtains on top of the curtain rods, etc.

You don't have to rearrange the furniture to be able to wash the windows. Use a squeegee with a pivoting handle along with an extension pole, if needed, so you can stand to the side of the window while cleaning it. But it would be easier if there were a bit of a path.

As you develop some expertise using a squeegee, window scrubber, and extension pole, you'll find you can safely clean windows without moving much furniture at all. Then you'll save even more time and hassle. But accidents will happen until you're used to these tools, so move everything well out of the way this first time.

Getting Started

Let's wash the first window. As long as you can reach all of the window, use a cleaning cloth dipped in your cleaning solution and partially wrung out. If the top of the window is out of reach, it's time to grab the window scrubber and use a long or short extension pole as needed.

If you're inside the house, shake or wring out the window scrubber, so it doesn't drip cleaning solution all over. If you're outside, a little splashed water doesn't matter. The idea is to transport just enough cleaning solution to the window to cover it completely. The window should be just wet enough, so it does not dry before you finish with the squeegee. If it's too wet, you'll make work for yourself later when excess water runs off the window onto the sill. To help manage dribbles of water, place a folded cloth on the windowsill before where the last stroke of the squeegee will end. It will catch any run-off and make drying the sill a snap.

Apply the cleaning solution with the cleaning cloth or window scrubber from top to bottom. Scrub a bit—just enough to loosen the dirt on the surface. But not too much scrubbing. Window dirt comes off very easily. Often, all you need to do is move the scrubber lightly over the window once. You're doing little more than getting it wet, yet the window is now ready to be squeegeed clean and dry.

Then return the sleeve to the bucket and *don't dally*. Time is of the essence because you have to start squeegeeing before the water evaporates from the window.

For the squeegee to work properly, it has to get a firm grip on the surface of the glass. That means *a dry blade has to be started on a dry surface for each stroke.* To accomplish this, dry a starter strip by hand at the edges of the window. Grab the cleaning cloth from your shoulder, and use it to dry a 2-inch strip across the top and both sides of the window. Professionals call this step "cutting the water." The top strip is where you'll start each stroke of the squeegee. The dry strips on the sides will help prevent water from oozing out from the window frames after the squeegee has passed by.

Now that you've dried the start strips, make sure the squeegee blade is dry too. Wipe the edge of the blade with your cleaning cloth.

Place the squeegee blade down in the dry strip at the top of the window. Using a steady, *light* pressure, draw the squeegee down for the first stroke. "Light pressure" means not to have a death grip on the handle. A light and even pressure is what's needed because that's what works. It also keeps you from getting fatigued from what should be a simple task. Hold the handle with your fingers and thumb rather than in the palm of your hand. Don't grab it like a hammer.

Stop the squeegee stroke a few inches from the lower window frame or bottom of the window. This avoids splashing water back onto the dry section of the squeegee were it to hit the small puddle of water on the window frame. Your last squeegee stroke will get this strip. (See the illustration.)

Wipe the squeegee blade dry.

Place it at the top of the window again, overlapping the first stroke by about 25 percent. Make a second pass with the squeegee down the window, again stopping a few inches from the lower window frame or bottom of the window.

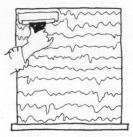

**Wash the easy side first.
Start at the top and hit all
the corners well.**

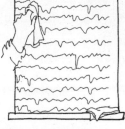

**Wipe a 2-inch starting strip
along the top and sides with a
cloth. Place a folded cloth in
the corner where most of the
water will end up.**

**Wipe the blade dry. Make the
first stroke. Stop a few
inches from the bottom.**

**Wipe the blade dry. Make the
second stroke, overlapping by
3 to 4 inches.**

**Wipe the blade dry.
Make the third stroke.**

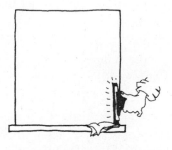

**Wipe the blade dry. Draw the squeegee
sideways for the final stroke.**

Wipe the squeegee blade dry again, and repeat the above steps until you
have moved all the way across the window.

You have left a wet strip along the bottom of the window. Get it now,
squeegeeing from side to side. That pulls the last of the cleaning solution into
the corner. This is the corner where your cloth has been sitting waiting to
catch this dirty solution. Smart, huh?

An equally fast way to wash the window is to make your squeegee strokes go across the window instead of up and down—provided that the window is not so large that you have to take steps while squeegeeing from one side to the other. You can go from right to left or left to right, depending on what's in the way. Cut the water on the top and on whichever side you'll be starting the squeegee. Start at the top and work your way down row by row. Remember to place a cloth in the corner of the sill toward which you'll be squeegeeing most of the water. If you produce prodigious puddles, wring out the window scrubber a bit more before doing the next window.

Small Matters

Occasionally, evaporation creates dry areas by the time you're ready to squeegee. So once you've covered the entire pane, you might have to give portions of the window a quick swipe with the scrubber to rewet them. Plan on using more water outside than inside because of evaporation.

If the top of the window is out of reach, cut the water with the squeegee instead of a cloth. Lift the squeegee at an angle so that only about 2 inches of one end of the blade rests on the glass. Unless you're very fussy, for *outside* windows, don't bother to cut the water on the sides of the window at all—just the top. The top is by far the most important area, since water dripping from there will travel all the way down the middle of the window. But if you skip the sides, the water that you miss will be scarcely noticeable.

Remember, the squeegee must be dry and must be started on a dry surface. Abuse of this simple rule is the main reason that people have difficulty with squeegees. The squeegee will not work properly if you start it on a wet surface *or* if its blade is wet when you start a stroke. In either case, the blade will sort of water-ski across the surface (hydroplane, to be more precise) instead of pushing the cleaning solution and dirt ahead of it, and streaks will appear without fail.

Also, *you've got to wipe the blade dry at the end of each stroke,* so don't fight it.

Pull the squeegee in a smooth, continuous stroke. Don't start and stop. If you lift the squeegee off the surface, you've got to redry it and start again in a dry spot *ahead* of where you stopped. You won't make a streak provided the blade is dry. Soon it will become a reflex to make a complete stroke from top to bottom without stopping or lifting the squeegee.

Very Large Windows

If the window is so large or the weather is so hot that the water evaporates too quickly to clean in a nonfrantic manner, just do half at a time. Start with the top half, of course. Squeegee as just described, but stop midway. Then wet the bottom half, and remember to start the squeegee in a dry spot. As long as you do this, it won't streak, and you'll have as clean a window as if you did it all in one step.

Window Frames

We like to clean the window frames as long as we're going to all this trouble. The bottom edges of a window frame get pretty grimy, and this is a great time to tackle them as we're getting them wet anyway. Do only the lower frames, not all four sides, unless they really need it. (This is in addition to the rinsing or vacuuming that you did earlier.)

Do the frames just before you wash the window glass. First, wet the lower frame by wiping with a wet cleaning cloth or passing one end of the scrubber over it. Now quickly run your toothbrush over the frame, paying particular attention to the corners. Pop your toothbrush back into your apron pocket, and wipe the frame clean and dry with a dry cleaning cloth. If you have trouble getting the dirt out of the corners after you've loosened it with your toothbrush, wash it out by squirting it full blast with Red Juice and then use a cloth to blot up the excess. Now wash the window. If a little cleaning solution gets on the frame as you wash the window, blot it up when you finish and move on.

Double-Hung Windows

If you have this type of window, nobody has to tell you that the outside can be a pain to clean. Here are four ways to clean the outside surfaces—most definitely in order of preference.

Method 1

Luckily, many double-hung windows are installed next to each other. This allows you to sit in one windowsill and wash and then squeegee the outside of the window next to it.

To follow this method, raise one lower pane as high as it will go to allow you to sit on the windowsill (carefully!). You may need a short extension pole for this chore. A variable 2- to 4-foot extender will work. Set the bucket close to you but off to one side, so you'll have a fairly good chance of not stepping into it later. Sit in the windowsill and reach to the neighboring upper pane to clean it first. The pivoting Ettore squeegee handle is perfect for this chore because it allows you to reach and clean at angles not possible with a fixed-position handle.

This is a time when it's a real joy to have an assistant to hand you things. If you don't have someone to press into service, be sure to locate all your equipment, so you can reach it *before* you've gone through all the gyrations necessary to get settled in that windowsill.

Cut the water using the edge of the squeegee if you can't reach the top of the window with a cloth.

Clean and squeegee the top and bottom of the window next to you. Climb off the windowsill (carefully!) and lower the window. Now trade places and sit in the windowsill of the window you just cleaned. Clean both the upper and lower panes of the second window from your new perch.

Precautions

If you're sitting on the sill holding on to the window frame for support, be sure the frame is strong enough to support you. It's not unusual for an old frame to have a nice coat of paint over it that effectively disguises visible signals that it's decayed and weak. If you're 15 feet or more above the ground, you should use a safety rope. Even with a safety rope, don't think you're invincible and lean out any farther or take chances you wouldn't ordinarily take. It's also a good idea to tie a string to the squeegee in a similar fashion, so it won't fall on someone if you inadvertently drop it.

Even if it can't hit anyone as it falls, the string will save the squeegee from ruin and will save you from having to retrieve it.

Please remember to use proper safety precautions. We cannot recommend

How Long an Extension Pole?

For out-of-reach windows, use an extension pole and a window scrubber. To determine how long the extension pole should be, measure the distance from the top of the windows to the ground, and deduct your own height. A 4-foot pole will suffice for most windows, while a 14-foot pole will reach most second-story windows. Use a window scrubber at the end of the extension pole to wash out-of-reach windows. Then replace the scrubber with the squeegee, and wipe the windows clean and dry.

that you hang out on a ledge 20 stories above a sidewalk just to clean your windows. If it's unsafe to do so, stay inside and do the best you can.

Method 2

If you're unable to use Method 1 because there is only one window or because the window has a difficult shape (e.g., a bay window), you will have to wash it from the outside. We much prefer to clean from the inside—as in Method 1—because it is easier, it is more comfortable, and there are fewer obstacles. But sometimes, you don't have a choice.

Method 3

If you can do neither of the above, you're down to your last two choices. For this method to work, both windows *must* move up and down for their full range of motion. If they cannot, skip ahead to Method 4—your last hope.

Many double-hung windows won't cooperate, especially if they've been painted a number of times or if the wood has swollen with moisture. This is particularly true of upper windows, which often only move an inch or two. *Don't force a stuck window!* The glass can shatter right in front of you. If windows must be repaired, call on a carpenter for help.

If both windows will open fully, here's how this method works. (Remember, this is all about the *outside* of the windows.)

Step A. First, pull the upper window all the way down. Next, raise the lower window high enough so there is just enough room for your arm to reach out between it and the top of the window frame. Wash and squeegee the top half of the lower window.

Step A   **Step B**   **Step C**

Step B. Push the upper window back into its normal closed position, and raise the lower window all the way. Sit on the windowsill and clean the upper window. Come back inside. It's a wonderful idea to have an assistant to hand you items such as the window scrubber or squeegee as you need them. It's quite discouraging to get settled—only to realize you need something from inside and have to climb in and out all over again. Once you're settled, it's far more gratifying just to yell at your assistant.

Step C. Last, pull the lower window back down until you have just enough room to reach out between it and the windowsill and wash the bottom half of the lower window. You're done.

Do your best with this awkward but workable situation. Please observe the same precautions as in Method 1. In addition, when you are reaching out at Step A, make sure your center of gravity stays *below your waist*. Or your assistant can hold you. For added stability, Step C is usually best performed while on your knees.

Method 4

Many—perhaps a majority—of older double-hung windows have lost their full range of movement. If you can't pull the upper window down far enough to carry out Method 3, there is one last chance (short of taking off the sash and trim and removing the window to clean it). However, this method requires nearly as much window movement as Method 3.

If they don't open, they don't open. It's not the end of the world. Call a window-washing company and go fishing.

Step A. Unlike Method 3, all the steps in this method are done while you are sitting on the sill. So raise the lower window all the way, and sit on the windowsill. Pull the upper window down as far as it will go. This allows you to reach up and wash the top half of the lower window. As with Method 3, this

| Step A | Step B | Step C |

is ideally done with the help of an assistant who will hand you items you need.

Step B. Without moving from the sill, push the upper window all the way back up to its normal closed position, and wash and squeegee it.

Step C. Finally, pull the lower window down until it just about touches your legs. This exposes the lower half of the window, so you can wash it now. Then all you must do is extricate yourself from your perch and go back inside.

Again, we must ask you to observe the safety precautions discussed above, plus any others that occur to you as a reasonable person.

Sliding Aluminum Windows

If your house has sliding aluminum windows, normally one side will lift out. It's the movable half of the window that lifts up and out. Some do so only if they are in a certain position—usually just an inch or two open.

The sequence to follow when washing them is first to remove the half that comes out. Set it on the floor to one side or the other of the stationary window. Turn it around as you set it down, so the outside is facing you. Be careful when leaning it against the wall because the top edge will mark the wall. Protect the carpet also, because the bottom of the frame is often filthy. Use a couple of old towels to protect the floors and the walls.

Wash the outside of the stationary half of the window. You will normally need a short extension pole. Use it only for the part of the window you can't reach by hand (see the next section).

Next, wash the outside of the window you removed. Clean it where you've leaned it against the wall, so you don't transport the window all over the house looking for a better place to clean it. Make sure it's stable, and use as little cleaning solution as possible to wash it. Then put the window back in, and clean the insides of both windows if you haven't done so already.

To clean aluminum window frames, use detergent and warm water. Even if the aluminum is pitted, be careful of using abrasives (steel wool, scouring powder, or green pads) because they will permanently scratch aluminum. Once aluminum is pitted, it's almost impossible to restore. If you would prefer the scratches to the corrosion, use a soap-filled steel-wool pad. Rinse the frames well to remove bits of steel wool that will later rust. Remember, you clean the frames before you wash the windows.

Most contemporary aluminum windows are anodized or permanently protected with a coat of baked-on enamel paint. Don't use anything on anodized aluminum except detergent and water, Red Juice and water, or a moderate clear ammonia solution.

Note: Auto wax or a silicone spray will help prevent aluminum corrosion and pitting. 3M makes a marine aluminum polish that may help.

The Extension Pole

An extension pole can make window washing a lot simpler and faster because you don't have to reposition a ladder constantly. But you do lose that direct hands-on control of the squeegee that you have when using it by hand. Accordingly, use the extender only for the part of the window that's outside your reach. First, wash all of just that part of the window. Then put the extender away and wash the rest of the window without it.

When using the pole, be even more cautious about what's behind you. Step back from the window to give yourself a comfortable position. Cut the water at the top of the window by using one end of the squeegee blade at an angle. If you're using a long pole, or if you're working in a tight space, this may prove difficult. The squeegee handle we use has an adjustable angle, which makes this job much more bearable.

Keep a mild, steady pressure on the pole. Sometimes it can begin to vibrate if the window is very high off the ground. If so, slow down the rate at which you are making a pass with the squeegee, and move your hands farther apart on the pole to give it more stability. As usual, wipe the blade dry at the end of every stroke. Don't dally or the window surface will begin to dry.

Extension Pole Etiquette

If you find that you've become downright dangerous with the extension pole, the problem is probably that you're using the pole to clean windows

> ## Should You Get a Second Extension Pole?
>
> **No. It's more difficult to manage a second extension pole than it is to take the squeegee and window scrubber off and on as needed.**

within reach. The pole is relatively harmless when deployed vertically—i.e., on high windows or on the top portions of tall windows that are out of reach. When you lower the extension pole too far, thereby poking it behind you, it causes havoc among the pets and accessories in your house.

Here's what to do. Use the pole first with the window scrubber and then with the squeegee on the out-of-reach window areas. Then set the pole aside (keep it vertical!), and clean the lower part of the windows with a cleaning cloth and the squeegee. Use this same technique when washing the outside windows. Finally, why tempt fate? Take a look around, and evacuate vulnerable animate and inanimate objects before you start on the windows.

Paint

The best way to remove dried paint splatters is with a clean, unpitted razor blade when the window is wet. There are several justifications for this rule: Ammoniated water will help loosen the paint; razors generally don't scratch a wet glass surface; and dry paint scrapings are often difficult to remove from a dry window. A dirty razor blade (for example, one coated with grease from the last time you used it) will leave a smudge behind, so use a clean one.

To avoid scratches, keep the blade at as low an angle as possible, and use very slight pressure. Needless to say, do not use a razor blade on a plastic window.

Squeegee Troubleshooting

If streaks remain after squeegeeing, there may be oil or grease on the glass. Try shifting to Red Juice, which specializes in cutting through oils. Then follow with a quick rinse with Blue Juice to remove any residue.

Another cause of persistent streaks after using a squeegee is a worn-out blade. Inspect the edge of the rubber blade carefully. Often you will find a small nick in the blade that will allow cleaning solution to be left behind as the squeegee is drawn down the window. If so, reverse or replace the blade. Also, keep a spare blade handy. They're inexpensive, and you need a good blade if you're going to do this right. The rubber in the blade can become brittle with age, which is another reason to replace it. To prolong its useful life span, store the squeegee away from oils of any kind and out of direct sunlight.

Another place where streaks often form is along the sides of the window-pane. This can happen if the squeegee puts insufficient pressure on the very ends of the blade or if the ends are rounded or torn. Again, replace it as needed. Another cause of streaks along the sides is one tip riding up on the window frame as you draw the squeegee blade down the window. Keep your eye on the end of the blade nearest the frame as you draw it down the window. Don't watch the frame or the squeegee handle. That way the blade won't wander as easily onto the frame. If you do leave a little water at the edge of the window, don't try to touch it up. Just let it dry, and you'll never notice it. People look out the middle of the window, and no one is going to inspect or notice the very edge of the window itself. If they do, hand them a squeegee.

Probably the most serious window problem, besides a Frisbee through the middle, is a persistent etching or fogging of the glass that resists any liquid cleaner or even the razor blade. It's not your imagination. Hard-water marks, auto exhaust, run-off from unsealed masonry, pollution, or acid rain could be at fault. You may have some luck with a professional acid wash intended specifically for such problems.

Touching Up

Generally speaking, don't. A drip of water in the middle of your clean window will dry to an almost invisible dot. But trying to wipe it off with a damp cleaning cloth whose loose ends are slapping against the window in several places can quickly turn that little unnoticed dot into a window that you need to start all over with.

If you have streaks or spots that you must correct, use a little cleaning solution applied with your finger directly on the offending area and then a completely dry cleaning cloth to wipe it off again.

Hard-Water Spots

To get hard-water spots off windows, if it's just a few small windows, Tile Juice or a similar acidic cleaner will work. Use it with a white pad or with #000 steel wool. Tile Juice won't harm many surfaces, but rinse well to be on the safe side. If the stains are large or are on multiple windows, I recommend calling a professional. Special acid washes that remove hard-water stains from windows are available, but they're used generally by professionals.

Note: Figure out what caused the stains, so they won't recur. The most common source is a sprinkler splashing water on the window. Adjust the sprinkler, so it can't happen again.

Squeegee Psychology

Cleaning windows with a squeegee can be an exasperating or a relaxing experience, depending on the pressure you are placing on the blade—and your nerves.

Inanimate objects typically do not respond well to force. The squeegee actually needs only the slightest pressure—just enough to keep it on the surface evenly. If you're pushing too hard, it will let you know and squeal as you move it down the window. It may also streak because too much pressure can cause the blade to distort and partially lift off the surface. Moreover, your hand will

Streaks

If you're already using a squeegee, streaks probably mean that you have to make just a small adjustment in your technique. There are five secrets to avoiding streaks.

Secret No. 1. Always start the squeegee on a dry area of the glass. After washing the window, create a dry "starter strip" for the squeegee either by wiping with a cleaning cloth or by using the end of the squeegee. If you stop the squeegee midway through a window, restart the subsequent strokes in the dry area.

Secret No. 2. Always use a dry squeegee. Wipe the blade dry with a cleaning cloth after every pass on the window.

Secret No. 3. Don't wash windows in the direct sun. The cleaning solution dries too quickly to avoid streaks.

Secret No. 4. Don't use any more soap or clear ammonia than is absolutely necessary. The more "product" you have in the water, the more likely it is that some of it will be left on the glass as a streak.

Secret No. 5. Make sure the squeegee blade is in good condition. A nick in the edge will leave a streak with each pull of the squeegee.

wear out in no time. So make a conscious effort to relax, and you may even enjoy yourself before long!

Super-Squeegeeing

Okay, you've got the basic squeegee technique down, but something's still missing in your window-washing life. You've noticed that hotshot professional window washers can squeegee windows in one long continuous stroke back and forth across the window. They don't ever stop or lift the squeegee. You are jealous. Or you just want to torment the neighbors by showing off. Whatever your reason (or lack thereof), once you've mastered the basic technique and would like to make some fancy moves with the squeegee, forge on.

The basic idea of the advanced technique is simple. It's just that working out the kinks will require a bit of practice. And a loose wrist. Sorry to report it, but it's all in the you-know-what.

This technique is really practical only if you're cleaning large windows. If they're smaller, the extra gyrations aren't worth the effort.

The plan is to complete the whole window with one continuous stroke of the squeegee, never picking it up off the surface of the window. First, cut the water a few inches on top and at both sides. Professionals use only their squeegee for this task—not a cleaning cloth.

Next, place the squeegee vertically along the side starter strip in the upper corner of the window. Move it sideways until you get near the other corner, and then angle the upper end of the squeegee into it. Now rotate the blade— without lifting it off the surface—and head back in the other direction, overlapping the first stroke by a few inches. As you reach the other side, pivot the blade again and head back across. You're making giant sideways figure eights without ever lifting the squeegee from the surface. Angle the squeegee again into the first bottom corner you encounter, and then do the last sideways stroke.

Of course, it's going to be awkward the first few times. If you mess up, just dry the blade and start up again on a dry part of the glass. The corners and pivoting are going to be the hardest spots. Just keep loose as a goose: Remember, no death grip on the handle—no white knuckles. Hold the handle more toward the ends of your fingers rather than the palm of your hand, which will encourage flexibility in your grip. And don't be afraid to move that elbow. If you can remember, keep a slightly greater pressure on the upper part of the blade as you move to the left or right, which will help eliminate streaks and skipped spots.

When you've mastered the technique, plan your ambush of the neighbors carefully. It will be worth all the practice to be able to show off your new expertise.

Big Decision 2: Times Not to Use the Squeegee

For the vast majority of windows, the squeegee is the way to go. But there are a few situations in which it is necessary to clean with Blue Juice and a cloth.

Blue Juice and a cleaning cloth are sometimes faster than a squeegee if one of the following conditions prevails.

1. **The window has an uneven surface (e.g., leaded glass or fake stained glass windows).**
2. **The window needs only a touch-up of (a fingerprint or nose print or two).**
3. **You have only a few very small windows.**

If a squeegee is ruled out, and you must use Blue Juice or any other spray-on cleaner, remember these simple rules: Spray as little as possible in an even pattern over the window; work your way from top to bottom with big side-to-side strokes, turning the cloth as needed; use your razor blade on impossible spots like dried paint; and to avoid streaks, keep wiping until all the liquid disappears from the surface. A streak is leftover dirt and/or cleaning solution. So use only the driest and cleanest cloths you have. And use the cloths generously. When a cloth gets noticeably damp, toss it and grab a new one. Using dry cloths makes the job go much faster. The cloths will all fit into one load in the washer anyway.

If the window is only slightly dirty, or if you need only to spot-clean a smudge or two, save time by spraying the cloth itself (lightly) and wiping (and then drying) just the smudge.

Spray-Cleaner Troubleshooting

One of the reasons we are so fond of squeegees is that a whole flock of problems can arise when using a liquid spray and a cloth. For starters, make sure you wipe carefully in corners and along the edges, because that's where most misses happen.

Sometimes, the spray cleaner will evaporate before you get to a section to wipe it. If so, just spray and clean the top half of the window before doing the bottom. While you're at it, because you will be overlapping the top and bottom, you can save time by not wiping the lower 6 inches of the top section. You will shortly be respraying it, so there's no need to clean it twice.

The same principle applies if you are cleaning adjoining windows. When you're cleaning the first window, overspray the next window about 6 inches so you can keep clear of the window you just finished when you move on to the next one. The idea is to avoid having spray drift back onto the window you just cleaned when you're spraying the next one.

This looks a lot more confusing than it is in practice. All you're doing is saving yourself work by not recleaning areas you just finished.

Screens

I vacuum my screens for several years before I resort to wet-cleaning them. Use the brush attachment of your vacuum cleaner. Do one side first in an up-and-down direction and then in a side-to-side direction. Repeat on the second side.

When they need wet cleaning, don't just squirt them with a hose (which is scarcely better than doing nothing). This is definitely an outside job, though. Mix a solution of liquid dishwashing soap and water in a bucket in the same ratio you use to wash dishes. You'll also need a brush, either a tile brush or a soft-bristle brush on a pole, so you can stand upright. Lay the screen flat on a hard surface, such as a deck or driveway. Use the brush to clean first one side and then the other, rinse, and allow the screen to air-dry. If you have an old piece of carpeting to put down first, you can wash both sides at the same time by laying the screen on the carpeting. Wet the carpet first, then as you scrub the top of the screen, the carpeting is rubbing against the bottom side and cleaning it also. This cuts your time in half. Before you replace the screens, remember to vacuum and clean where they were. Use Red Juice—and a toothbrush, if necessary.

Note: Remove and put in storage all the screens from windows you never open. This improves your view and reduces the number of dirty screens in your future.

Covetous note: I once read that Jacqueline Kennedy Onassis had screens that were installed directly below the windows of her Nantucket home, right in the wall cavity. Only when the windows were raised was the screen pulled up into view. That sounds like the perfect screen—expensive though they must have been. However, if you ever build a house and must make decisions about windows and screens, no matter how you must juggle your budget, get screens that can be installed and removed from inside the house. This will save an enormous amount of time and annoyance. It's simple enough to remove them one at a time, vacuum them, and then re-install them. Even when you must take them outside to clean, it's still much easier to carry them through the house instead of fighting with the shrubs and ladders.

Blinds

Dirty Miniblinds—Is There Any Other Kind?

I have strong opinions about miniblinds that you may want to read eventually. They are set forth directly after this answer, but for reasons that will be clear to you later, you should not read them if you are exceptionally fond of miniblinds. However, there are two general approaches to miniblind cleaning.

1. **If the miniblinds are grossly dirty, the first and by far best choice is to look in the yellow pages under "Venetian Blind Cleaners" or "Miniblind Cleaners." You will find quite a number of listings under one of these headings. (That ought to give you a clue to how nasty this job is.) Someone from one of these companies will race to your home in the morning, whisk your miniblinds away, and then rush them back to you in the afternoon sparkling clean and dry. Most of these companies use an ultrasonic cleaning process—the same type used by jewelers.**

2. **A distant second choice for very dirty miniblinds is to do it yourself. Be forewarned that cleaning them requires the patience of someone negotiating lasting world peace. There is much more surface area on these blinds than one imagines when innocently contemplating the cleaning thereof. Every square inch on every slat must be carefully washed to remove dirt and usually just as carefully dried to avoid streaks. Just thinking about it gives me the willies.**

For the brave of heart, there are two methods for hand-cleaning miniblinds.

In-place method. If you have only one or two miniblinds, consider yourself lucky. You can clean them in place. Cover the adjacent window and window frame with cleaning cloths or towels to protect them from overspray. Or you can ignore the overspray and wash them as well. Starting from the top, spray the miniblinds dripping wet with clear ammonia solution (up to one part ammonia to three parts water) or chandelier cleaner. Then turn the slats to expose the other side, and spray them again so both sides are dripping wet.

Unless you have very soft water, you must wipe each slat dry to avoid streaks and water spots. Use cleaning cloths to dry them, also working from the top down. When you're finished, raise the miniblinds and clean the frame and then the window behind the blinds. Then lower the blinds again to air-dry.

Remove-and-clean method. If you have a number of blinds, it's easier to remove them and make a single big mess elsewhere. The best place—if you have the opportunity and if the weather is accommodating—is outside, mounted against something. It's even better if there is concrete or grass below so you can use the hose without creating a swamp. The perfect spot is in front of the door or the wall of a garage. Use wire or rope to temporarily hang the fully extended blinds. In this case, it's easier to put the ammonia solution in a bucket and use a soft-bristled brush to scrub the blinds rather than spraying them with the cleaning solution. First, turn the slats to the down position to scrub them gently. Turn them around, and repeat the process to clean the back side. Now use a hose to rinse, if you can do so without making a muddy mess underfoot. If the water is hard in your area, let the blinds drip for a few minutes, and then wipe each slat dry to avoid spots and streaks. Alternatively, a final rinse by spraying with distilled water will allow you to air-dry the blinds with only minimal spotting. You will also gain quite a reputation in your neighborhood.

If you don't have such a site available, hang the blinds inside the shower, and clean them as described above. Or soak them in the tub. Good luck.

If the blinds are too big to fit into the shower or tub, put them, fully open with slats in the down position, on a flat grassy area. Clean with the same ammonia solution and soft-bristled brush, only now you'll need an extension pole to reach the middle of the blinds. Turn them over, clean the other side, and then rinse with a hose. Move them to another place to dry, or rehang them while still wet and dry them in place. This is not a project you would attempt in Boston in January.

Highly opinionated note: Whenever I answer cleaning questions, I know that at least one will be about dirty miniblinds. I try to answer these questions honestly and openly and to be helpful and courteous. But anyone who has ever cleaned house for a living dreads them. Each of the seemingly endless slats is horizontal and therefore catches every particle of passing dust. Then the dust gets wet from ambient moisture and redries as a miniature layer of adobe mud.

If you don't own any miniblinds now, keep up the good work. Don't be tempted even by a half-off sale. Your household cleaning burden will be forever lighter if you resist.

Note: Vertical blinds don't present the same problems. Consider installing them instead.

For the millions of suffering people who own miniblinds, I offer the following suggestions.

1. **Raise the blinds as high as they'll go, and leave them there forever.**

2. **If you must lower them, turn the slats so they are as close to vertical as possible.**

3. **Once they are clean, dust them regularly to prevent the adobe phenomenon.**

4. **Sell them at a garage sale, give them to anyone who will take them, or sell the house.**

Once they're clean, dust miniblinds routinely with a feather duster or with the brush attachment of a vacuum cleaner. When using a feather duster, use back-and-forth motions, not up-and-down motions. If dust starts to build up in spite of regular dusting, wipe the slats with a cleaning cloth moistened with Blue Juice. It's time consuming but less aggravating than waiting until you have to take them down to clean and less expensive than having them cleaned professionally.

Wood Blinds

Because of their vulnerability to water, your wood blinds can't be treated like miniblinds. They must be hand-wiped, one slat at a time. Use a polishing cloth dampened with furniture polish to wipe each slat. Use so little polish that you don't have to wipe each slat dry also. Streaks aren't as noticeable on wood slats as on the metal or plastic slats of miniblinds, but wipe carefully and thoroughly to avoid having to touch up dirty areas after you think you've finished.

Once you get them clean, follow the instructions for miniblinds, and dust them with an ostrich-down feather duster or the vacuum brush attachment. The key is to be consistent about the dusting. You can't just dust when company is coming, because a buildup over time will have to be painstakingly hand-removed. You don't have to dust every square inch of every slat each time you clean, but rotate them and dust some of them each time, or dust all of them in one room each time. As with miniblinds, wood blinds will stay cleaner longer if you leave them in the fully raised position as often as possible and turn the slats down whenever the blinds are in the lowered position.

Chapter 16 Washing Ceilings

We believe that most ceilings should be washed about as often as you have your appendix out. Dirty feet do not walk on them. Dirty hands do not grab or poke them. Dust doesn't settle on them. Paintings are not hung on them, so there aren't rectangular clean spots and nail holes every few feet. Besides, unless your room has lighting that draws attention to the ceiling, people generally don't look up nearly as often as they look down or at eye level. So entire catastrophes can flourish on the ceiling and scarcely be noticed.

If dirt is distributed evenly over the entire ceiling, leave well enough alone. To be able to see dirt on a ceiling that is uniformly dirty, you would have to wash a spot, so you could compare the dirty area to the clean area. Go ahead and clean or even paint the walls alone (if they need it). A nice, even coat of orange nicotine smoke damage will scarcely be noticed if left undisturbed. *You* may know better, but your guests will not, and you can gaze upward with a sublimely ironic smile on your face.

If you clean the walls (Chapter 17) without doing the ceiling, be sure not to disturb the ceiling's uniform appearance by wiping any little spots clean, trying to repair any little holes or other damage, or getting cleaning solution on it from the walls.

If you paint your ceilings off-white and your walls a different color, often you won't even need to repaint your ceilings when you repaint the walls. This saves lots of time because the ceilings are far more difficult and messy to paint, and you have to move the furniture much more extensively. I've painted my front room several times without touching the ceiling. The ceiling is dirty, I'm sure, but because it looks just fine, I'm leaving it very much alone. By having the ceiling a different color than the walls, you've created a color scheme in which the ceilings are *supposed* to look different from the walls. Wonderful! Make the dirt earn its keep.

Sensible Reasons to Wash a Ceiling

Uneven filth is another story. For example, mold on bathroom ceilings is in-considerate enough to flourish in conspicuous patches instead of even colonies. And cooking grease that builds up on kitchen ceilings often does so in a pattern that centers over the stove. In such cases, you have to do something about the ceiling.

Your course of action depends on a few factors. If the existing paint on the ceiling is gloss or semigloss and in good condition, your cleaning job is going to be easier. If it's flat paint, or the paint coating is damaged (peeling, blistering, water-stained, cracking, etc.), the balance tips quickly in favor of repainting the ceiling.

If the course of action is to wash the ceiling, read on!

The Choice of Cleaner

The choice of cleaner and list of materials to clean ceilings are essentially the same as those for cleaning walls. If you've already read these sections in Chapter 17, skip ahead.

We use clear ammonia for washing the ceiling. Clear ammonia is nonsudsy, nondetergent, and non–everything else. It is perfectly clear in appearance, not cloudy, and is generally sold only in janitorial supply stores. There are many other possibilities, but ammonia works as well or better than anything else we've tried. And it's downright cheap. Its major drawback—as in the case of all ammonia formulas—is its ferocious odor, but its superlative cleaning qual-ities are hard to pass up. With all types of ammonia, make sure the area you're working in is well ventilated.

Mix 1 to 2 cups of ammonia per gallon of water. If you use cool rather than warm water, fewer fumes will drift your way. Our second choice is Red Juice. Our third choice is TSP (trisodium phosphate), which we actually prefer to ammonia when we are washing the ceiling in preparation for repainting. The

TSP leaves the surface microscopically etched, which gives the new paint a better "bite" on the surface. The few streaks it leaves won't matter, since you're just going to paint right over them anyway.

Materials

1 cleaning apron
10 to 15 cleaning cloths
1 spray bottle of Red Juice
1 toothbrush
1 white scrub pad
1 quart of clear ammonia (or Red Juice or TSP)
1 Sh-Mop
6 to 12 Sh-Wipes (for the Sh-Mop)
1 stepladder (optional)
2 plastic drop cloths or bedsheets
1 pair of plastic gloves
1 double bucket (recommended) or single bucket

How to Wash Ceilings

Whether you are washing gloss or semigloss paint in the kitchen or bathroom, or flat latex paint in some other room, there are two ways to proceed. The fastest way is to use a Sh-Mop. We'll talk about that method first. The second way is to work from a ladder. We don't recommend using a ladder except when it's not possible to clean the mop. When might that be? If the ceilings are too tall for you to be able either to reach them or to apply adequate scrubbing pressure to the mop, then skip ahead to "Ladder or Chair Strategy" on page 208.

Getting Started

Tie your cleaning apron snugly around your waist. Hang the bottle of Red Juice on its appropriate loop, and put the toothbrush in its pocket. Load 5 to 10 cleaning cloths in a large apron pocket, and put 3 or 4 Sh-Wipes and the white pad into a plastic-lined pocket. Set the Sh-Mop and the cleaning tray with its extra cloths and supplies just outside the door of the room you're cleaning. Take the bucket and the clear ammonia to the nearest convenient sink.

Mix about ½ cup of clear ammonia in about half a bucket of warm water. (Adjust this formula according to how dirty the ceiling is.) We prefer using one side of a double bucket for reasons that will shortly become apparent. Carry the bucket to the corner of the room you're about to clean. It doesn't really matter, but for uniformity, we start in the left-hand corner of the room farthest from the door we will eventually exit from. Set the bucket down and spread a plastic drop cloth to catch the drips. Wet a terry-cloth Sh-Wipe in the ammonia solution, wring it out but leave it almost dripping wet, and put it on the Sh-Mop.

Washing an Area

The Sh-Mop should be wet enough to actually wash the ceiling well but not so wet as to provoke much more than an occasional drip: more like a light shower than a rainstorm. Be especially careful to avoid splashing water on the walls. Even though you may be washing them soon enough, dribbles of water left on the wall for a period of time make streaks that are difficult to remove. When you see water running down the wall, wipe it off with a cloth.

Clean a section of the ceiling (1 to 3 feet square) each time you dip a Sh-Wipe into the cleaning solution. Stand with your feet 2 to 3 feet apart, as though you were taking a long step forward. Clean with a back-and-forth motion with the mop. Work without actually taking any steps: Move the mop back and forth with your arms only, taking a step to the side only to advance to the next dirty area.

Drying Each Area

When you've cleaned a total area of about 3 by 3 feet, it's time to wipe that area dry. Put a dry Sh-Wipe on the Sh-Mop. Use it to dry that area somewhat, but it also will absorb any little round drips that would otherwise sit up there and dry into little round spots. Running the Sh-Mop over it this way also removes additional dirt (you'll see it on the Sh-Wipes) and other potential streaks that would become apparent after the ceiling dries. The idea is to dry the ceiling before it dries on its own.

When you advance to a new area to clean, overlap the last area by half the width of the mop head. Also overlap when drying. Be careful with these overlap areas—especially on latex paint. It is easy to end up with border marks that materialize later and draw a perfect map of each little 3-by-3-foot square for the whole world to see.

Optional Rinsing

If the ceiling is extremely dirty, you may have to rinse it. Normally, washing and then wiping with a cleaning cloth or towel is sufficient. Use your own judgment, but if you decide to rinse, this is how to proceed.

If you're using a double bucket, fill the second side with clear water. If you're using standard buckets, use a second one for rinse water. After cleaning each area, repeat, using the clean rinse-water side of the bucket. Dump the dirty water often, or you will just redistribute the dirt. As soon as the rinse water is dirty enough to be able to be seen on the ceiling, it's time to dump it out and refill it.

Don't rinse unless you're sure it's necessary, or you're not satisfied with the results without it. This step is seldom needed unless the ceiling is truly unspeakable.

Edges: If You're Also Washing the Walls

It's a little tricky to clean the ceiling along the edge, where the ceiling meets the walls. If you start your Sh-Mop directly against the edge when it's full of cleaning solution, it is likely to drip on the wall beneath, and you'll waste time having to stop to wipe the drips off. To avoid this difficulty, start with the mop about a foot away from the edge and work in toward the edge. (Painters call this motion "cutting in" when they're using a paintbrush.) Stand close to the wall while you're working.

Once you've worked the sponge mop against the edge, pay close attention to get that last bit of the ceiling. As long as you clean each edge leading into a corner, you will automatically clean the corner as well.

Edges: If You're *Not* Also Washing the Walls

The above method of cleaning into the corner and along the edges of the ceiling will also clean the top inch or so of the wall. If you don't want to wash the walls at this time, clean the edges and corners by hand to avoid that inch-clean streak at the very top of the wall. If you don't mind that, fine.

You'll need a stepladder or a chair to do the work by hand. Be careful climbing up and down the ladder with things in your hand. But you don't have to haul the bucket up the ladder, just one of your cleaning cloths. First, wet it in the ammonia solution, wring it out, and take it up the ladder with you. Use it to clean the last little area of ceiling near the wall, and then wipe the area dry with another cleaning cloth.

It's a bit risky to change from the Sh-Mop to a cleaning cloth because they clean somewhat differently and may leave a noticeable difference when the surface dries. This won't be a problem if you clean all but the last few inches of the ceiling with the mop. Then the small strip you hand-clean with a cloth will scarcely be noticeable—if at all. Clean as much as possible with the mop and as little as possible by hand.

How to Move the Furniture Only Once

Let's say you're working your way out from the corner and are about to bump into a chair that's directly in your way. If you're not careful, you'll end up moving that chair four times before you're done—especially if you will be washing the walls after you finish the ceiling. You will move it (1) out to wash the ceiling, (2) back when you come to it again, (3) back out to wash the walls, and (4) back again when you're finished with the walls.

Don't waste all that time. Move it once out and once back as follows: When you come to the chair in the first place, don't move it at all. Instead, first wash the ceiling over the spot to which you intend to move the chair—usually just 3 feet straight ahead. Wipe the area dry and move the chair. Then clean the ceiling over where it was, wipe the ceiling dry, and keep on going. *Don't* move the chair back yet. When you come back in the other direction, the chair will be in your way again. But since you've already cleaned above the chair, just skip ahead to the next dirty area on the other side of the chair. Leave the chair alone until you are finished with the walls—if you are cleaning them at all. If not, return the chair to its original spot.

Remember to throw a drop cloth over furniture or countertops when you are cleaning close to them. Those little drips of dirty water cause stains that can be tedious to clean up. Also keep a drop cloth on the floor in the area you're working in to protect the floor finish. For the floor, heavier cloths are much easier to manage—especially a real painter's canvas. They won't cling to you like plastic wrap when you walk on them. The lighter and thinner plastic ones are more suitable for countertops and furniture.

Light Fixtures

If you're lucky, you can usually figure out a way to clean around the light fixtures, using the same technique you use when cleaning a corner. Don't clean close to them when your Sh-Mop is still dripping, and move your body around the fixture to clean it from different angles. If you're not able to clean it from the floor using your mop, then resort to a chair or ladder. If so, use a cleaning cloth to clean and a second cloth to wipe the area dry. Since you're wearing a cleaning apron, you'll have a cloth in your pocket and won't have to climb back down the ladder to get one.

Ceiling Fans

Just how *do* you clean ceiling fans?

Forget better mousetraps. What the world really needs is a self-cleaning ceiling fan or, failing that, at least one that you can raise and lower like a flag. As it is, ceiling fans are much too difficult to reach. And when you do, they won't stay still.

If the fan hasn't been cleaned in some time, and the blades are as dusty as we suspect, it's best to rise to their level. Trying to clean a very dirty ceiling fan from the floor is exasperating and ineffective. Obviously a ladder is needed in most cases, but once you are there, the cleaning itself is easy enough. Position the ladder once, and then rotate the fan blades to clean each one in turn. Use cleaning cloths and Red Juice. Spray the cloth or the blade (it's easier and safer to spray the cloth), and wipe. Use one cloth to make the first wipe. This cloth will soon be a mess, but it will remove most of the dirt. Use a second Red Juice-dampened cloth for a second and final wipe.

Once you get the fan blades clean, keep them that way with regular maintenance cleaning. This can be done from the relative safety of terra firma. Use a flexible duster on an extension pole. The one we use is called a rabbit ear duster. It has a bendable, double-loop wire frame head (it looks as if it had ears, hence the name) that's covered with a thick 100-percent cotton-yarn head mounted on an extension pole. The tool allows you to clean out-of-reach fans, and you can bend and shape the "ears" to match the contours of the fan. Use the rabbit ear duster dry to remove the bulk of the dirt. If necessary, dampen it with Red Juice, and finish wiping the fan in the same manner.

Note: When installing a new ceiling fan, position it on the ceiling so you can reach it by ladder without having to move heavy furniture. For example, don't place the fan directly over a king-size bed. Install it close enough to the foot of the bed that it will be easily accessible by ladder.

Ladder or Chair Strategy

In some situations, you cannot avoid using a ladder when washing ceilings. If the ceiling is too tall, first try using the mop while standing on a chair. Or if the ceiling is so tall that your Sh-Mop is straight up in the air before you can reach it, then use a chair so you can work from an angle and avoid being right under your work area—and in the path of every drip. Select a chair that is sturdy and stable and not covered with anything slippery. If you need to protect the chair, cover it with a towel to ensure firm footing. If a chair won't do, use a ladder. We prefer wood to aluminum.

You probably already know a lot of the rules about using a folding stepladder. Don't stand on the top two rungs of the ladder. Don't use a stepladder unless the spreaders are fully opened and snapped in place to lock them. Set the bucket only on the little folding shelf that was designed for that purpose. Don't move the ladder while the bucket is still on the shelf. When working near a door, make sure the door is either wide open or else closed and locked. Don't lean your body off center to reach for something, or gravity will take over in a most unpleasant way.

An important aspect of ladder strategy is to do as little work as possible with a ladder alone. It's just about the slowest and most inefficient technique possible. Rather, we recommend that you set up a simple work platform to clean the ceiling. It will save having to move the ladder so many times, and it will mean you can clean the stairwell ceiling without risking life and limb.

Work Platforms and Scaffold Planks

Either of the work platforms we show you, or your own variations thereof, require a plank to stand on. Ordinary planks won't do. They aren't strong enough, wide enough, thick enough, or long enough to be safe. You'll need a specialized scaffold plank. These are 2 inches thick by 8 inches wide (nominal size) and up to 10 feet long (actual size). They also come longer than 10 feet, but the longer lengths require additional support in the middle— not something realistic for the present purposes. If you are also going to use the plank to paint, or perhaps use it outside for window washing, you might consider buying one at a lumberyard. Planks can also be rented at paint stores or many equipment-rental stores.

Here are two configurations that can be used to make life easier while working on ceilings or high walls—for washing or painting or wallpapering. One is a work platform. The other is a more specialized stairwell platform.

Work Platform

Unless your ceilings are unusually high, here is a simple work platform that will eliminate all those trips up and down the ladder and moving it so often. You may use a sawhorse plus your ladder, or two sawhorses. You can also use a chair, or even two chairs, as long as you follow the same rules that apply to the sawhorses and ladder: *Be sure the scaffold plank extends 1 foot beyond the edge of whatever it rests on.* Needless to say, the resulting platform must be level.

Don't make the whole thing unsafe by using something inappropriate to try to correct the height at one end of the platform—like a pillow (too wobbly), a pile of books (not wide enough), or a trash can (not strong enough). You get the idea. It's best to use a combination of things (sawhorse, ladder, and chair) so you don't have to add anything else to correct the height, which is just one more thing to take apart and move every time you need to change the location of the platform. If you must, a couple of safe things to use for leveling the platform are either a plank (2 inches by 6 inches or larger) cut into appropriate lengths, or one or two books if they are large enough (something like an encyclopedia).

Doing the Work on a Platform

Even though you are using a work platform, you proceed in pretty much the same way we described in the first part of this chapter. Prepare the same way, start in the same place, and use the same cleaning solution. However, instead of using a Sh-Mop, use a large handheld sponge. We prefer the synthetic kind because their rectangular shape and smooth sides apply even pressure over a larger area than does a natural sponge. If you have a little sponge by the kitchen sink, or a dirty old sponge that you've been using to clean the car, and it constantly sheds bits of sponge because it's rotting away, you must know by now that we aren't going to let you use it for this job. Spring for a brand-new sponge about 4 inches by 6 inches in size. But don't buy a cheap one with no spunk. Get a substantial one. You'll thank yourself more than once.

When working on a platform, place the bucket beside you. Which side you choose depends on what hand you use to clean. If you're right-handed, locate the bucket on your right so you don't have to twist and turn to reach the bucket when working. (Such movements aren't so simple as they might sound when you're on a narrow plank above the floor.) Then work your way to the left, so you don't run into the bucket, which could have spectacular consequences. If you're left-handed, kindly reverse these directions.

Rinse the sponge, wring it dry enough so that it isn't dripping, and use it to clean an area of the ceiling about 3 feet by 3 feet. Put the sponge back in the bucket, and take a cloth from your apron pocket, and wipe the same area dry. Even a very dirty wall or ceiling doesn't need to be rinsed using this method. Just be sure you wipe each area with a cleaning cloth right after you wash it with the sponge—and before the area dries on its own.

Stairwell Work Platform

Here is an illustration of how to erect a work platform in a stairwell in case that area has you stumped. Nothing else is different as far as cleaning procedures go, but please exercise extreme care when using an apparatus such as this in a stairwell.

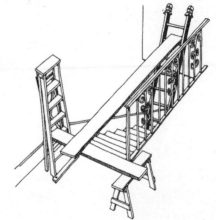

Porous Ceilings

If you have a fairly smooth, well-painted surface over a plaster or drywall ceiling (the most common types), you can usually clean it and be satisfied with the results without causing any noticeable damage to the surface.

Not so with many porous surfaces. Most of us are aware of how difficult acoustical ceilings are to wash—especially the blown-on variety. But stucco, some types of plaster, and textured concrete can also be damaged by your attempts to clean them. Or they may look no better. Don't try to wash these types of ceilings. Paint them instead or call in professional help. Or vacuum them if you're dealing just with loose soot or other particulate matter. You'll feel better. And then get back to whatever you were doing before the idea to wash them popped into your head.

If you have acoustical ceiling tiles, it is usually possible to wash them if you're careful and patient. There are specialty cleaning products for such ceilings, including dry sponges that rely on dry-cleaning chemicals and an absorbent surface material.

Those of you who have soft-blow acoustical ceilings know that they are just about impossible to maintain. The best you can hope to do is to use the soft long-bristle brush attachment with the vacuum to remove cobwebs and obvious dust or soot while trying not to dislodge more of the ceiling than is absolutely necessary. The only other possibility is to have it spray-painted. Hire a professional painter. Or move.

Maintenance

The proper way to maintain ceilings is largely preventive in nature. Unless the ceiling is unusually clean, you can't spot-clean it without a patch of cleanliness becoming very apparent.

Preventive maintenance involves finding and eliminating the source of recurring dirt. Chief offenders are undersized or clogged exhaust fans over kitchen stoves. Clean the fan filter religiously. It's not as hard as it looks: Pop it into the dishwasher. (See Chapter 19.)

Soot from exhaust vents is another annoyance. The first thing to do is check the filters in your heating/ventilating/air-conditioning (HVAC) system. If they're clean, it may benefit you to consult with an HVAC contractor to see what else can be done to reduce the soot level.

Mildew is a timeless enemy of ceilings. Moisture tends to condense on warm ceilings more than on other surfaces, and mildew needs moisture like we need air to breathe. Ventilation is your first line of defense. Use the fan if there is one. Make sure the bathroom window or door is kept open during a shower—or at least afterward, long enough to let heavy moisture dissipate. Mildew is a living organism, and once it takes hold on a surface, it is tenacious. When you have to repaint the ceiling, use an oil- or alkyd-based primer plus top coat, each with a mildew-preventing agent added. It really does help. You might also consider an oscillating room fan to keep the air moving, which the mildew will not appreciate at all. Aim it toward the ceiling.

Chapter 17 Washing Walls

It is an exceptional day indeed when you have to wash a wall completely. Certainly some walls would benefit from being washed, but it would be better to paint others instead, and some should be benignly ignored. Your decision about what to do will depend not only on the degree of uncleanliness but also on the type of paint and type of surface.

Gloss and Semigloss Paints

These are the exceptions to our general disinclination to clean walls. Gloss and semigloss paints call for a thorough cleaning much more often than a repainting. They wash and clean up far more easily than flat paint, which is a primary consideration for selecting them in the first place. In this chapter, we'll show you the fastest way to wash these walls.

Do a test area first to be sure that you will do no damage to the surface. The test also tells you whether or not the walls need cleaning to begin with. If they don't look any different after the test, relax and wait until next year.

Flat Paint

As you know, it's much more laborious to clean flat paint, and it's much less likely to come clean of fingerprints, stains, smoke, grease, and so forth. Nor does it do as good a job resisting damage by the chemical action of cleaning. The paint itself can be discolored or actually dissolved by the cleaning solution, or it can be worn right off the walls during the cleaning process.

Latex paints vary in several ways—ability to cover previous coats, resistance to fading, depth of color, resistance to running, and cleanability. Often, to excel in one dimension, the paint manufacturer must sacrifice one or more of the others. Cheaper flat latex paints are notorious for allowing stains to go right through the coating and for rubbing right off when you try to wash them. When you buy paint, ask about its rated ability to be cleaned. It's often worth the extra dollar a gallon to get a premium grade of paint that will save you hours of work in the long run. You can also check the periodic reviews of house paints in consumer magazines.

But even if you bought an excellent grade of flat paint, its chief maintenance advantage is not that you can wash the entire surface of the walls. Rather, you are much more likely to be removing stains and spot-cleaning the small areas around the light switches and thermostat—hundred of times during the lifetime of the paint, perhaps. But don't wash the entire wall! Only do this in case of emergency (like smoke damage) or your own personal choice—and to heck with our advice.

So what should be done with flat-finished walls that are thoroughly dirty? Paint them. Painting may not be cheaper, and it certainly involves hard work (as does washing them), but the walls will look so much better when you're finished. For a bit more effort, it's worth it and here's why.

Most of these flat-finished walls that you are thinking about washing have seen a fair amount of history enacted in front of them in their years of service. The wall behind the rocking chair has numerous little nicks where the chair has hit the wall over and over and over again. There's an infuriatingly visible scratch next to the picture frame that was gouged when you jiggled the frame as you were cleaning it. Then there are those holes in the wall where all the pictures used to be before you rearranged everything a couple of years ago—plus the holes left over from the Christmas decorations. Also the paint-free spots where you had taped up balloons for the birthday party last summer. Remember the sickening feeling when the tape took the paint right off the wall? Oh, and those oily patches where people lean their hands against the wall while they watch TV? And then there's the corner where the dog sleeps. And the red crayon stains that you can still see despite your best efforts.

Unfortunately, even after you've washed these walls, a great many of these eyesores will still be there. If you paint, they will be obliterated. With either job, you'll have to cover the furniture, move the furniture away from the walls, take down the pictures, and remove the drapes. This is a big chunk of work whether you're washing or painting. Paint. You'll be happier.

One exception to this rule is if you've had an accident in the room before all the normal wear-and-tear conflagrations have had a chance to transpire. Maybe some heavy-duty smokers turned the walls a shade of nicotine orange only a few months after you painted. Go ahead and wash the walls. Or maybe you moved into a house with walls so dirty that they have to be washed before you can even think of painting them. Or it may just be a matter of personal choice. If you feel better washing the walls, by all means, go right ahead. The instructions follow.

The "inconspicuous test area" is even more important with flat latex surfaces. The chances of a bad reaction between the paint and the cleaner are greater than with other surfaces. Don't take a chance without trying the cleaner in an out-of-the-way spot first.

The Choice of Cleaner

We prefer clean, nonsudsy, nondetergent, non-anything-else ammonia for washing walls. There are many other possibilities, but ammonia works as well or better than anything else we've tried. And it's downright cheap. Get *clear* ammonia, which is generally sold in janitorial supply stores. Its major drawback—as in the case of all ammonia formulas—is its ferocious odor, but its superlative cleaning qualities are hard to pass up. With all types of ammonia, make sure the area you're cleaning is well ventilated.

Mix 1 to 2 cups of ammonia per gallon of water. If you use cool rather than warm water, fewer fumes will drift your way. Our second choice is Red Juice. Our third choice is TSP (trisodium phosphate), which we actually prefer when we are washing walls in preparation for repainting. The TSP seems to leave the surface face microscopically etched, which gives the paint a better "bite" on the surface. The few streaks it leaves won't matter because you're just going to paint right over them anyway.

Materials

1 cleaning apron
10 to 15 cleaning cloths

1 quart of clear ammonia (or Red Juice or TSP)

1 Sh-Mop (or large sponge)

6 to 12 Sh-Wipes

1 spray bottle of Red Juice

1 toothbrush

1 double bucket (recommended) or single bucket

1 white scrub pad

1 stepladder or chair (optional)

2 plastic drop cloths or bedsheets

1 pair of rubber gloves

See If You Can Get Away with Spot-Cleaning

Usually, the only walls you ever need to wash are in the kitchen and bathroom. These rooms are normally covered with a gloss or semigloss paint that should respond well to cleaning. But often, there will be just a few streaks over a kitchen countertop, or a few lines on bathroom walls caused by condensation. Just wipe off these areas with Red Juice and a cleaning cloth when you're doing your normal weekly cleaning. Sometimes that's all that's really needed to keep them relatively spotless. The idea is to spot-clean absolutely whenever you can get away with it. If not, proceed with full washing. Most bathroom walls could use complete washing a couple of times a year and the kitchen once a year or so.

General Wallpaper Cleaning

Occasional removal of dust with a cloth or by vacuuming is all the general cleaning that's called for. Smudges and other small marks can be removed with a gum eraser.

Grease and Wallpaper

Most greasy fingerprints can be removed with Red Juice, a cleaning cloth, and gentle encouragement with a toothbrush (pretest). For larger grease spots, place a few white paper towels folded to cover the grease stain. Press the paper towels with a warm iron until the grease is absorbed into the paper towels. Keep turning the towels to a fresh area or replace them.

Nicotine on Walls

Nicotine comes off most surfaces nicely with a dilute clear ammonia solution or Red Juice. If the painted surfaces are cabinets, baseboards, window frames, and so forth, just spray with Red Juice and wipe with a cleaning cloth. Use a toothbrush to reach into corners.

If the painted surfaces are walls and ceilings, mix clear ammonia in a bucket (start with about 1 part ammonia to 10 parts water, and make it stronger only if needed.) Apply with a Sh-Mop or a large sponge. Wipe first with either one, and then dry with a cleaning cloth or dry flat mop cover.

Discouraging note: If the surfaces are covered with flat paint, and the paint and the nicotine stains are old, you may have to repaint. But wash them anyway to get rid of at least some of the odor. And ask your paint supplier how best to seal or prime the surface before repainting to avoid possible bleed-through of those lovely nicotine stains.

Soot

If the wall above your fireplace has noticeable amounts of black soot—if you're lucky—you'll get some of it off just by vacuuming with the brush attachment. For the hard-core soot that's remaining, there are specialized soot cleaners (e.g., Soot Solution, Red Devil, and one a chimney sweep I know swears by, Speedy White) available in most hardware stores, but I would just as soon use clear dilute ammonia solution. It's safe, effective, and substantially less expensive. Use a Sh-Mop or large sponge and cleaning cloths to wash the wall itself. Dip a mop cover or sponge into the cleaning solution, wring it out but leave it almost dripping wet, and clean an area of the wall. Use a second, dry Sh-Mop or cleaning cloth to dry each clean area before you move on.

Note: Soot on small, smooth areas can often be removed with a large eraser.

Brick walls covered with soot respond well to cleaning with trisodium phosphate (up to $\frac{1}{2}$ cup in a gallon of hot water) or Speedy White and a handheld brush. Dry with cleaning cloths. It would be wise to seal brick or stone walls near fireplaces to resist future absorption of grease and soot.

Fingerprints

We're often asked how to clean the hundreds of fingerprints that appear on household walls.

Well, if the fingerprints are on glossy paint, they're easy to remove. So we're going to assume that the fingerprints are on flat paint. Flat paint (more so than gloss or semigloss paint) can hold on to or even absorb stains with tenacity, making the job difficult for any cleaning agent. First try to wipe the fingerprints off with Red Juice and a cleaning cloth. If the wall is particularly dirty, you may need a white pad or a toothbrush. But be careful! Even the cleaning cloth can wear away the paint beneath the fingerprints, especially if (1) the paint is old, (2) the paint is cheap, (3) only one coat of paint had been applied, or (4) there's been a long history of scrubbing at this site.

If Red Juice doesn't work, or if the paint has been scrubbed away, the solution is to repaint. But be wily about this and repaint just what's necessary. If only the area around a switch plate is defiled, repaint only that area. Paint—especially if you have some from the same can—matches quite well for several years. If the new paint looks too different, paint up to a corner.

Preparation

If this is a kitchen or bathroom, there usually isn't much furniture to move away from the walls. But regardless of the room, move the furniture that will be in the way, and then pay particular attention to the small items. For example, move the garbage can out of the room, so you don't collide with it later. Move or cover trays of little items like makeup and perfume so cleaning solution doesn't drip on them. Move items on the kitchen counters away from you or out of the way in case you have to stand on the countertops as you work.

Take down the curtains or drapes. And then, unless they are nice and clean, wash them or send them out to be dry-cleaned. The only time you don't have to take them down is when you aren't washing the window frames. But since the frames are usually just as dirty as the walls, that won't generally be the case. Okay, okay! You can leave the drapes up if it's too much of a hassle because they are too heavy, you won't be able to put them back up, or you just don't want to bother. But be aware that they will slow you down as you try to clean the woodwork under and around them if they are left in place. Get miniblinds out of the way by pulling them all the way to the top position—or send them out to be cleaned also. (Look in the yellow pages under "Venetian Blind Cleaners.")

Remove all the pictures from the wall. Don't remove the nails. Be careful, however; the nails practically disappear from sight once the pictures are off, and they turn into deadly little pieces of metal that slice fingertips and rip sponges. You can protect yourself from them by hanging a cleaning cloth from each nail as you remove the picture. The cloth will remind you where the nails are, so you can avoid any mishap with them as you wash your way around the room. As you're using cleaning cloths anyway to dry the wall, you can put the cloths to work when you collect them back from the nails as you come to them.

If the windowsills and baseboards are even moderately dusty, vacuum them first with the brush attachment. It is extremely important that you take the time to follow this instruction. If your home is like many where the walls need washing, the baseboards and windowsills are also nice and dusty. You do remember what happens to dust when you add water to it. Mud. And it is much more tedious to remove mud by hand than it is to remove dust with a vacuum cleaner. Don't forget to vacuum the high molding. Cobwebs are much easier to vacuum away than to wash away—especially since they have a lousy little habit of swinging loose and landing smack in an area you just cleaned. Vacuum the walls themselves only if there is visible dust on a flat latex surface.

If You're Washing Walls after Washing the Ceiling

If you plan on doing the ceiling during the same session as the walls, do the ceiling first. (See Chapter 16.) If you've just finished washing the ceiling, go to the same corner in which you had started it. Since the ceiling is now clean, you don't have to worry about disturbing the uniformity of its appearance. This means you can safely continue to use a Sh-Mop on the walls all the way up to the ceiling.

Tie your cleaning apron snugly around your waist. Hang the bottle of Red Juice on its appropriate loop, and put the toothbrush in its pocket. Load 5 to 10 cleaning cloths in a large apron pocket, and put 3 or 4 Sh-Wipes and the white pad into a plastic-lined pocket. Set the mop and the cleaning tray with its extra cloths and supplies just outside the door of the room you're cleaning. Take the bucket and the clear ammonia to the nearest convenient sink.

Mix about ½ cup of clear ammonia in about half a bucket of warm water. (Adjust this formula according to how dirty the wall is.) We prefer using one side of a double bucket, for reasons that will shortly become apparent. Carry the bucket to the corner of the room you're about to clean. It doesn't really matter, but for uniformity, we start in the left-hand corner of the room farthest from the door we will eventually exit from.

Strategy

This is back to basics, but Clean Team Rule 1 (on page 6) applies—work around the room once without backtracking. Clean everything as you come to it—upper molding, door frames, windowsills, and lower molding—not to mention the walls also. Work to the right and from top to bottom as you proceed. Use the Sh-Mop to wash, and a dry Sh-Wipe or cleaning cloth to dry. As with ceilings, save time by not rinsing except in extreme cases.

Work from the Top Down!

Just about every book we've read on the subject, and every person we've ever talked to, says to wash walls from the bottom up. The stated reason is because streams of cleaning solution run down the wall and cause anxiety-provoking streaks. Right, but don't you have exactly as many dribbles of cleaning solution running down the wall if you work from the bottom up? Of course you do. The same number of dribbles is going to travel the same paths—in one case, on a dirty surface, in the other, on a clean surface. Streaks may appear to be catastrophic at first, but eventually they blend into the background as the cleaner takes effect on the whole surface. The only danger is when dribbles are left on the wall for a long period. In that case, you'll be making work for yourself by having to blend them into the back-ground. The correct technique is to *manage* the cleaning solution on the wall. When you see solution running down the wall, wipe it off with a cloth before it has a chance to cause trouble.

Besides, if you work from top to bottom, you don't have to retouch the bottom as much. For example, if you clean the baseboard first, and then clean the wall above it, there is no way in the world you can clean that wall without dripping dirty cleaning solution onto your nice clean baseboard. So you have to stop and wipe the baseboard you just cleaned. How much smarter and quicker to wash the wall first from top to bottom and then wash the base-board last—never having to worry about little drips splattering on your clean work. As Clean Team Rule 3 (page 9) says: Work from top to bottom. Always. Period. Don't argue.

Use the Sh-Mop

Stand a couple of feet from the wall, so you can reach into the area you are cleaning with the Sh-Mop. That is, don't try to wash the area right in front of you. Wash a strip about 3 feet wide, and proceed all the way from the top of the wall down to the baseboards before you move ahead to the next strip. Stop to rinse or exchange Sh-Wipes as often as necessary. If the room is too small, or the wall is too hard to reach because of immovable objects, you can use a cleaning cloth or Sh-Wipe by hand on small areas. Keep the amount of cleaning solution running down the wall to a minimum by wringing out the Sh-Wipe but leaving it almost dripping wet before each use.

Wiping Dry

Each time you finish a strip of the wall with the Sh-Mop, wipe that same area dry. This is the same technique used when doing the ceiling. Put a dry Sh-Wipe on the Sh-Mop, holding it the same way as you did when washing. It's important to keep the Sh-Wipes and cloths uniformly dry and uniformly clean, so the wall will have an even cleanliness after it dries. Wipe with the Sh-Wipe before the walls dry of their own accord or else you'll end up with streaks.

Lower Part of the Wall

After you clean the upper part of the wall that's out of reach, you will find it easier to stop using the Sh-Mop. At lower levels, the mop handle can start to become awkward to maneuver, especially in small or crowded rooms. You can remove the Sh-Wipe from the mop and use it alone or use a large sponge or a cleaning cloth dipped in cleaning solution. Dry as above.

Baseboards, Molding, Doors, and Windows

You have to wash them. They won't go away. And it's faster to clean them as you come to them. By cleaning them in turn, you don't waste time backtracking or making additional trips around the room to do them later.

Nooks and Crannies

Clean areas that are difficult to reach with your toothbrush. It works very well in the corners of windowsills or woodwork, around (and on) light switches, molding, and stubborn spots. No need to be dainty with it either. You can really agitate up a storm with it and cover a surprisingly large surface fast. Switch to a larger brush if you have to cover substantial square footage. Just keep it moving. If you need a little extra cleaning solution in an area, reach for your Red Juice rather than the bucket or mop.

Corners

These are easy. Just stand close to each wall in turn to clean all the way into the corner. First, do one side all the way to the baseboards and then the other side all the way down. Then clean the corner baseboards and wipe the area dry.

If you can't get into the corner all the way because of the size of the room or some other obstacle, grab a cleaning cloth and use that instead.

Spots and Stains

The toothbrush and Red Juice are your first line of offense against spots and stains. If they fail, recall that you are carrying a white pad. If you come upon a relatively innocent little black mark on the wall, say ¼ inch wide and 1 inch long, please *don't* grab your white pad and start scratching away at an area of the wall that measures a good 6 by 6 inches. That method may indeed remove the small black spot—the one that none of your friends could see without their glasses—or it could turn it into one that you can't miss from the next room. Be careful.

When using a white pad on a spot on the wall, the idea is to concentrate its effectiveness on the spot and not the surrounding area. This is accomplished by applying pressure with your finger on the pad on just the spot. You can even use something like the handle end of the toothbrush to concentrate the working surface of the pad.

We are frequently asked how to remove crayon marks from walls. Our method is to spray the area with Endust, agitate gently with the toothbrush, and wipe with a cleaning cloth. Then spray the same area with Red Juice to remove the Endust residue. Wipe clean and dry. The Endust works its way under the crayon mark and floats it off the surface. We have used this method on scrubbable painted walls as well as many types of wallpaper (especially vinyl). Again, you must pretest an area to make sure the procedure is safe for your particular wall surface.

Crayon Art

"How do you remove crayon marks from painted walls and wall-papered walls? Sigh."

Use lighter fluid, Gunk Remover, WD-40, Endust, or another mild solvent and a toothbrush to remove most of the crayon from the wall. Spray or wipe with the solvent and then, ever so gently, brush with the toothbrush. Use a cleaning cloth to blot away residue. Finally, spray and wipe the area with Red Juice to remove the last traces of crayon and solvent. Follow the same procedure on wallpaper after first testing for colorfastness and the effects of the solvent and Red Juice in that legendary inconspicuous place. Naturally, you should avoid saturating the wallpaper as well as scrubbing too hard with the toothbrush or cloths.

Next best bet: If the solvent fails the inconspicuous spot test or isn't effective, try paper towels and a warm iron. (See "Grease and Wallpaper" on page 216.)

Managing the Cleaning Solution

Change it often. If you don't, you will be able to see plainly the difference between clean and dirty solution on the walls.

You're Finished!

If you persevere, you will complete one trip around the room, which means that you're finished. Congratulations!

If You're Washing Only the Walls and *Not* the Ceiling

When you clean or paint the walls without doing the ceiling, be sure not to disturb the uniform appearance of the ceiling, or it will be painfully obvious.

The reason a dirty ceiling may still look just fine is that the dirt on it is undisturbed. For example, if you molest that even layer of smoke on the ceiling by splashing water on it or by inadvertently cleaning a streak here and there with the mop, you'll make some brilliantly clean spots that are much worse than nice even dirt because now you'll have to wash the entire ceiling. There are better ways to spend Saturday afternoon.

The way to avoid touching the ceiling when cleaning the walls is first to clean the top foot or so of the wall with a cleaning cloth or a Sh-Wipe (not installed on the Sh-Mop), using a second cloth to wipe the area dry. Then use the much faster Sh-Mop to wash the rest of the wall. Standing on a chair if you can—a ladder if you must—clean the strip at the top of the wall. But don't do the strip all the way around the room. Rather, clean a strip that you can reach from the chair and then move the chair ahead and wash the rest of the wall with the Sh-Mop. (You're just working from the top to the bottom before moving on.) Except for this strip, follow the wall-washing instructions that we have already described. Be very careful not to touch the ceiling at all.

Washing Walls Using a Ladder or Work Platform

There are times that you must use a ladder to wash walls. Let's say you don't believe us about how well the Sh-Mop method works, or the dirt is such that you can't scrub hard enough with the mop, or the walls are too high. There is no way to avoid a ladder. So be it.

The basic strategies are almost identical to those used while using a ladder or a platform to wash ceilings, which are discussed in Chapter 16. No sense repeating them here, but there are one or two considerations peculiar to walls that we should review.

Do the Top Half of the Wall First

Because the work platform will be in the way of cleaning the bottom half, you can wash only the top half of the wall on the first pass. As before, be sure to catch or wipe off streaks of cleaning solution that start to run down the wall. Clean the top half of the wall from one end of the work platform to the other, and resist the temptation to reach or lean past the end, or you may upset the whole apple cart. Then set the bucket on the floor near the first part of the wall you washed from the platform.

Move the platform by moving the plank first, and then each chair or ladder. Next, wash the lower half of the wall, including the baseboards. Then get back up on the platform and start again on a new section. Clean window frames, sills, door frames, and any other woodwork as you come to them.

Once again, after you've made one complete trip around the room, you're done.

Maintenance

The proper way to maintain walls is to keep them free of spots and fingerprints. Each time you do your weekly cleaning, have Red Juice at the ready for new spots that have appeared. Remove them by spraying and wiping clean with a cloth. Anything that gets on the wall that might result in a permanent stain should be removed whenever you see it. Don't wait until you clean the house again.

The other maintenance is preventive in nature. Especially when you wash a wall, you'll discover things that could have been done to make the job easier. For instance, if the furnace vent is making a black area on the wall above it, install an air deflector. Oily spots on the wall from hair can be avoided by locating a pillow at strategic spots on the couch. If the chair is hitting the wall, move it out and put something under the legs, so it doesn't move right back. As you clean house, be aware of spots being made on the walls that can be stopped by moving something. Then do it. It's a pleasant feeling to solve these little problems instead of just wondering about them as you're cleaning. You'll be grateful you did because the house will look better between now and when you wash or paint again—and those jobs will be that much easier too.

One other thing: This wall will not come perfectly clean very many times, so fix the fireplace; if the draft is too slow, the chimney needs cleaning, or something else is askew.

If you're thinking about cleaning the bricks that form the sides and floor of the fireplace, don't—just ignore them. If you're thinking about cleaning the bricks that form the interior of the chimney, they are cleaned with specialized tools inserted through the top of the chimney. You must first seal the fireplace 100 percent to prevent soot from pouring out of it. Try to visualize a layer of soot everywhere. Then call a chimney sweep.

Chapter 18 Other Types of Cleaning

More!?

For those of you who see all the time savings available in the preceding chapters but feel that your particular cleaning problem is still ignored and still overwhelming, you may be right.

Cleaning Categories

There are three types of household cleaning. One is weekly cleaning, which is the subject of the first part of this book. Unfortunately, there is also daily cleaning (clutter) and yearly (spring) cleaning. Clearly, you are going to have trouble dealing with the weekly cleaning if no one is doing the daily cleaning.

Daily Cleaning (Clutter)

Daily cleaning is putting things in their place—day in and day out. Moving dirty dishes from the table (or TV room) into the dishwasher. Hanging coats on their hangers. Tossing dirty clothes into the hamper. Setting out the trash. Putting away the toys. Here are a few suggestions.

The best solution for reducing clutter is to handle each item once, so it never gets a chance to become clutter. Put it away. Takes about 2 seconds. Try it. If that doesn't work, you have too much stuff. Add a room, buy more furniture, take it to Goodwill, or have a garage sale.

It may help to have designated "clutter areas." Once you have designated clutter areas, it's okay to throw things into them. Examples may be the corner next to the front door, one section of the kitchen counter, or the bedroom floor near the closet. After you get in the habit of putting things away in these areas, slowly reduce their size and then finally eliminate them.

Also, as promised in the introduction, once you start regular cleaning, these daily jobs will start to take care of themselves as a sense of pride in a clean home encourages everyone in the household to keep the home civilized between cleanings.

Yearly (Spring) Cleaning

Stripping wax from floors. Washing ceilings and walls. Or washing (heaven forbid) the windows. All those things that may need your cleaning attention once or twice a year. (Don't worry. We give helpful advice on how to do even these tasks quickly in Part 3.)

Chapter 19 Getting the House Ready for Weekly Cleaning

Learning Speed Cleaning techniques and then whipping through your basically clean house in an hour or so on a weekly or biweekly basis can be very different from cleaning it the first time around. This is especially so if the house hasn't been really cleaned in some time. (Let's not dwell on the amount of time—or why.) The difference is that Speed Cleaning methods are for cleaning on an ongoing (maintenance) basis. But often a variety of tasks have to be accomplished before you can even begin to maintain a clean home. If you've been keeping a perfectly clean house or move into one, you can dive right into the time savings offered in the first part of this book without tackling the tasks in this chapter. If not, this chapter will help you get started.

Organization Problems?

There are homes in which a reasonable person wouldn't (couldn't) attempt maintenance cleaning, but the problem is more a matter of organization than cleaning. For example, in the kitchen, the problem may not be a long-term collection of dirt, grime, and grease, but instead a fairly short-term collection of dirty pots and pans on the stove top and surrounding counters. And maybe there are dirty dishes from the past few days filling the sink and overflowing onto additional counter space, children's toys strewn about on the floor, a 75 percent complete jigsaw puzzle on additional counter space, and coats, clothes, and shoes on and around the chair in the corner. We're sure you could paint an even more complete picture.

Such a room needs to be picked up first, not cleaned first. There is a huge difference. You should fill the dishwasher—not haul out specialized cleaning tools. You should pick up the toys and clothes—not rent a floor machine. This is as much an organizational problem as it is a cleaning problem. (We tackle that subject in my book *Clutter Control.*)

You already really know what you have to do. Put things away before you start to clean. Threaten or cajole other family members to do so also. If you just put things away when you finish with them, your life will be transformed. Hang up your coat when you take it off instead of first tossing it on a chair for a day or two. It's easier and faster, your house will look better, and the rooms won't be cluttered all the time. But you already knew that. Now all that remains is to do it. You may have a little fight with yourself when you do, but go ahead and be organized in spite of yourself. Fake it until it's routine enough to become a genuine impulse. Now let's go on to some of the cleaning tasks you may have to get out of the way to be able to begin the easier weekly (maintenance) cleaning.

In the rest of this chapter, we'll talk about situations where routine cleaning gets out of hand: The shelves are too dusty to use a feather duster; the shower-door tracks have devolved into miniature snake pits; the fiberglass tub no longer responds to anything you try. In the other chapters in this section, we tackle the more serious and independent spring-cleaning jobs step by step.

This chapter builds on the methods we discussed for routine weekly cleaning, so for it to be most helpful, it would be best if you were familiar with the earlier chapters. This chapter is designed to help you get through the first-time cleaning of an especially dirty house—without repeating all the instructions in the earlier chapters. If you have any questions or problems on cleaning techniques, please call or write us. We will be happy to give you our personal attention.

The Bathroom

If the entire room needs cleaning from top to bottom, start by washing the ceiling and then the walls (see Chapters 16 and 17). Don't worry about the mirrors or the sink or the toilet or shower right now. Don't even worry about covering such things up. Just let the drips and splashes fall where they may, unless the room is carpeted. (In which case, you will need a drop cloth.) When you come to a light fixture (either over the sink or on the ceiling) put its glass bowl in the dishwasher unless it could be damaged. Most won't be, and the dishwasher cleans them very nicely. Remember, this is *not* routine Speed Cleaning. We wouldn't dream of hauling a light fixture off to the dishwasher during regular maintenance cleaning. We would just dust it, which takes a couple of seconds, and move on. Right now, we're as interested in smart cleaning as we are in fast cleaning. If the light fixtures themselves are old and rusty and an eyesore, throw them away and replace them. You don't have to be very handy to do this, and the fixtures are often inexpensive. The same is true for replacing glass bowls missing from the fixtures. Both of these steps can really enhance your spring-cleaning efforts.

After the ceiling and walls are out of the way, most of the rules of Speed Cleaning apply to a heavy-duty cleaning. It's just harder and more time-consuming. But taking the time to get the bathroom as clean as it will ever be will save you time in your maintenance cleaning all year long.

Use the toothbrush or a specialized grout brush liberally since it will get into long-neglected dirty corners and other areas that are difficult to clean or reach. If you use it correctly, you may wear out a couple of them the first time through. Fine—that's what they're for. Use them on dirty grout lines around the sinks and faucets, towel racks, switch plates, corners of mirrors, pictures, and anything else you come across. Spray with Red Juice, agitate with the toothbrush, and wipe with a cleaning cloth.

Shower Enclosure

When the shower is truly despicable, rely heavily on chemical cleaning power. That is, apply Tile Juice, wait (which means move on to something else to clean), and then scrub. You *must* have a tile brush to do this job properly. Rinse, reapply Tile Juice, wait again, and rescrub. You can use a razor and white pad to help remove heavy layers of soap and hard water from the glass shower door. Remember to keep the surface wet and the blade at a low angle. *And be careful!* Use the toothbrush in corners and on grout that you can't reach with the tile brush.

If the above methods don't work, shift to a pumice stick as long as it's a porcelain surface. Always use it on a surface wet with Tile Juice, Red Juice, or water. But keep it away from fiberglass or metal or plastic surfaces. *Be careful or you will damage the wall*. Test a spot on the wall first to be sure it's safe against scratches. The pumice stick requires very little pressure to work a minor miracle, so don't press hard.

The "black stuff" (or, less commonly, "red stuff") that people always complain about in bathrooms is generally mold. Most of it will be removed when cleaning the shower/tub area. What's left can be killed by spraying it with a little chlorine bleach. Just before you leave the bathroom after cleaning it, open a window and spray the bleach directly on any remaining mold. You can use it full strength or diluted up to three parts water per one part bleach. Chlorine bleach is a very powerful cleaning agent, and we are discussing its use only on areas such as ceramic tile that will not lose their color when treated with bleach. Treat bleach with utmost caution. After spraying it, leave the bathroom to avoid the fumes. Return in 20 minutes to rinse it thoroughly. Also, adjust the nozzle of the spray bottle so it squirts instead of sprays in a mist. This will help control the direction of application as well as minimize the amount of bleach vaporized into the air.

Shower-Door Tracks

It is a little-known fact that after God was finished creating hell, he had a few spare moments on his hands, so he turned his attention to shower-door tracks—thus creating a little branch office of hell here on earth. It's hard to imagine how so much dirt, sludge, soap scum, mineral deposits, and grunge can accumulate so fast in so small a space.

Advance Preparation

If you are organized well enough, you can cut down your time on this job considerably if you vacuum the tracks *when they are bone dry*. Use the long-nosed vacuum attachment along with a dry toothbrush to loosen up the grunge. You will also be getting rid of most hair plus some dried gunk, which causes a significant management problem when you're cleaning, and especially rinsing.

Cleaning

This procedure is messy, but it works for especially filthy and neglected tracks. Spray them liberally with Red Juice and clean with the tile brush. This big brush gets into both tracks at the same time. It also splashes Red

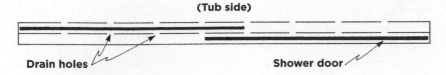

Juice and recently liberated grunge out of the tracks into the tub on one side, onto the floor on the other side, plus on you. This needs to be done just once, so persevere. Besides, you haven't cleaned the floor or tub yet, anyway.

If necessary, shift to more heavy-duty tools in this order: After the tile brush, try the toothbrush for those last hard-to-reach spots. Then try the white pad folded to fit into the track, and then the scraper with a cleaning cloth around it. Twist the scraper so it is tight against both sides of the track.

Rinsing

It's much more laborious to rinse the tracks than to clean them. Drain holes in the base of the middle rail between the two tracks are designed to drain water from the outside track to the inside track and then to the tub itself. Trouble is, they cross-feed rinse water and grunge back and forth between the two tracks until you're ready to have fits. Blotting up the dirty solution with a sponge or even cleaning cloths takes forever.

It's fastest to rinse with a shower wand or a specialized speed rinser. This will cause water to splash all over, but it will wash the loose grunge into the tub if you keep at it. Any water on the floor is potentially damaging to the floor covering, so don't get carried away. If you don't have a shower wand or speed rinser, use a large container to pour water into the tracks. An outdoor watering can works very well. Pour lots of water, so you're not really using all those drain holes that are probably clogged with grunge anyway. Instead, the water is running over the top of the tracks and carrying the grunge with it. Try to direct the water so more of it is running into the tub than onto the floor. This is easier said than done, however, so put down cleaning cloths or towels on the floor to catch the overflow as necessary.

Even rinsing as thoroughly as this, it is still difficult to stop grunge from moving back and forth and from side to side. Keep at it, and you'll get most of it. Don't even try to rinse away the very last of the grunge. Instead, use cleaning cloths to wipe out the last residue left over during rinsing. Resist the impulse to forbid anyone from ever using the shower again.

Recaulking

First a clarification of terms: We're using "caulk" to refer to the band of material that seals the junction between tile and the tub, or between the shower-door track and the tub, or other junctions where water might leak or collect. It's usually squeezed from a tube. We're using "grout" to refer to the plasterlike material between individual tiles that was rubbed in when the tile was installed. This section is about recaulking only. In Chapter 22, we say a few words about regrouting.

If the caulk is damaged or missing in areas around the tub, or if it has mold growing deeply in or behind it, take the time to repair it. If you don't correct this problem now, you will leave areas where moisture will be trapped and mold will flourish. Also, old caulk will continue to break loose when you scrub it. Repairing it will reduce your maintenance cleaning time all year long.

The time to get started on repairing the caulk is when you're cleaning the shower or tub area. Dig out the loose pieces of caulk. Or remove it all if you can. It's easier to replace it that way, and it looks better when you're finished. Use the scraper from your apron pocket.

Clean out the areas where the caulk was removed. Use Red Juice and the toothbrush and rinse thoroughly. Then finish cleaning the shower/tub. Spray the entire area you're going to repair with chlorine bleach. Do this after you've finished cleaning the whole room and just prior to leaving the room. Return in 20 minutes to rinse the bleach residue. Then *let the area dry thoroughly at least overnight*. Before anyone uses this shower again, recaulk.

Caulk for do-it-yourselfers is available at hardware stores and other mass marketers. Do the recaulking carefully. First, follow the manufacturer's directions to the letter. Do it their way. They want it to look nice, so you'll buy more of their product. Besides, they are bound to have more experience than you. Second, we have a recommendation about recaulking. Do the first line of caulk on the least conspicuous place—for example, the seam between the shower door and the tub. It's almost impossible to see this line from outside the shower, so this is a great place to practice. If you're not recaulking this area, choose the next least visible line on which to start. The same is true for caulking around the sink or the base of the toilet, where these same techniques can also be applied. (We never said this was going to be easy—but it is rewarding.)

Fiberglass

We get more questions from people on how to clean fiberglass than any other surface. Fiberglass is one of those products that is far more popular with its installers than with anyone who has to clean it. It is many times faster to install than grouted ceramic tile, but you'll notice that the installers don't stick around long enough to have to clean it, do they?

First, try not to neglect it. The reason we get all these questions is because it isn't easy to clean—so you are really compounding the problem if you let it go.

Manufacturers issue dire warnings not to use any sort of abrasive on fiberglass, and instead make utterly useless recommendations like using a mild liquid soap or detergent—which don't even faze a dirty fiberglass surface. Virtually every fiberglass cleaner on the market has abrasives, even though they may list them on the label as "earth minerals" or something else clever. There's nothing wrong with an abrasive as long as it's not too coarse, and you don't rub too hard.

We've heard all sorts of suggestions for cleaning agents—ranging from fiberglass specialty products to the rubbing compound you use on your car. The two we use most often are Tile Juice or Fiberglass Cleaner and Comet (the can swears it's now safe for use on fiberglass). Apply either with a cleaning cloth or white pad on smooth surfaces. For irregular surfaces, use the toothbrush or tile brush as well.

The most difficult cleaning problems involving fiberglass are to be found with floors that have very fine-grained strips designed to keep you from slipping. You can get these as clean as possible with your tile brush and Comet. (Because this finish is like sandpaper, you can't use white or green pads, steel wool, or cleaning cloths.)

To use the tile brush correctly (or any cleaning brush, for that matter), don't bear down as hard as you can to try to make it work better. You're only making things worse. That extra pressure splays the bristles to one side or the other, so they aren't really scrubbing anything—they're only rubbing the surface. This is a place where the "don't work harder, just smarter" concept is particularly true. Feel with the brush so that you are digging the individual tips of the bristles into the dirt lurking in the sandy, rough finish. If you do, you'll get results.

After you have cleaned the entire floor, if it still isn't as white as you'd like, try a little chlorine bleach. Open the window or door. Put a few layers of white paper towels on the shower floor and soak them with bleach. The paper towels keep the bleach from running directly into the drain. Toss the paper towels after half an hour or less (*carefully!*), rinse well, and your fiberglass is now as clean as it's going to get.

Mildew in Fiberglass Showers

Most mildew will be removed via weekly cleaning, using standard Speed Cleaning methods. In other words, apply cleaner (Red Juice, Tile Juice, or Fiberglass Cleaner as described above), agitate with a white pad and a toothbrush, and then rinse. This will remove soap scum and water spots, and it will also remove most or all of the mildew. If mildew remains, apply household liquid bleach solution. Use a spray bottle to do this, but adjust the nozzle so it squirts, rather than sprays, the bleach onto the mildew. This minimizes the amount of bleach in the air that you might breathe. (Also leave a window open if you can.) Leave the room immediately after applying the bleach, close the door if you don't appreciate bleach odor in the rest of the house, and return a few minutes later for a final rinse with cool or warm (not hot) water. Rinsing is not optional; chlorine bleach can eat away at chrome fixtures and other durable surfaces if left to its own devices. Grout, especially older grout, can begin to dissolve as well.

   Note: This method works for tile showers also.

Hard-Water Spots on Glass Shower Doors

If your glass shower doors are cloudy even after you've cleaned them with Tile Juice and the tile brush, it's time to up the ante. Clean Team Rule 7 (page 10) says: "If what you're doing isn't working, then shift to a heavier-duty cleaner or tool." In this case, shift to a white pad, possibly to a razor in a razor holder, or even to #000 steel wool. (Before using the razor or steel wool, test them in that legendary inconspicuous spot. Some shower doors that appear to be glass may actually be plastic, and the razor or steel wool will scratch plastic.)

   Another approach is to increase the amount of time the Tile Juice works on the hard-water spots before you go to work with these tools. Apply the Tile Juice, and allow it to soften the hard-water deposits by chemical action for 5 to 10 minutes. Rewet the area with Tile Juice a couple of times, if necessary. Use a scraper to remove mineral deposits where the tub and the shower

Preventing Hard-Water Spots

"It seems I spend half my life fighting hard-water spots. Is there a permanent solution that's legal?"

Yes. Install a water softener. Besides the visible hard-water spots on showers and elsewhere, hard water promotes soap deposits, scaly deposits in plumbing and appliances, and impaired cleaning action of soaps and detergents. Hard water's one good characteristic? It usually tastes better than soft water.

door frame meet. If a metal scraper leaves black marks, remove them with cleaner or use a plastic scraper instead.

Hard-water spots are a lot easier to prevent than to remove. Do this by squeegeeing away water that would otherwise dry and leave deposits. Hang a squeegee in each shower and make a new house rule: The last person to take a shower each day *must* use the squeegee to dry the shower walls and door. It takes just a few moments, but it will make a big difference. The shower walls, and especially a clear shower door, will stay clean longer and will be a lot easier to clean next time. If you have particularly hard water, take one more step, and wipe with a towel to remove any residual water after squeegeeing. If you take this short additional step, you won't have to clean the shower at all for weeks or months at a time!

Soap Scum

To clean heavy soap scum from bathroom tile, a heavy-duty liquid cleaner such as Red Juice should get it off. Manufacturers are fond of intimating that it takes a special cleaner to combat soap scum. It doesn't. Let the cleaner soak in for a longer period, and use a tile brush or a white pad with extra vigor. Resort to a razor blade in a holder if necessary, but the soap scum will come off without too much of a struggle.

If your efforts weren't successful, it could be that you're confusing soap scum with hard-water deposits, which are much more tenacious. The way to tell the difference is to scratch the afflicted area with your fingernail. Soap scum will collect under your fingernail and feel waxy. Hard-water deposits will stay put.

Shower and Counter Grout .

As you've no doubt discovered, grout is one of the most difficult surfaces to clean. It is both rough and porous at the same time. Rough surfaces are more difficult to clean than smooth ones, and dirt sinks into porous areas—out of reach of your cleaning efforts. Moreover, grout lines themselves are recessed, so most cleaning tools glide right over them. Some cleaning tools actually make the grout dirtier by pushing dirt from nearby surfaces into the grout. This is especially true when you clean a floor.

A brush, along with the appropriate cleaner (Tile Juice in showers and Red Juice on counters), is the best way to get at the grout surface and dig out embedded dirt. Use a tile brush or specialized grout brush in a shower and, depending on the area to be cleaned, a toothbrush or a handheld stiff-bristled grout brush on a counter. When cleaning vertical surfaces such as shower walls, you can really put some muscle behind a brush, but grout on horizontal surfaces like countertops can be damaged by hard scrubbing. Grease, oil, coffee, or chocolate spilled on a counter isn't moved along by gravity to a drain. Instead the grout becomes impregnated. Many household products weaken grout to the point that heavy scrubbing with a stiff-bristled brush will actually remove grout rather than clean it!

When cleaning countertop grout for the first time, go gently until you learn how strong or weak the grout actually is. If the grout has been soaked with various stains and has not been maintained well for a long period of time, you may not be able to get it clean again. Clean what you can without further damaging the grout. Let the cleaner sit on the grout a bit longer and gently use a toothbrush or other brush. Ultimately regrouting might be the best solution.

Protect new tile-and-grout countertops by being vigilant. Wipe up spills of all types—even plain water—promptly.

Note: A grout sealer can save lots of time by reducing the porosity of the grout. Apply it to new grout, and then reapply it every year or two. On old grout or when reapplying sealer, first clean the grout as well as you can and apply bleach if necessary. Rinse. Allow the grout to dry and then apply the sealer.

Toilet Bowl Rings

Assuming you've tried all manner of standard cleaning methods, including liquid bleaches, powdered cleanser, and Tile Juice, the solution may seem drastic, but it's safe and effective: a pumice stick. Pumice is a mild abrasive that's softer than porcelain (so it doesn't scratch it) but harder than the toilet ring (so it can rub it off). Make sure both the porcelain and the pumice stick are wet before starting, and then gently rub off the ring with the stick. You'll be amazed. If this is a persistent problem, think about installing a water softener.

Note: Toilet rings, which are caused by water evaporating and leaving behind tenacious mineral deposits, can cause permanent damage if ignored for long periods of time. If the stains aren't removed by pumice, and the porcelain surface is uneven in that area, you may have to replace the toilet itself to solve the problem!

Rusty Toilet Bowls

As you might expect, rust stains are usually due to iron in the water. Iron can also stain the laundry and add an unpleasant taste to the water. The most commonly used chemical to remove rust is oxalic acid. Examples of products with oxalic acid are Rust Remover, Bar Keepers Friend, and Zud. Oxalic acid is toxic, so follow the manufacturer's directions respectfully and completely. Don't use chlorine bleach on rust because it sets the stain and makes your problem worse. Another solution is to install an iron filter in the water line. Lastly, it's possible that your porcelain toilet has worn so thin over the years that the underlying metal is now exposed to water and is rusting. In this case, it's definitely time for a replacement.

Blue, green, or other unusual stains may be the result of corrosion or long-term cleaning with abrasive cleaners. They may be permanent. Chlorine bleach, peroxide, and oxalic acid products can lighten these stains, but you're probably better off replacing the fixture.

Disinfecting Toilet Bowls

Cleaning a toilet bowl by scrubbing with a toilet brush and a cleaner removes or kills nearly all bacteria. For a more complete disinfection, (1) use a powdered cleanser that contains bleach, (2) pour household chlorine bleach directly into the toilet bowl (½ cup is plenty), swish it around the bowl, then flush, or (3) purchase a specialized disinfectant. (For more about disinfection in the home, see page 426.)

Cultured Marble

Corian countertops are beautiful, but they are also a bit sensitive, so don't use anything abrasive. They can react to acids, so don't use an acidic cleaner such as Tile Juice. Instead, apply fiberglass cleaner, Red Juice, or marble cleaner or polish with a toothbrush, cleaning cloth, or a polishing cloth. Spray the surface liberally if you are using fiberglass cleaner or Red Juice, and get into the corners to loosen difficult dirt with the toothbrush (gently). Otherwise, wipe them clean and dry with a cleaning cloth. If you are using a specialized marble product, follow the manufacturer's directions. They usually tell you to apply it with a polishing cloth. Move items on the counter from left to right to clean an area, then dust and replace the items before starting the next part of the counter. Help protect the surface by sealing it.

Clogged Showerhead

To remove the hard-water accumulation, soak the showerhead overnight in a solution of one part white vinegar and two parts water. Dislodge the loosened deposits with a toothbrush. Repeat if necessary. If you have a detachable showerhead on a hose, you don't even have to remove the showerhead, just soak it in the bowl. Otherwise, it requires a wrench to remove the showerhead. Avoid scratching the chrome by putting a cleaning cloth or tape between the showerhead and the wrench.

Brass Fixtures

If your shower door has brass instead of chrome around the door, you can't safely use a strong cleaner on brass that has a coating of clear lacquer on its surface. Most brass bathroom fixtures have such a coating. Abrasive cleaners will scratch, damage, or remove sections of the lacquer. Those areas will then promptly tarnish. *Gently* clean with Red Juice or Blue Juice and a cleaning cloth.

Use brass polish only if the brass isn't protected with a lacquer coating. (Apply the brass polish after routine cleaning if you like, but it will retarnish very quickly because of the water, soap, shampoo, etc. it's exposed to daily.) Even if it's uncoated brass, powdered cleansers will scratch it and make it difficult to achieve a good shine. As you can tell, brass is tricky in bathrooms! So is gold, for that matter, but if you own gold bathroom fixtures, you probably aren't the one who cleans them.

Floor Grout

To get the grout in a ceramic tile floor white again, here's what to do occasionally, as a spring cleaning project. When the floor is completely dry, vacuum the grout lines well. Use the crevice attachment, if necessary, to remove all loose dirt. Now prepare a clear ammonia solution or use Tile Juice as is. About a cup of ammonia per gallon of water should do, but feel free to add more ammonia if necessary. Use a handheld grout brush, a grout brush on a handle (so you can stand up!), or a toothbrush to apply the ammonia solution. Dip the brush into the solution, position a row of bristles directly in a grout line, and scrub away. Use the ammonia solution sparingly, and remove the excess with a sponge or cleaning cloth as you go. If you own (or even better, if you can borrow from your neighbor) a wet-dry vacuum cleaner, it does a good job of picking up the dirty ammonia-and-water solution and saves a lot of time. Since this floor may be in the bathroom where bleach may occasionally be used on mildew, we will remind you to be careful *not* to mix ammonia and bleach together; they produce a poisonous gas that can have deadly results.

After the grout is as clean as it will get, apply grout sealer to make cleaning at least somewhat easier the next time. This method also works for dirty grout on floors in other rooms in the home.

Opinionated note: If you have a chance to choose the grout color for a new floor in your home, *don't select white*. Grays, browns, tans, and so forth are much easier to maintain.

Missed Targets

"How do you get urine out of the tile grout in the bathroom floors?"
Rewet the area with Red Juice. Scrub the area with a toothbrush and use cleaning cloths or paper towels to soak up as much as you can. Now spray with an enzyme cleaner such as Stain Gobbler. Enzymes are proteins that will break down the organic remains of the urine. This process also removes the source of any lingering odors.

White Film

If, after you clean the grouted tile in your bathroom, a white film spreads out over the cleaned area, the grout might be dissolving. The grout was not properly applied, the grout is getting old, the cleaner is strong enough to dissolve it, or you should rinse more thoroughly. Applying a grout sealer will greatly slow down the dissolving process.

If it's mildew that's built up in the white grout, first clean the grout as you clean the tiles to remove as much of the mildew as possible. Then squirt the mildewed areas with a bleach solution from a spray bottle. Leave the room and return in a few minutes to rinse off the bleach. Chlorine bleach kills mildew almost instantly.

If stains remain (and white grout often becomes permanently stained), a grout coloring agent (for example, Grout Whitener) can help. It covers up stains rather than bleaches them. These are the steps: Clean the grout, seal it, and then recolor it. The coloring product has its own applicator. Apply it, let it dry, and then wipe off any excess. Don't use this product on floors because it won't stay white very long, or on working countertops because of the various stain-producing spills that happen there. But it works well on shower walls. It cannot fix grout that is not there. That's up to you.

Mildew Prevention

Just like the old movie monsters that scared us as kids, mildew thrives in damp, dark, musty conditions. Short of the monster's foggy swamp, your bathroom couldn't be more perfect as a home for mildew. Here are some suggestions, however, to chase away mildew demons lurking in your bathroom.

1. **Keep surfaces clean. Dirt, grease, body oils, and so forth are all like Thanksgiving dinner to mildew.**

2. **Keep a squeegee in the shower, and use it on the shower walls, door, and floor after showering. Towel those areas dry after squeegeeing in extreme cases.**

3. Leave the shower door open or the shower curtains parted after you're done showering.

4. Open a window to keep fresh air circulating.

5. Leave the bathroom door ajar during showering.

6. Hang the towels, so they will dry completely before the next day's use.

7. Put a portable fan in the bathroom, and turn it on after showering to help exchange wet bathroom air for drier air from other rooms.

8. Get a dehumidifier.

9. Get really serious and install an exhaust fan.

Note: When building a home, install windows in the bathroom that are at least as big as windows in the other room of the house. Clear glass will make the room more appealing. If privacy is an issue, use the same window covering that you use on windows in other rooms—but not miniblinds.

Nonslip Strips

It's time to replace the grungy, worn-out, half-missing nonslip strips in your tub, but when you tried to pull the old ones off, you couldn't do it. Should you add new ones on top of the old ones?

No. If you double them up, the new ones won't adhere properly. The outside layer of those strips is impervious to almost all cleaning agents, so try to remove the top layer or two of the strips mechanically. Start by prying up one corner with a plastic spatula or fingernail. Try another corner if your first choice is holding tight. Or warm up the sticker with a hair dryer to soften the adhesive.

Note: A gentle heating softens the adhesive on many products, including tape, labels, and price tags.

Once you're down to the sticky residue (what's left after you get rid of the strip itself), use a solvent like Gunk Remover or lighter fluid. Allow the product to sit for as long as needed to soften the adhesive. But don't wait too long, or the solvent will evaporate, and the adhesive will reharden. Then rub with a cleaning cloth, or roll the sticker into a ball with your fingers to remove it. Clean away traces of solvent with Red Juice and a cleaning cloth.

If you can't pull off the top of the strip to expose the adhesive, use a spatula to lift the edges at least a bit. Now apply the solvent and let stand for an hour or more. It may take a while, and you may have to remove the sticker in stages, but it will give up eventually. When using a solvent, use only as much as is needed, and make sure the room is well ventilated.

Note: Before you apply new nonslip strips, prepare the surface by cleaning well with powdered cleanser. Rinse well and allow to air-dry before proceeding.

Acrylic Tubs/Spas

Acrylic tubs scratch relatively easily, but often the biggest problem is their size. Some of them are as big as a hot tub, which makes it nearly impossible to clean them without climbing in. For cleaning, most nonabrasive cleaners are fine: e.g., Red Juice, Tile Juice, Formula 409, Lime-A-Way. Rinse them away thoroughly. Avoid scouring powders like Comet or even Soft Scrub. Nor should you use a white pad, a green pad, steel wool, or a metal scraper. A soft-bristled brush on a swivel handle can allow you to do the cleaning without the risk of climbing into the slippery tub itself.

Note 1: Since acrylic tubs, hot tubs, and spas are so easy to scratch, the secret is never to let them get very dirty. Regular maintenance isn't an option if you want to keep the surface looking good. If you fall behind, it's nearly impossible to clean as aggressively as needed without damaging the acrylic surface.

Note 2: Acrylic surfaces respond well to protective wax products and specialized sealants such as Invisible Shield. Applying the protectant means an extra step, but dirt, soap scum, and hard-water spots can't cling to it as tightly as they can to the acrylic itself, making them all easier to remove.

Resurfaced Tubs

Here's the scoop. Naturally, the new surface won't be as durable as the original porcelain, so such relatively strong cleansers as Ajax and Comet shouldn't be used. Pro-Scrub, Bon Ami, and Soft Scrub are fine. Also avoid harsh chemicals that can react with the new surface, such as Tilex and X-14. Use Red Juice instead. Don't leave a rubber bath mat in the tub all the time. Take it out between uses, or it may bond with the new surface. And be aware that if you install nonslip strips, they can *never* be removed without damaging the new surface.

Shower Curtains

We have two good suggestions for speed-cleaning shower curtains. (1) Put the shower curtain in the washing machine. Throw in a couple of towels, and use warm water. Remove it before the spin cycle. (It won't be hurt if it goes through the spin cycle; it will just be very wrinkled.) Warm the curtain only slightly in the dryer (don't run the full cycle), and it will emerge close to wrinkle free. If you don't put it in the dryer, wrinkles will slowly disappear after the curtain is rehung. (2) Buy a beautiful cloth shower curtain of whatever design appeals to you. Line it with the cheapest plain white shower curtain you can find (about $6). If you trim the liner so that its hem falls about halfway between the top and the bottom of the tub, it will stay cleaner longer. When the liner starts to look dirty (in about 6 months), recycle it and install a brand-new, sparkling-clean liner. Twelve dollars a year seems a small price to pay to us, but if it doesn't seem that way to you, just wash them as above.

Note: Use only a white shower liner (or shower curtain if you have no liner) because that is the color of most hard-water spots and soap scum. Clear is the most laborious choice by far.

Streaky Mirrors

The secret to streak-free mirrors is to wipe them with a very dry cleaning cloth until they are completely dry. This usually means a few swipes beyond the point when you think you are done. You're probably wiping them with a cloth that is slightly damp and leaves just a bit of moisture on the surface. As that dries, it leaves traces of the cleaning solution as a streak.

Bath Mat Stain

"My bath mat left a colored stain on my linoleum floor that I can't get up. Any ideas?"

Yes, but we must be gentle in the telling of them. Some stains are permanent, and a stain that involves a transfer of dye from the mat or from the backing of the mat to a linoleum floor falls squarely in the permanent category. Linoleum is an almost extinct floor material that is more porous than tile or vinyl. We're not being cruel, merely truthful, when we say replace the floor, or cover the stain with a new mat.

If you still have streaks after drying the surface completely, dilute the Blue Juice or other glass cleaner with water. If the glass cleaner is more dilute, it's easier to wipe away without leaving a streak. Also, as when washing windows, never clean a mirror in the sun.

Hair Spray

Hair spray is lacquer. That's why it's difficult to remove. But rubbing alcohol, something you probably have right there in the bathroom, will remove it. Pour rubbing alcohol on a cleaning cloth or paper towel and wipe until the hair spray dissolves and is removed from a mirror or picture glass. Wipe with a dry cleaning cloth or spray with Blue Juice, and wipe dry to finish the job. It's safest not to spray Blue Juice directly on the front of the picture. It could damage the print and cause a stain if liquid is wicked up between the glass and the painting.

Note: Stand elsewhere when spritzing your hair. You know where your hair is, so standing in front of the mirror isn't absolutely essential. Once you have your hair properly coiffed, take a step or two back or to the side before spritzing.

Plants—Hanging or Otherwise

For undeniably noble and sentimental reasons, more people seem to have a dusty, dirty, decidedly unhealthy plant hanging in the bathroom than in any other place in the house. Most of these plants are at least three-quarters dead, and you really can't see the leaves through the ¼-inch layer of dust on them. Do the plant a favor and toss it. It's not really a family member, and you will still be a decent human being if you make compost out of it. And your bathroom will be greatly improved. If you miss the plant, get another one. Just promise yourself that you will take care of it this time.

Then go through the house with the same benign ruthlessness toward any other plants that merit it. My own mother has a split-leaf philodendron that is older than I am. And it looks it. (Poor thing.) In the living room, yet!

Plants get just as dirty as anything else in a room. They need cleaning as well as watering. If you wash or dust or otherwise maintain your plants, you may not have to dispose of them in 6 months. Unfortunately, many people seem to treat plants the same way they treat Levolors (miniblinds)—by doing nothing. Sorry, in both cases, you'll need to keep them clean as part of regular maintenance cleaning. You may not have to clean every inch of each plant or miniblind every time, but neither can you ignore them forever. The correct procedure is to do some of them each time you clean. Depending on the plant, a feather duster or a damp cloth is the instrument of choice.

The Kitchen

The same sequence applies to the kitchen as well as the bathroom: Clean the ceiling and walls first. Whether or not you wash the ceiling, put dirty light fixtures that you can safely remove, and that can stand it, into the dishwasher. Wash others by hand and replace. Clean the remaining part (the base) of the fixture when you come to it. If the track lights look terrible upon close inspection, clean them in place. Turn them off, let them cool, and spray and wipe with Red Juice. Resolve to try to remember to look up more often when you're cleaning and to dust them with the feather duster in the future.

Now clean the cabinet doors if they need it. This is also an appropriate time to clean out the cabinets, which you would do before cleaning the doors themselves.

Cabinets aren't easy to clean because they are usually neglected for many months. There is usually a buildup of grease, fingerprints, and other dirt that has made its way through your home and gravitated toward the kitchen.

For wood cabinets, we use a "furniture feeder"—a solution of a solvent and other cleaning and restorative agents. It cleans well and leaves a coat of carnauba wax to protect the surface until it needs cleaning again. Apply the furniture feeder with an old (disposable) cleaning cloth. Use a second cloth to wipe it away before it dries. Use fine steel wool (#0000), a white pad, or a toothbrush to help clean the cabinets. Use the toothbrush liberally if the wood has grooves or designs that you can't easily clean with steel wool and a cloth. Clean the inside of the door first. If you're lucky, inside the cupboard door may only need a touchup for the inevitable fingerprints and spots here and there.

If the cabinets have a gloss or semigloss painted surface (it doesn't matter whether it's wood or metal beneath), clean with the same clear ammonia solution you use on the walls (see Chapter 17), or use Red Juice in a spray bottle. These are often a bit easier to clean than wood cabinets. Use your white pad and toothbrush on any problem areas, but pretest this method on an inconspicuous area first.

The Stove

Another area that usually needs serious attention before you can attempt weekly cleaning of the kitchen is the *inside* surface of the stove. Beyond the pale of routine cleaning is the area under the top of your stove. Most stove surfaces just lift up by lifting up or sliding them forward a bit. If you have the owner's manual, check it for instructions. If not, you might call the customer service office of the manufacturer.

Under the stove top is one of those places to clean that illustrates your particular degree of compulsion. For instance, I barely care how much dirt and other grunge is accumulating there because I can't see it. However, I know people who practically lay awake at night worrying about this kind of unseen dirt. If there is a problem with pests (or "visitors," as pest control people delicately say), then you should keep this area clean regardless of how compulsive you are.

The way we clean this area is first to pick up any large pieces of debris (like dog biscuits or chopsticks) and then to vacuum it with the long-nosed attachment. Don't use a brush attachment, because there is enough grease here to ruin it for future use. Use the long-nosed attachment in conjunction with your toothbrush. Agitate with the toothbrush while holding the vacuum attachment close by to inhale the debris as you loosen it. After I have done this, I'm quite happy with the degree of cleanliness in this unseen area, and I replace the top and move on. If it takes additional cleaning to satisfy your individual standards, use Red Juice, a cloth, and the toothbrush.

Stove Tops

Here's the good news: you don't need to clean the greasy electric burners on your stove. You clean *around* them and *under* them, but not the burners themselves. If you have spilled something thick and sticky, first let everything cool, then clean the stove top with Red Juice, gently wipe the burner, clean under the burner where you may need a white or green pad or even #0000 steel wool, and finally turn it on to the highest temperature to burn off whatever remains. Have the exhaust fan on or the windows open to avoid setting off a smoke detector.

Glass and Porcelain Stove Tops

Streaks come from two sources. The first is that you're cleaning the stove top with a sponge and soapy water or with Red Juice or another general cleaner. Any of these products can leave a visible streak on glass. After first using one of these products to clean, respray the stove top with Blue Juice

> ## Drip Trays under Burners
>
> *"The trays under my stove's burners are nasty. Nothing gets them clean; even your dishwasher idea didn't make much improvement. Should I give up and throw them away?"*
>
> Yes! That's exactly what you should do. Replace these trays every few years when they don't come clean any longer or whenever they start to drive you crazy. As with aluminum filters for stove-top exhaust fans, you'll be surprised how inexpensive replacements are.

or another glass cleaner, and wipe it dry with a cleaning cloth. The second reason it may be streaking is that you may be cleaning it while it's still warm. In that case, the heat is evaporating the cleaner faster than you can wipe it off, and the result is streaks. Let it cool thoroughly first.

The stains on the stove top after cooking are probably caused by the pans you're cooking with. Wash the outside bottoms of your pots and pans well enough, so they can't transfer stains when you put them on the stove top or when you move them from one spot to another.

Exhaust Filters

If the aluminum filter in the hood of your stove has *never* been cleaned, it's probably a greasy mess. The situation may be hopeless, but you can always have hope. In this case, the answer is easy. Pop the filter into the dishwasher. You may have to run it through a couple of times, but it will eventually come clean. It pays to keep the filter clean because when it is, and the fan is on, it will pull in a lot of grease that would otherwise accumulate on nearby surfaces. And those surfaces can't simply be "popped" into the dishwasher.

Note: You'd be surprised how cheap a replacement filter is.

Greasy Backsplashes

Soap or detergent alone isn't strong enough for this kind of grease buildup, so you need Red Juice because it's a more powerful grease cutter. (You may find that a moderate clear ammonia solution works better than Red Juice on some types of grease.) Also, just as it helps to soak pots and pans that have baked-on grease, it helps to soak a heavy buildup of grease on tiles. To do this, spray the tiles with Red Juice; then go back and respray them a few minutes later. Keep the grease wet with Red Juice for 15 minutes or more before you start scrubbing. (Strategically position a few cleaning cloths to catch the runoff.) If the grease is especially thick, first remove most of it with a scraper; a plastic one is safe on all hard surfaces. Then use a stiff-bristled brush because bristles cut through the grease better than sponges or even white pads. They also clean the grout lines along with the tile. Continue wetting with Red Juice as you work.

If the tiles are plastic or if the backsplash is painted, the grease may have chemically interacted with the surface. If so, the paint or plastic will be permanently stained, and the grease can't be removed without damaging the tiles or removing the paint.

Greasy Bricks

Grease on a red-brick wall is no picnic to clean (at least, not any picnic *I've* been to).

If there's a stove in front of the wall, first move it away if you can do so safely. (Careful with the gas line and fixtures.) Trying to clean a wall while constantly reaching over a stove is more trouble than finding someone to help you move the stove to begin with. Next, liberally spray with Red Juice (or a moderate clear ammonia solution), and use a stiff-bristled brush to agitate the greasy area. Sop up the mess with cleaning cloths or paper towels. Try wrapping the brush with a cleaning cloth to make it easier to remove dirty cleaning solution from the brick's irregular surfaces. Because brick is porous, you'll probably have to repeat this process several times. The bricks may never get satisfactorily clean. You may have to paint them or otherwise cover them with a backsplash of some sort. A backsplash is a good idea in any event. It's a whole lot easier to clean than bricks.

Some types of old brick could be soft enough to be damaged by vigorous brushing and cleaning. Test, and if this is the case, just dust, wipe, ignore, or move.

Wood Cabinets

The beautiful wood cabinets on the walls of your kitchen are probably getting stickier and greasier with each year that passes. It sounds as if the time to take action has arrived. Here's what to do. Use a product such as Furniture Feeder. It's carnauba wax suspended in a solvent solution. The solvent removes the grease, fingerprints, splattered mustard and chocolate, long-dried spritzes of Pepsi, and so forth. The carnauba wax protects, reinvigorates, and adds new shine to the underlying coating on the cabinets.

It's a big job, however. Years-old kitchen grease does not give up without a fight. Apply Furniture Feeder to the cabinets by pouring some onto an old cleaning cloth. Starting at the top and in one corner of the kitchen, wipe the cabinets in small areas at a time. Dip a toothbrush into Furniture Feeder to clean corners, hard-to-get-at areas, or hard-to-remove spots. Add generous amounts of Furniture Feeder to your cloth regularly. Wipe each area clean, dry, and shiny with a separate cleaning cloth, or use a polishing cloth to achieve a bit more shine. This treatment with Furniture Feeder is a spring cleaning chore that comes up only once a year or so. During weekly cleaning trips around the kitchen, spot-clean the cabinets with Red Juice.

As you clean the cabinets, you will undoubtedly notice that the hinges are also filthy. That is another case where a simple toothbrush tool can quickly scrub away dirt, grime, and other gunk from the nooks, crannies, and crevices that make up a decorative cabinet hinge. Go ahead and clean all the hinges before you continue with the cabinets themselves. Just grab some Red Juice and spray, agitate with the toothbrush, and wipe with a cleaning cloth. If necessary, because of the design of the cabinet or hinge, open the cabinet door, and repeat from the inside. It's quick and nearly painless. You've probably forgotten how nice the cabinets looked when they were new.

Hard-Water Deposits on Glass Shelves

For mineral stains, say, those caused by water that seeped under a planter on a glass kitchen ledge, use Tile Juice. Squirt some on the glass, allow it to sit for a few minutes, and scrub with a white pad. Be careful! If the buildup is particularly thick, use a single-edge razor in a holder to scrape most of the Tile Juice and hard-water spots off. Then reapply Tile Juice. If possible to do so, it's safer and faster to remove the shelf to do this. Put the shelf on a flat surface, so it will be safely supported when you scrape with the razor. For general cleaning, and if they fit, put the glass shelves into the dishwasher.

Note: Don't use terra-cotta saucers directly on the glass because they aren't waterproof, and moisture seeps through. Even though water hasn't overflowed, a stain can be formed. Use a glass or plastic saucer instead of, or under, the terra-cotta saucer. Clean the saucers themselves when they look dirty.

Butcher Block

Here's the scoop. If you cut poultry on your butcher block (or plastic cutting board or other surface) and then prepare uncooked food on the same surface, you could transfer salmonella from the poultry to the other food. The salmonella on the poultry will be destroyed by proper cooking, but you and your family could be made seriously ill by the salmonella on the uncooked food.

Clean the butcher block between uses with warm, soapy water. I use a plastic scrub pad (S.O.S. Tuffy dishwashing pad) to scrub the surface. Then rinse the block with hot water, and wipe it dry. If the block is too big to move, wipe the suds off with a couple of paper towels, and then wipe dry with a final paper towel. Allow to air-dry thoroughly. You should be washing the knife (and your hands) as well. If you can remember to do it, use one side of the block for fruits and veggies and the other side for meats. While we're at it, wash your dish towels regularly. Wash and rinse sponges well, and allow them to air-dry.

Occasionally, treat the butcher block with a coat of walnut oil. Wash it well, as described above, and allow it to dry several hours or overnight. Pour walnut oil onto the butcher block, and spread it around with a paper towel. Use a bit more than is necessary, and allow the oil to remain on the surface for half an hour or so. Then wipe away the excess with several paper towels. It will look like new again for a few months.

Granite Stains

To research this topic, I went to San Francisco's preeminent stone dealer, Clervi Marble Co. It was my pleasure to meet Attilio Meschi, a man who has worked with granite, marble, and other types of natural stone for 40 years. He travels to Italy regularly to oversee his supply of raw materials, and he was a wealth of information. I wanted to apply for his job, but that's another story.

First, try to remove the stain with 12 percent hydrogen peroxide and a few drops of ammonia. (Hydrogen peroxide for bleaching hair is 12 percent; for first aid, it's only 3 percent.) If that doesn't do it, Mr. Meschi recommends a poultice: a cleaner or chemical mixed with an absorbent material and then applied to the stain. An organic stain should respond to a poultice of hydrogen peroxide and Bon Ami. You may substitute talc, white molding plaster, powdered chalk, whiting, or fuller's earth for Bon Ami. (Mr. Meschi actually uses 32 percent hydrogen peroxide and painter's whiting, which may make the work go a bit faster but are more difficult to find.) Mix the two ingredients to the consistency of cake frosting, and use a plastic scraper or spatula to apply it ¼- to ½-inch thick over the stain. Cover the poultice with plastic sheeting or plastic wrap, and tape the edges to the granite. (If you use a tape like blue Scotch masking tape that doesn't leave any residue, you won't have that problem to deal with later.) Allow it all to remain for 24 hours. Then remove the tape and plastic, and allow the poultice to dry for another 24 hours. Wipe off the poultice, clean the area with water, dry with a cleaning cloth, and inspect the stain. If it disappeared, great. If the stain is lighter, repeat the process. If it's not improved after three tries, give up or call a professional.

A poultice can also be made using cotton balls or gauze pads. For small stains, that might be easier. Put either over the stain, wet with the hydrogen peroxide (but not to the point of dripping). Then cover and tape as above. You can also substitute acetone for hydrogen peroxide. Actually, if the granite is quite dark, it would be safer to try the acetone first because of the very slim possibility of a bleaching effect from the hydrogen peroxide. As usual, it's also smart to pretest.

For oil stains, the poultice can be made with (a) baking soda and water, (b) poultice powder (e.g., Bon Ami) plus mineral spirits, or (c) cotton balls or gauze plus mineral spirits.

Note: Granite is far more resistant to stains and acids than is marble. But "resistant" doesn't mean that it won't stain at all. To guard against stains, most natural stone surfaces should be sealed and perhaps also waxed. Check with your installer or other professional for a recommendation about products for your particular stone.

Stained Porcelain Sinks

Since coffee stains porcelain, and pots and pans make black marks, put leftover coffee directly into the drain, and use a protective pad or position a sponge to keep the pans from direct contact with the porcelain. It makes sense to provide this sort of protection to reduce the number of stains and black marks you produce and that you must subsequently scrub off again.

Aggressive cleaning with harsh products damages the porcelain over time. Intensive, lengthy rubbing of a surface with practically any cleaning product (harsh or not) can damage the surface. Green pads, metal cleaning pads, or steel wool can be murder on surfaces. In most cases, the damage consists of small scratches in the surface in which all manner of stains get trapped.

Liquid finishes such as Invisible Shield are available for sinks (also tubs, shower walls, shower doors, fiberglass and acrylic spas, etc.). Such products provide a protective barrier. The dirt is easier to remove from the smooth surface of the protectant than from the rougher surface of the porcelain itself. As you might guess, protectants can also add a bit of shine to the surface. They are designed to be applied only occasionally—something like car wax. Although they save cleaning time, it will obviously take time to apply them. You'll have to decide if you're willing to put in a bit of extra effort to get nicer-looking and nicer-feeling surfaces.

Note: New sinks, tubs, tiles, etc., are free of scratches and therefore far easier to clean. In fact, plain Red Juice or other liquid cleaner is all you need for new fixtures. Don't use powdered cleanser or even "soft" cleansers on a new sink by habit. Wait until you actually need them.

Rusty Stainless Sinks

If your stainless steel sink shows signs of rust, it may be coming from the sink itself or from metal things attached to it (like the faucet or drain ring).

"Miracle" Mops

"What do you think of those exotic mops that are sold on TV every hour of the day and night?"

I hope you don't feel bad if you've bought one, but I think they're a waste of money. I suspect that not one of them has been offered because it represents a legitimate advance in the evolution of the mop, but rather because some marketing-driven company is out to make a buck—or a million of them—if they can talk us into buying one. A European-style flat mop (a Sh-Mop, for example) with a terry-cloth cover is so much better. The American version we use is quite similar. It's genuinely faster, it doesn't recycle dirty water back to the floor, and it reaches under appliances and into corners. Because its terry-cloth covers are washable, it's like a new mop each time you use it.

But the sink itself may be rusty. Stainless steel is still mainly iron, with up to 30 percent chromium. Even stainless steel deteriorates over time. It just takes longer than other steels.

Whatever the source, powdered cleanser and a white pad will remove most rust spots. Use a toothbrush on areas you can't reach with the white pad. If the white pad doesn't work well, try #0000 steel wool. The rust stains or rust in porcelain sinks, tubs, etc., can also be removed with a special rust-neutralizing product (e.g, Rust Remover, Bar Keepers Friend, Zud) that contains oxalic acid. Oxalic acid is the main weapon against rust problems of all sorts.

The Rest of the Kitchen

There usually isn't a lot of high dust in the kitchen. If so, and if it isn't greasy, and if you didn't wash the walls and ceilings already, make a trip around the room knocking it down. You can use a broom or the vacuum with a brush attachment. If the dust is impregnated with grease, don't knock it down. Either use the vacuum with no attachment to get the worst of it, or use the broom to catch it. But don't let it fall all over everything. Or you can keep cleaning normally and spray and wipe it off as you come to it.

The same techniques used in the bathroom with your toothbrush will help with difficult areas here in the kitchen. Hard-water problems are solved in the same way also, but don't use a pumice stick on a stainless-steel fixture.

Remember the poor plant in the bathroom? In the kitchen, it has been reincarnated as a dirty, stained, misshapen sponge by the sink. Sometimes, right next to it is a scrubber of some vintage that is barely recognizable as such anymore. Please throw them away. Ignore tips about how to rejuvenate or otherwise bring these poor things back to life. Bury them. Replace the sponge whenever the old one looks dirty or starts to stink. (I get them in packs of four for about 20 cents each.) Also replace the scrub brush, and then leave it under the sink instead of out with the sponge. They learn bad habits from each other.

When all these tasks are finished, you can start the normal/maintenance/routine Speed Cleaning trip around the kitchen. There is undoubtedly harder work to do during this initial cleaning, but routine Speed Cleaning won't go very fast until you're finished with the preliminary cleaning. Have an extra supply of Red Juice on hand, lots of cleaning cloths, and abundant perseverance.

The Dishwasher Rule

This rule applies to things found in any room of the house: *If it fits, put it in the dishwasher.* This includes light fixtures from any room or the front or back porch; the grease filter over the stove; many porcelain knickknacks that get filthy over time; any removable parts of the can opener, toaster oven, or other small appliances; some dish-drying racks; or any other items that you can think of that would not be affected by the hot water, detergent action, and heat of drying. The welfare of some of these items will require that you skip the dishwasher's extremely hot drying cycle. You may be amazed at how sparkling clean the dishwasher can get items that had caked-on dust or grease—especially ones with lots of little nooks and crannies that are murder to get at any other way.

Stinky Dishwashers

Your dishwasher should smell like the detergent used in it. I checked for advice with Al Hale, owner of Accurate Appliances in San Francisco, who has been keeping our appliances running for the past 15 years or so. He said the most common reason for an odor is an improperly installed garbage disposal! The disposal water line may allow food from the disposal to be thrown into the dishwasher line. If you've recently installed a disposal, that could be the culprit. Three other possibilities are (1) the rubber door gasket that forms the lower seal has started to disintegrate and is creating its own odor, (2) the heating element is burned out and gives off an odor when it cycles on and off, or (3) gunk has accumulated in the area between the lower front of the dishwasher and the door. This last possibility has a cleaning solution: Clean that area carefully with a toothbrush and Red Juice. Call in a professional—like Al—for the other possibilities.

After you've solved the problem, run the dishwasher with a quarter cup of white vinegar to help remove any lingering odors. Start the dishwasher empty of dishes or soap. When it fills with water the first time, open the door, add the vinegar, and let the cycle complete itself.

Dishwasher Stains

Hard-water spots can be removed by running vinegar through your dishwasher's cycle. As a mild acid, it will help dissolve these deposits. Start the dishwasher empty, and add white vinegar after it fills with water for the first cycle. Add as much as you can without causing an overflow—up to 2 or 3 cups. Vinegar is a weak cleaner, so you may have to repeat this process. Hard-water deposits generally don't harm the interior of the dishwasher permanently. But if the water has an extremely high mineral content, stains will start to appear on glassware and dishes and can damage the dishwasher pump. Consider installing a water softener. If you're not using liquid rinse agents (see below) already, I suggest you do so. The humane thing to do might be to give your venerable dishwasher a well-deserved rest, and start over with a new one.

   Note: When doing your regular kitchen cleaning, remember to open the dishwasher as you go by and clean the interior edges of the door. This area isn't cleaned by the action of the dishwasher, and it gets rather disgusting if ignored. Use Red Juice, a toothbrush, and a cleaning cloth.

Hard-Water Deposits on Dishes

At the grocery store, in the same area as dishwasher soap, is a product known as a liquid rinse agent. Add it to the dishwasher's dispenser for automatic rinse agents. My dishwasher has such a dispenser—right next to where I add the detergent. *Voilà!* No more hard-water spots. I've also learned that #0000 steel wool will quickly remove hard-water spots from drinking glasses.

Salt and Pepper Shakers

Ever notice how much time restaurant staffs spend cleaning salt and pepper shakers? Sitting there on the stove at home, they're collecting grease, grime, and splatters, plus enough heat to harden them into a film that's nasty to get off. However, Red Juice and a white pad will clean them nicely and with minimum effort. Then clean the holes with a toothpick.

Can Openers

Don't toss your can opener in the can just yet. If it's a hand-operated one, put the whole thing in the dishwasher. (First give it a quick scrubbing with a toothbrush and a shot of Red Juice.) If it's electric, slide the cutting mechanism away from the body of the opening, and put only that part in the dishwasher. The body can easily be cleaned with Red Juice, a cleaning cloth, and probably a toothbrush. *Any* small appliance with difficult-to-get-to knobs, buttons, corners, and molded parts is an ideal place for a tooth-brush to come to the rescue. Naturally, do unplug small appliances before you start bathing them in Red Juice or anything else.

The Rest of the House

Now that the "wet" jobs are out of the way, it's downhill from here. The biggest chore left before you can begin weekly cleaning is probably lots of vacuuming. Our general rule is to vacuum almost everything first if there is a heavy buildup of dust. Even if you're going to wash the woodwork or the windows, you should vacuum the woodwork and sills first to avoid having to remove all the mud you'd make. The vacuum will quickly remove the dust in the corners and on the woodwork, furniture, lamps, tables, etc. If you get that same dust wet, it's far more difficult to wipe it out of all the corners and tight spots.

Heavy Dust

Before we go on about dust per se, indulge us in a short rumination. We were astounded one day when somebody asked us what dust *is*. (Think about it. What is it, really—baby dirt? Will each piece of dust grow up to be a dirt clod?) Considering the fact that The Clean Team has collectively spent thousands of hours dealing with it, we really didn't have a ready response.

So we looked up *dust* in, naturally enough, the dictionary. We thought you might appreciate this remarkable definition from the *American Heritage Dictionary*. Starts out conventional and then gets pretty weird.

> **dust (dust)** *n.*
> 1. Fine particulate matter.
> 2. A cloud of such matter.
> 3. Such matter regarded as the result of disintegration.
> 4. Disturbance; confusion; excitement.
> 5. a. Earth, especially when regarded as the substance of the grave: "Dust thou art, and shalt to dust return." (Milton).
> 5. b. The surface of the ground.
> 6. A debased or despised condition.
> 7. Something of no worth.
> 8. *British.* Ashes, household dirt, or rubbish. [From the Indo-European *dheu-*: The base of a wide variety of derivatives

meaning "to rise in a cloud," as dust, vapor, or smoke, and related to semantic notions of breath, various color adjectives, and *forms defective perception of wits.* (Emphasis added.)]

Disintegration! Confusion! Debasement! Defective wits! All that having to do with lowly dust—who would have imagined?

But back to the practical side of the subject at hand. Routine dust management is a task for daily or weekly cleaning. As we discussed in the first part of the book, your main ally in the war against dust is a professional feather duster made of ostrich down.

But what do you do if you encounter a really nasty accumulation of dust—something beyond the capacity of a feather duster? Something like, let's say, under the refrigerator, in a storage room, or in back of the washer/dryer, or behind Aunt Sophie's hatbox collection in the closet? In such cases, the feather duster would not be able to absorb the volume of dust and would just spread it around.

The main objective, besides removing dust, is not to make work for yourself by spreading the dust into the air or onto other surfaces. There is a difference between "old dust" and "new dust": Old dust is the dust you are trying to remove. New dust is what will resettle 2 minutes after you finish cleaning. Keep *new* dust to a minimum by making as little as possible of the *old* dust airborne. This is best done during heavy cleaning by using the vacuum cleaner rather than the feather duster. The equipment of first choice is the Little Vac equipped with the long-haired brush attachment at the end of the hose. Use any other vacuum if you don't have a Little Vac.

Vacuuming

If there are very dusty rafters, ceilings, or heavy cobwebs in your home, you should make an initial trip around the room with a long vacuum wand or broom to speed up the job. It's surprisingly easy to crash into things while you're doing that, so be extra careful.

The way to vacuum heavy dust is to start in one corner of the room and work your way around the perimeter of the room. Start high to get the cobwebs and high molding, and then vacuum all the way to the floor molding. Be sure to vacuum pictures and small objects as you come to them. Carefully.

If the objects are densely spaced in an area, you'll have to vacuum one, put it down in a clean spot, and repeat these steps for all other objects in the immediate area. Place each object in the temporary area in the same relative position in which you had originally found it, so it will be easier to restore everything to the original positions. Then vacuum the shelf or area in which the objects were originally located, and restore the objects to their original positions.

Also vacuum lamp shades, mirrors, furniture, plants (as is possible, or shake them thoroughly), drapes, miniblinds, window frames and sills, shelves, shutters, and heater and exhaust vents. Make a special effort around the TV, VCR/DVD player, and sound system—especially their power cords. Vacuum the TV knobs and the cloth over the speakers. Move the TV out from the wall if you can manage it or if you can find some help. Vacuum the back thoroughly and the floor area where it was. In fact, move anything and everything in the room that you can when doing heavy cleaning. In the middle of the room, vacuum the furniture and light fixtures (including their chains). As with the other rooms, clean light fixtures in the dishwasher if possible. If the fixture has been broken for months, now is the time to get serious about replacing it. It's not fair to spend a day or two making your home sparkle and then have company notice mainly the broken fixture in the hallway.

If your vacuum doesn't have a long cord, use a 50-foot extension cord when vacuuming, so you don't waste time having to stop to unplug and replug it all the time. You can't imagine how much time this will save until you've tried it.

The vacuum may need your help under these heavy dust conditions. If you encounter large debris that may clog the vacuum, pick the debris up and pop it into the debris pocket of the cleaning apron. The vacuum doesn't like things like straw, string, or thread, even though they don't appear to clog the hose. They act as a trap for debris in the vacuum hose and can build up to a genuine clog in no time at all. So resist the temptation to inhale such things into the vacuum.

Check the vacuum bag. Please. Don't go through the effort of vacuuming the entire house without checking to see if the bag is full! It's a false economy to be too frugal with vacuum bags: Don't wait until the bag is bulging at the seams before you change it. A stuffed bag puts a significant load on the vacuum motor and interferes with its ability to clean. Worse yet, if the bag is full, the dust is being expelled back into the room! Most professionals change it when it's only half full.

While you're using the vacuum, pay attention to the noise of the motor. If it shifts to a high whine, stop and check the bag. If the bag isn't full, there's a clog in either the hose or the wand. To find out where it is, disconnect the

hose or sections of wand at various intervals and put your hand over the end.
If putting your hand over the end does not make any difference—that is, the
vacuum continues to be clogged, and you feel no suction—then the clog is
downstream: somewhere between your hand and the bag. If the motor sud-
denly jumped back down to its normal pitch when you disconnected the
hose—that is, putting your hand over the end made the motor whine again,
and you felt suction—then the clog is upstream: somewhere between the inlet
and where you separated the wand. This sounds more complicated than it is
in practice: It's just a matter of locating the clog, which is worth the effort.
We're amazed when people vacuum an entire house with a full vacuum bag
or clogged hose. It's hard enough to vacuum once, let alone having to do it
all over again and have it be an exercise in futility! Most clogs can be cleared
by reversing the direction of suction.

If you have a model with a motorized beater-bar attachment, one other
mechanical thing you might check is the condition of the fan belt. Once
again, some people are content to vacuum the whole house with the beater
bar inoperative. It may be due to a burned-out motor or bad connection of
the power cord, but the most likely cause is a fan belt that has hopped off its
tracks or snapped apart. If the problem recurs regularly, the suction of the
beater bar on the surface of the rug may be too great, and the fan belt may be
put under too great a strain as a result. If so, reduce the suction with your particular machine's way of compensating—usually an adjustable opening to let
more air in the wand. To replace the fan belt, be brave. Flip the beater bar on
its back and remove the backplate with a screwdriver. The rest is just common
sense. If all else fails, read the directions.

Chandeliers

A chandelier is one thing you do *not* want to take apart and pop into the
dishwasher. There are several specialized chandelier cleaners on the market
that allow you to clean them in place.

Whichever product you decide to use, it's just a matter of inundating the
chandelier with the sprayed-on solution from top to bottom. Then let it drip-
dry onto a layer of newspapers you've placed under it. A sensible precaution
is to lay down a piece of plastic or an old sheet underneath the newspapers.
The newspapers can become saturated and transfer ink to the carpet.

First, because the chandelier obviously has to be turned off during this exercise, arrange for alternate lighting, if necessary, so you can see what you're

doing. Since we assume you regard the preservation of life and limb as a high priority, we urge you to put a piece of tape over each electrical switch that can electrify the chandelier (and you!) during your cleaning efforts. Perhaps greater than the risk of shock is the risk that you might be startled while perched on the ladder and lose your balance. Who knows what you might grab as you fall? Remember that scene from *Phantom of the Opera* where the chandelier descends with such spectacular results? Need we go on? Actually we will, for the truly prudent will throw the circuit breaker or unscrew the fuse that serves the chandelier. This is the safest way to proceed. However, it will probably complicate providing a source of alternate lighting. (Time to find that extension cord.)

Before you spray the chandelier, vacuum or dust it if possible. Then, spray liberally. Aim straight at the chandelier or from slightly below it, but not from above. This will minimize the amount of liquid that soaks into the light sockets. As you spray, you will notice that a coat of dirt comes loose almost immediately and starts dripping onto the newspapers below. Continue spraying each area until the visible dirt has been rinsed off and clear solution is all you can see on the chandelier. You can approach the individual pieces from countless angles. Try to follow as many of them as possible while spraying. After you've sprayed it, you can enhance your cleaning job by wiping dry the pieces of crystal that are easy to reach and can be wiped safely—both for you and for the chandelier. Resist the impulse to fuss, and allow the balance of the chandelier to air-dry. If you noticed any rust while you were up there spraying cleaner all over the place, it would be a good idea to speed up the drying (and slow down the rusting) by turning up the heat or aiming a fan at the chandelier until it's dry.

Before cleaning any type of light fixture, make sure the bulbs are not only extinguished but are cool as well. When a bulb is hot, the filament is as frail as a piece of cigarette ash. One little jiggle, and the filament will be destroyed. Also a hot bulb may explode if you spray it with a cool liquid cleaner.

White Rings on Furniture

What most furniture rings have in common is that moisture has become trapped in the finish. It's a sort of permanent fog. If you can coax the moisture out with an appropriate restorative (e.g., Furniture Feeder, Howards Restor-A-Finish), the ring will vanish before your eyes. Shake the product well, and then pour a small amount on the spot or the polishing cloth according to product directions. Rub a small area of the ring gently but firmly with the polishing cloth. It's safest to rub back and forth with the grain of the wood, but try any combination, including against the grain, to remove the ring. After some moments—from a few to quite a few—that segment of the ring should start to fade and then disappear. If such is the case, continue as directed until the entire ring vanishes. If not, try the same procedure, only with paste wax this time.

If these preliminary skirmishes didn't work, hold your breath and apply the restorative with #000 steel wool instead of the polishing cloth. A word of caution: Intensive rubbing with either the polishing cloth or the steel wool can start to destroy the finish on many antiques, depending on the type of finish, its age, and its overall condition. Be sure to test that legendary inconspicuous spot first. Yes, I know that spot doesn't have a ring on it, but just test to be sure that you aren't damaging the finish with the cloth and solvent, and test it again if you up the ante to steel wool.

Note: I know it isn't easy, but don't be shy about offering coasters to your guests. It will save you from repeating this chore.

Artificial Plants

The fastest way to dust silk plants is to use the brush attachment of a vacuum. If the vacuum isn't effective alone, use it along with a handheld dusting brush. If the dirt on the silk plant is sticky and can't be removed by these methods, add a small amount of dishwashing soap to a sinkful of warm water, and *gently* swish the plant in the solution. Rinse *gently* with clean warm water and allow to air-dry. (Of course, first test for colorfastness on a potential candidate for martyrdom.)

Note: Some things are nonmaintainable. If your artificial plant is dirty, can't be satisfactorily dusted, or fails the inconspicuous spot test, it's time to toss it.

Dried Plants

When you first install a dried flower arrangement or wreath in your home, start dusting it carefully and attentively with a feather duster as you clean your way around the room. This will remove cobwebs and some of the dust.

But dried flower arrangements by their nature are too delicate to withstand rigorous cleaning methods. And accidents will inevitably befall them: Flowers will fall off, twigs will snap, and so on. Accordingly, dried flower arrangements have fairly short life spans. If you have one that is cherished, consider having a clear plastic dustcover made for it at a plastic shop. They're not very expensive, they're considerably easier to dust, and you can still enjoy the appearance of the plants. Otherwise, no matter how beautiful they once were and no matter how expensive they were when purchased, dried plants should not be considered heirlooms to be passed from generation to generation.

Lamp Shades

Lamp shades with their rough and complex surfaces are particularly good dust catchers. Get rid of the current serious accumulation with a dusting brush. Then routinely use a feather duster or the brush attachment of a vacuum during regular cleaning sessions.

Water-Stained Vase

This is one case when the put-it-in-the-dishwasher rule doesn't work. The dishwasher does a fine job of cleaning the outside of a vase but of course completely misses the inside. Instead pour enough white vinegar and water (1:1 ratio) into the vase to cover the stain line. Allow it to stand for several hours or overnight. Before emptying, insert a bottle brush and scrub. Then empty and rinse. You can speed up the process considerably if you substitute Tile Juice for vinegar. Tile Juice is more difficult to rinse, however.

Cleaning Ceramic Pieces

"I have a ceramic frog in a suggestive pose (dressed in a painted-on bikini). Yes, it's ugly, but I love it and want to know how to clean it. It's almost impossible to clean—nothing will fit into the hard-to-reach areas."

Put your ugly-duckling-but-beloved frog into the dishwasher. If it has a hole in the bottom of it, put it in bottom side down, so it won't fill up with water. If it has felt or other protectors on the bottom, you have a decision to make. You can (1) wash it anyway. If the protectors disappear, replace them. There are packages of protectors of all shapes and styles available at hardware stores. (2) Clean it by hand. Use Q-Tips or a soft brush along with a cleaner such as Red Juice to reach into all those places you can't otherwise get to.

If the opening or the design of the vase won't allow a brush, pour out almost all the solution, and add a teaspoon or more (depending on the size of the vase) of uncooked rice or beans. Cover the top with your hand, and swirl and shake the vase to allow the rice or beans to rub off the loosened stain. Repeat if necessary.

Oil Paintings

This is tricky business, and something we have little experience with, so we turned to a professional conservator of paintings—Carolyn Tallent, from Santa Monica, California—for her wise counsel. She advises: (1) Inspect every square inch of the surface—in search of loose or flaking paint, hairline cracks, or other damage. If any are present, take the painting to a pro. (2) Remove the painting to a flat surface, or lean it against a wall where you can work on it without fear of its falling. (3) Dust the surface. As Carolyn observes, you can imagine what a hallway mirror would look like if you hadn't dusted it for several years. That's the sort of schmutz your painting is covered with. So—how to dust? The trick is to use a soft brush. Some paintbrushes are too stiff; choose a natural-bristle brush with feathered tips or, even better, a soft camel-hair brush available at art supply stores. She suggests dedicating this brush for dusting your paintings only. (4) If the dust deposits are heavy, hold the long-nosed nozzle attachment of the vacuum cleaner a couple of inches from the surface as you work so the dust doesn't resettle. (5) Stop after a thorough dusting because further cleaning with water is fraught with disastrous possibilities. However, if the painting has no great value, if you feel like living dangerously, and if the painting needs further cleaning, roll (not rub) cotton swabs lightly dampened with plain water over the surface. Don't use *any* type of soap or household cleaner. If the painting has sentimental value, or if the monetary value of the painting is unknown, don't go beyond dusting.

Furniture Wax Buildup

Certain restorative solvents, such as Furniture Feeder and Howards Restor-A-Finish, for example, dissolve wax buildup. Apply the solvent to a disposable polishing cloth or directly to the furniture (pretest). Loosen and remove the old wax with the polishing cloth, assisted by a toothbrush in nooks and crannies. (Check first to be sure that the toothbrush doesn't scratch the finish.) During the removal phase, you can position the toothbrush over the cloth so the bristles poke the cloth into these same nooks and crannies.

Note: In the future, don't use wax on the intricate parts of wood furniture for more than one coat. Rewax only the flat tops and occasionally the flat sides.

Marble Bar

I've had great luck removing hard-to-remove things that you can feel from marble with a razor blade. First wet the surface with Red Juice, and gently scrape with the blade at a low angle. Use a fresh single-edge razor in a holder. For glass rings on a marble bar top, first try a combination marble polish and cleaner—or good old Red Juice. Apply either, and wipe well. You might also try leaving the polish and cleaner on the ring for several hours before wiping.

Stone International (Florence, Italy) says light rings or stains can be removed by applying a small amount of hydrogen peroxide or clear ammonia. Use #0000 steel wool, if necessary, "with a very light hand." (I suggest consulting a professional before having at it with steel wool.) At the very least, pretest. Afterward, wipe clean, let dry and, Stone International suggests, apply a wax such as Johnson's paste wax. I don't agree with applying wax, but a marble sealer is important.

Discouraging note: Marble can last for centuries (just ask the Romans), but it is porous enough to stain and is remarkably vulnerable to acids. Unfortunately, a great number of drinks are acidic (e.g., wine, citrus juices, colas, cranberry juice, and tomato juice). The same is true of fruits often found near a bar (e.g., lemons, limes, and oranges). So it's likely that something acidic has etched its way into the surface as a permanent feature. If so, it's not dirt at all, and no manner of cleaning will prevail against it. It's time to consult a professional who will work over the area with a buffer and a pumice or rottenstone abrasive. In the meantime, immediately wipe off *anything* spilled (rinse if the spill is acidic), and don't allow beverage glasses to be set directly on the marble.

Candle Wax

To remove candle wax from a table, first scrape 95 percent of it off with a plastic scraper. The wax will come off in chunks if it's cool, and it will peel off if it's warm. To collect the loosened wax, use either a whisk broom and

Steam Radiator

"I need a nifty device or an even niftier suggestion for cleaning dust and grime out from between the tubes (or whatever they are called) of an old-fashioned steam radiator. My dust cloth–and–yardstick method is getting old, and it doesn't work anyway!"

We do have something nifty for you: a rabbit ear duster. The "ears" of the duster can be bent into whatever shape you want, and they will stay put. Bend them to fit the part of the radiator you want to clean. Use them dry to dust, or spray them with Red Juice if the grunge is more serious.

dustpan, or a vacuum cleaner. You will get good at this and learn how to remove practically all the wax in just a few minutes. The second step is to spray the remaining bit of wax with furniture polish and wipe it off with a polishing cloth as you're polishing the entire tabletop.

Candlesticks can be cleaned approximately the same way. While holding a candlestick over a trash can or newspapers, use the same plastic scraper to remove most of the wax. Warm, soapy water and a sponge will remove the rest.

Note 1: Remove candle wax from a tablecloth using the same warm-iron-and-paper-towel method described in "Grease and Wallpaper" on page 216, except now you can put paper towels on both sides. Pour a little liquid soap on the spot and launder as usual.

Note 2: A glass ring called a bobeche (bo-BESH) slips over the candle, sits at its base, and catches most of the wax before it drips onto the table. It's found at good hardware stores and is downright cheap.

Louvered Accordion Doors

Clean these no differently from other doors. It only seems more daunting, and it takes longer because of all the louvers and hinges. In most cases, you aren't cleaning the entire door. Spray just the fingerprints and other smudges with Red Juice, and wipe them with a cleaning cloth. Use the vacuum brush attachment to remove dust from the louvers each week or at least occasionally.

When it's time to clean the whole door, spray it with Red Juice or use a bucket with a dilute to moderate clear ammonia solution, and wipe it from top to bottom. Use a toothbrush liberally around ends of louver hinges and other hard-to-reach areas, such as molding, corners, and handles, and on marks that don't come off with a cleaning cloth alone. Clean the frame around the door at the same time.

Mildew Lurking in the Closet

Chlorine bleach is the best and cheapest mildew fighter. If the walls are dirty besides being mildewy, first wash them with a dilute ammonia solution, and then wipe them dry with a cleaning cloth. Depending on the surface, the paint, and other factors, this may also remove the mildew. If not, wipe the mildew with a bleach solution, and wipe again with a wet cloth to remove most of the bleach.

WARNING: Don't mix the ammonia and bleach or use bleach before the ammonia has been wiped off and the walls are dry. Bleach and ammonia together are dangerous. If you prefer not to smell ammonia in such small quarters, trisodium phosphate or Red Juice will also work well.

To discourage the mildew from returning, keep the closet as clean and dry as possible. Leave the door open. Mildew loves dirt, so store only clean clothes and clean shoes in the closet. Allow space between clothes and shoes. (If the closet is overflowing, see our other book, *Clutter Control,* for a step-by-step plan for solving that problem.) Brush mildew off shoes regularly. Keep a light on in the closet for several hours a day or even continuously during the season when mildew growth is greatest. If it lacks both a light and an outlet, buy a droplight at a hardware store and *safely* hang it in the closet. Next time the closet is painted, ask the painter or paint supplier to add an antimildew agent to the paint.

Dog Dragging in Dirt

Your dog probably has a favorite sleeping spot in the garden somewhere. It's cool and comfortable there. Coax him or her to rest in a cleaner, more civilized outdoor location of your choice by putting a bed in that spot. Or put an old blanket or towel at the place in the garden where the dog sleeps. Two other things you can do: (1) Dedicate one entry for the dog and hang a brush near that door. (Don't just set it near the door. It will disappear before the week is out.) Whoever opens the door to let the dog in should use it to brush off the dirt/mulch mixture before the dog is allowed to enter. (2) Long hair catches mulch, so consider giving the dog a haircut—seriously— especially if the dog is also uncomfortably warm in hot weather.

Note: I assume you have doormats in place. Also, supplement the brush with a towel in wet weather. Use it to wipe the dog's feet before mud is tracked throughout the house.

Fleas

First, you need to understand the life cycle of the flea to understand what must be done. It's somewhat horrific, but as explained to me by my dog's favorite caregiver, San Francisco veterinarian Daniel Hershberger, it goes something like this: Adult fleas are homebodies. Once they're on the host, they prefer to stay there for the balance of their lives. They don't hop on and off. Flea eggs, however, do fall off the animal. The eggs hatch into larvae, which wiggle to a protected area—e.g., in or under the edge of a carpet. They dine on flea feces that fall in the same area. The larvae turn into cocoons that can remain inactive for months. This hard-cased cocoon stage is so well protected that it's resistant to some pesticides. But when conditions are right—including temperature, moisture, and availability of food (such as a dog or cat, or its owner, for that matter)—the cocoon can hatch into a full-size flea in as little as 60 seconds. Discouraging, eh?

The secret, then, to controlling fleas is to vacuum them up when they are in the egg, larval, or cocoon stages of their nasty little lives. This is easy enough to do in theory, but it requires attention and repetition. Flea eggs are about the size of a grain of salt, and the other stages are even bigger, so most vacuums will capture them in their dust bags. But vacuum the carpet slowly enough that the flea eggs, larvae, and cocoons can be pulled up and out of the carpet. Vacuum thoroughly. Go 6 inches or so under the edge of carpeting as well as completely under beds and furniture. Either put a chunk of flea collar in your vacuum bag, or remove the dust bag after each vacuuming, seal it (tie it up inside a plastic grocery bag), and discard it. In addition, wash the animal's bedding every few weeks.

If you also keep most of the fleas off the animals by regular washing with flea shampoo or with monthly pills (talk to a vet), your home will be essentially flea free with no chemicals at all, except for the shampoo. Can you say "flea free" quickly 10 times?

Wicker Furniture

What's difficult about wicker furniture, for cleaning purposes, is that dust settles in out-of-the-way places on the individual strands used to weave the furniture. Use the brush attachment of your vacuum. Better yet, use it along with a handheld dusting brush or paint brush. Loosen the dirt with the dusting brush while holding the vacuum close by to inhale the dislodged dust.

Note: There are those who swear that putting wicker furniture into the shower once a year removes lots of dirt and is actually good for the furniture: It helps keep it flexible or something. I have my doubts—unless you get in the shower too, and scrub the furniture with a soft brush and soap—but it may be worth a try. Just don't send us a bill if it all unravels.

Body Odor in Upholstery

To get body odor out of upholstered furniture, have it professionally cleaned. If you're not so inclined, use detergent and water or an upholstery cleaner. Use minimal amounts of cleaner, letting the suds (not water) do the cleaning, and agitate gently with a cleaning cloth (occasionally even a toothbrush). Blot excess moisture with fresh cleaning cloths. Work in small sections. There may be rental equipment available if you want to try that.

Rolltop Desk

To clean grunge in the little grooves between the wood slats that do the rolling, once again, the brush attachment of a vacuum cleaner comes in handy. Use it to dig into those grooves and remove all the loose dirt. Clean the remaining dirt out with Red Juice–moistened cotton swabs (Q-Tips). If you're still in the mood, a wipe with furniture polish should bring back the shine, and your desk should start to look like the heirloom it may become.

Minor Repairs

If you're spring cleaning, and you come across nicks or gouges in walls or door frames, think about patching them with spackle and spot-painting them as a follow-up to the cleaning job. This minor repair process may not be the same caliber as a professional would do. You may even redo it when you get around to painting the room. But for now, even if these spots look a little different from the rest of the wall (cleaner, or shinier, or whatever), the overall effect is quite positive. A spot that once bothered you practically every time you walked into the room will have disappeared.

Other simple repairs can make a big impact on the appearance of a room. Is one of the plastic electrical switch or outlet plates broken or missing? Have you wished they were all white instead of three different colors? Before you go to the store to get the spackle, count how many of each type of cover you need and pick them up also. These items are often less than 50 cents apiece. The cumulative effect of a small repair or two, changing all the switch plates to one color, and thoroughly cleaning the room can be quite gratifying.

Take a look around the house. Notice the things that bother you. You'll be surprised how many of those things can be corrected by cleaning them, easily repairing them, inexpensively replacing them, or simply tossing them or setting them aside for a garage sale. Good luck!

Maintenance

Now that the house is clean, you can start Speed Cleaning (weekly, or so, maintenance cleaning) on a regular basis. There is nothing left in the way to stop you from saving all the time that's possible. It's amazing how housecleaning can be reduced to such a short period of time using today's techniques rather than the full-time methods passed down from our grandmothers.

Chapter 20 Outside Cleaning Services

We've spent much of this book explaining our method of cleaning your home quickly. But what if you don't want to clean it at all? Or what if you just can't clean it because of outside circumstances? Hiring someone else to do the cleaning for you is appealing, but it also introduces a new list of issues, questions, and well, problems. There are three basic types of services, although their methods may vary considerably.

Type 1: The Wonderful, Old-Fashioned Cleaning Lady

Some families are lucky enough to employ a cherished housecleaner who has been cleaning for them for years and is considered a part of the family. Unfortunately, as this group of housecleaners retires, it seems there is no new generation coming along to replace them. Perhaps the number of people who view residential cleaning as a permanent career is dwindling. Maybe it just seems that way because there has been such an increased demand for cleaning services as millions of women have entered the workforce.

Type 2: Temporary Cleaning Persons

The demand is being filled by more people who are cleaning either temporarily or as a perceived last choice. There appears to be a disproportionate number of immigrants in this group who do not opt for more traditional employment because language difficulties or lack of legal status in the United States prevents them from obtaining other careers.

Even when someone comes along with an aptitude for and interest in cleaning, it may still be difficult to be a good cleaner because formal training is virtually nonexistent. Also, language barriers are real, and cultural differences can lead to interpretations of "cleaning" in ways you didn't anticipate, such as reorganizing your closets and drawers instead of actually cleaning the kitchen or bathroom.

Another component of this group that cleans on a transitory basis includes students, aspiring actors, dancers, artists, writers, and others who are cleaning until they get their diploma or big break, or until their ship comes in. But all these marvelously human situations are fluid, and as their fortunes rise or fall, you may lose your housecleaner.

Type 3: Cleaning Companies

In this case, a professional housecleaning company hires, trains (ideally), and manages the housecleaner. If the housecleaner quits or is ill, it's up to the company to find a replacement. Some companies send individuals; others send teams.

The quality and reliability of these companies varies enormously but is generally improving as more people appreciate the opportunities available in this expanding industry. As more companies enter the cleaning field, they increase competition, which tends to improve service—in important areas such as better training, customer relations, and reliability.

You might find the perfect cleaner in any of these groups, but before you even begin to look, there is a very important question that you must investigate. For whom does your housecleaner work? You or herself or himself? Once you've answered this question, you may know exactly in which of the above groups you want to look for a housecleaner. And if you already have a housecleaner, you may be inclined to make some changes once you've considered this same question.

For Whom Does Your Housecleaner Work?

This question has more practical importance than you may have imagined, because the answer to it may determine whether you are personally liable for back taxes and penalties when your housecleaners (former and current) reach retirement and apply for Social Security benefits. In many cases, if their Social Security accounts are deficient, the IRS has been regularly ruling that their Social Security payments should have been paid by the people whose homes they cleaned. The IRS is ruling that the housecleaners were actually employees of the person whose house they were cleaning. That means you, gentle reader, and having an employee has a whole new set of rules.

If you hire a cleaning company that pays or withholds the necessary taxes and keeps the records that are required of businesses by the IRS, you shouldn't have much to worry about. Likewise, if you find your cleaner through an agency, the cleaner is generally not your employee if the agency is responsible for who does the work and how it is done. But if you find a cleaner through an agency or association that merely provides a list of housecleaners and does not regulate the hours of work, collect the pay, or set the standards and methods of work, the cleaner may very well be your employee. Likewise, if you hire an individual on the basis of a referral from a friend or neighbor, it's very possible that the cleaner is your employee.

Employee versus Independent Contractor (Nonemployee)

There are good (or at least practical) reasons to prefer that your house-cleaner *not* be your employee: It's less complicated and less costly. When someone is your household employee, you must collect, report, and match Social Security taxes, and sometimes pay federal unemployment taxes. Workers' compensation coverage must also be provided.

Obviously, it's much easier for you to call the housecleaner a nonemployee or self-employed person. The proper term in this case is an independent contractor. If your housecleaner is an independent contractor, you do *not* have to withhold or pay any payroll taxes or file any employment reports or forms. All those things are the responsibility of the housecleaner—not you.

The Difference between an Independent Contractor and an Employee

Ah! There's the rub. A typical example of an independent contractor is a lawyer hired to write a will. Although you are paying the lawyer, you don't have much control over her work—for example, how to write the will or what specific hours to work. And as long as the lawyer is doing the job properly, it won't be simple for you to dismiss her until the job is completed. For the IRS, control over the work of another person is probably the most important single distinction between an independent contractor and an employee.

In the case of housecleaning, if a worker performs services that are subject to your will and control—in terms of both what must be done and how it must be done—then that worker is your employee. It doesn't matter if you actually exercise this control as long as you have the legal right to control both the method and result of the cleaning services. Nor does it matter if you call the housecleaner an independent contractor. Nor does it matter if the housecleaner works full-time or part-time.

Here are a few characteristics of an *employer* of a housecleaner:

- **Has the right to discharge the cleaner**

- **Supplies the cleaner with tools and a place to work**

- **Directs the cleaner's work by means of instructions**

- **Sets the hours or day of work**

- **Or pays by the hour or day, not the job.**

A ruling in any one of these traits may mean that your cleaner is an employee of yours. (For a list of all 20 factors the IRS takes into consideration, see IRS Publication 937—"Business Reporting." The IRS Web site is www.irs.gov.)

If you have treated an employee as an independent contractor, and you shouldn't have, it's possible that you'll get a bill for all of your housecleaner's Social Security taxes plus a fine of 100 percent!

Keeping a Secret

So, you ask, who cares about all this? You have no problems, right? You like your housekeeper, and he likes you, and your way of paying wages has been working out just fine. So far.

Problems can and do arise a few years down the line when your housecleaner reaches retirement age and wants to start collecting Social Security benefits. If no one has been paying into that Social Security account, the housecleaner has no basis for collecting benefits.

Of course, what happens next is a stimulating discussion between the housecleaner and the IRS representative: The housecleaner has spent the past 20 years cleaning houses, so where are the retirement benefits that she has worked so hard to collect? Let's assume the housecleaner had paid income taxes every year, as many do. But no one had ever paid into her Social Security account. Maybe nobody even thought about it. Well, one thing leads to another, and, after a few seconds of deliberation, the IRS determines that the housecleaner was a household employee all those years—not an independent contractor as you had supposed. All of a sudden, you may be looking at a sizable tax bill.

IRS Ruling on This Subject

To test these waters, I filed three sets of Form SS-8 with our local IRS public affairs officer. These forms are called "Information for Use in Determining whether a Worker Is an Employee for Federal Employment Taxes and Income Tax Withholding." Whew. The IRS officer let me fill out this form with hypothetical cases, and agreed to make hypothetical rulings based on my three examples.

1. **I filled out the first form as if I were the housecleaner. I described myself as an individual cleaner who cleans five different homes during the week, is expected to be there on a certain day, and is paid by the hour. I follow a list if left by the homeowner; otherwise I do the "normal cleaning."**

2. **I filled out the second form as if I were the homeowner. The working conditions were the same as in Form 1. I said I hired him because— on a different day of the week—he works for a neighbor who raved about his work.**

3. **I filled out the third form in exactly the same way as Form 2, except I said I hired the cleaner after finding a mimeographed flyer under my car's windshield wiper. In the flyer, the business was identified as "Ruth's Cleaning" and a phone number was given.**

The IRS ruled that the housecleaner in all three cases was a "household employee." They based their decision on the control factor alone. The IRS felt the client directed the housecleaner's work. That was enough for them—even in the case where the flyer was left soliciting business.

What the IRS Calls Your Housecleaner

It appears that the IRS regularly rules against many people who hired housecleaners whom they thought were independent contractors, ruling instead that they are in a special category called "household employees."

Here's the IRS's definition of the term.

A homeworker who works by the guidelines of the person for whom the work is done, with materials furnished by and returned to that person or to someone that person designates.

Unlike standard employees, you do not have to withhold income taxes on wages paid to a household employee for services performed in or around your private home (unless the employee asks you to, and you agree to do so). But if you pay a household employee $1,400 or more during a calendar year (2004 rules; it may change in future years), you must pay or match the employee's Social Security (FICA) taxes. Social Security is 15.3 percent of cash wages. You can pay it all, or the employee can pay 7.65 percent, and you pay the other 7.65 percent. It doesn't matter whether wages are based on the hour, day, week, month, or year. The value of food, lodging, clothes, bus tokens, and other noncash items given to household employees is not subject to FICA tax. The Medicare threshold is $1,000 in wages in any calendar quarter. Medicare taxes you must pay if you exceed the threshold are usually 0.8 percent of cash wages.

The IRS Will Make a Ruling for You

Tax regulations are almost always open to interpretation, and the employment status of your housecleaner may still require clarification before you feel confident how to proceed. You may request the IRS to make a ruling for your particular set of facts and circumstances by filling in Form SS-8—the same one I sent in with three fictitious examples. *However,* this is *not* confidential information. If the IRS rules against you, they may follow up on it to see if you made any necessary changes.

How to Comply: Federal Requirements

If it turns out that your housecleaner is your employee, it really isn't too time-consuming or complicated to comply with these tax requirements. We've listed below the basic steps and the IRS forms you'll need. The forms are available at IRS offices or by calling 800-424-FORM or visiting www.irs.gov. For additional general information on the subject, also request Publications 926 and 937 and Circular E. We must make the disclaimer that we're not tax experts, so be sure to check with the IRS, your accountant, lawyer, guru, or some other source if you have questions.

The Forms You'll Need

1. Employer Identification Number (EIN): Form SS-4.

2. Record keeping: Publication 926, page 4.

3. Social Security Taxes (FICA): Form 942 and Form W-2 for you and Form W-4 for your housecleaner.

4. Federal Unemployment Tax (FUTA): Form 940 (or 940-EZ) and Employer's Annual Federal Unemployment (FUTA) Tax Return.

5. Advance Payment of Earned Income Credit: Notice 797, Form W-5, Form 942, and Form W-2.

How to Comply: State Requirements

So far, we've not mentioned any state requirements. Check with your accountant, or place a call to your state employment or labor department to check the requirements in your particular state.

In California, for example, all homeowner's or renter's insurance policies must provide coverage for any household employees in your home. If you don't have such a policy, you are responsible for providing workers' compensation insurance coverage for your employee. It's not that unusual for housecleaners to hurt themselves while cleaning a home. A slip on a wet floor, a fall from a ladder, or a back thrown out from changing the bed or vacuuming could be a financial disaster if you don't have insurance for the housecleaner.

We've assumed throughout this discussion that the housecleaners are citizens or have legal status to work in the United States as aliens. If not, it's illegal for you to hire them as your employees. If they are working for a company or are independent contractors, you have no responsibility to determine their legal status. In that case, it's between them and the Immigration and Naturalization Service—not you.

Independent Contractors' Income-Reporting Requirements

The good news is that unless the payments you make to the independent contractor/cleaner are a business expense (i.e., use in the course of *your* trade or business), you don't have to report any payments made to them. In other words, if your housecleaner is not your employee, you do not have to file any report or fill out any tax form of any kind. If the payments you make to your cleaner are a business expense to you, report payments greater than $600 on IRS Form 1099.

No matter what the employment status of your cleaner, you still have the same goal: to get the house cleaned on a regular basis without having to do it yourself and with *less* grief and bother than if you did it yourself. Seems easy enough. Naturally, it's not. So now, let's turn our attention to the management skills necessary to get the most out of your cleaner or cleaning service.

Roadblocks to Your Goal: Problems with Housecleaners

Here are the problems I have heard most often in the 25 years I've been in this business. The housecleaner . . .

- **Breaks things**

- **Charges too much**

- **Doesn't accept responsibility for accidents**

- **Doesn't clean well enough**

- **Doesn't come on the day or time scheduled**

- **Doesn't follow (or forgets) directions**

- **Doesn't know how to clean**

- **Doesn't understand English well enough**

- **Eats the cupboards bare**

- **Is too much trouble to get ready for**

- **Is too nosy**

- **Quits, and you have to start over again**

- **Rearranges the furniture and doesn't put things back in their places**

- **Steals things**

- **Substitutes personnel too often**

- **Won't do extra chores (windows!)**

If you're tired of trying to correct these problems, and if throwing good money at them is beginning to seem like more trouble than cleaning your house yourself, we've got some suggestions. We realize that we're often asking you to change instead of the cleaner. It's not a perfect world. And sure, there are plenty of housecleaners who should be fired or should be, perhaps, truck drivers instead. But if you're willing, you can learn techniques to stay in charge, create a better workplace, and motivate your cleaner to get the job done the way you want it done. Basically, we suggest *managing* your house-cleaner as you would anyone who works for you in the office or at home.

The Benefits of Managing

Honing your management skills can really pay off, because most house-cleaners are ever so slightly less than perfect. That includes The Clean Team! But certain customers really know how consistently to get the very best we have to offer, despite our limitations. We've cleaned for some of these folks for years, with inevitable personnel changes on our teams. But these customers manage to get even the newer cleaners to perform as if they had been around for much longer, to work harder, to apply themselves more diligently, to agree to do extra tasks, to take pride in their work—and to do all this with a smile and a feeling that these clients are really special.

Naturally, this isn't just luck. These customers realize that their hiring options are extremely limited. They can hire only perfect housecleaners (quite difficult to do). Or they can hire and motivate someone with the potential to be a very good housecleaner.

Spencer Johnson and Kenneth Blanchard said in *The One Minute Manager:* "Everyone is a potential winner." Like the favorite clients I mentioned above, good managers promptly turn potential into hardworking reality. These clients are those "lucky" people who always seem to find a great cleaner or cleaning service (or contractor or dry cleaner or dentist). Exactly! They create that luck through good management.

Your Home as a Great Place to Work

Your home is the housecleaner's place of business. Is it a good place to work? The spirit or morale of your household is set by you. It's more than a matter of trying to get along with your housecleaner; the human relations between you and your housecleaner are grounded in job satisfaction and job performance. Friendliness without these other foundations inevitably results in poor morale. If you create a positive work environment in your home, your housecleaner will feel good about the work and will be free to do his best. People who feel good produce good results.

The best way to create good morale is to look for people's strengths. Peter Drucker, in *The Practice of Management,* said: "Nothing destroys the spirit of an organization faster than focusing on people's weaknesses rather than on their strengths, building on disabilities rather than abilities."

Motivating

Your housecleaner is a resource. However, the housecleaner has absolute control over whether she works at all, so your housecleaner as a resource has got to be motivated. Fear is not much of a motivator anymore. In a society able to provide subsistence to the unemployed, fear has lost much of its grip. Besides, firing people doesn't get the work done.

Motivating doesn't mean being autocratic or hard-nosed. Positive motivation is usually far more successful than negative. But purely democratic, participative, supportive, or humanistic ideals alone aren't enough either. Money is important, but it's largely a negative incentive; being unhappy with pay is a powerful disincentive, but satisfaction with pay motivates only when other factors are working. A high wage won't keep people motivated if they hate every minute they spend at work, or if they are belittled, or if they feel exploited.

1. **Start with yourself and set high standards.**

   - **Remember that you're the boss. A good boss is supposed to be wise, fair, and decisive. In this setting, these qualities are expected of you as the manager of this small enterprise—your home. Your housecleaner will find it hard to be motivated to excellence if the boss is disorganized, ill-prepared, disinterested, or inept.**

   - **Have the house ready, so the housecleaners can start upon arrival. If, for example, you have to pick up the house before they can do the cleaning, be sure it's done. Don't make them clean around any chaos.**

   - **Have all the needed supplies on hand, plus a spare bag for the vacuum or a new one installed beforehand.**

   - **Be sure your equipment is in good condition: no clogged vacuum wands, no empty spray bottles. Have a spare vacuum belt available, plus any tools and instructions needed.**

• Be sure to have meaningful work to be done. Even if you have to take time to plan, don't have just "busywork" to be done.

2. Give housecleaners all the information necessary to be in control of their work and to be able to deliver a responsive performance. The housecleaner has to know what you want done, how you want it done, where things go, what not to touch, and so on. This is how job satisfaction starts. There's almost no better way to destroy morale than not letting someone know how to satisfy expectations. One can try hard but never have it turn out to be right or enough.

3. Let your housecleaners know how important their work is to your home and/or family as a whole. Tell them how their contributions improve your home life, reduce stress, afford you valuable extra time, etc. Allow them to see your household as if they were responsible, through their performance, for some of the success of your household.

4. Allow the housecleaners to participate in the planning of the job. They are more likely to feel responsible for the results if they helped plan the job itself. Don't detail them to death with what you want done, in what order, and how to do it. To be motivating and satisfying, work needs some element of challenge, skill, and judgment.

5. Since we are often at work when the housecleaner arrives, establish and sustain rapport by leaving your housecleaners a note every time they visit; address them by name. Thank them for last week's extra work; explain that because the sink's a mess this week, they can skip it; swear undying loyalty; tell them Aunt Bunny is coming, and the spare room needs special attention; pass a good joke; tell them there's a treat in the cookie jar. Try to keep your notes upbeat. And you'll get answers. This is a dialogue—and dialogue is critical to managing and motivating. We have clients who look forward nearly as much to the weekly note as to the clean house.

  Leave your note every single time—not just when you have extra requests or a reminder or a complaint. Consider how you'd feel if the only words you ever had from your employer or client were negative. A note with no special instructions—such as "nothing special today, just the usual great job"—is just as important as the ones that are chock-full of instructions. But when you do need to work out a problem, it will be much easier on you both if it's part of a regular weekly note.

6. Probably the most effective motivators of all are the simple expressions of thanks and appreciation for work well done: "Fantastic job!" "I could not have done that better myself, and you know how particular I am about my kitchen." "Thank you so much for working so hard on those horrible shower walls." "Thank you for all your efforts. You make our home and life so much more comfortable and pleasant."

Praise doesn't have to be lavish, but people do need to know their efforts are noticed and appreciated. A good manager knows this and never fails to act on it. Invariably, a simple "thanks" will guarantee an even better job done the next time. Especially don't forget to acknowledge the effort put into a special request or project.

Rewards and small considerations are great if they are sincere and appropriate. Cookies, holiday cards, or candy are all effective ways to express appreciation or thanks.

Management If Your Housecleaner Is *Not* Your Employee

Management of a housecleaner (or a team) who works for a company is effectively the same as managing your own employee. Think of yourself as a midlevel manager. The difference is that you aren't directly in charge of the cleaners; you can correct their work only up to a certain point before you need to talk to their boss. This type of relationship limits your control. But it doesn't limit your using all your managing and motivating skills.

Proven Ways to Get the Most from Your Housecleaner

Selecting a Cleaner or Cleaning Service

Of course, the best way to know who to call is via a recommendation from a neighbor or relative or friend. If you were so lucky, you probably wouldn't be reading this.

Start with names from a friend, from a flyer in the mail, from the yellow pages, from an ad on a bulletin board, or from a billboard. Then call them up and interview them on the phone. Ask them to tell you what they clean and what they prefer to clean. For example, here in San Francisco, there are cleaners who clean only empty homes or apartments, who clean only after fires or other insurance-related events, who clean only on a one-time basis, who clean only carpets, and so on.

Ask if they clean in your neighborhood.

Ask about their experience. How long have they been in business? Have they had any formal training?

They should be able to give you a reference. Give them a couple of days to check with one of their customers to get permission to give their name and telephone number to you. But don't necessarily give up on a particular individual or company if they don't have a reference. Some people are reluctant to give out their names and telephone numbers to strangers.

Also check with the Better Business Bureau (BBB). Poor cleaning services accumulate a negative file with the BBB rather quickly. Bear in mind that individual cleaners are less likely to have complaints filed against them with the BBB.

If you're looking for ongoing household cleaning, the service should make an appointment to see your home in order to give you an estimate. You may prefer that they just come and clean your home once, so you can see if their work is any good. However, most companies really do need to know how much work there is before they can schedule you, and countless potential misunderstandings can be avoided by having them see your home prior to cleaning it the first time. Read on.

Rates: By the Hour

It's more important how much work gets done per hour than what the hourly rate is. But many people still shop by comparing hourly rates. It's no bargain to pay $4 per hour for 8 hours of work when someone else can finish the job in far less time at a higher rate—especially if the lower-paid worker is not very experienced, is a mediocre cleaner, or is unreliable.

If you have a housecleaner you like, it can be to your advantage to pay by the hour. Housecleaners will get faster and faster at cleaning your home as they do it over and over again. So after a few months, cleaning your home may only take them 3 hours instead of the 5 hours it originally took. For the same price, you can now have the housecleaner do some ironing, wash a few windows, polish some brass or silver, or do some other chore that wasn't originally included in the housecleaning.

What Should Be Done for a Fixed, Per-Visit Fee?

Many housecleaners or cleaning companies charge by the job instead of the hour, especially for ongoing cleaning. It might take them a little longer one time and a little shorter the next, but it averages out.

A fixed job price has many advantages: You know how much work will get done, you don't have to worry whether they work fast or slow or take breaks on your time. All you have to consider is whether the price is fair and your house is clean.

It also gives housecleaners a chance to earn more money per hour by concentrating on being efficient. This is a real morale-booster because they can earn the same amount of money in fewer hours. Working more efficiently and smarter doesn't mean that the quality of work suffers. In fact, quite the opposite is commonly true because the work that is done is given full attention.

A fixed price assumes a job description: exactly what work is going to be done for the price. Generally, the job description is for "light housecleaning," which should include all the things you would normally clean once a week or every other week if you were doing the work yourself.

Cleaning tasks not included in the job description include yearly or "spring cleaning" chores, such as washing windows, stripping wax off floors, polishing silver, cleaning ovens, washing walls and ceilings, and cleaning carpets. Expect to pay extra for many of these chores.

A job description has to assume that the house is ready to be cleaned, so the housecleaner can go right to work. People often joke that they have to clean up before the cleaners arrive. But what we're really talking about is picking up the house, so the cleaners can get to the surfaces they are supposed to clean. Picking up is daily cleaning, and a good example is the kitchen. We can't clean the sink if it's full of dirty dishes. That doesn't mean that they can't be washed; it just means that if you want to include a *daily* cleaning job like the dishes, you'll need to discuss it and expect to pay for it.

Giving Your House Key to a Stranger

Housecleaners usually will want to clean when you're at work. They need a reliable, fail-safe way to get into your home—usually a key.

There are a few alternatives to providing a key. A doorman, babysitter, neighbor, or landlord are all fine as long as they never leave the house. Our exhaustive experiments have shown that, without fail, the moment your neighbor runs to the store for a quart of milk, The Clean Team will arrive. It is surprisingly difficult to arrange fail-safe access via a third party.

Some clients attempt to solve their security fears by scheduling the housecleaners to clean when the clients have a day off. This is a great way to ruin an otherwise perfectly good day. It is very frustrating to have plans for your day off and then find yourself waiting for a housecleaner who has been delayed. Even if the housecleaner does arrive on time, you may quickly discover that you don't appreciate having someone underfoot.

Absolutely don't leave the key under the doormat! Not only do burglars know about this favorite hiding place, but if there ever were a burglary at your home, how would you know who did it? At least if the housecleaner or cleaning company has a key and something is missing, you have a good chance to collect from a reputable housecleaner or company.

Some cleaning companies provide the client with a lockbox and a key to open it. The client puts a key to the house into the lockbox, which is usually hung on the outside doorknob. The housecleaner also has a key to the lockbox and uses it to retrieve the house key, which is replaced upon leaving. We're not sure how much this improves security. If the housecleaners were dishonest, they could still go copy the keys and replace the originals in the lockbox without the client's knowledge.

Needless to say, it's scary to hand over a key, but there seem to be few other options that are any safer and yet still accomplish the purpose. Some people with deadbolts offer only the doorknob key; we have yet to find a client who does not then forget to leave the deadbolt unlocked. In addition, the house is left less secure that day with just the one lock in place, whether we get in to clean or not.

When The Clean Team asks clients to mail us a key, we advise them to take one precaution: not to put their return address either inside or outside the envelope. We tell them to identify the key by name or initials only. We watch for it and call them when it arrives. Once we get the key, we number it and file it in a safe with no reference to name or address. Even if a team should lose a whole ring of keys, they would still be useless to whoever found them.

Security Alarms

Teach the housecleaners how to arm and disarm the house's security system. There are two problems if you leave it disarmed on the day the cleaning service comes. First, of course, your home isn't as secure as it would be if the alarm were on all day. And second, you have to remember to disarm it. What you really have to do is to remember *not* to do something that you usually do—which is surprisingly difficult. Most alarm systems have special codes that are designed to be used by people who need occasional access to your home. Consider using that feature instead of deactivating your whole alarm system.

Insurance

That is a tough one. Most services can and should have a bond to cover employee theft, usually for a fixed dollar amount. The problem with bonds is that most require a conviction before the bonding company will pay a claim, and the evidence is likely to be circumstantial: You didn't see anyone take it, and there's no physical evidence that the housecleaner did it instead of a neighbor or a burglar.

It would also be nice if the cleaning company had liability insurance to provide for relief in case a Ming vase is broken or, heaven forbid, the housecleaner somehow manages to set your house on fire. Many cleaning companies don't have liability insurance to cover these disasters. The Clean Team is insured, but if your cleaning service isn't, there is a solution. Many homeowner's policies will cover damage done in your home by household workers. Call your insurance agent and ask.

Scheduling, Cancellations, and Lateness

From what we hear, the most common complaint about cleaners is that they don't show up on their appointed day. You'd better talk to prospective housecleaners about this one. They will say they're reliable. But ask them what happens if they don't show up on the appointed day. Will they guarantee a free cleaning as a recourse?

This same problem, as viewed by your housecleaner, arises when you cancel cleaning visits. If you call and cancel the cleaning on short notice, you have taken one giant step toward ruining your relationship with your housecleaner.

If a genuine emergency does arise, at least try to reschedule the cleaning for the next day or two. Housecleaners will appreciate your trying to protect their income by rescheduling rather than skipping a visit entirely. We have clients that use us even when they're on vacation: They can ask us to substitute some chores for the regular weekly cleaning—like washing windows or stripping floors—and we can also help keep the plants alive. This kind of loyalty shown to one of our teams by a client seems to motivate that team all year long.

Lateness is usually a problem only if you've been unable to find a way to arrange access for your cleaners. (They have no house keys, in other words.)

Breakage

The most common "breach of security" in homes with housecleaners is not theft—it's breakage. Who pays for it if the housecleaner breaks something? Ask. Your prospective housecleaner or cleaning service should have a policy for taking care of such events.

Our policy is that if we break something, we'll pay for it. There are two exceptions. If the item was already broken, we don't want to be held responsible, and we would like the client to tell us about it before we even touch it. (Make sure to tell new cleaners about your home's booby traps. Like that lamp shade that falls off a particular lamp if you look at it cross-eyed. Everyone in your family knows it, but when the unsuspecting housecleaner starts dusting the lamp, the shade comes crashing down. Even worse, it lands on several other items that weren't broken before, but they certainly are now.)

The second exception is when we clean something, using standard accepted methods ("due diligence"), and it still breaks. For example, we dust a picture hanging on the wall with a feather duster just as we've done many times before. This time, however, it crashes to the floor, which breaks it and our nerves. If the client hangs the picture with a thumbtack, the client pays for this type of damage.

Tell the housecleaner about any items in your home that are so valuable to you that if anyone ever breaks them, it had better be you. Many items are valuable for strictly personal reasons that no one could ever guess. Tell your cleaner not to even touch them—that they're very precious to you, and you will clean them yourself. You can use the same rationale to protect other frail objects, heirlooms, or artwork. Why give trouble an engraved invitation? It will usually invite itself in anyway.

Federal laws on working conditions say that if your housecleaner is your employee, you may not charge him or her for breakage unless you can prove gross negligence or a willful or dishonest act. The law is specifically written so that the burden of proof is squarely on the employer.

Complaints: Satisfaction Guaranteed?

Some people think there is exactly one way to clean a house—their way. If you have tendencies in this direction, try not to complain about your housecleaners' method when their actual results are acceptable.

But if the end result isn't satisfactory, any housecleaner or cleaning service should have some policy for handling complaints and ensuring your satisfaction. When you inquire, have strong doubts about hiring the service of someone whose reply is something like, "Oh, there's nothing to worry about. We never have complaints." Really?

Your housecleaner or cleaning service should handle your complaints the same way any other well-run business does. You should receive an apology and an offer to make it right. The Clean Team offers to come back the next day to correct any oversight. If customers don't want us to do that, they may reduce the charge for the next cleaning by an amount they feel is appropriate. Finally, if the customers are so upset that they don't want us to return, we offer a full refund.

If you're generally satisfied with your housecleaner but suspect she has overlooked something, you'll find you get better results if you fully consider your complaints. Before you accuse, stop and think. Maybe the floor that doesn't seem clean was an ungodly mess from your party the night before. Maybe the housecleaner cleaned it, but missed a spot or two. Accusing conscientious housecleaners of skipping something is tantamount to calling them a liar. If you sincerely think a complaint is justified, ask before you accuse.

But don't be afraid to mention something that needs more attention or that's not quite up to your standards or expectations. This can be done in a positive and beneficial way, if you'll just give your words some prior thought. The antidote to anger is gentleness. If your complaint is presented in an appropriate and supportive manner—"We're working on this together"—it will generally be quickly solved.

It's a good idea to state your complaint right away. If you wait until it's happened over and over, you'll weaken your own credibility. Would you like to be told you'd made a mistake over and over? Wouldn't you rather be told the first time, so you could correct it right away?

And try to balance a request for more or better effort with a few kind words about something else that is being well done. It's easy to begin to take consistent hard work for granted.

Here are some notes from one of our clients who does a good job of getting the very best from us. (She's actually complaining, but it's just about painless, and it gets the job done.)

"Maybe it's just that time of year, but there seems to be more dust around than usual. Would you give it your critical and special touch this week?"

"I've moved a few pieces of furniture out from the walls to make it easier for you to get into those hard-to-reach corners that seem to love dirt and grime."

"We would appreciate it so much if you could give some thought or ideas on how to remove the grease buildup around the top of the stove and the stove pipe. What do you think? Should we try a better cleaning agent? Do you have a preferred favorite? As always, thank you for your help."

Just as you need to be able to complain, so should the housecleaners. You will make giant strides in positive motivation if you make it clear that you are open to feedback also. Keep communication open.

Leaving Cookies and Milk: Is the Cleaner Welcome to Raid the Fridge?

If you provide your cleaner with lunch, the cleaner should eat what you offer. Whether or not you should offer lunch is an easy problem to solve. Just ask. The housecleaner's expectation will be made very clear to you. Until you discuss it or make an offer in one of your notes, the housecleaner should not raid the fridge. Offering something refreshing, a soft drink, for example, may enhance motivation, is appreciated, and isn't very expensive. And we've gotten notes from dieting customers who have a supply of cookies or cake on hand that is tempting them too much: "*Please* eat *all* the cookies."

Also, consider whether the cleaner is welcome to turn on the TV, radio, VCR, or the like. It is somewhat startling to turn on the stereo (which you had left tuned to the easy-listening station) and be blasted halfway across the room by acid rock. But some people do enjoy listening to music while they work. If it's all right with you, but not all right with your spouse, make some decision on the subject, and discuss it with the housecleaner. (The discussion beforehand with your spouse is important. It's demoralizing to the house-cleaner to get chewed out by the husband for something the wife explicitly said was okay.)

Who Supplies the Cleaning Products and Equipment?

The Clean Team supplies everything—mops, polish, cleaning cloths, cleansers, two vacuums, everything. We don't want to waste time looking for your supplies. As long as you don't object to particular supplies, it saves you time and money if the cleaners bring their own supplies. Careful: Two cleaning services may charge about the same, but one brings its own supplies, and the other expects you to buy them. That can be a substantial difference in effective cost.

They Can't Clean Every House on Friday

The cleaning service probably works Monday through Friday. This means they need to clean about 20 percent of their accounts each day and can't clean everyone's house on Friday. In a city the size of San Francisco, we can't afford to clean for someone on a certain day unless we're already in the neighborhood. To drive across town to clean one house would often take longer than the housecleaning itself. Besides, if the housecleaners come soon after a weekend instead of just before it, they can clean up after the mess made over the weekend, you'll enjoy your clean house for a much longer period of time, and you'll end up with more for your money.

Other Types of Security

There are ways that security can be breached that go beyond leaving keys.

I remember a client, a doctor, who had brought home some original patient files, test results, and x-rays to study at home. These items weren't supposed to have left the hospital. She smuggled them home in a paper bag. After she was finished with them, she replaced them in the paper bag and set the bag on top of the small wastebasket next to a desk. Naturally, we threw them away! And as fate would have it, the garbage was picked up before the doctor got home.

We've thrown away rings that had been mixed in with the cigarette butts left in an ashtray. We've heard of a cleaner who diligently stacked and straightened all the papers on an accountant's desk just as she did every time she cleaned. Problem was, on that particular week, the papers were tax records and expense receipts for several people. Once they were neatly stacked, it was almost impossible to figure out what belonged to whom.

Even when you completely trust your housecleaner, don't leave things lying about out of place. Besides the obvious temptation, you're asking for other headaches. The housecleaner might drop a ring left on the kitchen counter into a cleaning apron pocket, intending to put the ring on the bedroom dresser where it belongs. By the time he gets to the dresser, the cleaner has forgotten all about it and then tossed all the "trash" from the apron at the end of the day. An honest housecleaner, but you're missing a ring.

Protect Your Household's Privacy

Like any normal household, you undoubtedly have a secret or two that you hope and pray absolutely no one will discover. English author W. Somerset Maugham (1874–1965) said, "There is hardly anyone whose sexual life, if it were broadcast, would not fill the world at large with surprise or horror." Human nature being what it is, you might want to be sure that certain items are returned to the back of the dresser drawer, for example. Or that certain papers (especially financial ones) are replaced in the locked desk drawer. Certain pictures or videos should be put away. You get the idea.

Special Instructions

Let's say you know that the instant your housecleaner turns on the vacuum cleaner, your cat will head straight for the hall closet and will stay hidden there long after the vacuuming is finished. So tape a note to the closet door saying *"DO NOT CLOSE."* Your house is not the only one your house-cleaners work in. Especially on the first few visits, don't rely on their memory of everything you mentioned the first time you met. We all forget instructions occasionally, and most of us appreciate friendly reminders and warnings.

Other changes in your household from week to week may have little to do with security, but if handled incorrectly can make you feel as if *something* has been breached. A new puppy in your home or a school project in the middle of the living room are examples. If you were doing the cleaning, you would certainly know what to do about each of them. The housecleaners may not. Don't leave it to chance. Tell them.

Tipping

Since the housecleaner performs a personal service (like a haircutter, waiter, or cab driver), tipping is appropriate when deserved. A few customers leave a small tip each visit or for a special project or effort, but most leave some-thing around the holiday season. Some leave gifts like food or wine instead of cash. But a gift of cash—and not a check—is preferred by most house-cleaners. One guideline is to leave an amount equivalent to 1 month's cleaning charges. This amount would be split if more than one person does the cleaning.

Training

Training is a very touchy subject when it comes to housecleaners, particu-larly if they're in business for themselves and are not your employees. They already know how to clean and may not be the least bit interested in learning how to clean any differently than they now do—especially any faster if they are working by the hour.

However, many cleaning services are perfectly willing to consider ideas from other experts. They want to know about anything that may save them time, techniques that may save wasted energy, or products that may save their health. Naturally, we believe that suggesting or giving them this book and out-fitting them with an apron and some cleaning tools are excellent ideas.

If the person cleaning for you is your employee, you can train her any way you like. *Speed Cleaning* is custom-made for your situation. Your employee will be a better cleaner and will have more time available to do other things. Use our book as a training manual, and contact us if you would like to order any of the supplies we use. If you or your housecleaner has a cleaning question, call or go to our Web site. We're happy to help in any way we can.

Language Problems

It's most difficult to communicate if you and your housecleaner speak dif-ferent languages. Sometimes, translation services are available through the agency that sent the cleaner or through a few civic or religious organiza-tions. But there aren't enough of them and they aren't uniformly available.

Part 3: Keep It Clean

Chapter 21 Death, Taxes, and Maintenance

Unfortunately, books about home maintenance are usually "how to" or "fix it" books. They don't appeal to me because I have little interest, or patience, in trying to fix broken things. However, I do like to take good care of things, to keep them looking like new, and to keep them running well. But once they are broken, I prefer someone else to do the fixing: someone with the proper tools, work space, temperament, experience, and time.

This section is a guide to taking care of the items found in most homes. We're focusing on the contents of a home and not the home itself, although it's sometimes difficult to separate the two. For example, we'll talk about how to maintain tub/shower enclosures and central air conditioners. Whether they're part of the house or part of its contents isn't clear, at least to me, but we include such items in this book if there are important maintenance issues at stake. We do not include structural items like roofs, foundations, walls, and decks, or purely personal items like jewelry and clothing.

When I started my research, I thought that much of the best information would come from owner's manuals written by manufacturers. I was dead wrong.

Sales, manufacturing, and maintenance are not comfortable bedfellows. If you ask a leather-furniture salesperson, for example, "What maintenance does this leather couch need?" the answer is usually something like "What maintenance? Just wipe it with a damp cloth once in a while. Isn't the color great?

How many do you want?" Salespeople know only too well that too much talk about maintenance can kill the sale. Likewise with manufacturers. Successful maintenance by consumers will extend the life of products and could ruin obsolescence projections and future replacement sales. I'm not accusing anyone of anything, but it does seem that practical maintenance doesn't get the attention it deserves.

I quickly discovered that a better resource for finding out about maintenance is people who have spent years fixing the things other people didn't maintain properly. Plumbers know a lot about how to keep a water heater from breaking down: They fix or replace a whole lot of them. Someone who repairs major appliances knows exactly how to avoid ruining a clothes washer or dryer before its time. Much of the information in this section is from interviews with these knowledgeable people. It's the sort of information that is learned the hard way and is passed on from master to apprentice, but until now, it hasn't found its way into a book for consumers.

When should you start maintenance? Even before you buy the item in question. When you make a purchase, ask pointed questions about how to care for the product you're considering. You would not believe the number of calls I get from people who have just arrived home with something new and want to know how to clean or maintain it. Ask the salesperson. Persist until you get a full answer—not "Cleanup is a breeze" or "This unit practically takes care of itself." You *must* know what maintenance to perform and how to clean it (and with what product) as well as how often to schedule maintenance and cleaning operations. Besides that, ask if it will fade, stain, dent, scratch, rust, crack, splinter, shrink, peel, or rot.

Also, before you make a purchase, consider how much time this item will be adding to the total time spent maintaining the household. Each decision adds a bit more to the total unless you also get rid of something. Unless you manage these maintenance demands, ultimately, the amount of time required will be more than is available. Certain building materials, design elements, and new possessions require much more maintenance time than others. For example, shiny surfaces magnify every little fingerprint, whereas fingerprints on brushed surfaces are not even noticeable. Here's a partial list of high-maintenance items.

- **Any shower enclosure**

- **Bare aluminum window frames**

- Black-and-white floors

- Brass anything—whether lacquered or not

- Carpets in bathrooms and kitchens

- Carpets that show vacuum marks

- Chandeliers

- Cheap carpet that doesn't hold up

- Cheap paint that can't be washed repeatedly

- Cheap plastic that scratches

- Clear glass light fIxtures

- Clear glass shower doors

- Collections of anything large displayed in the open

- Collections of anything small displayed in the open

- DrIed flower arrangements

- Fabric lamp shades

- Fiberglass showers with sand-grain floors

- Floor-to-ceiling mirrors

- Glass doors

- Glass furniture

- Glossy, shiny floors

- Gold or brass plumbing fixtures

- Grouted tile counters

- Highly textured floors, walls, ceilings, or wallpaper

- Intricate beds

- Intricate cabinets

- Intricate knobs

- Intricate lamp shades

- Large bathroom mirrors

- Light- or dark-colored carpets

- Miniblinds

- Piles of pillows on furniture

- Practically any fabric-covered furniture

- Silk flower arrangements

- Soft wood

- Tiny hexagonal floor tiles (in many old San Francisco homes, unfortunately)

- Unfinished wood

- White grout—especially on counters and floors

- Wicker furniture

- Windows that can't be opened to clean

Obviously, you can't, nor would most of us want to, avoid everything on this list. But pick items for your home critically and judiciously. Otherwise, you'll spend excessive time on maintenance efforts for years to come.

One way to measure the difference between high-quality products and poor-quality products is the additional time it takes to maintain the latter. Buy as good a quality as you can afford in order to reduce maintenance time. Delay the purchase, if you must, to get items that will last. You'll remember and appreciate the quality of your purchase long after you've forgotten its price.

Once home, well-maintained possessions retain greater value, are more reliable (they don't leak, don't skip, aren't too hot or too cold, too fast, or too slow), look better, and continue to be more enjoyable as the years pass by. To give yourself an idea of how valuable maintenance can be, take a stroll through your home, and add up the cost of the things you see—stove, refrigerator, CDs, washer, carpets, furniture, books, art, and so forth. Proper maintenance means that should you decide to sell everything and move to Grenada, you'll get full value. Without it, you may have to pay someone to haul your possessions away.

Well-maintained things also reduce the number of crises you'll have to face. An air conditioner serviced at the start of the warm season is less likely to break down on the hottest weekend of the summer when the house is full of sweltering guests. Postponing maintenance means that a small problem will inevitably blossom into a more expensive, inconvenient full-blown nuisance someday.

This section will not, however, make you an expert on air conditioners, water heaters, CD players, or any of the other entries in Chapter 24. Rather, it will teach you what maintenance is needed to keep such things running well and/or looking good for the longest time possible. The philosophy is similar to the one I use when talking with computer experts about new software for my office computers. I tell them, "I don't want to know how it works. I just want to know which button to push." Inevitably, I have to remind them of this once or twice as the conversation proceeds. In this book, I have tried to follow my own advice and relate only what is needed to maintain an item. And that's where I stop. If you want to become an armchair expert on air conditioners, for example, you can find books about almost every aspect of them. What's previously been difficult to find is a book *only* about maintaining such things in the home.

By the way, since it might occur to someone to sue me (this *is* litigious America, after all), I have come up with my own warning.

> **Hey! The maintenance instructions in this book are generic and do not include important warnings and specific instructions contained in the owner's manual for the specific product on hand. You may be exposed to dangerous risks without those warnings and instructions. Before you proceed, please review the owner's manual or contact the manufacturer or other professional to protect yourself against injury or death if you have any doubt, question, or hesitation about any procedure contained in this book.**

After warnings, the next line of defense seems to be to tell consumers to perform certain maintenance chores so often that it seems obvious the advice is meant to shift blame from the manufacturer to the consumer if a problem ever arises. For example, manufacturers of fire extinguishers tell us to check the pressure gauge once a month. Do they tell us that because they stay up nights worrying about us, or because in the event of a fire, they can claim it was the fault of the consumer who, like most all of us, hadn't checked the pressure on the fire extinguisher for a year? They sort of have us over a barrel. We don't want to risk our family's safety, but we have only so much time in the day. Is it really, truly, absolutely necessary that we all mark our calendars every month for the rest of our lives to check the pressure on every fire extinguisher we own? Or are manufacturers giving us busywork while trying to ensure that they are protected from phantom lawsuits? Add in checkups on water heaters, refrigerators, freezers, electrical devices of all kinds, and pretty soon, there would be no time left in the day at all. In this book, we'll offer suggestions on how to live with generalized instructions and how to personalize them to your home and to your lifestyle—a refreshing dollop, we trust, of common sense. Most of us want to take care of our things, but we don't have any time to waste unnecessarily.

When you buy a house, especially if it's a used one, get as much information as you can from the builders or sellers about things in the house such as the furnace, air conditioner, refrigerator, stove, washer, and dryer. What maintenance has been performed to date? Ask for any owner's manuals. Ask what products have been used on wood floors and if tile and grout in the house have been sealed. Ask for the names and phone numbers of tradespeople such as plumbers, electricians, and appliance repair people who are familiar with the appliances in the house. While you're at it, ask for the names and phone numbers of roofers, gardeners, and any others that you may want to consult in the future.

Despite the poor quality and the lack of helpful information in many owner's manuals, save them all. Also save warranties, sales slips, and other literature that comes with the things you buy. Read them or not, but create a hanging file for them in your file cabinet. You never know! Every once in a while, manufacturers slide some valuable information into those papers. Besides, when your sister's children accidentally reprogram your VCR, you will have to read how to undo whatever they did to make the sound disappear.

Chapter 22 Prevention

The fastest way to clean is not to have to clean at all. You already knew that. Here are a few ideas about eliminating the maintenance burden before it gets a chance to accumulate.

Floors

- Save a spare piece of carpet when you've had a new one installed. It will give you something to practice on when people like us annoyingly suggest that you try out a cleaning treatment on an "inconspicuous" piece of carpet. Moreover, if the carpet becomes permanently stained or otherwise damaged, it is often possible to patch in a new piece rather than replacing the entire carpet.

- Your choice of colors for the carpet can be critical. Solid dark and solid light colors are the most difficult to maintain. Tweed browns and grays are among the easiest.

- Most carpets sold these days are synthetic and have good resistance to staining. Nylon is an especially cleanable floor. Wool rugs are among the most beautiful, but enzyme cleaners and alkalis can attack wool fibers.

- Don't buy a white resilient floor. It shows all the dark dirt.

- Don't buy a black resilient floor. It shows all the light dirt *and* smudges.

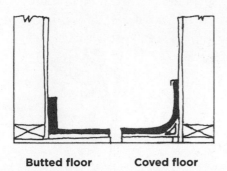

Butted floor   **Coved floor**

- *Especially* don't buy a black-and-white resilient floor. It shows everything.
- A smooth floor covering is much simpler to maintain than a textured one.
- Put doormats everywhere. An amazing amount of dirt is transported into the house on the soles of shoes. But don't use rubber-backed mats on vinyl or asphalt floors, or the floor may become discolored.
- Seriously consider leaving shoes at the doorstep—perhaps just in one or two rooms of the house, if you encounter too much resistance to the idea.
- Use as little floor finish as humanly possible.
- Seal the floor properly. It will save you a lot of grief later because dirt will not be ground into the flooring itself.
- If you are installing resilient floor coverings, cove the edge rather than butting the flooring against the wall at a 90-degree angle. A coved edge doesn't trap dirt and is much easier to mop.

Kitchen

- Replace inefficient countertops if you can afford it. Grouted tile countertops can be beautiful, but they're lots of work to keep clean. If you have to keep them, seal the grout with a professional specialized sealer. If you can replace them, give some thought to a high-grade Formica or another durable surface. As in the case of floors, see if you can have a coved edge installed to prevent dirt building up in corners and edges. You will thank yourself every time you wipe the countertop.
- Remove baked-on spills in the oven as they occur by spraying the spot with Red Juice, scraping loose all that you can with your scraper, and removing anything left with a pumice stick. Very fast and simple. You can avoid using oven cleaner again for a long time.

Dust

- Consider investing in a real air filter—not just the tabletop variety. One of our clients was required to have an air filter on doctor's orders to help alleviate symptoms of emphysema. It ran 24 hours a day in the hallway about 10 feet from his front door. There wasn't a speck of dust three rooms away. He got it at Sears. In-line air filtration systems can also be installed in central air-conditioning and heating systems. Check with a contractor.

• Put small items behind glass, especially collections of porcelain elephants, for example.

Bathroom

• If the grout between the ceramic tiles is cracked or has shrunk or is powdering, it's time to regrout. Get a can of premixed grout from the hardware store and rub it into the cracks, following the directions on the label. If the deterioration is serious, and you have to remove the old grout, a specialized grout saw will speed the job along considerably. It's like a small handheld hacksaw, except that the 2-inch angled blade has a gritty carbide edge that cuts right through the grout at just the right width. It's worth its weight in grout.

• After you've done such splendid work regrouting the tile (in any color but white, of course), it would be a shame to let it go to seed again. Do yourself a big favor. Do what professional tile-setters do: Seal the grout. We recommend a penetrating water-based sealer. The surface sealers are often formulated with silicone, which can start to look like dried-on glue after a while and peel off. To help maintain the wonderful appearance of your vertical fresh new grout, during your routine cleaning, make sure you rinse it with particular thoroughness to neutralize any cleaning agents that might eat away at it over time. Wipe horizontal tile dry instead of rinsing.

• Put a squeegee in the shower, and use it on the walls and especially on glass shower doors. It doesn't have to be a perfect job, and you don't have to squeegee every square inch, but 30 seconds of squeegeeing after a shower adds up to lots of time saved. It makes scrubbing the tile easier and will make intervals between cleanings significantly longer. Naturally, the bathroom will also look much better between cleanings.

• Mineral deposits around faucets or outside the shower door can be caused by leaks or by pools of standing water. Repair the leaks by recaulking or replacing washers, and wipe up standing water as needed. You'll avoid ever having to remove that difficult mineral buildup again.

• Open the bathroom window, so the mold doesn't flourish. If there isn't a window, use a fan. Leave the bathroom door open (or ajar) when showering. Leave the bathroom door open whenever it's not in use, and spread out shower doors or curtains fully, so they can dry.

- When the mood grabs you, you might want to take some Tile Juice and a white scrub pad into the shower with you—for the walls, not you. It's a fast way to do some quick touchups when company's on the way. Rinse thoroughly. If the buildup is heavy, don't try it because the floor of the tub or shower will get very slippery as the soap and mineral deposits are dislodged.

- Don't even think about installing a fiberglass shower enclosure. If it's already installed, replace it if you can afford to.

- If you have a persistent and otherwise unexplainable buildup of soap scum in your shower, it may just be the *soap*. Some of the bar soaps have a high fat content that will contribute to your cleaning burden. As an experiment, try different brands of soap—especially the newer liquid soaps—over a period of time. There are also totally fat-free, soap-free liquid skin cleansers such as Cetaphil Lotion (Owen Laboratories). You may be amazed at the difference.

Light Bulbs

- Put a drop of light oil (WD-40, sewing machine oil, Vaseline, etc.) on the threaded base of a light bulb before your screw it in. This will prevent the bases from getting stuck when it's time to unscrew them. You know what a hassle it is when you twist the glass right off, leaving the base welded in the socket. Aluminum-based bulbs are especially vulnerable. If you have the choice, get bulbs with brass bases. They're far less likely to get stuck.

Silver

- Keep items under glass if possible. Keep them away from sulfur-generating things (e.g., rubber, many fruits, some oak furniture) and salt. Store in tarnish-resistant cloth if possible.

The next two chapters go from the general to the specific. Chapter 23 reviews maintenance rules that apply to most household situations. Chapter 24 provides an alphabetical list of items likely to be found in your home. So if you would like to know what maintenance should be performed on your refrigerator, look under "R." For better or worse, that's where our responsibility ends. The next step is up to you, but it will be much easier to take that step with the confidence that knowledge provides.

Chapter 23 Maintenance Rules

I've distilled a few core principles or operating rules that have emerged as I've done our research on this subject. I hope they will be helpful in situations not mentioned here, so you'll be more equipped to develop maintenance solutions tailored to your specific household.

Maintenance Rule 1: Schedule your maintenance. Most actual (as opposed to imaginary) maintenance is scheduled for a definite date, not "next month," "when I get around to it," or "as soon as I have a free Saturday." Indefinite dates never actually arrive, and, as everyone knows, there is no such thing as a free Saturday. Some maintenance dates are determined by the season—for example, servicing the air conditioner before the warm season starts. But some dates are determined by your home and living style. If the manufacturer tells everyone in the world to clean the freezer's condenser coils every 3 months, test that advice for yourself. Go ahead and dust the coils (see **Freezers** on page 346) and then *check* them in 3 months. If the coils are dirty again, clean them again. But if not, recheck monthly until they really are dirty. Now you have a maintenance interval that's more meaningful than what the manufacturer said. Enter it into a maintenance journal (see Maintenance Rule 13 on page 307).

Maintenance Rule 2: Treating your belongings with care will reduce maintenance. In many cases, patterns of daily use are more important than maintenance in determining how long something will last. Be gentle. You can break almost anything if you try—purposely or not. Little plastic pieces are

305

sometimes the most important part of something and are easily broken off. An example is my hummingbird feeder. If the top of the plastic stem is broken, the whole feeder is useless. I know you're always in a hurry, but habitually stuffing 26 pounds of laundry into an 18-pound-capacity washer instead of doing two smaller loads will take years off the life of the washer.

Maintenance Rule 3: All things are not created equal as far as maintenance goes. By this, I mean that things used heavily need more attention than things used lightly. If you maintain the entire carpet on the same schedule, traffic areas will be worn out before the balance of the carpet shows any wear at all. Also over time, low-quality items often cost more to maintain, wear out more quickly, must be refinished, repaired, or cleaned more often, and must be replaced more quickly than quality items—which means they also end up costing more anyway. Don't settle for high-maintenance, low-cost items if waiting will allow you to afford better quality.

Maintenance Rule 4: Don't buy any product without knowing exactly what care it needs, how often it needs it, what cleaning it needs, and what product(s) to use.

Maintenance Rule 5: Cleaning is a major part of preventive maintenance and is often the cure for failures or problems. For example, the most common problem with CD players is skipping. The cause is almost invariably dirty discs or a dirty laser lens. The cure is cleaning in either case.

Maintenance Rule 6: Water is the enemy. Even seemingly small amounts of water are more dangerous than dirt to your house. A little drop behind the washer or a tiny leak in a shower will eventually ruin the drywall, then the studs, flooring, and joists. Ditto for water oozing in around windows, doors, and other outside openings. A leak is almost guaranteed to cost thousands of dollars of damage if ignored. Some of that water will eventually make its way to the frame underneath and start the inevitable process of deterioration. And water that soaks the soil underneath will attract termites and all sorts of other nefarious creatures.

Maintenance Rule 7: Ditto for direct sunlight. Keep most things out of direct sunlight. Carpets, wood floors, and many fibers fade; leather dries out; fibers are weakened; plastic warps, paper yellows.

Maintenance Rule 8: The more moving parts, the more imperative it is to keep the item clean. If a unit has moving parts, dirt is particularly dangerous. Moving parts also need lubrication unless factory-sealed.

Maintenance Rule 9: If you find yourself even thinking about it, it's time to change filters. It is just about impossible to change filters too often. They usually aren't expensive, so replace rather than clean regularly.

Maintenance Rule 10: Buy good floor mats. You've probably heard it be-fore, but everything they say about "good" floor mats is true. They can pre-vent lots of dirt from making it to places where it can cause damage. Good floor mats are not the cute little ones made of hemp or rubber that say *Welcome*: Good mats are the ones you see both outside and inside the doors of banks and other public buildings. They are big enough to take several steps on. They are made from nylon fiber or polypropylene fiber with heavy rubber backing, and they can be easily vacuumed to remove accumulated dirt. They belong both outside and inside all entrances to the home. Sources include jan-itorial supply houses and thecleanteam.com.

Maintenance Rule 11: Take advantage of a move or repair. Anytime you disassemble something or move something heavy out of place, clean every-thing carefully before reassembling or moving it back into position. So when the refrigerator is pulled out to be repaired, clean the floor where the refrig-erator was and vacuum the coils, the motor, and anything else that can't ordi-narily be reached.

Maintenance Rule 12: When in doubt, seal it. If instructions say to apply a protective seal on a product, do so. Grout of all sorts will last longer, stay cleaner, and resist stains and water damage far better if you do. So will various types of tile and natural stone products. Like making a bed or painting a room, sealants must be renewed at regular intervals.

Maintenance Rule 13: Keep notes or a journal of your maintenance ac-tivities. When you learn how often different maintenance chores need to be done in your home, write it down. Date each entry, so you know for sure when it's time to do it again. Include notes on anything that looks odd or sug-gests the possibility of a future problem. Identify major problems so that needed repairs can be scheduled in advance. You can use a simple three-ring binder or spiral-bound notebook, and file it with your monthly bills, so you have it in your hot little hands regularly to check for upcoming maintenance activities.

Chapter 24 Alphabetical List of Home Items

Air, Indoor

Today's homes are sealed much tighter than older ones, which slows the rate of air exchange with the great outdoors. This is fine if the great outdoors happens to be 20 degrees below zero. But without fresh air, a buildup of materials from furniture, carpets, construction, pets, and/or smoke can cause what would certainly be called smog were it outdoors. Improve the quality of the air in your home by following these suggestions:

• Regularly change the filter(s) that are used in the heating, ventilating, and air-conditioning systems.

• Open windows and doors whenever practical.

• Use exhaust fans routinely if your kitchen and/or bathrooms are so equipped. Clean or replace the filters in these exhaust fans on a preventive schedule.

Another potentially dangerous buildup in household air is moisture. Too much moisture promotes mold and mildew growth on and in clothes, walls, closets, and basements. Some research indicates that mold, when it can't escape from today's tight-as-a-submarine buildings, is the source of interior pollutants with the most widespread impact on health. Cooking, laundering, and showering can add 2 gallons or more of water a day to a house (Michigan State University Extension). Cool air holds less moisture than warm air, so you can rid air of moisture by (1) turning on the air conditioner, or (2) heating the house for a short time and then opening doors and windows to exchange the moisture-laden air for cooler and drier air. Granules that absorb moisture are sold in hardware stores and are good for damp closets, but they have limited impact on an area the size of a room.

Dehumidifiers reduce moisture in the air in much the same way that an air conditioner does.

Air Cleaners

Not having a *clean* filter in an air cleaner is kind of like having a car without an engine—it misses the whole point. So vacuum the foam prefilter with the crevice tool at least once a month, or wash it with dish soap and water, rinse and let dry. At the same time, vacuum or wipe inside the cabinet with a dampened cloth.

Most manufacturers suggest (1) cleaning ion-emitting needles every other month or so with a cotton swab dipped in alcohol, (2) replacing activated charcoal filters every 3 to 6 months, and (3) replacing HEPA filters once a year.

Run air cleaners continuously to get the greatest benefit. Position them near the source of dust if you can. The cleaned air will blow toward the middle or most-used part of the room.

Bathtubs

Most tub drains become clogged sooner or later with hair, even though most tubs have a removable plug in the drain. Clean the hair from the plug once or twice a year (depending on how quickly it starts to clog) by twisting or pulling the drain plug out, or by removing the lever that operates

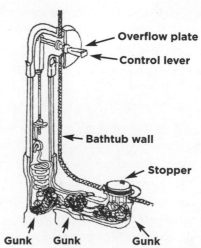

Overflow plate
Control lever
Bathtub wall
Stopper
Gunk Gunk Gunk

the drain plug's closing mechanism. Then you can pull out the stem and clean the hair (which has now turned into gunk) from the end of it.

Protect the tub from damage from tools, paint, trash, and so on when redecorating or remodeling by laying down a few towels or a tarp. Don't walk in the tub with shoes to hang shower curtains. Any grit—and there always seems to be some—caught between the tub and a shoe can cause a scratch in a moment.

Tub/Shower Enclosures, Caulking

Water or moisture in the wrong places is a threat to your house (see Maintenance Rule 6 on page 306). A common place for water to creep into areas of the house where it doesn't belong is around the tub or shower. Inspect the caulk every so often when you shower. Check the joints for cracks or separation between the tub and shower, between the tub/shower and the wall, and around the drain.

Caulk is one of the main defenses against moisture, but it was never intended to last as long as structural materials like wood and metal. However, if caulk is applied under building materials as the house is being built (so it isn't exposed to the air), it can last 30 to 50 years. Replace the caulk in any tub or shower joints when you notice it peeling, discoloring, shrinking, or developing gaps.

It is not particularly difficult to recaulk. The most difficult step is arranging to remove the bathroom from service for a few days. Contemplation can be converted to action by reminding yourself of the damage water does to your walls and floors *and* that your homeowner's policy will not pay for the repairs.

Before you start, clean the tub/shower enclosure thoroughly. Get rid of any soap scum buildup or hard-water spots, especially where you will be working. Then protect the tub with towels, a blanket, or a drop cloth. Remove all the old caulk you can, using a putty knife, screwdriver, metal pick, or a pair of pliers to pull it loose. Use a screwdriver or metal pick to rough up the surface of any caulk you can't remove, so the new caulk will adhere better. Try not to stab yourself or scratch the surrounding surfaces as you do.

Then vacuum with the crevice tool to remove loose caulk, dust, and debris. Wipe the area to be recaulked with a solvent (such as alcohol) to remove oils and other films. If mildew was growing anywhere in or around the old caulk, spray the area thoroughly with bleach. (Use undiluted household chlorine bleach, or dilute it with up to 4 parts water.) Rinse thoroughly after a few minutes with plain water, keeping excess water out of the newly exposed cracks. It will take a very long time to dry if excessive rinse water runs into the spaces that caulk used to fill. So take a break while it dries completely—usually overnight. If you're in a hurry, use a hair dryer to shorten the drying time, but don't recaulk before all surfaces to be treated are absolutely dry.

Caulks are now available that are pressurized and dispense without a caulking gun. Besides your not having to purchase or fuss with a caulking gun, they also make it a bit easier to get professional-looking results. For tub/shower enclosures, the best type of caulk is silicone because of its high flexibility and low shrinkage. If mildew grows in the shower even occasionally, choose a caulk with a mildewcide that will help subdue the mildew population for a year or so. There are dozens of different kinds of caulks to choose from. Shop where you trust the salespeople, explain exactly what you're going to do, and then buy the most expensive caulk if there are several to choose from. (It's worth it.)

Begin caulking at one end of the least visible joint. (Don't caulk the most visible area until you get the hang of it.) A continuous bead of caulk gives the best-looking results. Usually what stops you from applying a bead continuously is something in your way. So move stuff out of the way and do a dry run from one end of the tub to the other. Then fill the joint evenly without overfilling. If you must stop in the middle, overlap slightly and start again.

Produce a smooth finish by running your wet finger or a plastic spoon over the fresh bead of caulk. Depending on the type of caulk and temperature, caulk skins over quite quickly, so try not to dillydally. Rewet your finger as needed to avoid pulling the caulk out of position.

Allow the caulk to cure according to label directions (usually 36 hours) before using the tub/shower.

Note: Curing should not be sped up with heat.

Batteries

Alkaline

Alkaline batteries can leak acid even if they're unused. One appliance manufacturer reports that they've seen batteries fail and leak 2 years before the expiration date! If you have batteries in equipment such as a digital camera or camcorder, take them out if you don't plan to use the equipment within a week or so. Likewise, if you're using the AC adapter instead of the batteries, take the batteries out or check on them weekly. The damage that acid can cause to electronic circuitry far outweighs the inconvenience of removing or checking on the batteries.

Ni-Cad (Rechargeable)

According to Panasonic, today's nickel-cadmium batteries are virtually immune to "battery memory" problems caused by using a battery for a short time and then recharging it. They report that studies now show that repeated charging following a partial discharge can actually increase the battery capacity by as much as 10 percent. Don't use them immediately after charging, while they're still hot, and store them in a cool place when not in use. An unused corner of your refrigerator or wine cellar would be dandy.

If you haven't used your Ni-Cad batteries for 6 months or more, you may have to discharge and recharge them several times before the batteries are fully restored.

Note: The battery contacts of almost any battery-powered gadget don't have to be very dirty to interrupt the trickle of current. They can be cleaned with an ordinary pencil eraser, silver polish on a polishing cloth, emery board, or very fine sandpaper. (Rub gently!) Clean both ends of the battery as well as the battery contacts inside the appliance. If the batteries are failing to recharge for no apparent reason, or if replacement batteries don't seem to work, this is the first thing to try—*before* taking an appliance in for repair or tearing it apart. It may save you a trip or a few gray hairs. Manage pencil erasure droppings, so they aren't left in the unit. They could interfere with things that have delicate moving parts (e.g., tape recorders, CD players, etc.).

Bedding

Blankets

To reduce the number of times you have to launder blankets and quilts, vacuum them with the brush or furniture attachment a few times a year. Store unused quilts in large pillowcases, but not in plastic bags that don't allow air to circulate.

As long as the blankets are labeled as washable, pretreat spots and stains with a laundry prewash agent or with Red Juice. Keeping in mind the exception that you should wash only one blanket at a time, follow the instructions for washing pillows (see **Pillows** on page 314). Soak a very dirty blanket for 15 minutes or more before starting the wash cycle, and squeeze it by hand a few times as it soaks.

The procedure for drying blankets depends more on their type of fabric. Here's what Michigan State University Extension sources recommend for drying wool blankets.

Dry . . . on the high temperature setting. To absorb moisture and dry a blanket more quickly, place three or four dry towels in dryer. Preheat towels for 3 to 5 minutes. This helps absorb moisture, dry blankets rapidly, and avoid pilling caused by long tumbling. Place the blanket in the dryer with the warm towels. Set dryer control for about 20 minutes. Check the blanket after 10 minutes. Remove while still slightly damp to avoid shrinkage. Place blanket on flat surface such as a bed or over two [clothes] lines. . . . Stretch it to its original shape. When the blanket is completely dry, brush gently (with a soft brush) to raise nap. Press binding with a cool iron, if needed.

Hang the blanket over the shower door if you—like me—don't have those two clotheslines to drape it over.

For cotton and synthetic blankets, set the dryer to permanent press, and remove the blanket from the dryer as soon as it stops. Restretch to its original size, if necessary, before it cools off completely.

Blankets, Electric

Laundering is easy to do, so don't put it off until the blanket won't come clean. Follow the manufacturer's laundering instructions. If you don't have them anymore, start by presoaking the blanket in the washing machine for 15 minutes in laundry detergent and warm water. (One of the warnings in my owner's manual told me to unplug it before washing it. What was I going to do? Add an extension cord, so it would reach to the washing machine?)

Use your hands to squeeze soap and water through the blanket. Then launder on the gentle cycle for 1 to 5 minutes. It can be put through the spin cycle, but set the cycle to gentle as well. Dry it on the lowest temperature setting for 10 minutes and check. Remove it while still damp, and let it air-dry over the shower door or two parallel clotheslines. Have someone help you gently pull it back into shape while it is still damp and again when it's laid on the bed.

Note: Most electric blankets will shrink considerably if you dry them too long. Too much heat can cause electrical problems as well.

Down Comforters

Down comforters can be washed the same way as pillows (see below). The only problem is that many home washing machines aren't big enough to accommodate one. Take the comforter to a laundromat and use an oversize washer.

Pillows

Birds preen their feathers every day, and it's probably smart for humans to take the hint. So give your feather pillows a good "fluff" every time you make the bed. Wash the pillowcase and, if there is one, the removable cover regularly to prevent dirt and body oils from migrating to the ticking or filling. Leaving pillows in a crushed position can permanently damage the loft of a down feather, so don't wad them up or store them under heavy linens for long.

It's not unusual for feather pillows to be discarded without ever being washed, when, in fact, washing every couple of years is a good idea. As long as the label says "washable," they can go directly into the washing machine. Select regular agitation and spin cycles and use warm water and detergent. If you have a top-loading machine, first fill the machine, add the detergent, and either agitate manually or let the machine agitate briefly to mix the detergent and water. Then add the pillows. Push them down into the water because they will float. If you have a front-loading machine, add the soap, then the pillows, and then fill with water. Wash two or three of them in the same load. Let them soak for 10 minutes or so, and swish them around a couple of times during this period. Now let the machine agitate for 5 minutes or so before moving the dial ahead to the first spin cycle or to the rinse cycle if there's only one spin cycle. (Important!) *First* push in the dial or otherwise turn off the machine, then turn the dial ahead to the new setting before pulling it back out again to restart the cycle. Let it go through the rinse and remaining spin cycles. Set it for an extra rinse if available. (If not, and if the pillow still seems soapy to you, rinse again in the washer or sink and then put it through a final spin cycle.)

Pillows take a long time to dry, so be patient and start early. Set the dryer to low. Stop the dryer every half hour or so, and give the pillows a good shake to help dry, reshape, and refluff them. Be patient and try not to imagine they are dry before they really are. They must be completely dry, or they will be vulnerable to mildew.

Blenders

Blenders are designed for speed, not power (like a food processor), so they are easily overloaded. In other words, they can't move around a heavy volume of food. Be gentle.

To keep the bank of buttons from sticking, clean them by spraying very lightly—misting, really—with Red Juice. Use a toothbrush to agitate the surfaces of the buttons, the sides of the buttons, and the areas between the buttons. Dry with a cleaning cloth. Drape the cleaning cloth over the toothbrush to dry hard-to-reach areas like the ones between the buttons.

Disassemble the blender jar to clean. When disassembling or reassembling, protect the rubber gasket from damage. Nicks make the blender leak. Replace the gasket if it's dried out, cracked, or otherwise suspect.

Books and Bookshelves

Books should be removed from bookshelves and their tops vacuumed once a year or so (more often if the room is very dusty and less often if not). Do this in a methodical way. Start at one end of the highest bookshelf. Grab a handful of books with one hand and tilt them outward, so their tops can be vacuumed with the brush attachment held in the other hand. Keep the books closed, so dust won't fall into them, and vacuum from the spine to the edge of the book. Because of the design of some shelves, you first may have to slide the books partially off the shell before you can tilt them forward. If the books are too tightly packed to allow this, remove a few books to make some room. Set these books on the next shelf or on the floor until you're done with the shelf.

After you've vacuumed the tops of the books in a shelf, push them as deep into the shelf as they will go to expose the front part of the shelf, and wipe that exposed area with a Red Juice–dampened cleaning cloth. Finally, pull the books back out into their proper position, and move on to the next shelf. (An option is to remove the books completely, vacuum them, wipe the shelves, and restack the books. But since the books prevent dust from reaching most of the shelf area, this isn't usually necessary except on shelves with collectibles instead of books or in the case of unusually fragile books.)

Another enemy of books is moisture. So maintenance includes monitoring for possible mildew growth—especially if you have warm, damp summers. Check books occasionally for mildew growth on pages and covers—leather covers in particular. If mildew is a problem, install a light bulb or chemical de-humidifying crystals in any enclosed bookshelves and/or consider installing a room or central dehumidifier or air conditioner. (And check the roof, walls, or foundation for sources of leaks or condensation.)

To treat established mildew spots, a dab of hydrogen peroxide or alcohol may help. Use in moderation (a cotton swab is a good idea) and blot up any excess quickly. If the mildew has spread deep into the pages, sprinkle di-atomaceous earth (available at a garden-supply store or plant nursery) in the page, leave the book closed for several days, and then shake and vacuum the book out. Refer to *Cleaning and Caring for Books,* listed in Appendix B. For se-rious mildew infestation, you might want to consult a book/paper restorer.

Brass (and Copper)

The first thing to check, of course, is whether or not the metal has been lacquered to prevent tarnish. If so, polishes are out of the question. Just spray with Red or Blue Juice and wipe with a cloth as needed. If the lac-quer has begun to break down or has been rubbed off in areas, little patches or cracks of oxidation will begin to show up. Then it's time either to strip the lacquer off (with lacquer thinner) and begin to polish the piece regularly, or strip it and relacquer it yourself or have a metalsmith do it for you.

Brass and copper can be cleaned with specialty polishes or generalized metal polishes. If the polish you're using leaves a chalk residue, follow the steps out-lined for silver polishing to get rid of it. If the polish (e.g., Twinkle) calls for the object to be rinsed under water after polishing, resist your impulse to use hot water because it will hasten retarnishing. For the same reason, wipe all pieces completely dry after rinsing.

If you have a copper-bottom pot or pan that is particularly charred with heavy carbon buildup, lay an ammonia-soaked rag on the area for 15 to 20 minutes, and then scrub with a white pad and polish. Repeat as needed.

Brass Discoloration

Boy, do we get a lot of questions on brass. Let's get them all cleared up once and for all. There are two possible situations where you may need to get dis-coloration out of brass.

The brass is coated with clear lacquer. Lacquer keeps the brass from being exposed to the air and tarnishing as a result. So long as the lacquer coating remains intact, the brass will look newly polished. Clean it by dusting or wiping it with a damp cloth. Unfortunately, the lacquer can eventually (perhaps inevitably) peel or wear off. Just like paint, it gets nicked here and there, or the coating gets wiped or rubbed or scratched off during cleaning. Once the lacquer coating is compromised, the area of brass exposed to the air starts to tarnish while the rest of the brass stays shiny. That's when we get questions about discoloration.

There's no satisfactory solution to this condition other than one of the following: (1) Remove the rest of the lacquer with a paint stripper safe for use on metals. (Examples are 3M's Safest Stripper and Jasco's Speedomatic.) Then clean and polish the brass, and apply new coats of lacquer. Specialized (i.e., very expensive) clear lacquer in spray cans is available in many upscale hardware or paint stores. Be warned, however, that relacquering is a *very tricky* thing to do properly at home: Dust gets trapped in the lacquer, the lacquer runs, etc. (2) Remove the rest of the lacquer, polish the brass, and forget about relacquering. You will have to repolish it every so often for the rest of your life, until you sell it at a garage sale or until you decide that a little tarnish adds to its charm. (3) Pay a metal refinisher to strip and relacquer it for you. (Look in the yellow pages under "Plating" or "Metal Refinishing.")

Note: The secret of owning good-looking lacquered brass is to handle and clean it as gently as you would an egg. Take extreme precautions to ensure that nothing happens to nick, scratch, or otherwise remove even the tiniest bit of lacquer, because that's when the "discoloration" will start again.

The brass has no protective coating. In this case, the brass tarnishes uniformly. It will take on a darker and darker shade as the tarnish gets more and more established. Fingerprints show up startlingly well as the tarnish develops. The solution is to polish it with a brass polish as often as you must to keep it satisfactorily shiny. You always have the option of coating it with lacquer, but then you will have Problem 1 above. Oh, well.

Brass Sconces

Most sconces are protected against tarnishing by a lacquer coating, as are most brass knickknacks. So, most of the time clean them with only a feather duster. When the duster isn't effective, wipe them gently with a cleaning cloth dampened with Blue Juice or water. Then go back to feather dusting for as long as you can before the brass needs to be hand-wiped again.

Brass Film

If new brass fixtures have a film over them, leave them alone. It's the lacquer coating referred to in the previous two pages. It's conceivable that your fixtures were covered with a thick plastic film to protect them during shipping, but that should be easy to peel off.

Butcher Block Surfaces

A good one—preferably made of a hardwood such as birch—will last long enough to be able to hand down to the grandkids (if they ever develop an interest in cooking). The secret is maintenance, of course. Don't apply a hard finish such as polyurethane or varnish. Use an oil finish instead. There are differing opinions on which oil to use. Some prefer mineral oil because other oils (boiled linseed, vegetable, etc.) can turn rancid. I have always had great luck, however, with walnut oil. I like the feel of it, it gives the wood a beautiful finish, it lasts a long time, and it has never turned rancid in my 15 or so years of experience with it. Besides, walnut oil came from a hardwood tree to begin with. I keep a bottle of it handy for the butcher block, which means it's also available when a recipe calls for it.

To season a new butcher block, apply walnut oil with a paper towel. Be liberal with the oil, and cover the top and four sides while the block is resting on paper towels over a few layers of newspaper on the counter. It doesn't matter whether you apply it with the grain or across the grain. Wait an hour or more, and repeat. Keep applying until the wood seems equally saturated (usually several times). Then wipe thoroughly with a cleaning cloth or more paper towels, turn the block over, and repeat on the bottom.

Here's how to get a well-used butcher block ready for a coat of walnut oil. Scrub the surface with dish soap, hot water, and a white pad or a soap-impregnated steel-wool pad. Rinse and let dry. If the surface is rough, sand lightly, but unless this is a restoration, don't try to make the surface like new again. Wash once again after sanding and let dry. If the surface is still heavily stained or too dark for your liking, apply a solution of 50 percent bleach and water to the surface. (You can use up to full-strength bleach if you prefer.) Use gloves and avoid the fumes. Use the same plastic scrub pad to work the bleach into the wood. Wait a few minutes, then rinse, wash one more time with soap and water, rinse again, and let dry. Repeat this step to further lighten the wood. Do a final touch-up with fine sandpaper, if needed, and now you're ready to apply walnut oil as just described. Whew.

Wash the block after each use with dish soap and water, rinse, and wipe dry. Some of the walnut oil is removed each time the block is cleaned, so reapply additional walnut oil as needed—usually every few months or so—whenever it passes the particular threshold of drabness or dryness that bothers you.

Cabinets

During normal housecleaning, cabinets are just wiped around the handles, where fingerprints are most likely to appear. The rest of the cabinet surface—especially in the case of kitchen cabinets—needs a deep cleaning once a year or so. The specific cleaning steps vary depending on whether the cabinets have a natural wood finish, are painted, or are metal. If the cabinets aren't cleaned when needed, especially in the kitchen where grease is interacting with the finish of the cabinets, they may have to be refinished or repainted. Use Red Juice or a restorative such as Furniture Feeder or Howards Restor-A-Finish. Use a toothbrush to clean corners. In addition to this yearly cleaning, maintenance includes checking that hinge screws are snug and lightly lubricating the hinges with Teflon spray or WD-40.

If a screw has stripped the wood and can't be tightened any longer, here's what to do. After removing the screw, stuff the hole with wooden matches or toothpicks, and break them off flush with the surface. Now insert the screw and tighten. If the holes are so short that the matches or toothpicks won't stay in the hole, glue them in place before you insert the screw. Alternatively, you can use longer screws or fill the holes completely with epoxy putty, and start over again.

Protectors for cabinet doors are designed to cushion their stop against the door frame of the cabinet. These protectors often fall off or otherwise mysteriously disappear over time. Without them, the cabinets are noisier and the screws and hinges more likely to loosen or fail. Check how many are missing when you do a heavy cleaning of the cabinets, and then get replacements at a hardware store. They are available as self-adhesive plastic, rubber, felt, or cork dots. Take a sample, so you can pick one that has the same material and thickness as the existing protectors.

Camcorders

See **Video Camcorders** (page 401)

Cameras

Many maintenance problems with cameras are really accidents that happen as we're prowling about trying to get interesting photos. Use your camera case and its carrying strap to minimize the risks. Dirt and moisture cause many other maintenance problems. Go to extravagant lengths to keep them both out of the camera and off the film or compact flash card (digital cameras).

We all know we're supposed to remove the batteries when storing a camera. But most of us ignore this eminently sensible advice, so when you change batteries, at least clean the contact points with an eraser or similar means (see **Batteries** on page 311).

Likewise, everyone also knows they're supposed to clean their camera. There's no easy way out of this one, but fortunately, it doesn't take long. First, and this is important, remove loose grit with a few blasts of canned air (available at camera or electronics stores), a lungful of air, or the lens-cleaning blower brush lying unused in the junk drawer. Then, using a soft cloth, clean the lens, the viewfinder, and the face of the electric eye. Purists gasp, but I treat it just like a pair of glasses. First I breathe on the part to be cleaned, and then I wipe it with the cloth. There are special lens-cleaning fluids and lens tissues available where cameras are sold. Take a couple of minutes to perform this chore occasionally but regularly. If your camera accepts filters, install a haze filter over the lens to protect it.

When you get word that your first grandchild is going to perform at the White House, and you haven't used your camera for some time, take it out and test it. Clean the battery contacts and change or replace the batteries, or at the very least purchase a spare set—not a bad idea in any event. Give yourself time to get it fixed if anything is amiss.

Can Openers

The cutting wheel should be cleaned every few months. Usually, it will pull away from the body of an electric can opener and can then be put in the dishwasher. If further cleaning is necessary, use a toothbrush and Red Juice or fine steel wool. The cutting wheel will probably last a bit longer if you lubricate it with some cooking oil after cleaning. Dull cutting wheels that slowly open a can of cat food while the cat yowls feline expletives can be replaced with shiny new, inexpensive ones—often using only a screwdriver.

Between cleanings, watch out for paper or food getting caught in the drive-gear teeth. Such things caught here make the teeth slip, resulting in only a partially open can. Clean the teeth with a toothbrush and Red Juice also.

Note: Some small appliances mentioned in this chapter can't really be "maintained" because there's almost nothing that can be done in the way of maintenance—and when they break, they should be tossed instead of being repaired. If you're tired of "throwaway" appliances, (re)consider replacing them with manual appliances. I'm very pleased with the manual can opener I've had since my last 2-year-old, nonrepairable electric one croaked. My manual one is easy to use, easy to store (without taking up counter space 24 hours a day), and has a pleasing design, *and* I'm quite sure it will still be working decades from now. Also available are manual ice-cream makers, pasta makers, food mills, coffee grinders, and so forth.

Carpets and Rugs

Just like the floors they cover, carpets are susceptible to the plain old dirt carried onto them by shoes, feet, and paws, and blown onto them by gusts of wind through open doors and windows. Plain old dirt is mostly pulverized specks of broken rock. Imagine a crushed-rock driveway reduced considerably in size, and you can visualize what destroys most carpets before their time. Proper maintenance starts with minimizing the crushed-rock effect by installing mats inside and outside all entryways to the house (see Maintenance Rule 10 on page 307). And vacuum, vacuum, vacuum. Several times a week is about right for active households, at least in areas of heavy use. Speaking of heavy use, don't install carpets in kitchens (visualize peanut butter toast facedown), patios (imagine a bowl of the chef's not-yet-world-famous BBQ sauce upside-down on the ground), bathrooms (mascara and Mercurochrome here and there), or garage—you get the idea. Rooms that get moisture or heavy traffic, or are too involved in food preparation, shouldn't be carpeted.

I'm fond of the saying "There are only two kinds of dirt in the world; the light kind that's attracted to dark objects, and the dark kind that's attracted to light objects." This is particularly apt for carpets. Avoid single-color dark or light carpets. Pick grays, rusts, and browns in midrange colors to reduce maintenance. Patterns and designs, multiple colors, multiple pile lengths, and varied textures all help disguise the inevitable and make maintenance easier. Whatever color, place the carpet on a quality pad to cushion and extend its life.

Vacuum the backs of small rugs at least yearly. Spot-clean as soon as a spot occurs—and if it's wet, clean it before it dries. Blotting up a little spill of coffee with a paper towel will remove it almost completely. Follow up with a quick spray with Red Juice and another good blotting, and it's gone. That same spill allowed to dry will be a permanent stain on some carpets. This is a good example of Maintenance Rule 5 (page 306). Much as you would prefer to sit quietly and drink your coffee instead of worrying about the small spill, do it now. Then pour yourself a fresh cup and start over again—or take it to work with you if you're now out of time. Get a good spot remover, and store it with your cleaning supplies.

Shampoo traffic areas as needed. This requirement is different from one household to another, but several times a year is not unusual. The best method for yearly deep cleaning is a shampoo followed immediately by extraction, but there are options for cleaning traffic areas. (1) Very small areas can be cleaned by hand. Mist Red Juice evenly on the dirty area—like a heavy morning dew. Now wipe the misted area with a cleaning cloth. Turn often. The surface dirt, along with the Red Juice, is absorbed into the cleaning cloth. (2) Dry cleaning: This method uses an absorbent powder or other material impregnated with a cleaner or solvent. Sprinkle the powder on the dirty area, agitate by machine or by hand with a brush, and vacuum it away. Several brands are available at grocery, hardware, and home-supply stores. (3) The same shampoo/extraction method used for deep cleaning.

Shampoo (deep-clean) the entire carpet only as needed. The Carpet and Rug Institute recommends deep cleaning every 12 to 18 months depending on type, color, use, and the manufacturer's recommendations. In any event, no carpet-cleaning system gets out oil stains and dirt, so keep up with the spot-cleaning and err on the side of shampooing a little too often rather than not often enough. Arrange carpet cleaning when you can keep dogs, cats, kids, spouses, and so on, off it until it is completely dry.

I recommend hiring a professional to do the deep cleaning. The money saved doing it yourself seems insignificant when you consider the cost of the machine, detergent, and prespotter as well as picking up and dropping off the machine, moving and replacing furniture, and operating the machine. Professional equipment will routinely do a better job in a fraction of the time. And carpet cleaning can really take a toll on your aching back.

Change traffic patterns yearly, if possible, by rotating the rug. If you have wall-to-wall carpeting, rearrange furniture to change wear patterns.

Sun can damage carpets by fading the color and weakening the fibers.

Protect with blinds (vertical ones, preferably), tinted windows, plants (vines), trellises, and so forth.

Stop any frays before the vacuum or something else turns them into a ruined carpet. Trim them with scissors or stitch them with a needle and thread—even if the job looks less than perfect. Or hire a professional for a more seamless job.

Position castors under furniture legs. Or attach furniture rests to the bottom of the legs of furniture that is moved often or that rests on hard floors such as wood or tile (see **Furniture** on page 347).

Sprayed-on soil retardants such as Scotchgard actually work, although they have to be reapplied after cleaning. If such a treatment is an option when you purchase a carpet, take it.

Cast-Iron Cooking Utensils

If they haven't already been seasoned, that's the first thing to do. First wash and scour with cleanser or fine steel wool. Rinse and dry thoroughly. Liberally coat the inside with vegetable oil, and place on a burner at very low heat or in the oven at 250° to 300°F for 2 to 3 hours. Add more oil as needed. When finished, wipe off the extra oil and wash the utensil with dish soap and water. Rinse, and then dry first with a dish- or paper towel and then over a stove burner (a minute or less for a gas range or a few minutes for an electric range). Wash and dry in this manner after each use. Wipe with a thin coat of oil after several uses. To help prevent rust, once seasoned, store the utensil in a dry area without the lid in place. It shouldn't have to be re-seasoned if properly maintained, but do so if it starts to look stained or rusty.

Ceramic Tile

These tiles are essentially glass, so protect them against chipping by using a cutting board in the kitchen and avoiding hard blows. Perseverance is the key to maintenance. Don't let floors or showers accumulate dirt, grease, mineral deposits, or soap scum. Even if you don't mind the unsavory appearance resulting from deferred cleaning, and even though the ceramic tile can be made like new again with liberal doses of elbow grease and household cleaner (one of ceramic tile's great advantages), the all-too-visible grout that's between the ceramic tiles is likely to become permanently stained without regular maintenance cleaning. That is, the tile will look great again, but the grout will not (see **Grout** on page 354).

Christmas Trees

These maintenance ideas come from the National Christmas Tree Association.

1. **A tree should smell and look fresh. To test it, lightly grip a branch about 6 inches from its end and draw your hand to the branch tip, letting the needles slip through your fingers. Only a few needles should fall off. If the tree is small enough, you can pick it up and drop it on its cut end. Again, this should dislodge only a few needles.**

2. **Cut off a section of the tree's stem before placing it in water, and place the tree in water immediately afterward. It may drink a gallon of water in the first 24 hours, so check the water level often.**

Closets

Maintenance of closets boils down to organization—a big, big subject—especially if all your closets are filled to the brim, your drawers are overflowing, your garage is increasingly harder to fit the car into, and paper—articles, magazines, bills, junk mail, and so forth—is spread throughout the house. Household organization solutions for closets and many other problem areas are discussed in our book *Clutter Control* (see Appendix B). In the meantime, remember to open the door to dust and vacuum inside closets as you do your regular housecleaning.

Coffeemakers

My brother tossed away his coffeepot when its water flow slowed to a trickle. I wonder how many others have done the same. Mineral and scale buildup made his pot slow to a crawl and its demise practically inevitable (which he could have avoided by using a water softener or distilled water). Besides the slowdown, the coffee also often tasted bitter. The buildup should be removed periodically.

Most coffeepot manufacturers sell a decalcifying agent, but a solution of half white vinegar and half water works fine. Pour the solution into the water reservoir and turn the pot on. Let half the solution drip into the carafe, shut off the coffeepot, and let stand for half an hour or so. Pour the solution back into the reservoir, turn on the coffeepot, and run the full amount of vinegar solution through the coffeepot. Do this several times (with fresh vinegar solutions) if you are treating a severe buildup. Finish up by rinsing all the accessible parts with water and then running plain water through a cycle. *Popular Mechanics* magazine reports that at least some specialized coffeemaker cleaners work better—and *smell* better—than white vinegar.

Heated water passes through one or more small holes as it drips onto the coffee grounds. If the previous method didn't get the coffeepot up and running, it may be that hard-water deposits have completely closed these holes. If so, unplug and upend the coffeemaker to clean them out at least partially with a stiff wire or small nail. Now do the vinegar-and-water treatment just described to finish the job.

Coffee/Spice Grinders

When grinding, pulse the on/off switch rather than holding it down continuously. Don't run it for more than a minute or so without stopping to let it cool. And don't run it while empty, or it will quickly overheat. If the switch needs cleaning, use a pastry brush along with a vacuum cleaner to deep-clean it. Use the same tools to clean out the grinder when changing from grinding coffee to grinding something else.

CDs or DVDs

The data (music, images, movies, or computer info) are stored on a reflective metal layer located below a protective coat of transparent plastic on the bottom (unpainted side) of the disc. Microscopic pits in the foil surface create the digital "ons" and "offs" that translate back into something intelligible when read by a laser focused on the foil surface.

The protective coat is quite durable, so the digital information is fairly safe from damage. If you're lucky, fingerprints or small scratches won't affect performance because the laser focuses on the metal layer below. Many fingerprints turn into a harmless blur, and the player can actually interpolate and fill in short breaks caused by scratches. They aren't indestructible, but good maintenance means they can last for decades. Hold them by the outside edge.

Wipe dirt and fingerprints with a clean soft cloth and CD-cleaning fluid or alcohol. Or wash gently with dish soap and water and dry with a soft clean cloth. It's safest to wipe from the center out (like spokes on a wheel), but as long as you're using a soft clean cloth and the proper fluid, you can wipe any way that's convenient without worry.

Keep the discs away from heat. They will warp if left in a dashboard player that can reach well above 125°F. And warps can cause the laser mechanism to fail prematurely by requiring it constantly to focus and refocus on the uneven surface at its extreme range.

Note: Many scratches that affect performance can be repaired, as long as the scratch didn't reach completely through the plastic layer to the foil layer. Compact disc repair persons can mill the disc down by a few thousandths of an inch and then polish it back to its original smoothness. They claim that this process removes the scratches and allows the laser to read the disc as if it were new. It is undoubtedly less trouble and expense just to replace a damaged disc as long as copies are still available. Record stores also sell kits that will repair more minor scratches. Scratches from either side that are deep enough to reach the metal layer cannot be repaired.

Compact Disc Players or Digital Video Disc Players

Repair expert Daniel Bennett says there's little involved in caring for a CD or DVD player.

1. As with electronics in general, locate it in a cool location. The unit itself doesn't produce a lot of heat, but being kept cool helps ensure trouble-free operation.

2. CD and DVD players are sensitive to dust—especially smoky or greasy dust.

3. To avoid a variety of audio problems, double-check audio connections to be sure they are secure.

Even though CDs and DVDs rely on very precise optical readings of incredibly small stored information, they are remarkably robust. Even portable and automotive units that are bounced all over the place usually don't need optical realignment. This is why, at least in part, extended warranties aren't necessary (along with most other things in the world). You can clean the optical laser lens, however, with the CD-cleaning discs now on the market. They have a fuzzy side that gently brushes the lens to remove accumulated dust.

Take the player in for service only when something goes wrong. Here are some symptoms that indicate it might be time to take yours to a professional to be cleaned or serviced: (1) you hear audio noise, skipping, or sticking (make sure your discs are clean—see below); (2) it is taking longer to start a disc or to complete a search; and (3) loading or starting a disc becomes erratic.

While a dirty videotape can harm a VCR, or a dirty record can ruin a stylus, it usually takes a cracked or broken CD to damage a CD player. Of course, dirty CDs may give rise to audio problems, so clean them according to the directions given under **CDs or DVDs** (page 325).

Computers

Locate your computer and the monitor where they will remain relatively cool, dry, and dust-free, with plenty of room for air to circulate around each component. On particularly hot days, turn on a fan or air conditioner. Both the monitor and your eyes prefer subdued lighting. Don't put anything on the monitor that might block the ventilation grills on the top or rear.

At the risk of sounding preachy, I'm repeating the ubiquitous warning against leaving coffee, Budweiser, Diet Coke, or anything like it near the computer while you're surfing the Internet. If you do this 500 times, it's bound to spill at least once and ruin the keyboard or other components.

A few lights or an electric clock won't matter, but don't plug the computer into a circuit shared with a space heater, for example.

Besides installing a UL-rated surge protector to protect against electrical surges, it's wise to unplug your computer in the event of an impending thunderstorm. Also unplug the phone line to the modem. It's also prudent to unplug or at least turn off the computer if the weather is such that a power interruption is likely. If you don't, when the power resumes, all sorts of electrical aberrations can occur that you do not want your computer to experience.

If you're serious about computing, or if you are the frequent victim of blackouts, brownouts, surges, and electrical storms, you might consider investing in an uninterruptible power supply (UPS). It's essentially a constantly charging battery that activates in a fraction of a second to provide power to your computer when normal power fails. If the power goes down, it will sound an alarm and keep your computer and peripheral devices up and running—long enough for you to save your work and shut down the system in an orderly fashion. The UPS is usually connected to everything but the printer (which draws too much power for the UPS to sustain for long).

Dust is another enemy. Cover components when not in use. Wipe ventilation slots with a cloth, or gently vacuum them. If you remove the computer case, use a can of compressed air to remove accumulated dust from inside the computer. Clean the keyboard with the brush attachment of a vacuum cleaner when you do your regular housecleaning. Or use a can of compressed air, but protect yourself and other things in the area from flying dust. Also carefully vacuum out the printer to remove bits of paper and dust that have settled in it. Clean the monitor with a cleaning cloth sprayed with Blue Juice.

Keep unshielded speakers (i.e., the magnets inside them) plus any other magnets and electric motors away from the monitor. If the monitor becomes magnetized, it will display weird fluorescent colors and may even need degaussing (demagnetizing). Nearby power lines can also cause noticeable monitor interference—even electric wiring in the wall or behind the wall. Don't move your computer while it's on. The hard drive is particularly vulnerable. Finally, CDs and diskettes stored upright are less prone to accidental damage.

Computer Mouse

Under the theory that the more the part is moving, the more trouble it will cause, the computer mouse is one of those components that will require relatively more care over time. The main preventive step you can take is not to run it across dusty and gritty surfaces, where it will pick up and transport the grit and dust into its interior with great ease. In other words, do use a mouse pad rather than the desk surface and keep the pad dusted and cleaned.

If your mouse starts to freeze up or work erratically, it's time to clean it. With the computer off and/or the mouse disconnected, flip it over on its back and remove the cover plate that keeps the mouse ball in place. It will either twist or slide off. The ball can then be tipped out to clean. Don't use a strong solvent or ammonia: A plain damp cloth or one lightly sprayed with Red Juice should work just fine. Set it aside to dry.

Then turn your attention to the metal rollers in the mouse housing that are

spun by the ball. Wipe them with a cotton swab barely dampened with alcohol. If you have a can of air handy, it wouldn't hurt to give the area a blast or two. Then replace the ball and cover, wipe off any grungy fingerprints on the top, and your mouse is on its way again.

Convection Ovens

Like so many other things around the house, perhaps yourself included, the oven needs to vent. Leave a few inches of space around and over the oven for this purpose. Inside, make sure there's at least an inch clearance between the food being cooked and the sides, top, and bottom of the oven. Clean any filters in front of the fan every few months or as needed. Wash them in soapy water and allow them to dry before reinstalling. Clean the fan itself and the interior of the oven with Red Juice and wipe with a cleaning cloth.

Countertops

Whether your counter is made from tile, Formica, Corian, or marble, and no matter what the salesperson told you, protect it from hot pots, pans, or baking dishes taken directly from the stove or oven. Also, don't cut food on it. The countertop and/or the knife will be damaged. Liquids have a way of eventually getting to places where they cause great damage, so wipe up spills, including plain water, as soon as they occur.

Crystal Display Pieces

Crystal in all shapes and sizes, including crystal or glass sculptures, has some important maintenance considerations.

1. Surface protectors for crystal display pieces (such as vases, bowls, and sculptures) are doubly important because they protect the surface below as well as the piece itself. Use self-adhesive felt pads.

2. Wash by hand only. For smaller pieces, use a rubber mat in the sink. Since diamonds cut glass, remove any diamond rings you may be wearing. Use warm water and regular dish soap (ammonia can start to remove gold rims). Don't lift pieces out of the water to wash them. Wash underwater, where, if you drop it, it probably won't break. Dry by hand with a clean cotton towel. Clean larger pieces with a cleaning cloth and Blue Juice. Spray the cloth and wipe the piece clean and dry.

3. Use both hands when moving or using crystal. I once owned a crystal water pitcher that broke when it was lifted by its handle. I should have supported it with a second hand.

4. Change water every other day in small-necked vases and every day in large-necked vases or bowls of flowers. Remove lines left by evaporated water with a solution of half water and half white

vinegar. Fill the vase with the solution past the lines, and allow it to sit for several hours or overnight. Use a bottle brush to agitate, discard the solution, and wash normally.

5. Heat or cold can crack crystal. Don't let candles burn too low in a crystal candleholder. Prefill a crystal ice bucket with cold water. It's wise to avoid refrigerating or microwaving crystal pieces.

Curtains and Drapes

They take a beating from the sun and will eventually be ruined by its effects. Delay the inevitable by protecting them with awnings, outdoor trees or other plants, window film or tint, or similar tactics. (The same applies to furniture and other light-sensitive possessions.) Vacuum the tops of curtains and drapes as needed. Vacuum the rest of them yearly.

Dehumidifiers

A dehumidifier is an air conditioner that doesn't cool. Maintenance is therefore very similar to an air conditioner's. Vacuum the evaporator coils once or twice a year with the brush attachment. If necessary, use Red Juice and a toothbrush to remove grime, and spray with water to rinse.

Don't let water stagnate in the water container or run over into the base of the unit. Empty (or visually check) the water container daily. Wash it with soap and water, and allow it to air-dry (or put it in the dishwasher if it's safe to do so).

Wash or replace the filter once a month.

Dishwashers

Maintenance starts with correct usage. Scrape or rinse pieces of food off dishes and cookware. No matter what the salesperson or the TV commercial told you about not having to rinse or scrape, no dishwasher can successfully flush away a lot of food. Most can deal with only small amounts of undried soft food. And although some foods can be successfully removed by the dishwasher, they may discolor other items being washed or the inside of the dishwasher itself. Among the chief culprits are mayonnaise, mustard, and ketchup. All things considered, it's best to give a quick rinse or wipe to most dishes as you load the dishwasher. The disposer (or the garbage can) can deal with solid food a lot easier than the dishwasher's drainage system can.

Load the dishwasher in such a way that dishes and cookware face the center where the strongest water sprays can reach them. Place knives and other sharp or heavy items with care, so they don't cut the protective covering of the dishwasher racks. Once these are cut, rust will develop shortly. Glasses should be placed between prongs, not over them. Don't block the spray arm or spray tower.

Appliance expert Al Hale advises running the dishwasher once a week empty of dishes and soap, but with ½ cup or so of nonsudsing ammonia or white vinegar added instead. This treatment can remove and help prevent a film buildup that inevitably arises as residual dirt and grease are deposited on interior surfaces during everyday use. Wait until the water is being pumped into the machine, then open the door and pour in the vinegar or ammonia (but not both!) onto the floor of the machine. If the interior is stained because of hard water, run the empty dishwasher with 2 cups or more of white vinegar as just described.

If you have hard water, you'll get better performance if you regularly use a liquid rinse agent. (Look for it in grocery stores in the same area as dishwasher soap.) It's added to the dishwasher's dispenser for rinse agents, usually located next to the dishwasher's soap dispenser. You don't need a rinse agent if the water is naturally soft or if you have a water softener.

Keep the pump screens free of small food particles and other deposits. The pump screens are usually located in the well at the base of the unit. Some units don't have screens, so if you don't see an obvious opening in the bottom of the dishwasher with a screen on it, don't worry about it. It doesn't have one. If it does, check for large food particles. Remove them and then scrub the screen with a toothbrush.

It's possible that the holes in the rotating spray arms, especially the lower ones, are clogged with food particles. Using a paper clip, pin, or thin wire, try to get under food particles and *pull* them out through the hole rather than pushing them back in the hole where they will reclog as soon as you run the dishwasher. (Both the pump screen and spray-arm holes should stay clear and unplugged if you rinse and load as described above.)

The dishwasher requires fairly hot water (around 140°F). If you're in doubt, check the water temperature with a candy or meat thermometer. Allow the dishwasher to run through one fill-and-pump cycle, and let the dishwasher fill with water a second time. Then unlatch the door and slowly open it. Place the thermometer in the water toward the middle of the tub. Don't rest the thermometer on the floor of the dishwasher, or you'll get a false reading. If the temperature isn't between 120° and 140°F, you will not get good washing results. Hot water is essential for dissolving grease and activating detergents. Raise the temperature setting of the water heater and retest (see **Water Heaters** on page 406). If this doesn't result in a higher temperature at the dishwasher, or if the water heater is already set at a high enough temperature, have the heating element of the dishwasher checked. (Not all dishwashers have one, but a heating element is designed to boost the temperature of the hot water delivered from the house's water heater.)

The detergent dispenser must open and close freely. If detergent builds up here, the dispenser will not open and close on schedule, and the dishes won't get clean. Remove any leftover soap. Then clean thoroughly with Red Juice and a toothbrush. Rinse and wipe dry. And naturally, when running the dishwasher, use only detergent made for dishwashers, and don't use it if it's "lumpy." It gets that way fairly quickly, sometimes within a week or two (especially if stored in a damp location, like under the sink), and then it won't dissolve during use. Also, don't add detergent until just before you're ready to run the machine. You've probably already figured out that you don't need the heat cycle to dry the dishes. The dishes get almost completely dry without it. Not using it means less chance of a breakdown, and you'll cut down the electric bill as well.

By the way, if you see a puddle of water at the bottom of the dishwasher after use, don't worry. It's standard procedure in many models for water to be left there at the end of its cycle.

Doors and Door Hardware

Exterior doors are a particularly expensive and important part of your home. One of the most important steps to ensure their long-term health is obvious, but it happens often enough that it bears stating: Don't slam them. They will crack. They will stick or be difficult to close. Stucco walls will crack. Hinges will loosen; locks and doorjambs will fail.

Paint wooden doors every 4 to 6 years. Use a fungicide additive if mildew is a problem. Varnished doors may have to be recoated more often. Remember that doors have six sides, and each one needs equal protection by paint or varnish.

Keep doorknobs, locks, and hinges operating smoothly and quietly. Once every year or two, use graphite powder or Teflon spray (e.g., Tri-Flow or Borden's) for locks and doorknobs. Graphite comes in a small squeezable plastic bottle that allows you to apply it into tight spots. Although it's usually black, graphite is also available in white, which is less messy for indoor applications.

Only the tiniest amount of graphite is needed. If you use more, it gets on keys, hands, clothes, and so on. Squeeze or spray the lubricant into a lock, and then insert the key and work it back and forth a few times to spread the lubricant to all the interior surfaces. In general, don't use oil on knobs, locks, or hinges. Even though it does help at first, it also attracts dirt and grime that can gum up these devices and cause them to wear out prematurely.

Install doorstops on all interior and exterior doors to prevent wall damage from doorknobs. If the bottom of the door isn't suitable for a doorstop, install it at the top. If a door handle still touches the wall, even with a doorstop on the bottom, put another doorstop at the top of the door. If you don't like doorstops, use a pair of hinge stops. They attach directly to the hinge pins and are less noticeable (if you are one of the few people who notices doorstops at all).

You might consider removing extra interior doors. Our home in San Francisco had doors between the hall and the living room and between the kitchen and the dining room. Neither door had been closed for 5 years, so I put them in the garage. We have saved time dusting and vacuuming ever since, and we now have more space in each room.

Sliding doors usually get more and more difficult to operate. Clean the runners as needed with a vacuum, then with a toothbrush, Red Juice, and a cleaning cloth. Check to be sure weep holes are open. Then apply Teflon spray or other lubricant, and the door should slide easily again.

Drains

A sink, shower, or toilet drain is shaped to create a "trap" that holds water and forms a barrier or seal against sewer odors and gas that would otherwise enter the house from the drainage system. It is commonly called a "P-trap." A brilliant invention, actually; a fully functional seal with no moving parts. Infrequently used drains such as those serving a spare shower or basement sink should be refilled by turning on the water briefly to replace evaporated water and to ensure that the water barrier is in place.

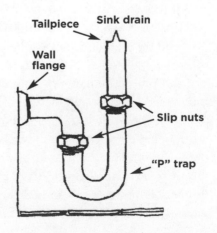

Because of their shape, drains are susceptible to clogs. I've had people tell me they were actually surprised that cotton swabs and matches clog drains. Other obvious examples of things that don't belong in drains include—but are not limited to—grease, oil, hair, and any paper other than toilet paper. The list includes practically everything you can name besides wastewater.

Plunger Use

Next to prevention, the best approach for cleaning a clogged drain is still the venerable plunger. Here's how to use one.

1. **Plug any sink overflow vent with a wet cloth. If it's a double sink, close or plug the other drain. It's best to have a helper hold the wet cloth firmly in place.**

2. **The plunger's rubber cup must cover the drain opening completely, and standing water must cover the cup's edge halfway or so up its side. Add water if necessary, but remove extra water to avoid giving yourself a splash bath. Use a cup or a bucket to remove all but 2 to 3 inches of standing water. Tilt the plunger so most of the air under it can escape as you put it into position.**

3. **Work the plunger up and down 15 to 20 times. This method builds up the pressure needed to break the clog loose. You can increase its ability to build up pressure by smearing a little petroleum jelly on the rim of the plunger. Repeat the sequence several times, if needed.**

4. **If the water starts to slowly trickle out, take a break while it does and then refill with hot—better yet, boiling—water, let it drain out, and try it again with the plunger.**

If this procedure has been unsuccessful, the next step might be one of the following: renting a plumber's snake, removing the P-trap itself, or calling a plumber. The snake is fraught with difficulties, because it's quite easy to poke it through the surprisingly thin wall of a drainpipe (especially after a few years of corrosion). And it can be surprisingly difficult to reassemble the drainpipes properly. Unfortunately, this is one of those problems that may not have a simple solution. A pipe can be filled with debris all the way to the sewer or septic tank, or it may be so badly invaded by roots or grease that it has to be replaced. You may also have to start a maintenance schedule with a rooter company. My personal recommendation is to call a plumber.

Some drains are old and corroded or installed so close to level (instead of downhill) that they clog fairly regularly despite your good habits. Further maintenance is required. There is great disagreement whether it's okay to dump lye-based drain cleaners into the drain once a week or even once a month. On one hand, if you ask almost any consumer advocate, these drain cleaners are toxic chemicals, they eat into pipes, and they destroy beneficial bacteria in a septic system. If you ask the manufacturer, they are quite safe if used according to directions.

Well, they do contain dangerous chemicals, and they are effective when used as a maintenance aid to keep a sluggish drain working. I have used them that way in an old house in San Francisco with very touchy drains. However, you can often keep a prone-to-clog drain open just as well by pouring boiling water (½ gallon or so) into it once a week, once a month, or according to what you have learned about the drain (i.e., before it clogs). Follow up in 10 minutes or so with a minute or two of hot water from the tap.

Enzyme drain cleaners are effective and safe but are rather slow-acting. Therefore, they aren't good for emergencies but are fine as maintenance. Use these when you go on vacation or can otherwise take the time necessary to let the enzyme cleaner work, because some of them take overnight to work. One caution: They are not usually very effective on hair.

Dryers

The complete and unrestricted venting of hot, moist air from a dryer is critical to its operation, its long life, and your safety. Therefore, the single most important maintenance step is keeping the lint screen clean. So, just like the directions always say, clean the lint screen after each use. In fact, if you are drying a very linty load, clean the lint screen partway through the drying cycle. Whenever the screen is clogged, the dryer will run longer. It can be working at less than half its normal efficiency, so it costs that much more to operate, and it will wear out that much more quickly. Also keep the lint screen in good condition. If it is bent, punctured, rusted, or no longer fits properly, replace it.

The antistatic sheets that are tossed into the dryer by many of us with each load may not be such a good idea, according to appliance guru Al Hale. If they lodge in the lint screen, they will block the flow of air just as if you hadn't cleaned the lint screen to begin with.

Every few months, remove the lint screen and vacuum behind it to get at the lint that manages to sneak behind it. Poke the vacuum hose into the opening (with or without the crevice tool) to remove as much lint as you can.

Check and clean, if necessary, the vent duct once a year by disconnecting it from the back of the dryer. Use the vacuum or a specialized dryer vent brush. Also, the duct should have no sags, which can trap water, or sharp turns, which can trap lint. Make sure the duct was not squished (even partially) when the dryer was pushed into place. Any obstruction can build up heat within the duct and can shorten the life of your dryer. Vinyl ducts have been known to catch fire, so when it's time to replace yours, change to a flexible aluminum one. In many cities, aluminum ducts are now required by code for new and retrofit construction.

Finish the inspection of the dryer by checking the far end of the duct at the exhaust hood once a year. Make sure that air can flow freely out of it and that the vent flap opens and closes properly. You should be able to feel a strong exhaust when the dryer is operating. Birds, spiders, and other unwelcome housemates can try to make their home here but should be encouraged to relocate. Also, lint can build up within this hood. Check with a flashlight and remove any accumulation with a screwdriver or similar device. If there is not a strong exhaust, remove the vent cover to investigate. If you don't find anything, go inside the house and pull the dryer away from the wall to get at the near end of the duct. Disconnect the vent duct from the dryer and from the exhaust port (where the vent duct attaches to the wall or floor). Clean the duct by first vacuuming what you can. Then take it outside and flush thoroughly with water and hang it up fully extended to dry. If yours is a rigid metal duct in sections, separate the sections and clean inside each section with the vacuum and the brush attachment or with a dryer vent brush. Use the crevice tool to vacuum into the dryer and into the exhaust port as far as you can. Clean the floor and vacuum the back of the dryer with the brush attachment. Before you move the dryer back into position, reattach the exhaust duct and recheck the exhaust volume. If it's still weak, call for service.

It may help motivate you to inspect the dryer's venting pathways and to clean the vent screen after each use by observing that lint is extremely flammable. The instant it can't get out, a potentially dangerous situation arises. Likewise, don't vent the dryer underneath the house. Lint accumulating in the crawl space, attic, or basement is highly flammable.

The soap, pretreatment agents, chlorine bleach, ammonia, rust removers, and so forth that can corrode a washer's surface can do the same thing to a dryer.

Some of these products will corrode both the painted surface and the plastic controls as well. Wipe up such spills promptly, and try not to use the dryer as a work top. Just use a sink instead of the dryer (or washer) top, and rinse the sink after use.

Overloading also wears out the dryer before its time. Besides, your clothes will dry faster and will emerge with fewer wrinkles if you give them some breathing room in the dryer.

Dust

If you're interested in lowering maintenance in the house by reducing the overall amount of dust, here are some subjects to check on:

1. Filters (see Heating and Cooling Systems, on page 356).

2. Effective floor mats (see Maintenance Rule 10 on page 307).

3. Weather-stripping around doors and windows.

4. Lint from your dryer.

Electrical Maintenance

Ground-Fault Circuit Interrupters (GFIs or GFCIs)

You probably have this type of electrical device in your kitchen, bathroom, basement, pool area, deck, or anyplace where water is likely to be present. GFIs detect a short circuit (caused by water or any other reason) and will shut down the circuit within a fraction of a second—faster than electrical current can travel to your heart, where it poses its greatest danger. A fuse or circuit breaker protects the house's wiring. A GFI protects you.

The manufacturers request that you test GFIs once a month. This is easy enough to accomplish, because there is a test button right in the middle. Push it. You'll hear a little click, and the circuit will be interrupted. Push the reset button to restore power to the outlet or circuit. I don't expect to live long enough to meet the person who actually does this every month.

Overloaded Circuits

If you have a circuit that regularly trips the breaker or blows a fuse, find out if it's due to an overload. If it's not, call an electrician. Ignoring it could result in a fire. And even if it is an overload, unless you solve the problem by redistributing the appliances that are plugged into that circuit, you may want to talk to an electrician to learn whether additional capacity is needed.

Electronics

(Also see individual electrical components.)

Allowing unhampered air circulation through all vents is critical to avoid overheating. The rubber feet under most electronic devices provide the minimum gap between adjoining units, so don't remove them or defeat their purpose by setting the unit on carpeting. It's also smart to keep cabinet or closet doors open when using the components inside. Vacuum the vent openings occasionally to keep dust from clogging them. Keep electronics away from open windows, high heat, and the cat.

Naturally, electronic gear will stay cleaner longer if you cover it when not in use. If you do spill something on a piece, turn it off, unplug it, turn it over, and wipe it to remove what you can. Then wait a few days before you plug it back in. If it works, fine. If not, it's usually smarter to start shopping rather than take it in for repair.

If you have invested a great deal in the equipment, proper maintenance includes having a lightning arrester professionally installed. Connect the equipment to its own ("dedicated") electrical circuit, and install a rated surge protector as well.

Here's a bit of useful information from Sony Hawaii (see Appendix B). Not using a unit for a long period could cause premature component failure. An electronic unit should be used once a month or so to help ensure that it stays in proper working condition. Turning it on will electrically energize the components, which in turn can help prevent premature failure. Ordinarily, electronic components should last for about 5,000 hours of use. But you can't quit using something for years and still expect it to work—or at least to last 5,000 hours. So it's counterproductive to store electronic equipment for the sake of prolonging its life.

Fans

Box and Oscillating Fans

Clean the blades when you can see dirt, because an accumulation can unbalance the blades and wear out bearings. Clean them with a vacuum or open the fan and wipe with Red Juice and a cleaning cloth. Align blades (metal ones only) by measuring and bending into position as needed. The motor shaft in unsealed motors should be lubricated with lightweight machine oil once a year or so.

Ceiling Fans

Whenever you find yourself cleaning a fan (which we recommend you do about once a year), check that the fan is still tight and not working its way loose from the ceiling mounting. Constant vibration when running and/or from a pull-chain switch can eventually loosen the entire fan. Check that fan blades are tight also. Blades should turn freely with the power off. If they don't, have the fan serviced.

You can stretch the period of time between cleanings by purchasing a specialized duster for ceiling fans. The one we use is called a rabbit-ear duster. It bends to fit around the fan and remove dust better. However, until they invent a brake to keep the fan blades stationary during the dusting operation, cleaning attempts will be only partially successful—even with the right tool.

If the fan starts to wobble when running, the most likely cause is that a balance weight has fallen off. The next most likely cause is that it needs an additional balance weight. The solution in either case is to add a balance weight. First try to eliminate these other possibilities.

1. Take a good look from below to make sure no blades or blade holders are askew.

2. Check that the screws through the blades into the blade holders are tight.

3. Check that all blade holders are tightly attached to the flywheel.

4. Check that all blades are equidistant from the ceiling.

If the fan is askew or if the blades aren't level with the ceiling, have it serviced. If none of these things is the problem, here are the steps to determine where to place a balance weight. (Most manufacturers provide a blade-balancing kit. Excavate yours from the tool cabinet or purchase a new one.)

1. **Select one blade and place a balance clip midway on the blade on the rear edge. (A balance clip is part of the manufacturer's balancing kit. If you do not have this kit, use a medium-size metal washer, and tape it in place.)**

2. **Start the fan. Note whether the wobble is better or worse. Stop the fan and repeat on each blade noting the blade on which the greatest improvement is achieved.**

3. **Select the blade that gave the greatest improvement, and move the clip outward or inward on this blade. Test each to find the position where the clip gives the greatest improvement.**

4. **Remove the clip and install a balancing weight on the top and in the center of the blade near the point where the clip is positioned. (If you don't have a balancing weight, firmly tape the washer in place.)**

5. **If the wobble is not completely gone, you can start over again and apply additional weights.**

Two cautions should be mentioned. Allow the blades to stop between each test. It's easy to get impatient and reach up too soon. Either the balance clip or the metal washer could fly off if not secure.

Exhaust or Vent Fans

Ceiling or wall exhaust fans in the kitchen and bathroom eventually get grungy—even if you vacuum or brush their grills regularly. When there is a visible buildup (or once a year if you can't see into the unit), remove the grill by removing the screws that hold it in place. (First, turn off the power and ensure it can't be turned on accidentally by flipping the circuit, removing the fuse, or taping the power switch off.) Put the grill and filter, if any, into the dishwasher or soak in dish soap and hot water in the sink. Replace the filter after it's been washed a few times. Use the crevice tool to clean the housing and a Red Juice–dampened cloth to clean the fan blades. Reassemble.

Faucets

Leaky faucets do more than merely waste water. If the hot-water faucet leaks only one drop per second, it means paying monthly for 200 gallons of hot water from which you received no soothing hot bath. A little trickle is more like 6,000 gallons a month—a waste of precious resources as well as money. Besides, if it's hard water, some of it undoubtedly will evaporate and leave tenacious or even permanent mineral deposits and/or stains.

Washers

Usually, it is a worn washer that's causing the drip. If the faucet has no washers, it is probably a cartridge type. The latter lasts longer but still must be serviced periodically. Learn how to replace either one. This isn't quite a fix-it; I prefer to call it maintenance when the alternative is to call in a $70/hour plumber to install a 15-cent washer. Here are some very basic how-to-change-a-washer instructions. Because of the subject of this book, there's a lot of ground that we're not covering. (And there are any number of excellent home-improvement books that cover the subject in great detail.) But we want to give you the basic idea and a dose of encouragement, so you can see that the task is not insurmountable. If you feel reasonably comfortable that you could tackle disassembly of a faucet—armed with a screwdriver, adjustable wrench, and a pair of pliers—we'll help you get it back together again (sans drip).

1. **Determine that a store with everything you may need is open. Make sure that it will still be open if you are delayed or if the project takes longer than expected (practically a certainty, at least the first time).**

2. **Turn the water supply to the faucet off, and open the faucet to drain the line.**

   Note: If the faucet doesn't have a shut-off valve under the sink, if the faucet is very old, or if it's a shower faucet in a wall—for

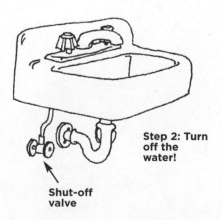

Step 2: Turn off the water!

Shut-off valve

heaven's sake, put your feet up, call a plumber, and turn on Oprah instead. You'll live longer. It's just too likely that something will go wrong that costs more than the 15-cent washer.

3. As you disassemble the parts, place them on the counter in the precise order in which you removed them. Always take worn parts to the store for exact replacements. If you have the slightest doubt, make yourself a diagram or Polaroid shot and then take everything to the store. Also, make a note of the manufacturer's name if it's not clearly shown on the part.

4. Put a stopper in the sink. Otherwise, the very thing that pops loose will head for the drain. (This is not a superstition; the drain is, after all, the lowest point in the sink.) Also place a towel over the sink to protect it from scratches. The next few steps will diverge a bit, depending on whether the faucet has a separate handle for hot and cold or is a faucet (ball, cartridge, or disk) with a single pivoting handle. The following instructions are for conventional faucets unless otherwise noted.

5. Remove the handle. Many faucets have a decorative cap that can be removed by prying it off with a screwdriver or knife. Then remove the screw keeping the handle in place. For single-handled faucets, the setscrew underneath the faucet handle must be unscrewed before the handle itself can be removed.

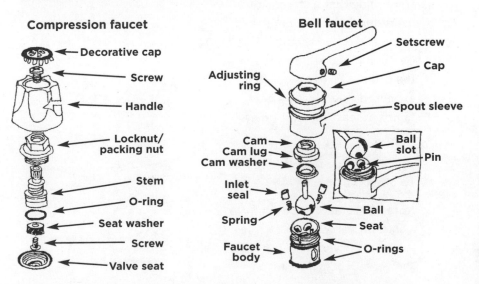

Compression faucet

- Decorative cap
- Screw
- Handle
- Locknut/packing nut
- Stem
- O-ring
- Seat washer
- Screw
- Valve seat

Bell faucet

- Setscrew
- Cap
- Spout sleeve
- Adjusting ring
- Cam
- Cam lug
- Cam washer
- Ball slot
- Pin
- Inlet seal
- Ball
- Spring
- Seat
- Faucet body
- O-rings

6. Remove the packing (or bonnet) nut with an adjustable wrench. Especially if this nut is tight, hold on to the faucet for dear life with one hand as you turn the wrench with the other. To avoid scratching visible parts (and even chrome scratches rather easily), wrap the faucet with tape or a cloth.

7. Unscrew the faucet stem by hand. The washer is located at its far end, held in place by another screw. If the stem looks like it's in good condition, remove the washer and replace it. If the stem looks worn, leave the washer alone and get thee to a hardware store with the whole assembly (stem and washer). The friendly clerk at the hardware store is much more likely to remain friendly if you do so. Some washers are flat and others are beveled. The clerk will be able to make more sense of the whole affair if you bring in the worn stem and washer together. For single-handled ball faucets, remove and replace the rubber seat and spring; remove the faucet spout; remove and replace the O-rings. For cartridge faucets, replace the cartridge. The same friendly clerk will help you select replacement parts.

8. Screw the faucet stem back in (but not too tightly). Replace the packing nut. For a single-handled faucet, replace the ball assembly as well as the spout.

9. Turn the water supply back on. Check for leaks. Adjust the packing nut as needed. Finally, replace the handle.

Ceramic Disk Faucet

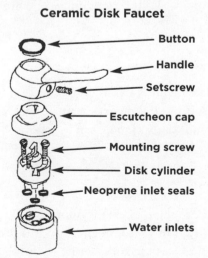

- Button
- Handle
- Setscrew
- Escutcheon cap
- Mounting screw
- Disk cylinder
- Neoprene inlet seals
- Water inlets

Cartridge Faucet

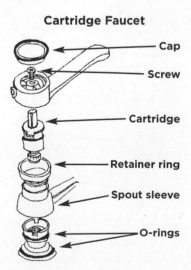

- Cap
- Screw
- Cartridge
- Retainer ring
- Spout sleeve
- O-rings

If you happen to be home while a plumber is installing a new faucet, ask him how to replace the washer. Also ask if you can buy a spare washer or two. If you're also willing to change the P-trap (see **Drains** on page 333), ask to buy one or two of them, and ask for a short demo of how to replace it. According to expert plumber Jeff Meehan, the only types of P-trap that will really last are 17-gauge brass or ABS or PVC plastic.

While you have his attention, why not ask for recommendations on draining or flushing your water heater (see **Water Heaters** on page 406) or whether or not the plumber offers a regular maintenance agreement?

Don't clean faucets (or anything else you don't want to get scratched) with a green pad. The green pad removes a layer of chrome or brass along with the dirt each time you clean.

Aerators

Found in kitchen and bathroom faucets, aerators add air to water to reduce splashing. As debris works its way through the water line, it will get trapped behind the aerator. Hard water will also restrict the flow of water. Unscrew it from the mouth of the faucet. Use a pair of pliers and a cleaning cloth or piece of tape wrapped around the aerator to keep it from being scratched. Rinse the filter and washer, replace them in their original order, and screw the aerator back on the faucet. You will learn how often this has to be done, but the most obvious sign is that the flow of water is reduced or misdirected.

If the deposits in the aerator filter don't rinse off, they are probably hard-water deposits. To remove these deposits, soak the disassembled aerator overnight in a solution of equal parts water and white vinegar.

Fax Machines

Go over the keyboard with the brush attachment of a vacuum cleaner as you do your routine vacuuming. Find out (from the owner's manual) where the glass is that covers the scanner portion of the fax, and clean it once a year or more with alcohol and a cotton swab.

Fire Extinguishers

Recharge or replace the unit if it's low. That's the easy part. Manufacturers recommend checking the pressure monthly. If this recommendation is really necessary, and I doubt whether it is, the hard part is remembering to do it—

and remembering where the extinguishers all are. If you have trouble re-membering, start checking the pressure while you're cleaning the house. As you pass a cupboard where an extinguisher is stored, open it and glance at the pressure gauge. Locate extinguishers in a visible—or at least very acces-sible—place, which will make it all that easier to check on their pressure as you do your routine cleaning. Exhume them from the back of cupboards and out from under the garage workbench, where they have been buried for years. And don't allow clutter to displace the fire extinguishers over time.

Take the time to make sure that other family members know where the ex-tinguishers are. It doesn't help much in an emergency if you're the only one who knows where to find the extinguishers, and you don't happen to be home.

Also give a lesson to family members on how and when to use a fire ex-tinguisher. They are a quick defense against small home fires only. Teach youngsters to call 911 first. Most home extinguishers are rated multipurpose (ABC), which means they can fight all classes of household fires. A is for ex-tinguishing trash, wood, and paper; B, liquids and grease; and C, electrical equipment. To use a fire extinguisher, pull the pin or other release mechanism and aim at the base of the fire. Squeeze the handle and sweep from side to side until the fire is out. You should always have an escape route available if the fire gets out of hand. Also be alert that extinguished fires don't flare back up.

Fireplaces

Call in a professional chimney sweep after 2 to 3 years of use in a new home and before the first year's use in a used home. He can clean the chimney, if needed, and advise you on how often cleaning should be repeated.

If your chimney doesn't have a chimney cap, have one installed. It protects the interior of the chimney from slow disintegration from rainwater, it breaks up sparks coming from the chimney, and most important, it prevents animals from nesting in or otherwise exploring your chimney. Call a chimney sweep, mason, or roofer to order one. If it's difficult to look up (or down) your chimney to be sure it's clear, a mirror and a flashlight will usually solve that problem.

Creosote buildup in chimneys is the principal reason for dangerous chimney fires. To reduce the amount of creosote collecting inside the chimney, burn hardwood (broadleaf flowering trees—such as oak, maple, and fruit trees) rather than softwood (conifers—such as pine, spruce, hemlock, and fir).

Food Processors

Besides normal cleaning, to keep yours running well and to avoid bending the blades, add food in small amounts, and don't process items like ice, grains, dried fruits, and coffee beans unless the manufacturer okays it. If the blades get bent or pitted, replace the blade assembly rather than trying to bend them back into shape or polish them.

Freezers

Freezers work most efficiently in a cool, dry location. The ambient room temperature shouldn't go much below 40°F for manual-defrost freezers and much below 60°F for frost-free freezers. Don't crowd things around the freezer; leave some room on both sides, the top, and the back for air exchange. Adjust the leveling as needed. An upright freezer should be tilted very slightly back, so the door swings shut on its own when released.

For manual-defrost models, defrosting should be done annually or when the frost is between ¼- and ½-inch thick. Turn the freezer off and unload the food into cooler chests or into boxes lined with plenty of newspapers or blankets. (Or do it when it's freezing outside—and just set the food on the deck. Somebody should keep an eye on the dog, however.)

If your freezer has a defrost drain, remove the drain plug from inside and place a shallow pan underneath. Have a second shallow pan handy or place a bucket nearby for easier emptying. Lacking a defrost drain, use a large sponge or turkey baster. Place a bucket nearby to wring or empty into. A few towels to catch drips are a good idea. Put pans of hot water in the freezer with the door open, and direct air from a fan (placed outside the freezer) into the freezer to speed defrosting. Reheat the water when it cools off. Use a plastic spatula or scraper to remove frost when it starts to melt.

If you own a wet-dry shop vacuum, there is an easier, faster way to defrost. Melt the ice by blowing air into the freezer, then use the shop vac to suck up the water. Once the frost is removed, clean well with Red Juice and a cleaning cloth. Inspect and clean the door gasket. You might as well wash the outside at the same time.

Note: Manufacturers recommend emptying and cleaning even frost-free models on an annual basis. As with other manufacturer's recommendations, adjust them to your home's conditions.

Move the freezer, if needed, to brush or vacuum the condenser coils. Frequency of cleaning depends on location, dirt, number of animals in the household, and so forth. In general, it should be done often enough to keep the coils reasonably free of dust and hair (see **Refrigerators** on page 374).

In the event of a power failure, *don't* open the freezer for any reason except to stave off starvation. The food will stay frozen correspondingly longer if you don't open it "just to check." Especially with an upright freezer, when you open the door, the cold air literally falls out, and the contents will warm up quite quickly from that point forward. Adding dry ice at the rate of 2 pounds per cubic foot of freezer space will keep foods frozen for up to 4 days, according to a recent Whirlpool owner's manual. Speaking of such cheery events, a freezer alarm that will alert you to a power failure is a good idea, especially if you have a freezer full of New York strip steaks and Alaskan king crab legs. If at all possible, put the freezer on its own electrical circuit, and, of course, don't select a receptacle that can be turned off with a switch or pull chain.

Furniture

Position furniture so there is enough room between it and the wall (or anything else) for the vacuum head to fit. If you don't leave this space, the furniture has to be moved or the vacuum disassembled just about every time you clean.

The scratches and gouges furniture legs inflict upon floors of all types are abundant, ugly, and expensive (if not impossible) to repair. Yet there is a cheap and easy solution—surface protectors. Even though the legs of most furniture have a metal, plastic, or rubber protector preinstalled at their base, it is there to protect the leg and not necessarily the surface below. However, there is practically no furniture with legs, almost none with wheels, and even some with neither (for example, speakers) that doesn't need a surface protector installed to protect the floor below.

Surface protectors of all types are available at hardware and other stores. For furniture legs on hard floors (wood, vinyl, tile, stone) I prefer carpetlike protectors that can be permanently attached to the legs so they don't have to be repositioned whenever the furniture is moved. For furniture legs with wheels, a coaster is called for. Furniture on carpeting also requires a coaster, with or without spikes to keep the carpet from being crushed. Cork pads work well on stereo speakers because they also help improve the sound in addition to protecting the surface they're sitting on.

Note: Even with protectors in place, especially with carpet or felt protectors that can trap grit and grime, don't slide heavy furniture if you can lift it instead.

The following are additional maintenance subjects for specific types of furniture.

Fabric

Apply a stain-resistant product such as Scotchgard. If it's an option when you purchase the furniture, take it.

Glass

Although glass used for tabletops is heavy and strong, it can all too easily be scratched—especially by jewelry, utensils, or even other glass. This fact, and their perpetual need for cleaning, is a big drawback to glass tabletops. They are beautiful when new, but they will get scratched soon after they're exposed to life outside a showroom (besides showing dust and fingerprints vastly more than any other type of tabletop). A standard coffee mug can wreak havoc on a glass tabletop if it's carelessly moved across its surface. Moving most other hard items across the glass will also scratch without fail. Use coasters, place mats, hot pads, or even newspapers if that's all that's handy to protect glass from these subtle and nearly constant assaults. Don't place a lamp, candlestick, picture frame, or other item on a glass surface without first putting surface protectors on its bottom. The same self-adhesive felt or flannel protectors used on picture frames will work just fine.

Leather

Manufacturers have widely different opinions about how to maintain leather. I suppose this is due to the widely varying qualities and finishes available, but here are some steps that are generally agreed upon.

1. As with fabric furniture, if you're offered a pretreatment option when purchasing leather furniture, take it! This treatment contains protectors against staining and soiling. It also helps keep the leather soft and supple. Some of them (such as Guardsman, when applied professionally) offer a warranty that covers stains, cracking, and even cuts, rips, and burns. Be sure to ask if and when the piece needs to be retreated.

2. Don't position leather furniture in direct sunlight or very close to a heating vent or fireplace. This is especially important for aniline-dyed or unfinished leathers. Their light color fades quickly.

3. Dust or carefully vacuum when you do your regular weekly or bi-weekly housecleaning. Dust and dirt are just as abrasive and damaging to leather as they are to the other surfaces in a house. In fact, dirt may be even more damaging to leather because it migrates to and concentrates at seams. These seams are bound together with thread, and if the grit isn't removed regularly, it can cut right through them—something that happens with auto seats with distressing regularity.

4. Once every year or two, clean with a leather cleaner. Or alternate between cleaning the entire piece and cleaning just those areas exposed to sweat and oily hair. There are at least two types of leather cleaners: surface cleaners and soap cleaners. Find which works best for your furniture by testing both. You're also testing for colorfastness, so conduct the test in that world-famous inconspicuous place. Allow the leather to dry completely after the first test before starting the second test.

Product instructions should include whether to use a sponge or soft cloth. You should dab or gently wipe, but not rub, the surface. Don't forget to slip a sheet of plastic under the furniture before starting this project. Don't let moisture get underneath the legs of the furniture, where rust can develop and stain the carpet. Tip the leather chair or couch forward (supported by its arms or by a coffee table or ottoman), so you can work on the back. This also creates a convenient place to put the cushions to clean. Do them first, starting with the edges and then the top and bottom. Set them on wax paper (or plastic wrap or a garbage bag) or lean them against a wall similarly protected, and let them dry. Clean the back and tilt the furniture into its upright position. Stand behind it to clean the top of the back cushions. Then clean the rest of it except the lower front panel. Finally, tip the furniture onto its back, and clean the front panel without having to get on your hands and knees.

Note: Leather is much more vulnerable to stretching and other damage when it's wet or damp.

Follow up the cleaning by reconditioning with an agent to restore oil and nourishment to the leather. This will remoisturize leather, keep it soft and pliable, and make it more resistant to cracking and scuffing. Some say to use one that contains wax, which protects leather in the same way that it protects paint on a car. Again, pretest to be sure you like the feel on your furniture.

Whether the leather is color-coated (what most of us have) or has a dyed "unfinished" look (usually called aniline or semi-aniline) makes a big difference when there is a spill or other accident. Color-coated leathers are quite resistant to stains. Aniline and semi-aniline finishes are next, and suede and other rough unfinished leathers are practically nonmaintainable. Unfinished leather readily absorbs liquids (like red Kool-Aid) and greasy, oily stuff (from Grandfather's hair when he falls asleep after Thanksgiving dinner, for example). The good news about oily spots is that they're often so completely absorbed into most types of leather that they eventually disappear. Because of the surface and nature of unfinished leather, even leather creams can cause blotches. Vacuum and/or wipe unfinished leather with a damp cloth or an untreated dust cloth regularly, and protect it from accidents with particular care.

Call in a professional if the leather has a serious stain such as ink or red wine—especially unfinished leather. But here are the steps to take if you want to spot-clean the furniture. (Pretest any procedure once.) Some dirt can be removed with an art gum eraser, but be careful—you don't want to make a clean spot that will be more visible than the dirt was.

Greasy stains. Wipe off any surplus stain as quickly as possible with a cleaning cloth or paper towel. This is the type of spot that should eventually disappear into the leather. If you wish to hurry up the process, use soap and water. Dampen the area and dab gently, then rinse with clean water and stop. Don't soak through the leather. Absorb liquid with a cleaning cloth, allow to air-dry, and then polish the surface with a dry soft cloth.

Water-soluble stains. Dab with a sponge saturated in clean warm water. Dab an area larger than the stain, and absorb the water with a clean dry cloth. As with a stain on the carpet or other furniture, work inward toward the center of the stain. Place the piece of furniture off-limits until it has completely dried. Don't hasten the drying process with heat. After it's dry, polish the area gently with a soft dry cloth.

Wicker

Dust regularly with a dusting brush or vacuum with the brush attachment. Spills can soak into the wicker and stain permanently, so remove them promptly. Rain, direct sunlight, and dew are all damaging. Indoor heat dries wicker and makes it crackle and creak when sat upon. An occasional wiping with a damp sponge may help, but it's probably too late once it gets dry. Better maintenance involves placing it away from direct heat and sun and maintaining an adequate level of humidity in your home.

As startling as the idea may seem, raw wicker (other than bamboo) should be literally washed every couple of years. Either move the item outside or put it in the shower, and then gently scrub with a soft brush and a bucket of warm water and dishwashing detergent. Rinse with a garden hose or the shower nozzle. It's important to dry the chair quickly, so put it in the sun, and/or use a hair dryer or fan. Don't use the chair for several days while it continues to dry. Then check for new sharp or fuzzy places caused by the washing. Remove them with fine sandpaper, and put the chair back in service.

Note: This procedure is for raw wicker. Painted wicker may start to peel if washed. Some wicker has wooden parts. If so, don't wet these either. Wash both with a sponge dampened in sudsy water. Then wipe with a sponge dipped in clean water and allow to dry thoroughly.

Wood

It's the finish of the wood that determines what sort of maintenance must be performed. Be sure to ask about the finish when you purchase furniture.

As mentioned, different finishes require certain products to maintain them. Once you've started with one type of product, don't switch unless you have a compelling reason. For example, if you apply oil to a finish that has polish on it, you will end up with a gooey mess that's difficult to get rid of. Clean the surface thoroughly or, better yet, remove the finish entirely before changing furniture care products.

Oil finishes will benefit from an additional coat of oil rubbed in once a year or so. Polyurethane's plasticlike finishes are much more resistant than traditional varnish to moisture, spills, heat, and the other dangers lurking in our households. Accordingly, they don't need a protective coat of furniture polish or wax. Just dust regularly and wipe occasionally with Red Juice as needed to remove fingerprints and so forth. Varnish and shellac are perked up by an occasional application of furniture polish, but no more than a couple of times a year. (An exception would be furniture that gets very heavy use, such as a varnish-coated dining-room table that should be cleaned and polished after each use.)

Garbage Disposers

It's unwise to throw everything in the kitchen into the garbage disposer just because it's there. Save fibrous things such as artichoke leaves, corn husks, carrots, and banana peels, plus grease, clam/oyster shells, and bones for the garbage, and of course, plastic, porcelain, and any type of metal. The disposer drain will clog just as easily as other drains, but don't use drain cleaners in the disposer's drain. And don't leave food in the disposer for hours on end. Seemingly benign tea leaves or coffee grounds have enough acidity to eventually corrode the blades or housing itself.

Not using enough water or not running the water long enough after grinding are two main causes of clogs in the disposer's drainage piping. Turn the cold water on before you turn on the disposer. Continue running water until all the material is ground and the disposer is running freely. The people at In-Sink-Erator—who know more about ground-up crud than the rest of us care to imagine—recommend keeping the cold water on (at full blast) for 15 seconds after grinding is finished, but with the disposer still operating. Keep the water running a few moments longer after turning off the disposer. These steps are especially important if you happen to be grinding up some stale rice or pasta that can swell after being water-logged. (One of our customers ground up a half a bag of rice in a disposer and then immediately turned off the disposer and the water. The next day, he returned to find a solid mass of swollen rice paste from the sink to the main waste line. It was not a fun morning.)

Avoiding clogs is quite easy if you follow the above guidelines. If your disposer has a problem, however, here's what to do. If you know that the jam was caused by a solid object like a spoon, shut the power off and remove the object with tongs.

If the spoon is impossible to remove, or if it's jammed because of fibrous material or another hard object, you'll have to work the flywheel free by moving it back and forth with the power still off. This is easy enough to do with disposers that came with a six-sided wrench inserted in the bottom of the unit. If yours didn't come with this handy-dandy wrench, next best bet is a specialized tool (available for $8 or so at hardware stores) that has a handle on top and a lever of sorts on the business end. The last choice is your own pry-bar of some kind. The most popular choice—based on availability and proximity—is a broom handle. In either case, the idea is to rotate the flywheel backward, thereby freeing it along with whatever had jammed it. This seems easy enough to do in theory, but the trick is to figure out backward from forward. First, go find a nice, strong flashlight. Aim it so you can see what's going on down

there—like what direction the thing
was going in when it jammed. A helper
would be nice—if for no other reason
than to give a second opinion about the
state of affairs, which of course, will be
the exact opposite of yours.

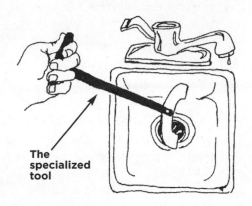

The specialized tool

The broom handle is a somewhat
dangerous lever because of its length.
It's quite easy to loosen plumbing connections or even the whole unit if you
apply too much leverage with a broom
handle (or any of these tools, in fact).
Just don't be too stubborn about your
interpretation of backward and forward. If your prying isn't loosening the jam,
try the other direction—preferably before your efforts succeed in loosening
the plumbing.

One of these methods should release whatever it was that caused the jam, and
it can now be lifted out with tongs. It really isn't smart to reach into a disposer—
even if the power is off—although I have to admit that I do it myself. If there
are toddlers around who might turn on the switch, unplug the unit or tape the
switch in the off position.

If the disposer still won't start after you've cleared the clog, the motor may
be overheated. Wait 15 minutes, make sure the power switch is off, and then
press the reset button. (Most disposers have a red reset button on the underside of the unit.) No luck? Check the circuit breaker or fuse. Still no luck?
Call the plumber.

Having been warned about what not to put into the disposer, you may be
surprised to read that experts recommend grinding up certain hard materials
to scour out the inside of the unit. Al Hale, who has been in the appliance business in San Francisco for more than 40 years, recommends grinding up a few
handfuls of ice cubes once a month. This will scour the disposer clean and help
keep it smelling fresh. Grind ice the same way you would grind anything else.
Lest you think Al is a bit odd, one reputable manufacturer (In-Sink-Erator) recommends grinding up small bones and fruit pits for the same reason.

Specialized products are available for cleaning the inside of the disposer.
Disagreeable odors are the tip-off that this needs to be done. However, it
shouldn't be a problem if you use the disposer properly and grind ice occasionally. You can also clean it yourself as follows: Turn it off, tape the switch in
the off position, and/or unplug the unit. Use a scouring pad (I suggest a white

pad impregnated with dish soap), and reach down to clean the underside of the
rubber baffle and as much of the interior of the disposer as possible. Then put
a stopper in the disposer opening and add water to the sink, along with a generous dose of baking soda. Mix this solution with your hand or a wooden
spoon and unplug the disposer. Let the solution wash away the loosened food,
grease, and so on, but don't turn on the disposer until you need it again. In the
meantime, the remaining baking soda will continue to deodorize the interior.

   If you have a septic tank, use the garbage disposer about as often as you have
your appendix removed. Not many home septic systems were designed for
the volume of waste that a disposer adds. If you run much food through it,
you incur the very real risk that the entire septic system could become
plugged up and quit working prematurely (see **Septic Systems** on page 378).

Granite

See **Stone Building Materials** (page 387).

Grout

Most grout is made of sand and cement, so it's rough and porous. And the
pores are easily filled with soap scum, dirt, coffee, or any number of other
household stain-makers. Maintain grout by filling the pores with an appropriate sealer *first* (check at a good hardware, paint, or home-supply store).
Sealing makes the grout easier to clean and reduces permanent stains from
dirt or mildew—whether you use an acidic cleaner or not (see Note,
below). Reseal every 2 years.

   The alkaline cement in grout, like marble and some other natural products,
is attacked by acidic cleaners. An acidic cleaner (e.g., Tile Juice and others) can
slowly erode the cement from the grout and eventually make the surface
rougher and therefore harder to clean. It may also affect colored grout by
making it lighter or mottled.

   Note: Because my house has very hard water, because acidic cleaners work
best on hard-water stains, and because the damage it causes to sealed grout is
minimal and gradual, I continue to use a mild acidic cleaner (Tile Juice), but
I'm careful to rinse thoroughly when finished.

Hair Dryers

Hair dryers have an air intake that eventually becomes clogged with hair
and lint, which is why they often smell like burning hair. In fact, most small

appliances with a fan quickly become incredibly dusty and dirty. If it becomes clogged, the hair dryer motor can burn up in short order. You can usually keep it clean without disassembly by using a toothbrush and vacuum cleaner. If you do disassemble it (usually requiring only a screwdriver), clean the fan blades and remove hair wrapped around the base of the fan or tangled around the heating coil. Clean dried hair spray with alcohol and cotton swabs or paper towels. To reassemble, first make sure the cord is properly seated, then start all screws, then go back and tighten them.

Heaters, Electric

If the cord of any type of electric heater gets hot, take the heater in for servicing.

Baseboard Electric Heaters

Once installed, there's not much to be done to keep a baseboard heater working properly. It's a good idea, especially if you have pets, to vacuum or brush the heating elements thoroughly at the start of each heating season. Dust, pet hair, spiders, cobwebs, and the like that collect inside will be cooked until they're sizzled, but during the process, it will be rather stinky.

Portable Electric Fan Heaters

These can be convective or ceramic, but in either case, they have to pull air in through vents to operate properly. These vents must be kept open or the unit will overheat. If the heater has a filter, remove it when it's dirty, wash it with dish soap and water, and allow it to dry thoroughly before replacing it. Remove dust from the fan and grilles with the brush attachment of a vacuum. Accumulated lint and debris can ignite, so remove interior dust with the vacuum's crevice attachment. Before storing the heater for the summer, protect the cord from accidents by wrapping it up neatly. I prefer to store things that are used only part of the year in a box or a garbage bag—clearly labeled, of course—so they won't gather dust while they're out of service.

Radiator Oil Heaters

They're easy. No significant maintenance. Just clean with a vacuum or wipe with Red Juice and a cleaning cloth when doing your routine housecleaning.

Heating and Cooling Systems

Household heating, ventilation, and air-conditioning (HVAC) systems include the furnace and air conditioner, ducts, return-air vents, room vents, and filters. Newer home construction often includes a single unit that both heats and cools. Whether your system is gas, electric, or oil, the following general maintenance steps apply. Hot-water heating systems and steam-heating systems have different maintenance requirements and are not discussed here.

Furnace

Change or clean the filter monthly during the heating season. Keep a supply on hand, so you don't have the excuse that you don't have time to run to the hardware store to get one. Change the filter even if it doesn't look very dirty. By the time a filter is really visibly dirty, you've waited too long. At that point, air circulation has decreased, and the amount of dust put 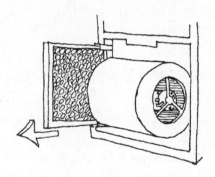 back into circulation has increased. In fact, if your house is particularly dusty and/or you have pets, filters should be changed even more often.

Vacuum the blower (usually located behind a filter) yearly or every 6 months if needed. This can be an easy or a difficult chore depending on the type of furnace you have, its age, and its design. There are often one or more spots on motors (especially on older furnaces) that need a few drops of oil once or twice a year. Have your furnace serviced by a professional before the cold season, either yearly or every other year.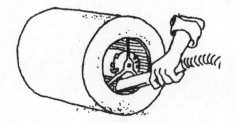

Note: If you would like to perform annual maintenance on the furnace and perhaps other major appliances yourself, the advice from here is don't try to learn how from the owner's manual. It's apt to not be of much help. Instead, hire a professional to do the service, then observe, ask questions, and take notes.

At least for any that you can access, check ducts for loose connections and repair with duct tape. It's surprising that they come loose, but the force of the air and its drying effect create leaks and make duct tape separate over time. Not only do leaks waste hot (or cooled) air, they allow pests of all sizes to take up residence. I've had mice as well as a full litter of kittens find their way into the ducts of my home. Much, much smaller things accumulate in ducts even if there are no leaks. Mildew, mold, dust mites, and bacteria are examples. Cleaning inside the ducts is not a part of the annual or biannual servicing of a unit, but they should be cleaned by a professional every 7 to 10 years. If you suffer allergies or asthma, you may have to have them cleaned more often to remove allergens.

If the system has a standing pilot light, keep it burning all year. It will help keep the furnace dry and help prevent corrosion, and the furnace will be ready to use during any unexpected cold snap.

An *electronic air filter* can be added to most modern HVAC systems. It does a great job of removing pollutants to make indoor air healthier. It also greatly reduces the amount of dust (and, it logically follows, the amount of time spent dusting) in a home. Its metal filters are washable and also require monthly cleaning during the heating (and cooling, if appropriate) months. After turning off the power, remove and wash the filter with soap and water—or put it into the dishwasher. Rinse, then allow to dry completely before reinstalling. These filters aren't expensive, so replace them whenever they get damaged. Once a year, slide out the electronic cells and carefully wash them in the same way.

Note: As with all filters, no matter how efficient they are at removing particulates from the air that passes through, they stay efficient only if they remain clean. An electronic air filter may be rated at 90 to 95 percent overall efficiency, but the rating applies only when it has a clean filter cell! Efficiency ratings fall off dramatically when the filter is not kept clean.

Another unit that can be added to existing HVAC systems is a humidifier. According to Janice Papolos in *The Virgin Homeowner,* central humidifiers must be cleaned weekly during the heating season, or they can become a breeding ground for mold spores and germs. She suggests sticking to a room humidifier if your schedule doesn't allow for this maintenance. A room humidifier also needs weekly cleaning, but at least it is more accessible (see **Humidifiers** on page 362).

Central Air Conditioners

As with window air conditioners, your central air-conditioning unit should not be installed in the direct sun. Don't let vegetation around it obstruct its air intake.

Have a professional look at it every 1 to 3 years, depending on usage and age. Here are a few guidelines: If you use it 24 hours a day for extended periods of time, or if it's also a combination furnace/air conditioner that operates throughout the winter, have the unit serviced once a year. If you use it only during the day, and it is fairly new, you might have it serviced every third year. The average life span is 15 years. After 10 years or so, have it serviced annually regardless of use.

Double-check with the service person about how to reach the parts to be cleaned and about any other routine maintenance (such as oiling the motor) that should be performed before she returns.

Here's what you should do if you don't have the unit serviced, or in the years that it isn't serviced. Prune back plant growth that could impede airflow to and from the unit, but leave growth that will help shade it. Use a brush and/or hose to clean the outside condensing unit. This involves removing a panel and/or the fan grill. Use a high-pressure nozzle and water to remove leaves, dirt, and so forth. Squirt waste from inside out and from outside in. Remove debris from the inside floor of the unit. If needed, use a fin comb (available from appliance stores) to straighten condenser coil fins. Wipe fan blades clean.

The second part of the air-conditioning unit contains the evaporator (cooling) coils. They're usually located inside the house at the top or bottom of the furnace (although if your furnace and air conditioner are a single unit, they could be on the furnace side of the outdoor unit). The drain pan should be cleaned once a year and the plastic drainpipe checked to be sure it isn't clogged. It's normal for water to drip from this pipe, so it's important that it isn't clogged and that the water flows to an appropriate drain. (If the evaporator unit is outside, also check to be sure that wasps or other critters haven't taken up residence in the pipe during periods of nonuse.) It's also possible for this pipe to be plugged with algae. If it's plugged, remove the pipe by removing the tape holding it in place or by sawing through it. Clean the pipe with a hose and either spray it thoroughly with 50 percent bleach solution or soak it in that solution for a few minutes. Rinse, and reinstall the pipe with tape.

Also inside the house, vacuum discharge registers as often as needed to keep them free of dust and lint. Remove them once a year to clean the back.

Vacuum inside the duct as far as the vacuum wand will reach.

Check and be prepared to clean or replace air filters monthly during the hot season (see Maintenance Rule 9 on page 306). Needless to say, this will be easier to do—not to mention more likely to happen at all—if you keep spare filters handy. Don't run the unit without a filter in place, and allow any filter you just washed to dry completely before reinstalling it.

If your system has an electronic air filter, it must be cleaned as described under **Furnace** (page 356).

If you don't use the air conditioner for months on end, turn it on once a month during the off-season to keep the condenser happy. It has a tendency to stick after long periods of inactivity. Sticking in this case means the air conditioner won't start in the spring when you need it, and a repair visit will be required.

Window Air Conditioners

If you install a window air conditioner in a cool and shady spot instead of one that's in the hot afternoon sun, it will run less, cool better, cost less to operate, and last longer.

No matter where it's installed, make sure the mounting is well sealed. Air leaks are an expensive waste of energy, and they are an entry point for rainwater, which will damage the wall. Foam stripping and/or caulk were usually applied when the air conditioner was first installed. If you're doing the installing, put 1 inch of foam rubber or some similar material under and over the unit. This will also reduce noise. Check all four sides annually and repair or replace foam rubber or other weather-stripping material as necessary.

Remove the unit in the winter or make the installation more permanent by replacing the original fair-weather plastic side panels with plywood. Then caulk around it and paint it.

Starting up the motor of an air conditioner puts a heavy demand on the electric circuitry. Window air conditioners generally aren't on their own ("dedicated") circuit, but it's a good idea if possible. Otherwise, be careful what shares the circuit with the unit, and don't plug anything into the other half of the same wall outlet. Also, keep the doors closed in the room to be cooled. Turning on ceiling fans will stir up the air and make it at least seem cooler. Window air conditioners can't cool the entire house. If you try, the result is apt to be a house that isn't comfortably cool, a higher electric bill, and an air conditioner that wears out before its time.

According to Franklynn Peterson's *How to Fix Damn Near Everything,* air-conditioner problems can arise from too many people adjusting the thermostat too often. Once you have set the thermostat where you want it, pull the knob off and hide it if necessary. When you're home and it's hot, you can change it as needed. This seems a bit severe, but it's a maintenance option.

Don't obstruct the flow in or out of the front of the air conditioner. Curtains, houseplants, and furniture should be 2 feet or more away from the front grill. Keep outdoor obstructions 2 feet away also. Running the unit when the temperature is below 60°F outside can also block airflow by frosting the coils.

If certain parts of an air conditioner get dirty, it may not provide cool air. Here is a list of annual maintenance tasks to keep it running well. Remember to unplug the unit before performing maintenance.

1. Clean the front grill. It's best to have someone work with you because to do this, you may have to slide the machine out. (You may also have to refer to the owner's manual to find out how to remove the front grill. There are usually screws or release clips, but they may be hidden from view.) Slide the unit out of the window far enough so you can get at the parts that need maintenance. Move a table into place to support the air conditioner during this time. Wash the front panel with Red Juice, a toothbrush, and cleaning cloths. There are plenty of little grills and louvers, so the toothbrush comes in quite handy. This is the part that's usually so dusty and dirty that it makes a 1-year-old unit look like it's 15 years old, so take the time to clean it well.

2. Clean the coils and fins. You must remove the wraparound housing to do this, but it usually takes just a screwdriver or a socket wrench to do so. If the screws are difficult to remove, apply a few drops of penetrating oil. Use a brush, the vacuum with a brush attachment, and/or Red Juice and a cleaning cloth to clean the condenser coils and fins (at the rear of the unit) and the evaporator coils and fins (toward the front of the unit). Bent fins should be straightened with a fin comb, which is available at appliance parts stores. Wipe the fan blades and straighten any bends.

3. Check the rubber or plastic drain tube and/or drain hole at the same time. If either is clogged, flush a 50 percent bleach solution through the tube with a turkey baster. (Wear old clothes.) Position a bucket to

catch the solution. After a few minutes, flush water through the same tube to purge the bleach. If flushing doesn't work, insert a wire into the tube and dislodge whatever might be there. If the unit has a drain pan where water collects, also flush it with the bleach solution to kill algae and inhibit their regrowth, and once again finish by flushing with water.

Running an air conditioner condenses water, which can give rise to unpleasant odors. If the air conditioner starts to stink halfway through the season, you may have to reclean the areas just described. In other words, once again unclog the drain hole and the drain tube. A toothbrush or thin bottle brush may come in handy. Then pour in a cup or so of the same bleach and water solution, and then rinse the drain pan.

4. Inspect for rust during the cleaning operation. Remove rust with steel wool and touch up bare metal with rust-resistant metal primer. Some air conditioners need lubrication for the blower motor. If yours does and you don't provide it, the motor will get progressively noisier and start to have other problems within a few seasons. Check the owner's manual for what to lubricate, and then either do it or have a professional service it every year or two.

Change or clean the filter behind the front grill once a month during the season it's in use. Clean metal mesh or foam filters by washing in hot soapy water, rinsing, and drying. Replace disposable filters.

Heat Pump

Clean the coils once a year. Turn the power off and remove the top and side panels to access the coils. Use a garden hose with a high-pressure nozzle to remove leaves, dirt, and debris. Aim the nozzle from the inside pointing out and from the outside pointing in. Use your fingers or tweezers to remove leaves and so forth that resist the water and remain stuck in the coil fins. Don't use a screwdriver or other tool that could damage the fins. For the same reason, use a fin comb to straighten coil fins rather than a screwdriver.

Hinges

See **Doors and Door Hardware** (page 332).

Hot Plates

If the plug is detachable from the base, plug it into the hot plate first and then into the electric outlet. Spilled foods can cause shorts or other electrical problems, so don't overfill cooking containers, and wipe up spills ASAP. Use Red Juice and a cleaning cloth, along with a toothbrush and a white pad, if necessary.

Belt evaporative humidifier

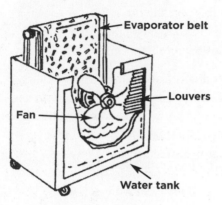

Humidifiers

Without careful maintenance, some humidifiers can spew mold, fungi, and dust into the air that you and your family breathe. Therefore, it's particularly important to replace filters and clean the tank with a bleach solution according to the instructions in the owner's manual. Some humidifiers have hard-to-clean foam belts and drums that also need cleaning in a bleach or other antibacterial solution.

Some have evaporator pads or belts, water trays, and other parts where hard-water deposits accumulate. Remove these by soaking in a 50 percent white vinegar and water solution overnight. You can go all the way to 100 percent vinegar to speed up the process.

Inspect the pad and other parts of the humidifier weekly until you know how often different parts need sterilizing (the bleach solution) or cleaning (the vinegar solution). Replace evaporator pads when they are no longer soft and spongy. Using distilled water will greatly reduce maintenance problems due to mineral buildup.

Don't place wood furniture or anything electronic too close to humidifiers. Also keep videotapes, computer disks, and paper well away from them, because humidifiers can promote the growth of black mildew.

Irons

It's best to empty a steam iron while it's hot, so heat will dry out the water reservoir. Store it upright. This will help prevent rust and pitting of the soleplate, but it doesn't help with hard-water problems.

Most problems with irons come from hard-water (mineral) deposits left inside the appliance. If your iron has a self-cleaning feature to remove hard-water buildup, use it with every ironing job. If not, when your iron starts to show signs of buildup—by spraying erratically, for example—it will probably benefit from the same treatment used to rid coffeemakers of hard water. Pour a cup of 50 percent water and 50 percent white vinegar solution into your iron, and run the entire amount through the steam mechanism—but not while ironing clothes, of course! Instead, place the iron bottom on a metal rack over a broiling pan. Then rinse by refilling with plain water and run that through the same way—again before ironing any clothes. Mineral deposits that are visible in the steam vents in the bottom of the iron can often be forced out using a strong wire.

Some manufacturers recommend distilled water for irons; others recommend plain tap water. It depends on how your particular model generates steam. If you have hard water in your neck of the woods, using distilled water will help avoid the hard-water buildup that clogs nozzle holes and causes the steam mechanism to work improperly.

Note: Water processed through a water softener isn't a substitute for distilled water. The water softener adds salts to the water that could harm the iron as well as your clothes.

If the metal sole of an iron gets encrusted with burned-on starch or dirt, clean it off with #000 or #0000 steel wool and Red Juice. Steel wool will also remove small scratches. Avoid creating scratches in the first place by not ironing over buttons or zippers.

Lamp Shades

I've noticed that lamp shades are one of the things that seem to be invisible to some housecleaners—the same way miniblinds and houseplants often are. For fabric lamp shades, use a dusting brush and/or a vacuum with a brush attachment, and dust them as you do your regular cleaning. Hard-surface lamp shades—parchment, plastic-coated, fiberglass, mica, and so on—can be vacuumed in the same way or can be feather-dusted instead. They should also be wiped a few times a year with a cleaning cloth sprayed lightly with Red Juice.

If it's been a number of years since anyone dusted a fabric lamp shade, it should be washed—or tossed, if it's not worth the effort. Do one or the other, but don't continue to ignore it. Wash it by filling a sink or large bucket with enough warm water to cover the lamp shade. Add some dish soap, swish around to mix well, and then dip the shade up and down in the water. Gently. (If parts are glued to the fabric, either sew them on before you start this process or reglue them afterward—the former being the better choice.) When the solution gets dirty, replace it and repeat. Rinse in several changes of water. Hang the shade up to drip-dry. You will feel amazingly virtuous afterward.

Leaks

See **Faucets** (page 341) and **Bathtubs** (page 309).

Light Fixtures

It seems that if you look at it from the right angle, nearly every glass part of every light fixture in the world has a dirty film on it. Remove it rather painlessly by washing them in the dishwasher every few months or so.

Mattresses

Mattresses (and pillows and fabric furniture and carpets) are places where dust mites are fond of congregating. As we discussed on page 75, dust mites aren't usually a problem unless a family member is allergic to them. Even so, you don't have to ignore them—and regular vacuuming of a mattress gets rid of a few zillion or so at a time. Use the furniture attachment and be thorough. Switch to the crevice attachment to deep-clean around buttons.

A good mattress cover keeps the mattress from being soiled and allows you to wash away a few trillion more mites. Get one that you can wash in hot water and that is easy to install and remove.

If a mattress does get dirty, wash it with upholstery shampoo, following package directions. As with other upholstery, the trick is to use soapsuds (not soap and water) to do the cleaning and thereby avoid getting the mattress too wet. Clean a small area with a medium-bristle brush, blot well with a cleaning cloth, and move to the next area. Naturally, you must wait for the mattress to dry completely before using it again. A fan blowing across the mattress speeds drying, as does warm dry air.

In these days of mergers and acquisitions and national and multinational companies, it's increasingly rare to see an independent business of any kind. But there's one near my office on Market Street in San Francisco: McRoskey Airflex Mattress Co. Old building, old people, and wonderful handmade mattresses (not just my opinion, either). Just thinking about the company makes me smile. They've been making quality mattresses since 1899, and I hope they're still at it in 2099. Tony Uruburu, who helped me select at least one of my three McRoskey mattresses, and the rest of the staff have definite opinions on how to care for a mattress. Here's what they say to do:

- Do not bend the mattress from side to side or in half. A gentle "horse-shoe" bend from head to foot is harmless (and is a great help in elevators and restricted entrances and when turning your mattress).
- After 2 weeks of initial use, flip the mattress over from head to foot.
- After another 2 weeks, spin the mattress around from head to foot (i.e., don't lift or flip it this time).
- Continue this sequence for a cycle of four turnings.
- After 4 weeks, reverse the box spring from end to end. (My suggestion: Vacuum it while it's exposed.)
- From here onward, occasional turnings are helpful.
- Vacuum or brush the surface and occasionally expose the surface to air.

Any questions about mattresses? Call Tony or anyone else on the McRoskey staff (800-760-9600).

Microwave Ovens

As with a conventional oven, it's smarter to catch spatters right away than to let them land on all four sides of the oven's interior. When a loose cover will prevent spatters, use paper towels, plastic wrap, or waxed paper. Put a paper towel or plate under food cooked directly on a shelf or the floor of the oven (e.g., a baked potato).

Microwave ovens seem to develop a unique B.O. Keep it to a minimum by opening the door to let it air out for a few minutes after cooking. Spray and wipe the inside with Red Juice and a cleaning cloth whenever you clean the kitchen. If odor continues to be a problem, an occasional wipe with baking soda and water does wonders.

Trying to microwave something too big could expose you to leaking microwave radiation or could damage the door or hinges. Check the gasket regularly to be sure it seals properly when closed. Meters that test for leaks are available for less than $10.

Miniblinds

In my grumpy opinion, the ideal maintenance solution to the scourge of miniblinds is to avoid buying them in the first place. They're nearly impossible to maintain. Even if you win a complete houseful on *Wheel of Fortune,* opt for cash instead. (Just in case Mr. or Mrs. Levelor is reading this and feeling bad [or mad], it's only the horizontal blinds that are so difficult to maintain. I think vertical ones are perfectly dandy.)

The first step in any effective maintenance program is to leave them in the fully "pulled up" position as often as possible. That is the only way to avoid the dust that otherwise collects, gathers moisture, and becomes more like a coat of adobe than a layer of dust.

The next maintenance necessity is regular dusting. Start within days of hanging them, so you never get behind because maintenance will not work if you ignore them until they have a visible, tenacious layer of dust. (Then they have to be washed, and that delightful chore is explained on page 198.) I prefer to dust them with the brush attachment of a vacuum cleaner. Other options are to use a feather duster or a dusting cloth. You need not dust every square inch of every slat each time you clean house, but dust some of them every time. For example, dust one or two rooms of blinds each time you do your regular housecleaning. Don't put this job off, telling yourself that you'll do them all in some marathon burst of cleaning fervor. There's too great a chance that such an energetic high may not arrive quite soon enough.

There are two other maintenance points of interest. One is that the blinds should be stabilized with one hand when dusting or handling so that they don't bang against the window frames. If they do, they will probably chip paint off the window frames and/or the slats themselves. Finally, don't bend a slat to peek through the blinds. Once a slot is bent, it's got a lifetime crease.

Mirrors

Here's what the National Association of Mirror Manufacturers has to say about caring for mirrors.

1. **Don't use heavy-duty, harsh commercial "cleanup" solutions on mirrors. Most of them contain abrasives, alkalis, or acids—all of which are harmful to mirrors.**

2. **Do use any of these three types of recommended cleaners.**
   - **Weak (5 to 10 percent) solutions of rubbing alcohol and water.**
   - **Weak (5 percent) solutions of household ammonia and water.**
   - **Weak (5 percent) solutions of white vinegar and water.**

3. **Don't use dirty or gritty rags, knives, scrapers, emery cloths, or other abrasive material for cleaning.**

4. Do use a clean, soft rag or paper towel when cleaning mirrors.

5. Don't abuse the "critical edges" of the mirror. Most mirror failures are at the edges, where spillover solutions attack the backing at its most vulnerable point.

6. Do protect the edges and frame from spillover by applying the cleaner to the cloth rather than to the mirror. Also, it's a good practice to wipe exposed edges clean and dry after cleaning.

The most important considerations are Numbers 5 and 6. Don't let cleaners, or even water, get into the crack between the frame and the mirror, where it will be wicked up and attack the backing of the mirror. We've all seen the result—misshapen dark stains spreading inward from the frame. One more thing: Blue Juice and any general glass cleaner in the known world are just fine for cleaning mirrors (except for plastic ones). It's not necessary to make your own cleaning potion from alcohol, ammonia, or vinegar.

Mixers, Handheld and Standing

To avoid serious damage to the rotating mixers, use a rubber spatula—not wood or metal—to scrape the bowl during use. Blocked air vents on the motor housing can cause the motor to overheat. Clean them with Red Juice and cotton swabs and/or vacuum with a brush attachment. The number one cause of mixer failure, according to California Electric Service in San Francisco, is overloading the mixer with too much dough.

Ovens

If it weren't for laziness—or thoughtlessness, I suppose—ovens wouldn't get dirty! Think about it. Ovens only get dirty from food that overflows its container and becomes baked onto the oven floor and walls. Change behavior (i.e., use large enough cooking containers), and the oven will stay clean. Aluminum foil won't solve the problem if the containers are still too small. Many ovens don't heat properly if foil is laid on the bottom or if the foil is too large or improperly placed. Foil on the racks themselves generally causes poor baking results. Even broilers shouldn't be lined with foil unless your oven manual gives the okay. (It's the same problem as lining underneath stove-top burners. It concentrates the heat and can cause damage to the pan.) Use a large enough container or two smaller ones. Maintenance will be a snap because little is required. If it's already dirty (non–self-cleaning type), use Easy-Off or other oven cleaner to get it clean. Then change your behavior. Use the cleaning cycle of a self-cleaning oven—don't use an oven cleaner.

As with other appliances with doors, check and keep clean the gasket around the oven door. If it's damaged, replace it. Don't clean the gasket of a self-cleaning oven. Just brush it with a toothbrush.

No matter how good the idea seems at the time, don't use an oven for temporary storage of things—most especially plastic things. The fateful day will come when you (forgetful) or someone else (unsuspecting) preheats the oven and . . .

Paintings

Situate a valuable painting on a wall that doesn't get direct sun or heat. Don't hang it over a heat register or a fireplace. Moderate temperatures and moderate humidity are best. Don't hang or store valuable paintings in or near a bathroom. Store them upright and let them lean forward when hung to limit the amount of dirt that settles and allow air circulation.

Dust the painting and the frame with an ostrich-down feather duster each time you dust the rest of the house. Use a soft-bristle dusting brush or the brush attachment of a vacuum occasionally to remove dust from intricate frames. Don't vacuum the painting itself. Whether you should even dust the painting depends on the condition and/or value of it and the softness of the brush.

For paintings protected by glass, spray the cloth with Blue Juice, and wipe the glass clean and dry. (But make sure it's really glass: Any glass cleaner that contains alcohol shouldn't be used on Plexiglas. Instead use a specialized plastic cleaner.)

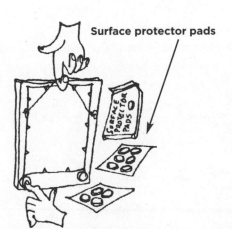

Surface protector pads

If the painting is yet to be covered, UV-resistant glass or Plexiglas is usually also a good idea.

To protect the walls from being scratched by the frame, install surface protectors on the back of at least the two lower corners, but all four corners is better. Self-adhesive flannel, plastic, cork, or velvet surface protectors—

precut as dots or in sheets—are inexpensive and widely available in hardware and other stores.

If you have an extensive collection of art, the following is old news (goes along with your old money, perhaps), but if you're just starting to acquire a few art pieces, read on. Specific valuable items in a household—for example, the *Mona Lisa* or the crown jewels of England—are almost certainly not covered by your homeowner's insurance policy. A special rider to your policy may be required for you to be fully protected. At the very least, make a call to your insurance broker, and store receipts and photos of such items in a safe-deposit box.

Pets

Whether we pet lovers admit it or not, pets add a lot to home maintenance. And though size is a factor, the worst offenders can be quite small. Oddly enough, The Clean Team's least favorite, most time-consuming pets to clean around are birds. As you perhaps suspected, big dogs are next. Here are a few strategies.

1. **Train pets to enter through just one door. This door should be the one that's the most protected from weather, has the best and largest mats, and is farthest from mud and related ilk. Use a door from the garage, if possible. Leave a towel and/or brush there to use when the pet enters the house. If pets come to the wrong door, go to the correct one and call them to you. They will quickly learn, because they're often quite motivated to get inside.**

2. **Encourage your pets to stay in one area of the house (or at least to spend most of their time there) by providing a comfortable bed in a protected corner. Beds (at least their covers) must be removable and washable. If you allow your pets to sleep on their—or your, for that matter—favorite chair, cover it with towels or something else easily washable.**

3. **Protect and select pet-proof surfaces. Dogs rub against the walls, so paint them a color that can disguise a little dirt and that can be washed a number of times. Pet hair comes off leather furniture effortlessly, whereas many fabrics require you to practically pluck each hair off one at a time. Don't let bird droppings get on any floor or any furniture at all. Cover anything at risk. For almost any pet—**

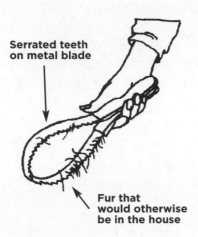

Serrated teeth on metal blade

Fur that would otherwise be in the house

except perhaps a fish—a vacuum with a good rotating beater brush is essential.

4. Feed pets from low-slung, heavy bowls that can't be tipped over. Ditto for water bowls. Put a towel under the bowls. Leave the towel unfolded, so it will cover a larger area. Remember to toss the towel into the laundry regularly. By the way, humans tip over pets' water bowls more often than do pets, so put them someplace where that won't happen so often. If you give pets treats, *only* do it in one area—such as in the kitchen—where slobber and droppings are easiest to clean up. In particular, don't feed pets human food at the dining-room table. If you do, bits of chicken fat, grease, butter, etc. will continually find their way into your carpet.

5. Give dogs a shower once a month or more often if they start to smell or when fleas or itching is getting to them—or you. The simplest way to do this (other than sending them to the doggy "fluff and fold" every other Wednesday, as The Clean Team's venerable Rudy Dinkel does with his overindulged Shih Tzu) is to install a showerhead with a Speed Rinser or a flexible hose. Especially with dogs, keep their claws trimmed to reduce scratches on hardwood and other floors. Ask your vet for a lesson if you haven't done it before.

6. Unless you want to vacuum every day, especially during the seemingly never-ending shedding season, brush dogs and cats every day instead. It's by far the shorter of the two operations, and you'll be amazed and gratified at the amount of hair the brush is picking up. Better in the brush than on the sofa! Not any old brush will work. Too many of them immediately become clogged with hair and are useless from that point on. Especially for short- and medium-length hair, use a rubber horse brush or a metal brush with a serrated blade. Obviously, it's best to do the daily brushing outdoors. I do mine during our daily walk at the point where we're the farthest from home.

7. Litter boxes (kind of like toilets) are designed to be emptied after use. If the box gets too full, the cat will eschew it and will go somewhere else in your house instead. Covered ones limit the amount of litter that ends up outside the box. I've noticed self-cleaning ones in the catalogs, but I suspect that proper maintenance, even with that type, is still a daily event.

8. Keep Red Juice, a cleaning toothbrush (see Appendix A), and paper towels handy for quick wipe-ups of spills, food droppings, slobber, etc. By the way, check out the slobber habits of the dog breed you're considering living with for its lifetime. With some breeds, that's the hardest maintenance job—and they never outgrow it. (Maintenance Rule 4, on page 306, applies: Ask before you buy!)

Pewter

Pewter is susceptible to pitting and staining by acids and other chemicals in foods, so don't leave food on pewter any longer than necessary. Wash right after using. You probably know that it is quite soft for a metal and gets scratched and dented easily. So don't get carried away when polishing it, or the piece will deform in your hands.

Pianos

If your piano is important to you, you probably already know to avoid extreme changes in humidity. If you can't avoid these changes, you may need a humidifier or a dehumidifier. Sudden changes in temperature affect both the tone and the wood, so be careful about locating the instrument close to a heat register, radiator, or window, or either the humidifier or dehumidifier.

If you have them, follow the manufacturer's instructions for cleaning. These are the general guidelines: If the finish is lacquer (usually black), wipe with an untreated dust cloth. Lacquer finishes are usually not waxed, but you may apply wax to other wood finishes. Heavy dust accumulations can be removed with a brush attachment and the vacuum—very gently, however, because lacquer scratches easily. Also vacuum the keyboard regularly.

Real ivory keys yellow with age. There's nothing you can do about it. Clean them with a cloth dampened with alcohol. (Soap stains ivory.) Modern pianos have plastic (acrylic) keys that can be wiped with a cloth moistened with Red Juice.

Vacuum inside the piano once or twice a year. Use a dusting brush along with a vacuum to catch the dust before it settles farther into the piano.

Plants

Dry, Natural, and Artificial Plants

Some folks put dry or silk flower arrangements into place and, since they don't need watering, fertilizing, pruning, or repotting, then forget about them. But they need regular maintenance. Dust them each time you clean. Use a feather duster, a dusting brush, or (very carefully) the brush attachment of the vacuum. However, they can't be maintained in like-new condition. Dried plants break. Brightly colored dry plants will fade no matter what and will fade rather quickly in the sun. Both will eventually get dirty in spite of regular dusting, and they may or may not look good after washing. If you want them to look great for a long time, put them in a glass or plastic display cabinet or box.

Indoor Plants

There are two maintenance concerns. The first is to protect the house, and the second is to keep the plant alive. There aren't that many homes without a water ring or some other plant damage somewhere or other. Some good friends of mine have an awful 12-inch-diameter water stain on their otherwise stunning hardwood floor. My parents' orchid plants have left their mark—literally—on windowsills and on carpets all through the house. This is serious, expensive damage, often requiring refinishing or replacing floors or carpets. Such damage is so common because you usually can't see that a saucer is leaking in the first place, and the leaking water gets trapped under the saucer where it can't escape and evaporate. Thus, the floor surface is kept wet for a long, damaging period of time. Sometimes the leak doesn't start until after you've checked. Or sometimes it seeps through the saucer itself, as with terra-cotta, so you can't see the leak in any event. Don't let this disheartening damage happen in your home.

1. **Use saucers that are 100 percent waterproof and that have ample capacity for excess water. (This usually means plastic.) But don't use inexpensive plastic liners. Use heavy-duty saucers that are unlikely to**

crack when hit by the vacuum cleaner or otherwise distressed by active household events.

2. Don't put a saucer directly on any surface. Use a wooden trivet available from a nursery or from your kitchen drawer. Avoid metal ones, which will rust. No matter where the trivet comes from or how much it costs, it's worth the price compared with the potential damage you're trying to avoid.

3. Check after the first few waterings to be positive there is no water leaking, seeping, or oozing. Move the plant and lift the saucer and trivet to check. Check again periodically.

4. After each watering, remove standing water from the saucer by pouring it out or using a turkey baster to draw it out.

Excess water is also the most popular way to kill plants because most houseplants left in standing water will die. So don't fill your bathtub with water and put the houseplants there when you go on vacation. Get either a self-watering pot or some other automatic watering device, or ask the neighbors to water them for you.

Of course, the second most popular way to kill houseplants is to underwater. The best way to water is to put the plant and pot in a sinkful or bucket of water for 15 minutes or more until the soil is saturated. Remove, allow the water to drain, and replace the plant on its saucer. If plants get severely dried out because of hot weather or skipped waterings, this is about the only way to get the dirt saturated again. A simpler method is simply to water the entire soil surface slowly and thoroughly. After watering, remove any standing water that has collected in the saucer, as just mentioned. Wash the saucers when there is a visible buildup of salts, which can also damage the plant.

Follow fertilizer instructions because it's easy to overfertilize houseplants. Two teaspoons are not better than one. Cut back or stop fertilizing during the winter. Most plants require indirect light but can't take full sun, so unless it's a cactus, it is unlikely to survive in a window in the direct sun. Dust plants with a feather duster when you do your routine housecleaning. Wash them occasionally, if possible. It's often easiest to do this outside, but don't leave them in the hot sun to dry for more than a few minutes.

There are two additional maintenance steps for plants. Trim or prune them as needed to remove dead leaves and diseased or damaged shoots, to shape them, or to thin them out. Finally, even though most houseplants like to be fairly tight in their pots, they will eventually become hopelessly root-bound and start to decline. This may take less than a year or up to several years. When it does, you have three choices:

1. **Repot into a larger pot.**

2. **Remove the plant, trim its roots, and replant in the same pot.**

3. **Start over again.**

Option 3 isn't selected nearly often enough in my opinion. Plants have a natural life span, and they often don't look all that great during their entire life. You do not have to cling to them until the bitter end. Replace them when they start to look like something you wouldn't even buy at a garage sale, let alone a nursery.

One of the least fussy houseplants is pothos (*Scindapsus*), a viney plant often with attractive variegated leaves. Other low-maintenance plants include most varieties of philodendrons and dracaenas, Chinese evergreen (*Aglaonema modestum*), English ivy (*Hedera helix*), grape ivy (*Cissus rhombifolia*), and India rubber plant (*Ficus elastica*).

Refrigerators

The most important maintenance operation is to keep the condenser coils free of lint, dust, and pet hair. These coils are located either behind the unit

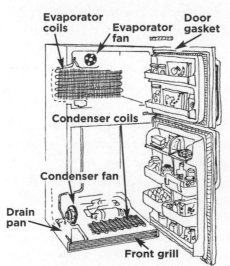

Brush and vacuum these areas

(especially in older models) or underneath it. Coils get dirty faster if they are underneath the refrigerator. A heavy accumulation of dust and hair is, unfortunately, an excellent insulator. The refrigerator will continue to run with this extra insulation, but it prevents the coils from dispelling heat. This, in turn, makes the refrigerator run longer. The refrigerator might even run constantly or, if it overheats, fail completely. So if your refrigerator doesn't seem as cold as usual, you've been delivered an early warning that it's past time to clean the coils.

But don't wait for symptoms to develop. Clean the coils regularly. Most manufacturers recommend cleaning them three or four times a year. However, these same manufacturers haven't visited your home, and you may have to clean the coils more or less often than they recommend. The coils in your refrigerator are probably downright filthy now, as they are in just about everyone else's, but clean them right away and mark the date on a calendar. Check on them in 3 months. If they're still relatively clean, check monthly until there's a buildup. Now you know the maintenance interval for your particular fridge. Indeed, use this same approach when evaluating general maintenance instructions for other appliances.

Finally, even though cats like to sleep in front of the refrigerator's warm air vents, do encourage them to sleep elsewhere or the recleaning interval will shorten by about half.

One good excuse for not cleaning the coils behind the refrigerator is that you can't get at them without moving it. Low wheels can be installed under the refrigerator, so you can move it relatively easily. I highly recommend them, so your floor won't become adorned with gouges.

The best tool to use is a long-handled brush designed for this job, which looks like a very long bottle brush. It's called a coil or refrigerator brush. Using this brush and the vacuum is the best option, because quite a bit of dust can get stirred up. Use a long-handled brush designed for removing snow from a car's windows, along with the brush attachment on the vacuum if a refrigerator brush is not available. Use the brush attachment and vacuum alone if neither is available. I'm sure you know that, once damaged, these coils usually can't be fixed by mere mortals, so use caution and be gentle when dusting or vacuuming them.

If the rear-mounted coils are greasy, wash them with warm soapy water. Use towels to catch drip water on other parts of the refrigerator and the floor.

When you move the refrigerator back into place, leave enough space behind it so it's not touching the wall. If the coils are rear-mounted, leave even more room. Most models also require several inches of clearance between the top of the refrigerator and any cupboards above. (Check your manual or call the manufacturer.)

Many newer refrigerators have an "energy-saver" switch that turns off a special type of heater located between the freezer and the refrigerator compartments. Most of us are all in favor of saving energy, so we turn this switch on and don't think of it again—ever. But now the heater is off, and condensation can build up between the compartments. This can result in the growth of mildew and eventually rust. Either don't use the energy-saver option at all (Al Hale suggests it probably saves only a few cents a year!), or go ahead and use it but keep alert for moisture between the freezer and refrigerator compartments. If moisture appears, turn the energy-saver function off.

Keep the gasket that seals the door scrupulously clean. Mold growing on the gasket can make it rot. If a sticky layer starts to pull on the gasket each time the door is opened, the gasket will be pulled out of position. It will eventually tear from being repeatedly stuck and then pulled loose each time the door is opened. Wipe the gasket itself and also wipe where it seals against the refrigerator frame each time you clean the kitchen. If this task is neglected long enough, the gasket can pull itself completely out of position.

Inspect the gasket visually for tears. Check also for brittleness and cracks. Close the door and check for any obvious gaps. Test to be sure it is sealing properly by closing the door on a dollar bill. There should be tension on the bill as you pull it out slowly.

If the door of your refrigerator doesn't close automatically or if it failed the dollar-bill test, the refrigerator should be tilted back slightly. Do this by having someone tilt the refrigerator back while you adjust the feet or rollers to raise the front just slightly. The idea is to add a little bit of closing force to the door's swing.

If your refrigerator drains to a basin that collects water, the basin must be emptied and cleaned often enough to keep it from overflowing and/or getting funky. Paper bags or towels in a refrigerator are dangerous because they quickly disintegrate, and their remains soon plug up that drain. Indeed, Al Hale refers to paper products as the "silent killers of refrigerators." If there is a drain opening inside the refrigerator, once a year, use a turkey baster to force through enough hot water to keep it clear. If the refrigerator leaks water, something is wrong. Check the drain opening first. If that's not it, call an appliance repair shop.

According to *Reader's Digest New Fix-It-Yourself Manual,* you should check the temperature of both the refrigerator and freezer compartments occasionally. (I'd think that once would be sufficient, unless you suspect that the temperature might have changed.) To perform the test, cool a glass of water in the refrigerator for 24 hours. Then put a refrigerator-freezer thermometer (available at houseware- or restaurant-supply stores) in the water. The optimum reading is between 34°F and 40°F. In the freezer, insert the thermometer between two frozen packages. The optimum temperature here is between 0° and 4°F. Reset the temperature setting(s) as necessary and retest.

Clean the insides of the refrigerator and freezer compartments when they need it. If you routinely clean up spills in the fridge, and if you remember to clean one shelf occasionally as you do your regular housecleaning, a special separate cleaning may never be needed. It's safest to unplug the refrigerator before cleaning it, but since this can often be impractical, just be careful with liquid cleaners around the light, switches, and controls. Use Red Juice and a cleaning cloth. If the fridge smells bad, even after cleaning it, install an open box of baking soda at the back of the top shelf. If necessary, replace every 3 months (when the season changes). If there is an odor problem in the freezer, do the same thing there.

For most efficient day-to-day operation, don't stuff the refrigerator full. The same is true for the freezer. Air must be able to circulate in both, and they work much harder when overfilled. If you have temporarily overfilled it (e.g., on Thanksgiving Eve), be sure that the door closes completely and the gasket is properly sealed. Don't put things in the refrigerator that don't have to be there. In particular, check condiments to be sure they have to be refrigerated. If you have seven partially full containers of various mustards, some of which date back to your bell-bottom era, ask yourself how many more years you want to pay to refrigerate them.

If you're leaving home for a long vacation, eat or give away the food in the refrigerator. Unplug it or turn it off, clean, dry thoroughly, and leave the door ajar so air can circulate. Food that spoils while you're on vacation may grow mold and mildew and create odors that penetrate the refrigerator's insulation so deeply that the only solution is to discard the refrigerator entirely. For shorter vacations, use up the perishable food but leave the refrigerator on. In either case, manually turn off the icemaker water line and lift the arm on the icemaker to stop its operation.

Remote Controls

If you get in the habit of laying remote controls upside-down after each use, they'll stay cleaner longer. And if someone does manage to spill something on one, it's less likely to be damaged. Vacuum them with the brush attachment when you do your normal vacuuming. Clean battery contacts with a pencil eraser occasionally—or at least when you put in new batteries.

Security Systems

The burglar alarm system is so important that I recommend having your alarm company perform an annual inspection. They can test the door and window sensors, motion detectors, glass-break sensors, tamper switches, and backup batteries, and clean the smoke detectors.

If you're doing it yourself, one of the most important tests is to be sure that all the circuits to the sensors at the doors and windows are working. Your owner's manual can help you, but one way is to open a door or window with a sensor, and check that a light is displayed at the control panel. This is accomplished a lot more easily by two people yelling back and forth rather than one person traipsing back and forth.

Avoid false alarms by practicing until everyone knows how to use the system. Purchase wireless "keys" that allow you to arm and disarm it if someone in the household has trouble operating it without triggering a false alarm.

Septic Systems

Properly maintained, a modern septic system will last 20 years or more. But with just the right sort of neglect, you can manage to destroy one in short order. The cost of replacement, especially if local codes have changed since it was originally installed (and they've changed considerably in many areas), can be staggering. Replacement or repair construction can also wreak havoc on other expensive things such as landscaping, driveways, and sidewalks.

Here are some steps you must take on a day-to-day basis to make sure your septic tank functions properly—at least until you move. The first step is simple, if a bit annoying: Don't use your garbage disposer. Get rid of garbage the old-fashioned way—in the garbage can. Okay, you can run small amounts of debris through the disposer to help keep the sink from clogging. And if your mother-in-law uses it steadily when she visits, it won't necessarily doom the septic tank. Otherwise, practice great restraint. It's not that the bacteria in the septic tank won't dissolve this waste pretty much the same as they do the human waste in there; it's just that the extra garbage-disposer material can overload and/or overfill it before its time—in as little as a couple of years, from what I've read.

You shouldn't pour grease into a sink in any event, but be particularly careful of grease getting into the septic system. Grease is not easily broken down by the bacteria, and it plugs up leach lines. As you know, paint, varnish, polyurethane, gasoline, oil, paint thinner, pesticides, antifreeze, and the like are all off-limits to the septic system. Ditto for paper towels, disposable diapers, napkins, and tissues (i.e., all paper except toilet paper), plastic products, rubber products, and cloth. Likewise, no sanitary napkins or tampons. Here's an easy summary: Don't put anything other than the effluent from sinks, toilets, and washing machines into the septic system.

It's unwise to flush large amounts of water into the septic system in a short period of time. So, for example, try to space out bouts of laundry. Since the washing machine is a major contributor to water volume entering the septic system, the next time you replace your washing machine, you might consider choosing a front-loading machine, which uses only a fraction of the water that a top-loader does. Several American manufacturers produce full-size front-loaders.

For septic systems, it's extra important to fix any leaking toilets or other fixtures that are continually adding water to the system. If you don't get around to fixing a leak right away, at least turn off the water supply to the leak in the meantime.

Whether or not to regularly use enzyme additives is an open question. They are intended to increase the bacterial population that breaks down solid waste in the septic system. They can't hurt the system, but the U.S. Department of Health and Human Services' Manual of Septic Tank Practice reports that none of the dozens of products on the market have proven to be an advantage in properly controlled tests. More important is preventive maintenance: limiting the types of waste and the amount of water you put into the system.

Have a septic system inspected right after moving into a used home unless a septic inspection was part of the presale building inspection. You can wait up to 4 years with a new home. Then ask the inspector when and how often it should be emptied. It's possible that it will need pumping more often, especially if the tank is undersized; more likely, you will find that you need not pump it more than once every 5 years or so.

Showerheads

If you have naturally soft water or have a water softener, no maintenance is required. But hard water eventually stops up showerheads, often so slowly that you don't really notice. Keep them running freely by soaking overnight in a 50 percent vinegar and water solution on a preventive basis. This can be accomplished without removing the showerhead. Put the vinegar solution into a plastic bag and tape it over the showerhead overnight.

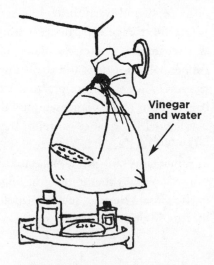

Vinegar and water

Showers

See **Bathtubs** (page 309).

Silver

If you want to find out about silver, go to Gump's in San Francisco. It's easy to get slightly intoxicated by the beauty of the Buccellati and other silver services there, but we managed to complete an interrogation of their exceedingly patient and knowledgeable silver specialist.

The two biggest care issues for silver are cleaning and storage. As for cleaning, the procedure is governed by the unavoidable fact that silver is a soft metal with a vulnerable finish. Accordingly, it's almost obligatory to wash and polish good silver (or any silver you are fond of) by hand. Forget about silly schemes involving aluminum foil and chemical baths in the kitchen sink.

Is the dishwasher safe? The simple answer is no. In addition to being exposed to harsh dishwasher detergent, the silver may knock against other metal items or be stained by food inside the dishwasher. It's far better to wash silver in hot soapy water as soon after use as possible, and then dry the pieces by hand immediately afterward. Polish is not needed every time you clean a piece.

When it comes time to polish, the brand is not all that critical, although you should avoid abrasive polishes and those that claim to work instant miracles through modern chemistry. Don't rub too zealously; you may also remove a dark patina or finish that was deliberately applied or that gives the silver much of its depth and warmth.

Careful storage is particularly important for silver, because an oversight in this regard can do serious damage. The great enemies of stored silver are rubber, salt, moisture, and the sulfur fumes given off by many foods as they ripen. One of the more practical storage solutions is a treated cloth storage bag. You can make your own (buy flannel treated for silver storage—*not* regular flannel—at a fabric store) or buy them ready-made at places like Gump's (800-444-0450).

When all is said and done, one of the best things you can do with silver is to use it. What's the point of having a fine piece of silver if you stuff it away in the closet? Besides, regular handling will create that fine luster and patina that are so prized in silver.

Do-Nots

The first "do-not" warning is not to use any of the quick electrolytic methods you may have heard about—you know, submerging the silver in a chemical potion in the kitchen sink with aluminum foil at the bottom. The method works almost instantaneously, but it does its job too well. It can strip the surface of the deep patina that develops over time on silver and can leave it dull and porous-looking. It can also strip the oxidation deliberately applied by the silversmith—darker areas that emphasize detail and create depth.

Likewise, many authorities frown on another fast method: silver dip. Although highly reputable companies sell the product, it is considered to be too harsh on the silver's oxidation and may leave an unnatural finish.

Silver experts are united in their opinion that heavy rubbing must be avoided to prevent scratches. A high-quality polish will do its work without bearing down on the surface. Relax and let the polish do its duty. Similarly, machine-buffing—even by a jeweler—is frowned upon. And nobody has to tell you not to use heavy abrasive powders on silver. Every silver polish that we have seen has abrasive powder as one of its ingredients, but it is an exceedingly fine powder almost like talcum. The same idea, but a far cry from Comet, Ajax, or even Bon Ami.

Choice of Polish

If you visit a good hardware store, you'll be confronted with a dazzling array of polishes. The first decision is between polishes specialized for silver versus those suitable for many metals.

Specialized polishes split into ones that are rinsed off underwater and ones that are wiped off. Goddard makes a particularly distinguished line of silver polishes, several of which are recommended by various authorities.

Those who have pitched their tent in the camp of the generalized metal polishes prefer to have fewer specialized cleaning products cluttering up the house. Provided that the polish does not do too harsh a job on the silver surface, generalized cleaners can do excellent work.

You may have noticed that we're being somewhat noncommittal on this subject. Personal choice and traditions are large factors here. Also, silver can vary so widely in composition, age, and use that it is difficult to make an absolute recommendation. Rather, we will spend most of our efforts discussing methods of polishing silver rather than picking out the polish itself.

So Fast It's Almost Cheating

If the silver is not heavily tarnished, you may be able to get away with a cute trick. Just spray the piece with Red Juice and wipe off with a cleaning cloth! Many liquid cleaners can work minor miracles. We *did* say minor. It won't make much difference if it's been neglected for a year or so, and it won't impress the Queen. But you will remove a thin layer of surface tarnish—enough to let you squeak by unless Betty and Phil are stopping by.

The Real Thing

Okay, it's time to bring out the polish and have at it. Put on some old clothes that you won't mind getting splattered with polish. Clear off an ample work surface, and cover it with something to protect it, if needed. Newspaper is not the best choice because the newsprint can transfer to the silver. Old towels or rags would do nicely and would soften the damage if you were to drop a large piece on the table. First, make sure the silver is not covered with any sort of grit that could be ground into the surface by polishing. If needed, give the silver a preliminary bath under running water or with Red Juice sprayed freely.

Regardless of the polish you have selected, our general approach is the same. Apply the polish sparingly with a soft cotton cloth. We prefer flannel, but small pieces of terry cloth are fine. If you're using a liquid polish, it's faster to pour a little polish into a shallow dish, so you don't have to pick up the bottle over and over. If the silver is only moderately tarnished, just rub gently with the cloth.

If the tarnish is heavy or if the surface is irregular, rub gently with a real toothbrush. The bristles of our heavy-duty brush are too thick and stiff to be useful here. Make sure the toothbrush you use is rated *soft*. Alternately, both Goddard and Hagerty sell a specialized silver brush made of hair.

By now, you've made a fine mess of polish and tarnish. Don't wait until it dries to powder. Wipe it from the surface with another soft cloth. If it's a flat surface, that's all you may have to do. If it's irregular, another step is needed. Spray the surface with Red or Blue juice to rid it of residual polish that is about to dry into a visible powder that will plague the little nooks and crannies of the piece and interfere with its embossed areas. Wiping while the polish is still wet can save you a considerable amount of time. If the polish dries, leaving conspicuous white areas, the fastest remedy is to buff them out with a soft clean brush.

Ornate Objects

Certain items pose a few problems for the happy polisher. Some are too detailed to allow for a reasonable polishing effort. Others have felt on the bottom (e.g., candlesticks) or on the back (e.g., silver picture frames).

Provided the object is not too tarnished, the speediest remedy is to use a silver polishing cloth, which comes already impregnated with a polishing compound. It really works. Just grab hold of the object (presuming it is free of abrasive grit) and rub lightly. Goddard makes an excellent one that costs around $7. As with any standard polish, if the object is intended for eating or drinking after being polished, it must first be washed. Otherwise the tea may taste mighty peculiar. For heavy tarnish, use silver polish instead.

Prevention

Happily, in spite of the various precautions one must observe about and around silver, there are a number of preventive steps you can take to minimize the time you will spend polishing it.

- Keep the silver behind glass. It will tarnish far more slowly than if exposed to the variety of airborne substances that hasten the process. If the silver is exposed to salty ocean air, it is especially in need of such protection. Make sure the piece was polished well, preferably using a tarnish-retarding formula (which really does work). William Meyer, a San Francisco antique silver dealer, has kept pieces behind glass for up to 1½ years without being repolished!

- Many foods are a serious threat to silver. Tarnish is accelerated by salt and eggs in particular, but also olives, salad dressings, vinegar, some meats, and many fruits. Many of these foods are either acidic or sulfurous in nature. If these foods are displayed or dispensed in silver, try to use a glass liner or at least rinse and clean the silver tray soon after use.

- Sulfur is the great chemical enemy of silver. It is the single greatest cause of tarnish in most homes. Sulfur is given off by deteriorating rubber, so don't store silver grouped together with rubber bands. The damage may not be reparable. Purists also don't wear rubber gloves when cleaning silver. (So that's why butlers wear white gloves!) Chamois also gives off hydrogen sulfide, so don't store silver wrapped in it either.

- When storing silver, it's best to use antitarnish protection strips and cloth bags. They contain a chemical tarnish preventive that will neutralize the hydrogen sulfide in the air. The strips are rated for about a year, the cloth bags for several years. Both Goddard and Hagerty have a line of such products. Camphor blocks are another traditional way of deterring tarnish if you don't mind the smell. Don't store silver in plastic bags or plastic wrap—both of which can trap moisture that could damage the silver.

• If your silver candlesticks are plagued by dripping wax, and you don't have the time to remove it every time you use them, consider buying round glass drip-catching disks traditionally called bobeches (bo-BESH). (Annoy the in-laws with *that* one!) They have a hole in the middle through which the candle is placed. The glass surfaces are much more easily cleaned than ornate silver candlesticks—for example, with a cloth soaked in hot water. Or you can pop a clean one on the candlestick in a second if company is coming. There are times when The Clean Team seriously considers giving a set of these to all its customers whose candlestick and candelabra problems have become ours instead. Candle shops or good hardware stores should carry them.

• Other steps you can take to minimize candle wax on silver (or any other) candlesticks are: (a) Use pure beeswax candles. They drip far less than other candles, if at all. Get the solid kind (they're hard as blazes to find now), not the kind that looks like beeswax directly from the hive.
(b) Keep the candles out of a draft, which makes the flame burn so rapidly that it can't burn off the wax in time to avoid drips. (c) If you are using thick candles, consider installing brass candle tips that are typically used in churches and synagogues. These little upside-down cups shelter the flame from drafts and enable the candle to burn slowly and evenly. Available from religious-goods dealers.

Sinks

Thou shalt not pour grease down kitchen drains. Pour it instead into an empty can and store it in the refrigerator until it's solidified or the can is full. Then put the can into a plastic zippered bag (or one sealed with a rubber band) before depositing it in the trash.

In sinks, tubs, or showers where hair is washed, use a plastic or metal hair strainer or screen to help keep most hair out of the drain. Quite possibly, the only civilized purpose served by a used cotton swab is to twirl it around in the screen to remove accumulated hair.

Don't let a small sliver of a soap bar get into the drain. It's worth 3 cents, but can cost you a $300 plumber's bill if it gets stuck in the trap.

Porcelain Sinks

Scraping metal utensils or pots against porcelain will ingratiate you only to sink suppliers. Plastic mats will help protect sinks from scratches and stains caused by pots and pans. They also provide some protection from accidental breakage while washing dishes.

Acids can etch sinks if allowed to remain, so rinse away the remains of acidic foods like lemons, cranberries, tomatoes, and vinegar. Tannins in coffee and tea create difficult-to-remove stains in short order. It's a good idea not to let any food debris accumulate in the sink. Either run it through the disposer or put in the garbage. On the other end of the pH scale, strong alkalis such as household bleach also attack porcelain, so use sparingly and rinse well.

It happens all the time, so I suppose it bears repeating: Don't use the sink as a handy spot to store tools, paint cans, and so on, when you're redecorating or attacking some other household project. Hammers are dropped and permanent nicks are created. Why tempt fate? Cover sinks and other fixtures before projects get under way.

Stainless Steel Sinks

For starters, don't even try to maintain the brushed finish or the cute little swirls or grain lines created by the manufacturing process. That would only drive you crazy because it's not humanly possible. I suppose you could preserve them for a year or two if you washed the sink with nothing but stainless steel cleaner and a soft cloth. I much prefer to wash them with whatever is used to wash the other sinks in the house.

As with porcelain sinks, mats will cut down on marks caused when washing pots, cutlery, and pans. Stainless steel sinks are particularly vulnerable to scratches from green cleaning pads, so don't even think of using them on this type of sink.

Smoke Detectors

Blow out dust with canned air once a year (more often if you live in a dusty area or have had false alarms in spite of annual maintenance). First, remove the cover and aim the canned air as best you can to blow dust away from the middle of the detector. However, no matter which way you aim the air blast, the dust particles can easily trigger a false alarm. So especially if you're perched on a ladder, it's wise to be mentally prepared for the possibility that the alarm may commence blasting. Don't let it blast you off the ladder.

A pair of earplugs is a good idea. (And, of course, forewarn your cohabitants and read up on how to shut the thing off if it activates.) At the same time, check or automatically replace batteries of detectors not hard-wired into the household current. If there's a chance you won't remember to change the batteries, make a maintenance schedule book that lists the different activities that must be done. This is not an optional maintenance chore, yet you read every year about entire families wiped out in a fire in a house equipped with smoke detectors with dead batteries.

Speakers

According to Franklynn Peterson in his book *How to Fix Damn Near Everything,* the single most common ailment in listening systems of all sorts—stereos, transistor radios, and even TVs—is a bad connection caused by corrosion, loose wires, or wear. That being the case, maintenance should be geared to protecting these connections from danger. Start off by installing wires correctly. San Francisco audio expert Lewis Downs reminds us to leave enough slack in wires so components can be moved to clean around and under without straining the connections. But it's not a good idea to have too much excess wire. Especially if the excess wire is arranged in a coil, it could turn into something like an antenna. Don't pull plugs out by the wire; pull on the plug itself. Don't let wires or other connections get damp, and don't locate them where they are in even the slightest danger of getting wet. Use the best wires and connectors you can afford. Besides creating future maintenance problems (see Clean Team Rule 3 on page 9), low-quality wires can pick up hum and interference. Don't hook up additional speakers unless you know what you're doing. If you do it wrong, you could end up with no speakers at all.

It doesn't hurt to remove a speaker's grille cloth and frame (it usually snaps on and off) to vacuum inside the speaker and both sides of the fabric. Just be gentle with the paper-thin speaker membrane. If the cat (or anything else, for that matter) ruins the speaker fabric, replace it with loosely woven "sound-transparent" cloth available at stereo or electronics stores. Most contemporary speakers have no wood in the cabinet surface (it's vinyl), so furniture polish isn't really necessary. Just wipe with Red Juice and a cloth. Polish it only if you want to add shine.

Steamers and Rice Cookers

Other than washing them after use, the most important maintenance issue involves nearby items. Don't use steamers or cookers directly below kitchen cabinets because moist air can be trapped underneath the cabinets and eventually cause mischief—usually in the form of black mildew.

Stone Building Materials

Mother Nature was kind enough to provide natural stone building materials that are stunning and original works of art. To protect and preserve these beautiful and costly materials, preventive maintenance steps are critical but not complicated. Here are four considerations.

1. **Contrary to what we may think, and even though the physical properties of various natural stones vary widely, they are all absorbent—even granite. So they will all soak up water, and if the water contains dirt, the dirt will end up inside small fissures in the stone and permanently darken or stain it. Many stone surfaces will soak up oils with similar dire consequences.**

2. **Polished stone, until recently the most popular choice of consumers, has a highly reflective surface that allows it to show off more of the unique color, grain, and contrasts that make the stone so beautiful. That glasslike polished surface is also correspondingly vulnerable to scratches and chemical damage that can make it look dull, white, or lifeless. Reduce ongoing maintenance by selecting less highly polished finishes on floors (e.g., "flamed," a rough finish) and counters (e.g., "honed," a smooth but not glasslike finish). Honed finish in particular is becoming increasingly popular. It still shows off the beauty of the stone but requires less upkeep.**

3. **Some natural stones (marble and limestone, for example) are vulnerable to acids, including very mild acids like those found in many soft drinks, oranges, lemons, and tomatoes, or even fingerprints.**

4. **Hard water can be very damaging to natural stone. If your home has hard water, and stone was installed inside the tub/shower areas, you'd be wise to install a water softener.**

Maintenance requirements depend on the type of stone (slate versus granite, for example) as well as its use (marble as a bathroom counter or a kitchen floor, for example). Stone is a natural product, and as such, its properties vary widely; even two different marbles may have widely different properties. Before you make a purchase, ask about specific properties (especially weaknesses) that could increase maintenance efforts. For example, one tile expert told us that green marble is not suited for installation in wet locations, whereas other types of marble are less vulnerable to moisture. Here are three specific maintenance steps.

1. Seal the stone. This can actually be done before installation, but if not, wait 1 to 2 weeks after installation until the stone and grout are completely dry. Use a penetrating or impregnating sealant that will repel both water and oil. Don't use a surface sealant that just coats the surface. Select a sealant that will not alter the color or change the gloss of the surface unless that's the effect you want. Therefore, it's vital that you make a complete test—usually on a representative sample of stone—to be sure. Some sealants require a second coat right away, and most sealants should be reapplied once a year or so to maintain full protection. A number of good sealants are on the market. Consult a local stone dealer or even a home-supply store for help in choosing among them.

2. Avoid using an acrylic floor finish on natural stone, because it can add a plastic or artificial look. If additional protection is desired (besides sealing it), use wax.

3. Keep it clean. The secret of beautiful natural stone is mainly to keep it clean after sealing. Complicated cleaning agents, maintenance procedures, or restoration steps will never be needed if the surface is cleaned regularly. Abrasions and stains, especially on floors, will take their toll if cleanliness is not maintained. Mats are particularly important. Use nonslip mats or rugs. Vacuum, sweep, dust mop, and/or damp mop daily, if necessary. Regular washing with a natural soap (not a detergent) such as Murphy's Oil Soap or Ivory Liquid not only cleans but also enhances the appearance of many types of natural stone and helps seal it. A specialized stone soap such as Marbalex Stone Floor Cleaner (available at hardware stores and stone dealers) is also recommended. Because stone absorbs

liquids, change dirty mop water often and rinse the mop often. Dry the floor if streaks remain after rinsing.

Use coasters or other protection on countertops or tables. Be vigilant about spills (remember, lemonade and anything else even slightly acidic will etch marble and some other stone surfaces), and wipe them up right away. Wet again with water and wipe a second time to remove any traces of acid.

If your shower is lined with natural stone and hard water is prevalent in your area, the regular use of a squeegee to wipe standing water from the shower walls is mandatory. Don't use an acidic cleaner (Tile Juice included) to remove hard-water spots. Any nonacidic cleaner that works for you is fine. Hard water and natural stone are a bad combination. Don't use stone in a shower in that case. If it's already there, a water softener may be the best solution.

Granite

It will absorb oil and water, so it usually should be sealed, but it is harder than most other stones and is resistant to food acids. This makes it a favorite choice for kitchen counters.

Limestone

It has the same weaknesses as **Marble** (below).

Marble

Polished marble requires careful maintenance when used as a floor (it's easily scratched) or as a kitchen countertop (it's absorbent and vulnerable to acids). In addition to applying a sealer, consider using paste wax (liquid or solid) for extra protection when marble serves as flooring or when installed in the kitchen for any purpose.

Note: If you're considering a purchase, marble is not recommended for either place. Polished marble is more suited for vertical surfaces, and granite is superior for horizontal surfaces in the kitchen.

Slate

Slate is softer than most natural stones and is thereby fairly easily scratched. But it's still quite durable, and the wear is concentrated on the high spots of its textured surface. If a reflective look is desired, select a sealer or wax that will produce one.

Stains on natural stones are more thoroughly explored starting on page 387, here's an overview: Start by washing well with dish soap and water or by spraying and wiping with Red Juice. If that isn't effective, try removing oily stains (grease, butter, cream, etc.) with alcohol. For tannin or dye stains (coffee, tea, soft drinks, etc.) use 12 percent hydrogen peroxide (hair-bleaching strength) straight out of the bottle. When using hydrogen peroxide on dark stone, test first. Stubborn or deep stains will require the application of a poultice (see page 251 for the thrilling details).

Storage Areas

Don't store valuable possessions in the far reaches of your home for months or years on end without checking on them occasionally. Check once after a couple of months, and then once a year or so. Attic storage is subject to extremes of hot and cold, so don't store anything there that could be damaged by such violent changes in temperature. If there are louvers or vents in the attic, they were deliberately installed to allow warm moist air to escape. Don't cover them. Basement storage may encourage mildew growth, even inside boxes. Put desiccants inside the boxes, if needed. Whether it's the attic, basement, garage, or closet, creatures such as spiders, bugs, and even mice will move in soon after the activity of bringing in the items dies down. Check after a few months of storage, and add mothballs, repackage, or move the items to solve any problems.

Stoves

Stoves should be level so that flames burn uniformly, pilot lights work properly, and the oven doesn't produce lopsided desserts! If you moved your stove for any reason, recheck to be sure that it's level when you put it back into place. Nearly all stoves have a built-in adjustment pod at each corner.

Stove Tops, Enamel

To make a stove top last and to keep it working efficiently, use the lowest temperature possible for each cooking procedure. The drip trays under burners also serve as reflector bowls. They reflect heat back up where it's needed for cooking. High heat can crack or permanently stain the enamel on reflectors and make them less efficient. Plain old food spills can also make permanent stains, so proper care also includes keeping these drip trays clean. When cooking, use a big enough pot or pan to provide enough head space to avoid spills and boil-overs. Wipe up any spills as soon as practicable. As my Aunt Ruth used to say, "The cookder they get, the harder they are to remove." It's okay to move hot pots directly from a burner to the stove top because the porcelain enamel can take the heat. But since the porcelain can be scratched, it's even safer to move the pot to a trivet, spider, or different burner instead.

It's not a good idea to cover or wrap the drip trays with aluminum foil. This can trap heat and make the drip trays overheat or even melt. Use store-bought liners instead if you are so inclined.

If you've led a charmed life, the metal trim, the drip pans, the broiler pan, and the oven racks will all fit into the dishwasher. If so, maintain these items with minimal effort by popping them into the dishwasher occasionally. Don't ignore the knobs like 90 out of 100 people do when cleaning. Red Juice and a toothbrush will keep them looking like new.

Note: Speaking of knobs, sometimes their painted marks wear off so you can't tell high from low, or they get pulled off the stove by little hands. Ditto for metal trim around burners, drip pans, and so forth. These parts can be replaced via GE's Parts Master Program (see Appendix B)—usually whether your appliance is GE or not. Spruce up old appliances with new knobs, trim rings, and so forth. Replace filthy appliance filters, pumps, switches, and valves if you're so inclined. Have the appliance's brand name and model number handy, and call 800-626-2002. If the part is available, you can order it and have it shipped directly to you, or they can tell you where to get the part in your area. Lots of big cities have appliance parts stores as well.

Stove Tops, Smooth Ceramic Glass or Black Glass

The important maintenance concern with glass stove tops is that they are susceptible to scratches and stains. Dirty or wet pots can burn a stain right into a stove top. Pans made of soft metal (such as lighter-weight aluminum pans) can rub off on the harder glass surface, leaving gray or black marks.

To keep glass stove tops in best shape, follow these simple suggestions: Use clean and dry pans when cooking; lift rather than slide pans when moving them; clean the stove top (after it has cooled sufficiently) after each use with a soapy sponge or a white pad and a paper towel; wipe spills immediately after they occur if you can safely do so; and finally, try to prevent spills by using large enough pots and pans and leaving plenty of headroom for boiling and stirring. It's virtually impossible to remove all streaks from black glass (or black appliances). Don't buy them if you have a choice.

Stove Hoods

Clean the inside of the hood regularly. If you let grease build up, not only is the hood a chore to clean but it becomes less efficient at attracting grease to the vent. Grease that isn't drawn into the vent settles on other surfaces throughout the kitchen and the house. (Take a quick look under there, then imagine that stuff settling on your couch, for example.) Wash the inside of the hood with a clear ammonia/water solution (25 percent or more ammonia) or Red Juice. Use a brush or white pad if there is a buildup of grease (also see **Exhaust or Vent Fans** on page 340).

Teakettles

As in coffeemakers, mineral deposits will form inside a teakettle if you have hard water in your area. To remove this buildup, combine equal parts of water and white vinegar, and fill to the normal water line. Bring to a boil, remove from the heat, and let sit until cool. Rinse well. Repeat if necessary. It helps if you empty the kettle after each use rather than leaving it partially full of water all the time.

Telephones, Cordless

To maintain proper charging of the all-important batteries, periodically clean the charge contacts on the handset and base with a pencil eraser. If the charge doesn't seem to last very long, try running the battery all the way down before recharging.

Cordless phones will have less interference if not located next to heating appliances and devices that generate electrical noise (for example, TVs, motors, power lines, other telephones, and fluorescent lamps). If an appliance causes interference, move the phone base to a different electrical circuit. Moving the base upstairs often improves reception also.

Vacuum the telephone keys with the brush attachment when you are doing your regular housecleaning. Remove fingerprints and dirt by wiping with a Red Juice–dampened cloth.

Telephone Answering Devices

My experience has been that there's little you can do to maintain these machines. They quit working soon after the expiration of their warranty, and they cannot be fixed—only replaced with a sparkling new, unimproved, more expensive model.

For your illumination (it isn't maintenance), San Francisco audio expert Lewis Downs swears that you can improve the audio quality of the outgoing message, in spite of the tiny and cheap microphones being used these days, by doing the following: Drape a towel over your head, and hover close to the microphone during the recording session (just don't let anyone take a picture of you doing so). We tested it, and he's right. It does work.

Televisions

Protect your TV by plugging it into a surge protector.

Ask any repairman, and you'll hear horror stories about what they find in TVs, stereos, VCRs, and so forth. Roaches, geckos, dead flies by the score, coins, mountains of dust, spilled soda, animal fur, and urine (usually from a cat), to name a few. Keep food and drink away from the unit entirely to avoid spills as well as to avoid attracting uninvited insect and mammalian visitors. If you can't control the dust or the cat, place a cloth over the set when it's not in use (after it has cooled off) and/or install an air cleaner nearby. Install the TV in an enclosed cabinet if you can, but if the back of the cabinet is sealed, keep the doors open after use to dissipate residual heat.

The picture tube needs cleaning occasionally to remove the never-ending buildup of dust that's electrostatically attracted to it. When you're doing your routine vacuuming in the area, use the brush attachment to remove 99 percent of the dust. While you're at it, vacuum the knobs and any cooling vents you can reach. A light spray with Blue Juice and a swipe with a cleaning cloth will finish the job. Don't use any liquid cleaner on projection screens or screens that aren't perfectly smooth. Just vacuum or dry-wipe only.

Note: I've been told that Endust acts as an antistatic product to help cut down on the amount of dust that's attracted to electronic stuff—for example, the dust that's always on your TV screen.

Termites

Termites are attracted to wood in any event, but small leaks or drips that make wood and the dirt below it wet will create a hugely inviting welcome mat—and convenient entry point—for the nasty little critters. (Moisture also attracts hordes of other bugs and pests, not to mention encouraging the start of dry rot, but let's not get sidetracked on those cheery subjects, shall we?) Order a termite inspection for your home annually. The damage that termites can cause is so great compared with the cost of an inspection that it's a critical maintenance step. Look in the yellow pages for an inspector (licensed, if appropriate, in your state). In states such as California, pest control reports are public documents available to anyone who asks for a copy. The idea is that if a swarm of winged or crawling creatures is invading the neighborhood, you have a right to know. If you see a "Ted the Termite Terminator" van parked in front of the neighbor's house, ask him what's going on, or go to City Hall to get a copy of the report if the two of you haven't spoken since he ran over your garbage cans 17 years ago.
If you live in a known termite zone (practically anywhere, unfortunately), you can go a step further and hire exterminators to treat the perimeter of your home on a preventive basis. If you want to do inspections yourself, a number of good do-it-yourself books are available, such as *The Virgin Homeowner* by Janice Papolos and *The Complete Guide to Four Season Home Maintenance* by Dave Heberle and Richard Scutella.

Thermostats

Remove the thermostat cover once a year or so. It usually twists off if round and folds down if rectangular. Carefully vacuum or blow out accumulated dust and lint with canned air from an electronics or video store. (Do this task at the same time you clean the smoke detectors, since both jobs call for a blast of canned air.)

Replace batteries in programmable thermostats once a year.

Toasters and Toaster Ovens

If you remove the crumbs after each use, a good toaster or toaster oven can last a lifetime. After the appliance cools and just before you put it away, either remove the crumb tray and empty it, or turn it upside down and shake the crumbs out into the sink. Or use a dusting brush to loosen the crumbs and then shake them out. Wipe the crumb tray with a damp cloth occasionally. If your toaster smokes despite this regimen, there are probably a few doesn't-quite-fit-unless-you-really-push-it bagel scrapings and Pop-Tart chunks stuck on the heating elements. Once the appliance has cooled and been unplugged, *gently* loosen and remove these scrapings with a toothbrush. Keep an eye on the condition of the cord and plug—especially if the appliance is more than a few years old. Test it after use by running it through an empty toast cycle three times. Then check the plug and cord to see if they're hot. If they are, you should have the cord replaced.

Remove burned-on globs and melted-on plastic bags from the outside of chrome toasters with a razor blade (in a razor holder) and Red Juice. Spray the area with Red Juice and hold the razor at a low angle to avoid scratching the finish. Only the lightest of pressure is needed. Finish up by spraying with a glass cleaner such as Blue Juice and wiping dry to leave a streak-free surface.

Don't try to turn a toaster oven into a full-size oven. Use it to warm things, to bake small items such as potatoes, to cook frozen dinners, and so on. Wash racks in soap and water or in the dishwasher, but not in a self-cleaning oven.

Toilets

Toilets can and, therefore, eventually will leak in a variety of places. The good news is that the replacement parts—at least if the toilet isn't more than 20 or so years old—usually cost only a few dollars. Despite protestations about not being a do-it-yourselfer, I make an exception when the parts are this cheap—and plumbers so far in the other direction. And don't worry, this won't put the plumbers out of business. We'll all need them for other, far graver emergencies sooner or later.

Occasionally, a suspected leak may only be condensation dripping from the tank to the floor. Wipe the tank dry to see if this stops the leak. The most common leaks in a toilet don't make water drip where you can see it. One leak is the type that you become aware

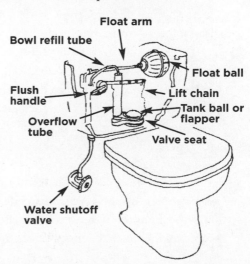

Float arm

Bowl refill tube

Float ball

Flush handle

Lift chain

Tank ball or flapper

Overflow tube

Valve seat

Water shutoff valve

of when water is heard continuing to run long after the toilet is flushed. Most of us "fix" this problem by jiggling the flush handle. This leak is caused by the tank ball or flapper not seating properly. Jiggling the handle maneuvers the ball or flap into a tighter fit on the valve seat and so prevents the water from draining out. To correct this type of leak, the lift chain may have to be moved to a different setting on the flush handle, so the tank ball or flapper will settle squarely onto the valve seat on its own. By the way, if the toilet doesn't flush at all, and the handle doesn't have any resistance when you touch it, the culprit is probably that lift chain. It has become separated from the flush handle and simply needs to be reattached.

Another common leak happens when water continues to run into the overflow tube after the tank is full, and the float ball is all the way up. (Lift the tank lid and look.) Jiggling the handle won't stop this. To fix this type of leak, bend the float arm slightly so that the float will be a bit closer to the bottom of the tank.

A third type of leak becomes apparent when the water comes on for a few seconds every so often for no apparent reason. This is also caused by water leaking between the tank ball and the valve seat. First try correcting it by cleaning both of these parts. Turn off the shutoff valve (clockwise turn) and flush the toilet. Clean both parts where they meet by wiping with a cleaning cloth or white pad. If this doesn't solve the problem, get replacement parts.

It's safest to take the old tank ball or flapper with you to the store. I recently replaced my 6-year-old tank ball and *no* tools were required. I bought plastic parts that could be removed and installed by hand. I picked up two sets while I was there (they were less than $5 each) to save myself another trip sometime in the future. I don't know if that was such a great idea. Now I'm sort of looking forward to another toilet having the same problem.

If a toilet threatens to overflow, first turn off the water. Then quickly remove the tank lid and press down on the tank ball or stopper to prevent water in the tank from getting into the overflowing bowl. This is a drainage problem and requires a plunger, snake, or plumber (see **Drains** on page 333).

Wire brushes can leave black marks on porcelain that are difficult to remove (use cleanser and a white pad), so I recommend all-plastic toilet brushes for everyday cleaning.

New low-flow toilets use less water but do a worse job of flushing. Make sure yours is using as much water as it was designed for by removing the lid and checking the water level. If it should hold more water, bend the rod that supports the float (the metal or plastic ball) upward. Even if the water amount is correct, if you flush disposable diapers in a low-flow toilet, faithfully follow the directions that come with the diapers, or you will surely plug the toilet. If you continue to hold the handle down for a few seconds after the flush, you'll get a somewhat more effective flush—a "superflush," as I believe it's called. (Don't do this every time because it uses more water.) In any event, keep a plunger on hand because you'll probably need it—see **Drains** on page 333.

Toilet Seats

The hinges will eventually start to rust—especially if the seat was cheap to begin with and if it wasn't cleaned properly and regularly. Faithfully clean hinges—along with the other toilet surfaces—with Red Juice and a toothbrush. By cleaning the hinges with a toothbrush, you will remove any remnants of urine that encourage rust. Wipe with a cleaning cloth.

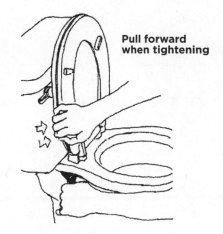

Pull forward when tightening

When replacing the toilet seat, get the type that attaches to the toilet with plastic bolts because they make both installation and future removal simpler. First, remove the old seat, which can be difficult if bolts are rusted and frozen. If they are, apply penetrating oil such as WD-40 (place paper towels to catch drips) and let it sit overnight. The next day, use a long-handled wrench, if available, to add leverage. Don't hit the bolts or the wrench with a hammer: The toilet is like glass. As a last resort, a hacksaw may be necessary. Clean the newly exposed area well, using a white pad and Red Juice or cleanser such as Comet. While tightening the mounting bolts, pull forward on the new seat and cover. If the seat is pushed all the way back when it is tightened, it may not stay up when lifted because it will hit the toilet tank lid at the wrong angle.

Trash Compactors

Other than keeping the compactor clean, the secret to long life is to compact correctly or not to compact at all. Here's a list of things not to compact (it seems pretty obvious, but you never know): paint, lacquer, paint thinner, kerosene and other flammables, aerosol cans, insecticides, fireworks, and ammunition. Don't compact things that aren't empty, such as hair spray in a pump spray container, iodine, and so forth. If you don't recycle glass, you can compact it by placing it on its side on top of other garbage, keeping it away from the sides of the compactor.

Remove the entire drawer every 6 months or so and check behind it. Most drawers can be removed by pulling them out and then lifting up. Pick up the debris that has collected here, and then spray and wipe the area. Wash the drawer and replace it.

TVs

See **Televisions** on page 393.

Vacation Maintenance Checklist

Going on vacation for a week or more? Here's a short list of things for you to do before you leave. The idea is to help you relax and not worry about what you might have forgotten to do. You're on your own about stopping mail and newspaper delivery and turning off the coffeepot.

1. Turn down the water heater to the vacation setting (see **Water Heaters** on page 406).

2. Turn off the hot-and-cold-water supplies to the washing machine (see **Washing Machines** on page 404).

3. Depending on the length of your vacation, empty the refrigerator either completely or partially (see **Refrigerators** on page 374).

4. Turn off the water supply to the automatic ice-maker (see **Refrigerators** on page 374).

5. Turn the water softener to the "bypass" mode.

6. Pour enzyme drain cleaner into slow drains (see **Drains** on page 333).

7. If you can get a relative or neighbor to help with access, this is a great time to have the carpets shampooed (see **Carpets and Rugs** on page 321).

8. Especially if neighbors or relatives are coming over to feed the cat or water the plants anyway, also have them check to be sure the power to the freezer is on when they're in your home.

Vacuum Cleaners

Overfilling the dust bag can actually cause dirt to be beaten back into the carpet! That's because when the bag is overfilled, it doesn't work as efficiently and can't pick up the dirt. It just whips it in and out of the vacuum's beater head a few times as you pass over an area with the machine. Most vacuums also suffer a decrease in suction performance, and many start to spew more dust back into the air. So replace the vacuum bag when it's only three-quarters full. Allowing the bag to get completely full doesn't even save money because doing so overworks the motor and shortens its life in the long run.

Remember Maintenance Rule 8 (page 306): Dirt is the enemy of moving parts. A vacuum motor has moving parts, and it's certainly involved with dirt, so keep filters that protect the motor meticulously clean. These filters are quite inexpensive. Considering that they are so important to the life of the vacuum motor, replace them whenever they start to look the least bit dirty.

Most vacuums depend on rubber belts to transfer motion from the motor to the beater head. This belt wears out for various reasons, but the most common is just plain old age. "Old" for a vacuum belt may be less than a year. Belts take a real beating when you vacuum up something that stops the beater head from spinning (e.g., rug tassels, a paper clip, a piece of string, too many Christmas tree needles). Since the motor continues to run, the belt can heat up, become glazed, and/or melt. Some belts don't break; they merely loosen and quit working. Even if you somehow *don't* notice that the vacuum is no longer picking anything up, you should be able to hear that the motor sounds different when the belt is broken or loose and the beater head is no longer turning at all or is turning at a much slower speed. Listen for the difference. Also learn to change a belt. The first step is to keep one on hand. See the illustrations on page 400 or your owner's manual for typical belt-changing steps. While you're poking around in the vacuum changing the beater belt, clean misguided dirt, lint, string, gravel, hair, and so on, from anyplace you find it.

After each use or at least regularly, flip the beater head over and remove hair or string wrapped around the beater bar itself and where the bar attaches at each end. Inspect the brushes on the beater bar and replace them when they are worn. If you replace them, replace them all—not just some.

Here's how to avoid clogs: (1) When vacuuming heavy accumulations, slow down. Allow the beater head to pick up everything in its path and regain its normal speed before moving on. (2) Don't even try to save time by vacuuming up paper clips, pins, collections of leaves or pine needles, anything wet,

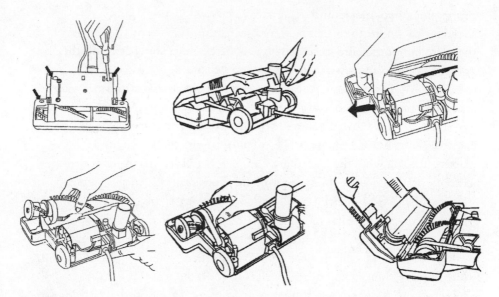

carpet fringes, rocks, marbles, wire, and the like. An otherwise innocent tooth-pick, for example, will create a clog when it lodges halfway through the hose, and other items start collecting around it. As already mentioned, notice what the vacuum normally sounds like because its pitch gets higher when it's clogged. If you continue to vacuum in spite of a clog, you will burn out the motor or ruin a belt in short order. It's the equivalent of a car attempting to pull too heavy a trailer up a mountain. The car's engine will work as hard as it can, but will make no progress and eventually will burn up.

To unclog the beater head of a canister vacuum or an upright vacuum, you must dismantle it—usually the same way you would when changing a beater bar belt. If the clog is in the neck of the vacuum leading to the dust bag, you may have to dismantle it further and/or remove the dust bag. If the clog is in the flexible hose of a canister, try to remove the clog by first disconnecting the hose from the vacuum. Then turn the hose around and hold its reverse end to the air intake of the vacuum and let the vacuum suck the clog back out. If that doesn't work, try using a broom handle or something similar to push the clog back out—in other words, insert the broom handle from the direction opposite the airflow. If the broom handle is too short, try a garden hose instead (without water, of course).

When you unplug the vacuum, don't try to save time by pulling the plug out of the wall from the vacuum end of the cord. This doesn't actually save any time because the plug will eventually break or the cord will short-circuit. Speaking of the plug, if your vacuum has an automatic rewind, don't let the cord come speeding back into the machine. The mechanism will eventually break when the plug end of the cord stops the rewind mechanism abruptly. Hold the cord and guide it into the rewind mechanism in a controlled manner.

Unless you have a wet-dry vacuum, don't attempt to vacuum up water or anything remotely moist.

VCRs (Video Cassette Recorders)

Manufacturers used to advise us to clean VCR heads once a year as preventive maintenance. Since then, changes in tape formulations and equipment have led to a different rule of thumb: *Don't* clean them unless you have to. The heads are usually clogged by damp, worn-out, or cheap videotapes (which is often a roundabout way of saying rental tapes). If you don't play such tapes, your VCR may run for years without having to clean the heads. So proper maintenance is pretty simple: Use tapes with a reputable brand name in good condition, and keep them that way by proper storage (see **Videotapes** on page 402). Otherwise, protect the unit from spills, allow air to circulate around it, and vacuum vents when you do your normal vacuuming. Shoo the cat or dog away from the unit so fur doesn't accumulate within. If you play a steady stream of rental tapes, you may have to count on more frequent maintenance.

Video Camcorders

To keep them working in good condition for as long as possible, avoid using them in very dusty, humid, or wet conditions. When you move from hot to cold or cold to hot areas, allow time for the unit's temperature to adjust before operating. Don't aim at the sun or very bright light, both of which can ruin a camcorder's sensitivity to low light. According to Sony Hawaii, this can happen even when you're not using your camcorder—when it's strapped over your shoulder, and the viewfinder is by chance pointed directly toward the sun. The viewfinder acts like a magnifying glass and focuses the sun's light, burning a large permanent spot. This is an expensive repair. Don't leave a camcorder in a hot car for any length of time. If you have to protect it during use and its case isn't handy, pop it into a plastic bag.

Remove the battery pack after use (see **Batteries** on page 311). Most camcorders have two batteries: a main battery and a clock battery. According to Keith Bianchi, who has been in the electronics business since long before camcorders were invented, if the main battery is left in place, the camcorder will switch to the main battery to run the clock—at least until it's drained to 1.3 volts. Then it switches back to the smaller clock battery, but by then, it will have drained the main battery. And when you reach for the camcorder . . . well, you know the rest.

To clean the lens, first remove grit and dust with compressed air or a soft lens brush or blow on it. Then apply lens-cleaning fluid or breathe on it, and wipe with a lens tissue or a clean soft cloth.

Most maintenance tasks that apply to full-size VCR units also apply to camcorders (see **VCRs** on page 401). But, as Mr. Bianchi observed, you would do well to remember that camcorders must be treated far more gently than full-size VCRs. For one thing, their motors and other critical parts are much smaller. If you encounter a sudden problem in a previously well-functioning camcorder, there are two things to try before heading for the repair shop: (1) Try a different or a new tape. If a tape exceeds the camcorder's tolerances even slightly, it can activate the camcorder's self-protective defenses, and the machine will shut down. (2) Turn off the automatic features (e.g., autofocus), and try to operate it again on manual settings. This may take care of the problem instantly. (Automatic functions on camcorders have been known to fail.)

Videotapes

No matter how expensive your VCR is, the quality of its picture and sound will be only as good as the tape you use. You can easily spend much more getting your VCR fixed or cleaned than you save by using bargain tapes. In order of increasing quality, the classes of tape include HG (High Grade), SHG (Super High Grade), EXG or HGK (Extra High Grade), and PRO (professional). The higher the grade, the fewer the dropouts and (sometimes) the better the oxide coating and/or binder. Consumer magazines review VHS tapes from time to time, but within the video industry, the buzz is that it's hard to go wrong with Fuji tapes.

Keep a spare tape on hand, so you can immediately replace a tape whenever it shows signs of decay. Better yet, use seven tapes—one for each day of the week—which will head off family crises that arise when someone (not you, of course) tapes over a program that someone else hadn't watched yet. Replace all seven when one of them starts to wear out, or after about 200 record/play sessions.

Leaving a tape on pause for longer than 30 seconds or so can damage the tape as well as clog a VCR's heads. As Mr. Bianchi observed, tape heads are small but also sharp as knives, and they rotate at around 1,800 rpm. Most newer machines will take themselves off pause after a while, but why tempt fate?

Uneven tension can harm a tape, so it's generally not a good idea to store a tape stopped in the middle of its run. It's also best to eject a tape before shutting off the machine (i.e., don't leave it in the machine overnight). Store tapes on any edge (just not lying flat on their side) to minimize settling, misalignment, and damage to their edges. Invest in dust- and moisture-resistant cases for your prized tapes. These are now available at all sorts of stores and video rental outlets. To avoid a variety of problems, it's wise to "exercise" an unplayed tape at least once a year. Fast-forward it to the end, stop the tape, and eject it. Next year, you can rewind it.

Wallpaper

The most important maintenance step is to control moisture, which can rapidly shorten the useful life of wallpaper. Open windows, use the exhaust fan, or install a dehumidifier to remove and control moisture. Please see the information on furniture placement and for water stains in **Walls and Ceilings** (below).

Walls and Ceilings

Touch up painted walls regularly. Keep some leftover paint from each paint job specifically for this purpose. You can make the paint last much longer if you transfer the leftover paint into a quart container. Even better, transfer it into several pint-size cans. Empty cans are available from paint stores. Label and date each can. Use inexpensive throwaway paintbrushes that are nothing more than a bit of foam rubber on a stick. You can get several of them for a dollar. Whenever there is a ding or scratch or mark, dab it away. You will keep an old paint job looking like new for years if you do.

Protect walls from furniture banging into them. Situate the furniture far enough away to prevent banging, or put a piece of wood between the wall and the furniture legs to prevent movement. Or add a rail to the wall at chair height. With wooden or plastic corner beads, you can protect wall corners from being dinged again and again. They are available at home-supply or hardware stores.

Look for water stains, especially below an exterior window or on the ceiling below a bathroom. They may indicate a need for weather-stripping or caulking around the window, or for plumbing repairs in the bathroom.

Washing Machines

Ever notice how the tops of many washers are corroded and rusted? Such damage is usually caused by laundry products. Soaps and detergents are corrosive when spilled and left moist for periods of time. Chlorine bleach, ammonia, stain removers, rust removers, and prewash sprays can be even worse. Wipe up such exterior spills, drips, and dribbles promptly. If any of these products find their way to rubber parts (e.g., the door gasket), rinse them off with water or Red or Blue Juice and then wipe. Don't use the washer top as a workplace for stain removal. Perform such operations over a sink and rinse it afterward.

Most owner's manuals tell us to turn off the hot and cold water faucets between uses to reduce pressure on the filler hoses and thereby reduce the possibility of the hoses bursting. These are sensible and prudent reasons, but I've yet to meet anyone who does this. My experience has been that I would have to move the washer even to be able to reach these faucets. Besides, plumbing expert Jeff Meehan says regularly turning the faucets on and off can, over time, actually loosen the valve spindle, which could then pop off and flood half of creation. This is eerily similar to the problem the owner's manuals want us to avoid!

Follow the owner's manual if you wish. Also inspect the hoses regularly for cracks, bulges, and splits. But my preference is to replace the plain rubber hoses with a new set of hoses wrapped in stainless steel mesh (approximately $22 a pair). Retighten new hoses at both ends after the first and second wash loads. Replace even stainless steel hoses every 5 to 7 years. As added insurance, do turn off the hot and cold water faucets when you go on vacation. A broken hose while you're away can cause spectacular damage. (Close your eyes and visualize what your hardwood floors would look like under 2 inches of hot water.)

For the ultimate in protection, have a plumber install a deep drip pan (with an overflow line to a drain) under the washer. Similar to what's installed under most water heaters to catch any leaking water, a drip pan is especially appropriate when the washer is installed on an upper floor.

There is a filter washer on one or both ends of the hot and cold supply hoses. Even small amounts of debris caught in the screen will make the washing machine take forever to fill. Turn the water off, unscrew the hose, and use a screwdriver or needle-nose pliers gently to extract the filter washers.

Keep a towel handy to catch the inevitable dribbles of water from the hoses. Clean with a toothbrush and by blasting water through the screen backward. Or just replace them (they're cheap) if they're difficult to clean or if they were punctured when you removed them. Be sure to check both ends of the hoses for filter washers. Check the filter washers if the washer takes longer than normal to fill with water, or whenever you replace the hoses.

Motor-driven appliances such as the washer should be level to help protect the motor bearings. In addition, for a washer at least, when the machine is in its spin cycle, it's important for it to be level to help keep it from vibrating or "walking." Walking is a major cause of failure of the filler hoses because the vibration or movement can stretch and stress them. Leave enough slack in the lines to allow for this (even if the washer is level).

Use a level to be sure your washer is installed properly. If you move the washer for any reason, relevel the machine when you put it back into position. At least the front two corners will each have a leveling foot. Place a level on the top of the washer. If only one leg isn't touching the floor, try extending that leg first by loosening the lock nut and then unscrewing the foot until it is solidly in contact with the floor. Often that's all you need to do. If not, adjust each leveling foot until the level bubble is centered front-to-back and side-to-side.

Don't change the controls of the washer (or dryer) while it is in midcycle. In other words, if you remember that you wanted to set it on the gentle cycle, but the machine is merrily proceeding though the normal cycle, don't just grab the dial and twist it to the new setting. First pull out the dial or whatever you do to stop the machine and only then change to the new setting. The gears will appreciate it.

Don't habitually overload the machine. You may think you're getting away with it, but you're actually wearing out the machine at a much more rapid clip—including the gears in the transmission, which is the most expensive part of the machine. If the wash should be done in three loads, don't try to do it in two. Usually the owner's manual will list the machine's load capacity in pounds. But who has the time or scales to figure out the weight of a load? Instead, judge by the space the load takes up. Don't crowd. Mix small and large items together, and don't wrap large items around the agitator. Most of our mothers taught us to separate the wash by color. It also helps to separate lint producers (towels, chenille, throw rugs, etc.) from lint attractors (synthetics and permanent press items). If your machine has a lint filter, clean it after each use.

Even though you've asked other family members to clean out their pockets before putting clothes in the hamper, check pockets before putting clothes into the washing machine. Washing coins can nick the enamel, and rust will get a foothold. Besides, one coin will eventually get stuck somewhere and have to be removed by a pro. Washing (and then especially drying) crayons or other items that melt or stain should also help convince us to take the time to check the contents of pockets before adding the item to the washer. Also zip up zippers and fasten hooks.

Note: Appliance touch-up paint is available at appliance dealers and repair stores. If rust has already started, remove it with steel wool or sandpaper and prime the spot before repainting.

When you're done with the day's washing, leave the lid open at least long enough for the inside to dry completely. This helps prevent rust from getting started.

Water Heaters

A properly maintained water heater should last 13 to 20 years. Considering that a replacement can cost $1,500 or more, it's important to extend its life as long as possible.

A service agreement with a local company to perform annual maintenance on the hot water heater, the furnace, and the air conditioner is an excellent value. It may even be worth it to have three separate service agreements, but if you can find a company that can do all three or more, it's well worth the peace of mind.

Maintenance books and owner's manuals recommend that hot water heaters be drained (flushed)—either partially or fully—every 6 months to a year. Few homeowners bother to do this. Even if the homeowner is willing, the heater

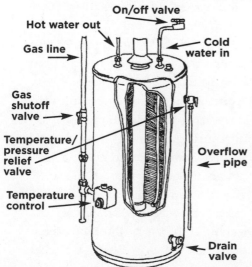

On/off valve
Hot water out
Gas line
Cold water in
Gas shutoff valve
Temperature/ pressure relief valve
Overflow pipe
Temperature control
Drain valve

may or may not be easy to drain even though all water heaters have a hose connection and drain valve at the bottom. And, as expert San Francisco plumber Jeff Mehan has found time after time, the drain valve can become clogged with accumulated debris as the water heater is drained, which makes it difficult or impossible to reclose. Also, unfortunately, the drain valves used on most water heaters are notoriously poor in quality. The result is an emergency phone call to a plumber.

Especially if the water heater hasn't been drained in several years, draining it may cause more problems than it solves. Unless you started a regular draining schedule within the first year or so of a water heater's installation, I recommend having a plumber do it for you, at least for the first time. Also have the plumber check the drain valve and replace it with a higher-quality one if needed (a full-port gate valve) as well as test the temperature/pressure relief valve (see below).

If you're ready to drain the water heater, here is how to do it:

1. Shut off the cold-water supply to the tank.

2. If it's an electric heater, turn off the power. If it's a gas heater, turn the water temperature control to the pilot or vacation setting.

3. Screw a garden hose onto the drain valve, and position the other end at a suitable drain site. (If a garden hose is not feasible, drain the tank into a bucket only until the water runs clear—not until the heater is completely empty, as in the following directions.)

4. Open the drain valve. When the tank is empty, turn the cold-water supply on and off a few times to create a few blasts into the tank to wash out additional sediment from the bottom of the tank.

5. Close the drain valve, refill the tank, and reset the gas or turn the power back on.

The usual recommendation is to operate the temperature/pressure relief valve once every 6 months or year. As with draining, however, a bit of sediment can lodge in the valve and prevent its closing. If you want to perform this test, lift the pressure valve stem (near the top of the tank) for a second or two and allow some water or air to escape. A good time to do this is when you've just refilled the tank with cold water. If the valve doesn't release properly or if it won't reseat after the test, have the heater serviced immediately.

If the unit is taking an unusually long time to heat, if the water just won't get hot enough, and especially if you hear a crackling/rumbling sound as it heats the water, it's definitely time to call a plumber.

Here's other maintenance you should perform:

1. Vacuum around the base for dust, dirt, and lint on a regular basis.

2. Visually inspect the venting system of gas water heaters. Look for obstructions, damage, or deterioration of the venting cap or pipe, or

rust flakes around the top of the water heater. Remove any obstructions. It's amazing the things someone might have left on top of it during the preceding year. If you see rust flakes or deterioration of the vent, call the utility company or a plumber to clean and replace the flue and venting system.

3. Inspect the burner in gas water heaters. Check for sooting, which is not normal and impairs proper combustion. If you find soot, call either the utility company or a plumber to service the unit.

4. Insulate it. If the water heater feels warm to the touch, it will work less and last longer if you install a water-heater blanket. Kits are available at most home improvement and hardware stores. A blanket with an insulation value of at least R-11 is recommended. Newer water heaters are already insulated and don't need a blanket, so check the manufacturer's guidelines and warranty criteria before adding more insulation. (A blanket may actually void the warranty.) *Do not* insulate the top or bottom of gas water heaters. Insulation can interfere with the flue draft and/or cut off air to the pilot light. Insulate only the sides. However, the top and bottom of an electric water heater *should* be insulated.

Here are other energy-saving things you can do to lighten the load on the water heater and so help to lengthen its life:

1. Insulate the hot-water pipes. Your home is a good candidate for insulation if you use hot water frequently, if the pipe runs are long, and if the pipes pass through an uninsulated crawl space or basement.

2. Make sure the water temperature setting is correct: 120° to 140°F meets most household needs. This is a setting between "low" and "medium" on most water heaters. (See **Dishwashers,** page 330, for instructions on measuring the temperature of the hot water.)

3. Turn it to the lowest temperature setting (often labeled "vacation") when you leave for a week or more.

Water Softeners

A modern water softener doesn't require much maintenance other than keeping the unit properly filled and refilled with salt. Clean out the salt compartment before each refill. Wash the brine intake with a toothbrush and fresh water. Empty any brine or salt residue (or use a wet-dry vacuum) and rinse with fresh water. Turn off the water softener's timer, and turn it to "bypass" mode when you go on vacation.

Water Supply

Once a year, test the main water supply shutoff valve by closing and opening it to be sure it hasn't stuck in the open position. Do the same thing with fixture shutoff valves that supply water to sinks and toilets. Both the main valve and fixture valves must be operable so water can be turned off in an emergency or when plumbing repairs are necessary. Label these valves, so you and others can locate them next year.

Pipes

If the hot-water pipes are covered with insulation, inspect them annually. Replace or reposition loose insulation, but be careful. If it's not visibly the do-it-yourself type of tubular insulation, and especially if it is old and looks like it contains plaster, there's a good chance it also contains asbestos. In such a case, consult a plumber or asbestos-abatement contractor. (Also see **Drains,** page 333, **Faucets,** page 341, **Sinks,** page 384, **Toilets,** page 395, and **Water Heaters,** page 406.)

Whirlpool Baths

Most are made of fiberglass, so don't use abrasive cleansers. Be patient when filling the tub, and wait until all the jets are covered by water before you start the motor. If the motor operates dry, you run the risk of burning it out. Use no soap—or minimal amounts of it—while the whirlpool is operating. Occasionally rinse interior pipes after use by refilling the tub with freshwater and turning on the motor. Once or twice a year, open and vacuum the compartment that contains the motor and the motor vents.

Windows

To continue to have easy-to-open, easy-to-slide windows, you should clean and lubricate them regularly. Open crank, awning, or jalousie windows to expose the extension arm. Remove dried grease, paints, and so on, with a wire brush. Clean with Red Juice and wipe dry. Spray a Teflon (or other) lubricant on the moving parts. (Use a piece of paper to keep the lubricant off painted areas.) Sliding window runners should be vacuumed with the crevice tool. Spray lubricant can be applied also. Wood windows will continue operating smoothly if you apply a very thin layer of paste wax or paraffin.

Caulking and/or weather-stripping windows and doors saves money and makes the house more comfortable. I've read that a ⅛-inch opening around two door frames lets in as much cold air as a 12-inch window opened 6 inches. The money you spend on caulking and weather stripping is usually recovered in one heating season or less. And your home will be noticeably more comfy and cozy come winter. But most important, a house must remain waterproof to avoid the very serious problems water can cause when it gets into walls and floors.

Caulk around exterior window and door frames where they meet the siding. Weather stripping should be applied around a window or doorjamb or at its threshold. Caulk is flexible when applied, but it eventually cracks, dries out, and has to be replaced. Weather-stripping materials include vinyl, rubber, metal, and foam rubber, most of which can also dry out or wear out and need periodic replacement.

Pick a day to caulk outdoors that is neither too hot nor too cold. Easier said than done, but it's nearly impossible to caulk properly except in moderate and dry weather.

Caulking Instructions

Everything must be clean, or the caulk won't adhere properly, and you'll be wasting your time. Remove the old caulk (at least as much as is possible), loose paint, and dirt. Use a scraper, a wire brush, or sandpaper, depending on the surface. Apply caulk with a caulking gun or a pressurized can (see **Tub/Shower Enclosures, Caulking,** page 310, for additional information). Get the best silicone caulk that money can buy. This is not the place to save a buck or two. Besides, it's a false savings. Cheap caulk will have to be replaced more quickly, which automatically multiplies its actual price—and that's nothing compared with the value of your time.

Fill any deep cracks with expanding foam sealant to within ¼ to ½ inch of the surface, and use caulk as a top layer. Cut off about ½ inch of the cartridge tip at a 45-degree angle, and puncture the interior seal with a nail. You can use the nail later as a stopper for any unused caulk. Don't caulk around the front door

or the most prominent window first. Start
where your work won't be noticed, because
you won't be as skilled on the first door and
window as you will be on later ones.
However, with a steady hand and a little
practice, it's relatively simple to learn how to
lay a uniformly wide bead that overlaps both
sides for a good seal. Finish the job with a
moistened finger, plastic spoon, or finishing
tool (which you can buy at the same store
where you bought the caulk and caulking
gun). While you're in the mood, check for
any openings or cracks around dryer vents,

Metal weather-   **Foam weather-**
stripping   **stripping**

water pipes, exhaust fan outlets, lighting fixtures, window air conditioners,
heating and cooling ductwork, garage doors, attic doors, and wires. Also check
where porches attach to the house, the foundation, water spigots, TV cable, telephone lines, AC wires, seams between masonry and siding, chimney bricks and
siding, and corners. Any opening should be sealed with caulk, foam sealant, gas-
kets, or weather stripping. Try to seal things (pipes or wires, for example) that
penetrate a wall both on the inside and the outside.

If you feel a draft of air between a window and its frame, the gap should be
sealed with weather stripping. (Air entering between the window frame and
the wall indicates the need to caulk.) There are a number of choices, but the
most durable (and most expensive) weather-stripping products are the smartest
choices. They include bronze, aluminum, steel, rubber, and adhesive foam strips.

Condensation on the inside of windows or between windows and storm
windows is another indication of the need to weather-strip (or to add storm
windows). If you do caulk around storm windows (which may make them in-
operable), make sure the weep holes at the bottom of the storm window
frame are clear, so moisture can escape. You can also reduce condensation by
turning on the bathroom and kitchen exhaust fans. High humidity in the
house contributes to buildup of condensation on cold surfaces like windows.
It's worth checking the indoor relative humidity in your home if it seems too
humid to you. Around 30 to 50 percent relative humidity is optimal during
the heating season.

Locate the origin of excess moisture, if present. A wet crawl space or basement may have to be covered or waterproofed. Moisture is also a by-product
of combustion. If you can't find any other source, have your heating system
and chimney checked.

Sliding window tracks should be vacuumed at least once a year. These tracks generally have weep holes to allow rainwater to escape. Check to be sure they're clear as you vacuum. Teflon spray, paste wax, or paraffin may make opening or closing windows easy again.

Wine

Maintenance of wine is not a concept that needs any particular discussion in my family—we drink it before the bottle even needs to be dusted. The same goes for any partial bottle left at the end of a meal. I suppose households with wine cellars don't spend time discussing wine maintenance either—at least once the cellar construction is complete. But there are a few maintenance considerations for the balance of the wine-drinking population.

Wine likes to be stored cool (the ideal is around 55°F) without frequent temperature fluctuations and without vibration or frequent movement. Of course, this describes the wine cellar we all don't have, so just use this as a guide. The first choice for storage is a nice cool place. If you have a reasonably consistently cool place, store the wine there—in cardboard boxes to help insulate against temperature fluctuations. Storing on a concrete slab can help keep bottles cool. If you can't locate a consistently cool place, at least pick one that doesn't get hot. If you can't find a place like that, put your wine in the refrigerator (including red wines too), or at least keep it there during hot spells. Storage in a refrigerator is not a substitute for a wine cellar, and it should not be used for permanent wine storage. But the problems that arise from storing it there take a long time to develop, and they are less injurious to wine than letting it get cooked in a hot location.

Ideal storage involves laying the bottles on their side, with the cork end tilted slightly down.

There are a few options for maintaining partial bottles of red wines. Red wines start to taste like vinegar a day (more or less) after they're opened unless you take steps to preserve them. (For white wines, just replace the cork and store in the refrigerator.) Here are several choices for preserving a partial bottle of red wine:

1. Pour a half-full bottle into an empty *half* bottle and tightly recork. The less air left in the half bottle, the better. Oxygen in the air is what turns the wine into vinegar.

2. Wine authority Ronn Wiegand says to freeze it right in the bottle. When you're ready to finish it, let it thaw to room temperature. He

says you can even microwave it to speed up the thawing as long as you don't let it get warm.

3. There are at least two inexpensive products that work. My personal favorite is Private Preserve Wine Preserver. It's an aerosol can containing a safe, inert gas that blankets the wine as it forces out the offending air. Then just recork the bottle or use a special stopper to keep air out, and set it aside until you're ready to finish it. Heidi Yorkshire, author of *Wine Savvy* (Portland, Oregon: Duplex Media Group, 1995), favors a Vacu-Vin. It's a simple plastic device that allows you to pump most of the air out of the bottle. Special stoppers replace the cork and prevent air from getting back into the bottle. She says wine stored this way will keep for at least several days, which is similar to my experience with the Private Preserve Wine Preserver. Both products are available at wine specialty stores and by mail order from the Wine Enthusiast Catalog (800-356-8466).

Wrought Iron

Don't do anything with it other than keep it clean by dusting or wiping—unless it starts to rust. If that happens, remove the rust with steel wool or by chemical methods. Reprime and repaint. Depending on how long it took to start to rust in the first place, you may be able to retard the return of rust by applying a coat of Rust-Oleum. Being thorough when removing all the old rust before repainting is more important than applying new paint.

Chapter 25 Environmental Impacts of Household Cleaners

As most of us learned long ago, dirt and grime don't just roll over and give up when they see us coming. So consumers have often turned to powerful cleaning agents to help the cause. These agents can have potentially harmful consequences on the environment long after they're washed down the drain.

This is a time of transition—when many formerly cholesterol-happy cooks are turning to tofu. Likewise for cleaners' technology—people are seeking ways to turn from hazardous cleaning agents to relatively benign ones. But this transition in technologies has only just begun. Accordingly, many recommendations in publications on the environment turn out to be personal beliefs or preferences that are not backed up with scientific data. We've sifted through these recommendations and integrated them with our own experience, and we list below our review of the products we use in terms of their probable environmental impacts. We have also listed alternatives in case you have other preferences.

It is important to distinguish between hazards to individual health and hazards to the environment. The two are often inextricably entwined, but not always. For example, a product can be an irritant to an individual but can biodegrade quickly and thoroughly enough to pose little environmental hazard. On the other hand, a product may not be much of a personal irritant but may promote excessive growth of algae downstream in the waste cycle. By and large, when there's a lack of environmental data, some publications shift to descriptions of personal hazards. Until the environmental data are in, one way of reasoning is that if a little of a product is personally hazardous, then a lot of it is likely to be environmentally hazardous too. That's not always the case, but it's often a good start.

Our own selection of the products we use (The Clean Team supplies our own products) was motivated by a strong desire to avoid products that caused health problems or irritation to ourselves. Our teams are exposed to five or more complete household cleanings every workday, so if there's a problem with a product, it's readily apparent. None of the products we have recommended in this book, when used as described, have caused our team health problems. Admittedly, that may not be an accurate index of their environmental impact, but we take it as a favorable sign.

Alternative formulas for brand-name cleaning products are being proposed by environmentalists as safer—both environmentally and personally. Some of these formulas are mixtures of several ingredients. Many environmentalists seem to believe that if one cleaner is good then several mixed together ought to be that much better. But that's often not true. When you combine a second or third active ingredient, you can generate a chemical free-for-all, especially considering that there are so many trace compounds in ordinary tap water to begin with. In addition, mixtures of ingredients can work at cross purposes— such as mixing an acid and an alkali in the same formula. Unless a mixture of multiple ingredients has been thoroughly tested by someone with a competent background, stick with single-ingredient alternatives.

One of the most famous and dangerous combinations of household cleaners is chlorine bleach and ammonia, which produces potentially harmful chloramine fumes. And mixing chlorine bleach with other cleaning agents such as acids—vinegar and phosphoric acid, for example—can liberate chlorine gas, which can be as toxic as chloramine.

Face Masks

By the way, you may be tempted to wear a face mask when working with cleaners to avoid exposure to fumes. But most cheap particle masks filter out only large dust particles—not vapors. To block vapors from cleaning agents, you would need a cartridge-type or industrial-grade mask with an air supply (both of which require medical consultation before use if you are overweight, smoke, or have a heart condition). In most cases for household work, a mask seems unnecessary if you've provided the abundant ventilation that is called for in the directions for just about all cleaning products.

Rubber Gloves

Wearing rubber gloves, by contrast, is almost always a sensible idea when working with strong household cleaners. Unfortunately, many consumer varieties don't effectively resist strong cleaning agents. We use a very thick type that resists even formaldehyde—not that we use it in our house-cleaning activities! They're also 16 inches long, which helps a great deal to avoid those clammy dribbles down our arms and inside the gloves when cleaning.

General Considerations

Before we consider individual products, let's review a few ideas about environmental impacts that apply to many cleaners. Often the easiest way to clean in an environmentally sound way is simply to reduce the amount of the product used: Use one paper towel instead of three; apply a tablespoon of Comet rather than half a cup. And use durable tools instead of disposable gimmicks: brushes, not disposable swipes.

Several products require reasonable caution when disposing large amounts down the drain—notably chlorine bleach and ammonia. The P trap under the sink is made of relatively thin metal, and undiluted chlorine bleach can eat right through it if given the chance. So keep the cold (not hot!) water running if you pour a quart or more of bleach down the drain. Actually, the toilet is the preferred means of disposing of reasonable amounts of cleaner, except for ammonia (see below). To comply with laws for disposal of significant quantities of bleach or other potentially hazardous substances, contact hazardous-waste authorities in your area for the recommended procedure.

For your personal protection, provide abundant ventilation when using any strong cleaner. For prolonged exposure to powerful fumes like those of ammonia, bleach, and pine-oil cleaners, knowledgeable sources recommend exhausting the fumes out the window with a fan. (Presumably, you are prudent enough not to be situated between the window and the fumes.) Another way to avoid respiratory exposure is to use pump-spray products instead of aerosols. This applies especially around children.

Labels

Most of us believe we can get reasonable information from labels regarding environmental and personal hazards. But consumer labels are not required to disclose many, many potentially dangerous substances. Why? The Consumer Products Safety Commission (CPSC) has limited jurisdiction. They can require a listing of an ingredient on a consumer label only if the substance is defined as a hazardous substance by one specific law (the Federal Hazardous Substances Act). And they can ban an ingredient only if an adequate label cannot be written for that listed ingredient (e.g., if adequate first-aid instructions cannot be given on a label).

What is covered by this federal law? Only substances that pose an acute (immediate) hazard—not chronic (long-term) hazards. Swell. If it doesn't knock you over on the first whiff, you don't have to be informed about it (with one or two exceptions—such as asbestos). What does this exclude? Oh, merely *carcinogens* (agents that cause cancer), *mutagens* (agents that cause genetic mutations), and *teratogens* (agents that cause birth defects)! And just because the Occupational Safety and Health Administration (OSHA) itself declares something to be a contaminant doesn't mean you have to be informed about it on the label of the product you'll be using in your home.

Such ingredients must be listed for industrial usage via something called a Material Safety Data Sheet (MSDS). You can request an MSDS for a retail product from the manufacturer, who will usually voluntarily comply.

There's little point in jumping all over the CPSC, because their jurisdiction is limited by law. Their budget isn't increased often, and it's an amount that the Pentagon probably spends in 5 minutes. The people to contact live in the White House and work in the House and Senate. Tell them that consumers need fuller disclosure on consumer labels, so we can make up our own minds about what we're introducing into our own homes and bodies. Thank you.

Red Juice

We started looking for a nonirritating general-purpose cleaner within a few days of starting The Clean Team. The grocery-shelf cleaners made most of us cough, especially in confined spaces. Our search led us to a unique product from Oregon.

It's no accident that our Clean Team Red Juice is environmentally safe. It was designed to be that way. Dirt clings to surfaces like a stretched elastic

MSDS (Material Safety Data Sheet)

MSDS stands for "material safety data sheet." MSDSs are documents that detail what chemicals are contained in a product, what immediate and potential hazard(s) they may pose, precautions for handling and storing the product, first aid in the event of exposure, what to do in an emergency, and so forth. Federal OSHA regulations require them to be available to anyone who asks. Their original purpose was to protect employees from short- or long-term negative health consequences from exposure to chemicals they might come into contact with on the job. But interested consumers may request an MSDS for any cleaning product from the manufacturer or distributor. They are not standardized and can be difficult to decipher, but you'll find that they have important information (including emergency telephone numbers) if you take the time to study them.

membrane. Without getting into too much chemistry, Red Juice is basically a unique blend of surfactants—compounds that reduce the surface tension of the goop clinging to surfaces. The surfactants in Red Juice break this surface tension and allow the dirt to float away.

The surfactants in Red Juice are derived from sea kelp, among other things. What is *not* in it is also important: It lacks the surfactant in many janitorial and retail general-purpose cleaners—something called Butyl Cellosolve (2-butoxyethanol or closely related compounds). Butyl Cellosolve was formulated 25 to 30 years ago. According to California law,[1] it was listed as a "chemical contaminant" and described as being easily absorbed through the skin. (Maybe that's why it irritates the lungs so quickly.) It injures the kidneys and liver, irritates the eyes and mucous membranes,[2] and is listed as "very toxic" by an established textbook on toxicology.[3]

Needless to say, we were delighted to find a cleaner that didn't contain a drop of Butyl Cellosolve. Red Juice has the USDA's highest approval classification (A-1), meaning that it can be used on equipment in which food is made and on all surfaces of meat and dairy processing plants. It is nontoxic, odorless, and quickly and easily biodegradable (in 4 to 7 days).

Red Juice cannot be registered as a disinfectant because it lacks "killability" (thank goodness): It does not kill living cells on contact. But it cleans so well that bacteria and fungi have just about nothing to feed on, so the microbe count after cleaning a surface is close to zero.

We like Red Juice so well that we diluted it and colored it blue to make Blue Juice, which is the way we use and sell it. Its weaker concentration is all that's needed for cleaning glass surfaces. Both the red and blue dyes are included in the USDA A-1 approval. If you'd like to try our Red or Blue Juice, see Appendix A.

Alternatives

A solution of white vinegar and water is recommended by some sources. (Start with ¼ cup white vinegar to 1 quart water.) Or try 4 tablespoons baking soda per quart of water.[4] Don't expect either of these alternatives to have much cleaning strength.

Chlorine Bleach

We recommend the use of only a tablespoon or so of laundry-strength chlorine bleach—and then only if there is a mildew problem in the bathroom. We also dribble it on other mildewed surfaces—we don't spray it in a fine mist. This amount of bleach thus applied, especially rinsed with sufficient cold water afterward, does not appear to pose a significant environmental threat. Although chlorine bleach can be an individual health hazard in large enough amounts, we found no data on the environmental effects of the release of household-level amounts of chlorine bleach. Chlorine bleach in household quantities rapidly breaks down to a variety of common salts when it gets past the sink's P trap and enters the common drainage system.

Clorox states that its bleach is safe for septic systems—at least in standard household amounts. Its chlorine bleach is registered with the EPA as a disinfectant and contains no phosphates.

If you are concerned about the use of chlorine bleach in your home, consider using a more dilute solution. Clorox recommends a dilution of 1 part Clorox to 21.33 parts water (that's ¾ cup per gallon of water) for anti-mildew operations, which is much more dilute than what we use (1 to 4). If you are concerned, you could experiment to find the most dilute solution that is still effective against the particular species of mildew in your home.

Alternatives

If you prefer not to use chlorine bleach at all, the alternative most commonly mentioned in the literature is a solution of borax and water. For example, Greenpeace[5] recommends a dilution of ½ cup borax per gallon of water. Powdered borax is available in the laundry section of larger grocery stores. We found no data showing that borax is effective against mildew or safe for the environment either, but it is less irritating than chlorine bleach for personal use.

Mildew can actually thrive in a mildly acidic environment, so vinegar and other acidic solutions that have been suggested for mildew treatments are not sensible alternatives.

Clorox recommends that no other cleaner—including baking soda—be mixed with bleach except a small amount of detergent as an option.

Comet

The active ingredient of environmental consequence in Comet and many other powdered scouring cleansers is a small percentage of chlorine bleach. We recommend its use but in much smaller amounts than most housecleaners are inclined to use.

If you want to reduce your exposure to bleaching cleansers, use chemically resistant gloves, be careful about ventilation, and rinse the surfaces with cold water. (Steam from hot water may carry the chlorine into the air.)

Alternative

If you want to use an unbleached scouring powder, try Bon Ami, which is a relatively mild abrasive powder without chlorine or any other type of bleach. Some sources recommend baking soda, but it's an alkaline substance that can damage vulnerable surfaces itself if left unrinsed. And it often dissolves as it is being scrubbed on surfaces just when you need it most.

Paper Towels

As you've read, 100 percent cotton napkins are our first choice for spray-and-wipe operations. Cloth diapers are a distant second. Our third alternative is paper towels.

The quality of consumer paper towels varies enormously, and we believe it is a false economy to use the bargain brands because you'll end up using more of them to do the job. We prefer the Bounty brand. No inks or dyes are used in their manufacture, as is the case with most other pure-white paper towels. In addition, only materials approved by the Food and Drug Administration are voluntarily used in their manufacture. (Paper towels are normally not regulated by the FDA.) According to their manufacturer, there are no dioxins in this paper product—measured to one part per trillion.

Few, if any, unbleached paper towels are available in grocery stores. Many environmental workers are concerned about the effects on our water supplies of dioxins produced by the bleaching of wood pulp. Bleaches are added to pulp to purify it and make it more absorbent, among other reasons. The bleaches are not the problem. But they can lead to the production of dioxins when they react with certain ingredients of natural wood pulp. It is the dioxins that are the problem. The good news is that the paper industry is developing new technologies, including ones that use oxygenated bleaches, so dioxins aren't produced. Other operating and processing innovations have been or will be introduced, so the risk of dioxin release should be greatly diminished or eliminated for this industry.

Alternative

Clean with reusable 100 percent cotton cleaning cloths, such as the white table napkins used in restaurants.

Ammonia

Anyone who has used ammonia cannot long remain unaware that ammonia is a powerful irritant to the lungs, eyes, and skin. But from an environmental point of view, sources differ considerably on its use. Some recommend it as an alternative to traditional strong cleaners like oven cleaners. Others say to minimize its use because it is an irritant. We could find no data on the environmental impact of household levels of ammonia. But it is a compound that occurs spontaneously in nature—especially that part of nature near cat boxes. And it is an eminently biodegradable product.

Used in the amounts we recommend for washing floors, it is hard to conceive of it as an environmental threat. But be careful about pouring it down the toilet! If you installed a dispensing chlorine product in the toilet tank, keep the ammonia entirely away from the toilet.

Alternatives

We use a pH–neutral floor cleaner called Sh–Clean. You might try a solution of ¼ to 1 cup of white vinegar per gallon of water for most types of floor. But test in an inconspicuous spot first, because some types of floor (e.g., marble) do not like to be cleaned with any type of acid—even a mild one like vinegar. Although vinegar is recommended by several manufacturers of flooring material, we do not recommend it. Vinegar is not a cleaner, so floor dirt (especially greasy dirt) is only smushed around and not lifted off the floor.

Oven Cleaner

We use the standard formula of Easy–Off oven cleaner, but we ask that it be applied the night before without heating the oven, so we don't have to deal with any fumes. And we use long, heavy industrial gloves when wiping out the oven. By the way, please ignore well-intentioned but misguided suggestions in some environmental publications to apply oven cleaner when the oven is already warm after cooking (to save energy). If you've misjudged and sprayed an already hot oven, you could be exposed to very harmful fumes. Better to spray a cool oven, close the door, and then heat it—if called for per instructions.

   The active ingredient in many oven cleaners is a serious compound: sodium hydroxide (lye). We found no data on environmental harm caused by household concentrations of oven cleaner. However, most formulas are notoriously caustic, which means they can burn and destroy skin tissue. Easy–Off is now sold in at least two noncaustic varieties that contain no lye, and Arm & Hammer also has a noncaustic variety. All of these formulas are sold in manual pump-spray containers, not aerosols. They require a heated oven and overnight application. One or more of the formulas are so mild that their label instructions say you don't even have to wear gloves, but it's such a messy job that gloves would still seem to be a good idea.

Alternatives

The alternative to oven cleaners most often recommended in publications[6] is a bowl of ammonia left overnight in the oven. Add ¼ to ½ cup ammonia in a shallow glass or porcelain (not metal) bowl, plus about the same amount of warm water. Place the bowl in the oven and close the door. The idea is that fumes from the evaporating ammonia soften the crud in the oven overnight. Make sure the kitchen window is wide open before you lower the oven door the next day, because you will be greeted by obnoxious ammonia fumes. Wet the surfaces with Red Juice or the equivalent before scrubbing, and follow the procedures described in Chapter 11 for cleaning an oven.

The best way to reduce the amount of oven cleaner used is prevention, of course. Positioning a large baking sheet beneath the item being baked is one of those splendid ideas that one always remembers after the fact. Putting a piece of aluminum foil on top of that same tray is the other great idea.

Tile Juice

Most liquid tile cleaners that are designed to remove soap scum and mineral deposits are formulated around some type of acid—typically phosphoric acid.

Phosphoric acid does biodegrade, but unfortunately it biodegrades to form phosphate salts. Phosphates indirectly kill fish and other aquatic life by promoting the growth of algae that use up the available oxygen in rivers and lakes. Depending on where you live and how wastewater is processed and disposed of, this may or may not be a problem in your area.

If phosphates are a problem in your area—and err on the side of caution if you're not sure—we've discovered an effective non-acid tile cleaner called Scum Bum.

Alternatives

An alternative is white vinegar—another acid, but this time it's 5 percent acetic acid (the weakest type of acid). If you want to try vinegar, mix it half and half with water. To increase its effectiveness, use it full strength. Apply and scrub like Tile Juice, and rinse afterward. The white pad might be better than the tile brush for a thin liquid like vinegar. Some environmentalists suggest a paste of baking soda as an alternative (see Note 4 on page 428). And there are new environmentally oriented product lines[7] that use citric acid (plus other ingredients) instead of phosphoric acid in their tile cleaners. Similar products are listed in *The Green Consumer*.[8]

Yet another choice is to stick to traditional powdered cleanser—chlorinated or otherwise—scrubbed with the tile brush. It's considerably more difficult to manage than a liquid cleaner, but it is not an acidic product.

Prevention is one of the wisest environmental steps you can take in terms of tile cleaning. The buildup from hard water is one reason that tile is difficult to clean, so consider installing a water softener. Or wipe down the shower walls and doors after each shower with a quick swipe with a squeegee left in the shower for that purpose. If soap builds up quickly on your shower walls, changing soaps may help. For example, switch from a hard bar soap to a liquid soap or one that is milled with oils instead of fats.

Furniture Polish

The furniture polish we have used for years has never caused us breathing difficulties. We find that the manual pump-spray formula works better than the aerosol (they are different formulas). It's fortunate that the product that works better is also safer environmentally.

There is concern that furniture polishes can cause harm to children who inhale their vapors. Polishes that have a high concentration of low-viscosity (thin) oils can, if inhaled, coat the lungs and seriously interfere with a child's ability to breathe. Our formula has relatively little oil (less than 10 percent), and the oil is of high viscosity. If it is inhaled, the probability of causing respiratory distress is slight. If drunk, it is usually nontoxic. But needless to say, it and all other furniture polish and household cleaners in general must be kept away from little ones, and any significant accidental exposure warrants medical advice.

Alternatives

If you prefer to use an oil instead of wax, you might consider plain walnut oil. After all, it came from wood to begin with. (We are absolutely amazed that some environmental publications recommend using mineral oil on wood furniture.) Many aficionados of fine wood furniture eschew oil in favor of paste wax. You can reduce airborne exposure to the oils in furniture polish by using a paste wax. Kiwi Bois and Goddard's are two excellent brands.

Water

One of the major issues in terms of environmental impact of household cleaning is the conservation and protection of the drinking supply. In a few years, we'll probably look back in wonder that we used to flush our toilets and water our lawns with drinking water. But for now, our goals are more modest: to use as little water as reasonably possible and not to damage the available sources.

We believe that our Speed Cleaning methods minimize the use of water in several ways: by not using sponges, which require frequent rinsing; by avoiding the use of scouring powder on areas that are difficult to rinse; by training you not to rinse or wipe until the proper time (Clean Team Rule 5 on page 10); by training you to work from top to bottom, which eliminates needless re-washing and rerinsing (Clean Team Rule 3 on page 9); and by using a cotton scrub mop (the Sh-Mop) that requires far less water to clean floors.

Biodegradability

Essentially all liquid cleaners are biodegradable by loose definition. *Webster's* says only, "capable of being decomposed by natural biological processes." As we all know by now, it's the *length of time* that something takes to biode-grade that's important. In addition, research at landfill sites shows that you must consider the circumstances in which an item will biodegrade. For example, some plastics may biodegrade within a few days in the direct sun but will essentially last forever if buried in a landfill. And don't forget, even a biodegradable cleaner may be packaged in an ecological disaster. In response to the public's rising concern for the environment, many manufacturers with a marketing department even half awake print a big, bold, colorful BIODEGRADABLE across their cleaner's label to appear to be as ecofriendly as possible. Whether these cleaners or their packaging are environmentally friendly is not at all clear. Until manufacturers are held to a stricter defini-tion, a top priority for The Clean Team is to start with products that are "personally friendly"—that is, products that are safe and nonirritating to the human being using them. While sometimes similar, "environmentally" friendly and "personally" friendly are not always the same thing. But if you make sure you have products that are personally friendly around your home, you're well on your way to being environmentally friendly as well.

Concentrates

You might be a little surprised at how much water you're instructed to add to your concentrated liquid cleaner—it's practically all water.

We think all that water is one reason concentrates have not been generally available until recently. Manufacturers were nervous that it would lower our "perceived value" of their products. But the fact is, most liquid cleaners are 90 percent or more water. That's okay. The important test is whether they work, not how much water they contain. Concentrates are a good idea. Besides saving money, they reduce packaging that ends up in our landfills, and they save trips to the store. Use them in good conscience.

Note: Many people use more concentrate than the directions call for in the commonly held belief that if a little is good, then more is better. That's not true in this case. Using extra concentrate almost never improves effectiveness, but it does cause you to have to purchase the product again more quickly. Save the most money with concentrates by following the directions exactly.

Are Disinfectants Necessary?

For regular housecleaning, disinfecting doesn't work the way you probably think it does. Even when a communicable disease is loose in your home, the items to disinfect are the shared things, such as the phone, eating utensils, and so forth, not every surface in the house. Here's why disinfecting isn't usually helpful in a household setting:

1. Germs (bacteria, viruses, fungi, et cetera) need warmth and moisture to survive. Simply wiping with soap and water removes nearly all of them: The very act of cleaning results in a clean and dry surface hostile to their growth.

2. Even if a disinfectant is used, because a home is not a sterile environment, germs start growing again almost immediately.

3. Most disinfectants have to be left wet on a surface for 10 minutes or so to be effective anyway. If you rinse before the full 10 minutes (which nearly everyone does), what remains are the hardiest bacteria, viruses, etc. If you continue to encourage the hardiest and strongest in this way, you can create a "super" bug (like what sometimes happens in hospitals) and make your home into a "sick house."

4. Disinfectants work because they are poisonous—not only to bacteria and viruses but to larger living things, such as human beings. If you do use them, take steps to protect yourself (e.g., avoid breathing fumes and wear rubber gloves). Here's what my friend, Boston-area physician Geraldine Somers, says on the subject: "In general, the health risks from many commonly used disinfectants hugely overbal-

ance the almost imaginary risk from the organisms they are intended to kill." She adds, "As for toilet bowls, the bacteria in feces that cause disease have to be swallowed in order to cause infection—they don't jump out of the toilet bowl at us. (By the way, most organisms are species specific, so dogs are safe drinking toilet water—unless of course the water is full of toxic cleaners and disinfectants.)"

5. Children, who are being "protected" by their well-meaning parents from the nearly nonexistent threat of sickness from household bacteria and viruses, are not well served by the regular use of disinfectants. Turns out, for children to have fully developed immune systems, they need to be exposed to the normal (bad) stuff that exists in households.

My viewpoint is simple: Keep the house clean, and don't resort to routine use of disinfectants. Your home is not a hospital. That said, there is, as usual, another point of view. If you are one of those who believe you're really not adequately cleaning if you aren't slaughtering every last little bacterium as if you were Rambo himself, go right ahead. Two simple, effective, and inexpensive disinfectants are chlorine bleach and hydrogen peroxide—provided the surface will tolerate their bleaching effects. Geraldine reports that chlorine bleach kills bacteria, viruses (including HIV and hepatitis), fungi, and TB. Hydrogen peroxide (her favorite because it's the safest disinfectant around) kills bacteria, viruses, and fungi, but it doesn't kill TB. She also says that alcohol in 50- to 95-percent strength kills yeast, bacteria, many viruses, and TB, but it does not kill hepatitis B.

Disinfecting Cleaning Brushes

"What should I do to disinfect my toilet brush and my cleaning toothbrush before I put them back in my tray?"

Rinse them in clean water, shake well, and allow them to air-dry. As long as you allow them to dry thoroughly, nearly all harmful microorganisms will perish. As an alternative, you can spray them with a disinfectant or bleach solution.

Having dedicated toothbrushes is also a fine idea. Leave one under the sink in the kitchen and another in each bathroom, so they are handy between weekly cleanings. Put another one in your carryall tray to use in other parts of the house.

Further Reading

Environmentally safe cleaning is obviously a complex issue; much more can be learned. If you are interested in reading further, please see one or more of the references below. One of the most complete presentations of the environmental perspective to date is the *Guide to Hazardous Products around the Home* by the Household Hazardous Waste Project.

Whatever your choices about cleaning products, remember that *the method is more important than the products.* We can assure you that the Speed Cleaning method we've described here works well with a whole range of products whose ultimate selection is up to you.

Notes

1. *California Code of Regulations,* Title 8, *General Industry Safety Orders,* Sec. 5155.
2. Proctor, Nick H., James P. Hughes, and Michael L. Fischman. *Chemical Hazards of the Workplace,* 2nd ed. Philadelphia: J. B. Lippincott, 1988.
3. Gosselin, Robert E., Roger P. Smith, Harold C. Hodge, and Jeanette E. Braddock. *Clinical Toxicology of Commercial Products,* 5th ed. Baltimore: Williams and Wilkins, 1984.
4. Household Hazardous Waste Project, *Guide to Hazardous Products around the Home,* 2nd ed. Springfield, MO: Southwest Missouri State University, 1989. (901 South National, Box 108, Springfield, MO 65804. $9.95. 178 pp. Shipping/handling included. Missouri residents add 61 cents sales tax.)
5. Greenpeace Action. *Everyone's Guide to Toxics in the Home.* (1436 U Street NW, Suite 201-A, Washington, DC 20009. 4 pp. Or request from your local chapter of Greenpeace.)
6. Center for Science in the Public Interest. *The Household Pollutants Guide.* Albert J. Fritsch, ed. Garden City, NY: Anchor Books, 1978.
7. Ecolo-Clean, Inc. 800-373-5606.
8. Elkington, John, Julia Hailes, and Joel Makower. *The Green Consumer.* New York: Penguin, 1990.

Appendix A: How to Order Tools, Equipment, and Supplies

It makes little sense to us to write about cleaning aprons and cleaning solutions if we don't offer some way of enabling you to find them. However, we're not advising you to discard your present cleaners. Use them up, and then if you want to try some of the things we've found to be fast, effective, and personally safe, see below.

Because we use cleaning products daily and test new ones regularly, we have developed very definite opinions about them. We know what works, and we won't tolerate anything that doesn't.

Some of the products have higher initial costs, but they last two to three times longer than the cheaper alternatives. Others have replaceable parts that save money in the long run. And others cost more but just plain work better. For example, even if those cheap chicken-feather dusters you see in the grocery stores were free, we still wouldn't use them because they don't work. We much prefer to use ostrich-down feather dusters that work and that save time week after week.

Sometimes the products we select are the least expensive. For example, our synthetic-bristle whisk broom is less than $2. A whisk broom with natural bristles that continually break off as you use it costs in the $8 range.

Overall, if something new comes along that works better, we change products. We aren't committed to any brand name or manufacturer—only to excellence.

One way to save time in your own housecleaning is to skip all the tests and trials of products that we do. But even if you know what products you want to use, it still takes time to purchase them—especially if they're not carried at the local grocery or hardware store, as is true of many of the professional products we use.

Our catalog can save you time on both accounts, because you can make your choices without leaving your home. The only products we offer are the best ones we've found so far—and we're still looking after all these years.

If you would like a free copy of our catalog, please write us at
The Clean Team
206 N. Main St.
Jackson, GA 95642

If you're in a hurry, call us at 800-717-CLEAN, and we'll mail you one the same day. Or call us or visit our Web site, thecleanteam.com, anytime for solutions to your toughest cleaning questions.

Appendix B: References

If you're feeling a need for more detailed information, here are a few sources for you to explore—via the Internet as well as plain old magazines and books. Our apologies in advance if the Web sites are inoperative: It is the nature of Web sites to be in transition. And we are being by no means thorough here: Reference sources are scattered far and wide, but these are among our favorites.

Web Sites

www.msue.msu.edu/msue/lacmain.html This terrific site is operated by Michigan State University Extension. It is the A-to-Z great-grandmother of all Web sites for home care and maintenance. After reaching the home page, click on FAMILY RESOURCE MANAGEMENT (twice), then HOME MAINTE-NANCE AND REPAIR DATABASE, then HOME MAINTENANCE AND REPAIR.

www.popularmechanics.com An exceptionally well-organized site, this is the Web site of *Popular Mechanics* magazine. From the home page, click HOME IMPROVEMENT, then HOMEOWNER'S CLINIC or SMART CONSUMER or HOME IM-PROVEMENT (again).

www.onthehouse.com This is the Web site of the Associated Press syndicated column "On the House" by James and Morris Carey. Always a pleasure to read, the Carey brothers' columns are clear, thorough without being overwhelming, and well illustrated. They usually discuss repair and remodeling projects, but their maintenance articles are right on target. From the home page, click on NEWSPAPER COLUMN or TIP OF THE WEEK. Or enter "maintenance" as a search term.

www.pacificharbor.com/whpier/pdd The Web site of Pete Prlain, who hosts a syndicated TV and radio show called "How-To with Pete." It offers direct, helpful, and down-to-earth entries on maintenance. From the home page, click on HOW TO or ASK PETE at the bottom of the page.

www.hometime.com This is the Web site of the TV series *Hometime*. From the home page, click on HOME MAINTENANCE, or go to the bottom of the home page, click on SITE SEARCH, and enter "maintenance" as a search term.

For AOL subscribers click on KEYWORD on the top bar, then type "House-Net." Click on the HOME IMPROVEMENT image (not title). All sorts of topics will pop up; REPAIR/MAINTENANCE is particularly helpful.

mkennedy@primenet.com For help with scratched compact discs, contact the Compact Disc Repairman at this e-mail address.

www.service@sonyhawaii.com A good source for answers to your questions about electronic equipment.

www.ge.com/appliance This is the Web address for the GE Parts Master Program. Contact them with the name and number of the appliance for which you need parts.

Magazines

Fans of hers will already know this, but *Martha Stewart Living* can be a gold mine of information on home maintenance. Articles on the subject can be found anywhere in the magazine, but they are typically found in the "Homekeeping" section. Ms. Stewart and her staff are particularly good at finding and interviewing just the right expert (often with decades of experience).

Another essential magazine for home maintenance is *This Old House.* Not an issue goes by without a tantalizing article on a major maintenance topic. They are especially well researched and illustrated. As with *Martha Stewart Living,* a resource section will guide you to sources of products mentioned in the articles. And the more traditional sources should not be overlooked either—especially *Popular Mechanics.* Their regular "Homeowner's Clinic" department is usually the place to check.

Our Previous Book

We couldn't resist the temptation to give our own book a mention. Besides, it's chock-full of good information for any busy person having to deal with any aspect of housekeeping.

Clutter Control (New York: Dell Publishing, 1992): This book addresses the subject of household organization: how to keep the house from being overwhelmed by paper, products, and other modern detritus, how to keep track of the things within the house, and how to keep the household civilized enough to tackle the weekly cleaning chores.

Other Helpful Reading Material

American Institute of Maintenance. *Carpet Selection and Care*, 3rd ed. Glendale, CA: American Institute of Maintenance, 1982.

Bigelow-Sanford, Inc. *Commercial Carpet Maintenance Guide*. (Bigelow-Sanford, Box 3089, Greenville, SC 29602).

Brandt, Herb. *How to Remove Spots and Stains*. New York: Putnam, 1987.

Feldman, Edwin B. *Supervisor's Guide to Custodial and Building Maintenance Operations*. Irvine, CA: Harris Communications, 1982.

Garstein, A. S. *The How-To Handbook of Carpets*. Monsey, NY: The Carpet Training Institute, 1979.

Herberle, Dave. *The Complete Guide to Four Season Home Maintenance*. Cincinnati: Betterway Publications, 1993.

Massey, Frederick R. *The Professional Window Cleaning Manual*. Valley Center, CA: MBM Books, 1983.

Papolos, Janice. *The Virgin Homeowner*. New York: W. W. Norton & Co., 1997.

Peterson, Franklynn. *How to Fix Damn Near Everything*. New York: Bonanza Books, 1989.

Reader's Digest Association, Inc. *Reader's Digest Do-It-Yourself Manual*. Pleasantville, NY: Reader's Digest, 1977.

Reader's Digest Book of Home Do-It-Yourself Projects. New York: Putnam, 1996.

Sack, Thomas F. *A Complete Guide to Building and Plant Maintenance*, 2nd ed. Englewood Cliffs, NJ: Prentice Hall, 1963.

Sandwith, Hermione, and Sheila Stainton. *The National Trust Manual of Housekeeping*. Harmondsworth, England: Penguin Books, 1984.

Shep, Robert L. *Cleaning and Caring for Books*. London: Sheppard Press, 1982.

Shrode, Terry. "Installing a Sheet-Vinyl Floor." *Fine Homebuilding* (August/September 1984): 44–49.

Wright, Veva Penick. *Pamper Your Possessions*, rev. ed. Barre, MA: Barre Publishing, 1979.

Yorkshire, Heidi. *Wine Savvy*. Portland: Duplex Media Group, 1995.

Acknowledgments

Bill Redican, editor and friend, was my writing collaborator and partner in this effort. He contributed much of what is good, clever, and fun here. We both wrote chapters and then passed them back and forth to edit, correct, and make sensible. It's been a fun effort (practically all the time), and our friendship remains intact. Bill has a curiosity about the world and everything and everyone in it that's astonishing and refreshing, and a memory that seemingly works as easily and as quickly for him as it does for my computer. He has been a wealth of professional information in many sections of this book, and his editing skills are once again appreciated. Thank you.

Keith Taylor, with his special skills and dedication, kept The Clean Team cleaning and patiently helped resolve disputes about techniques and products. Thanks again.

Mike Curry, Eric Ernsberger, John Redding, and other members of The Clean Team cheerfully offered their consultation based on an expert involvement with their work.

Neal Devore, owner of Economy Sales in San Francisco, together with his great staff, shared their extensive knowledge of products and procedures with us.

Miguel Cosio, manager of the custodial staff of the City and County of San Francisco and instructor of custodial classes, shared the experience of a lifetime involved in this profession.

Frank Gromm III, of Gromm's Rug and Upholstery Cleaners, Montara, California, offered excellent advice on carpet spotting based upon his 25+ years of experience.

William B. Meyer, purveyor of fine antique silver in San Francisco, offered generous and expert advice on polishing and caring for silver.

Lorraine Umphrey, Hardsurface Products Manager of L. D. Brinkman Co., Ontario, California, was kind enough to help with information on linoleum and other resilient floor coverings.

Sarah Lazin, our agent, is one of those bright, successful, busy professional New York women that everyone reads about. She's always understood that our method of cleaning was meant to include professionals like her, and she's very good at explaining that to the right people.

I also don't know what we would have done without the maintenance knowledge provided by the craft and repair people we were fortunate enough to meet and talk with. Each of them had the rare kind of knowledge that can only be attained from years of hands-on experience repairing and working with the appliances, furniture, drainpipes, faucets, CD players, air conditioners, and so forth that we all have in our homes. By sharing their knowledge, they helped solve little (and not so little) mysteries right and left that make a home seem a bit more comfortable and manageable.

Daniel Bennett is an owner of Omega Television in San Francisco. Since 1974, he has sold and serviced all types of audiovisual equipment and has seen music, sound, and images change from purely mechanical units to today's sophisticated electronics. He has a rare depth of understanding about VCRs, for example, because he sold them when they were first introduced, then started repairing those very first models when they started breaking down.

Keith Bianchi has been in the electronics business in sales, repair, and manufacturing since 1953. He had to restrain himself just so we could keep up with his stream of experienced advice. He is a wealth of knowledge and generous about sharing it. Thank you.

Lewis Downs is an independent audio expert who has been in the industry since 1963. We think he discovered and was recommending Endust as a good antistatic product for electronic audio and stereo equipment before Endust even knew it. Now that Endust has found out and introduced a specialty product just for that purpose, I only hope they send him a nice fat royalty check.

Al Hale, owner of Accurate Appliance, once again took time out of his schedule to share more of his encyclopedic knowledge about appliances. Accurate Appliance was founded by Al's dad in 1939. Al joined the business in 1953 after returning from the Korean War, and his daughter signed on and has been working with him for the past 15 years. I think I can safely say he knows as much about appliance maintenance as anyone in the business.

Jeff Meehan is a partner of Cabrillo Plumbing in San Francisco. His company was rated number one in the country in 1996 and is consistently one of the finest plumbing and heating companies in San Francisco. That kind of great service seems rare these days and makes his achievements that much more admirable. Jeff's enthusiasm and his knowledge are much appreciated.

Tony Uruburu of McRoskey Airflex Mattress Co. works at one of the last great independent businesses in California. Thanks for sharing knowledge learned from years of experience.

After working with her on five books, I think of illustrator Axelle Fortier as an old friend. Since our books were all illustrated, I check out other illustrated books and make comparisons. No one does it better. Her illustrations help us learn and, just as important, they often make us smile. Thanks again.

Jesus Omila Jr., in spite of his own busy schedule, once again helped us stay on schedule by keeping food on the table, drinks in the refrigerator, and the dogs patted and fed.

Also, for the fifth time, thanks to Mike Curry, Rudy Dinkel, Phil Nordeng, and my other partners and friends at The Clean Team.

Index

Boldface page references indicate illustrations. Underscored references indicate boxed text.

A

Acetic acid, 28
Acrylic bathtubs, cleaning, 243
Acrylic floor finish, 16, 137
Acrylic High-Gloss Floor Finish, 16, 135, 137, 142
Aerators, cleaning, 344
Air, maintaining quality of indoor, 308–9
Air cleaners, cleaning, 309
Air conditioners, cleaning
    central, 358–59
    window, 359–61
Air filters, cleaning or changing, 67, 308, 357, 361
Alarms, home security
    cleaning, 377–78
    professional cleaning services and, 285–86
Alcohol, 16–17, 133, 427
Alkaline batteries, maintaining, 311
Aluminum windows, cleaning sliding, 191–92
Ammonia
    for ceiling cleaning, 203
    chlorine with, avoiding combining, 31, 267
    environmental concerns, 421–22
    general uses of, 17
    safety issues, 31, 267
    water and, 44–45
    for window cleaning, 181–82
Amps for vacuum cleaners, 96–97
Anger, avoiding cleaning when feeling, 32
Annual cleaning, 87–88, 227
Antistatic sheets for clothes dryer, 335
Apron, cleaning, 6, 9, 18–19, **19**

Artificial plants, cleaning, 262, 372
Asphalt tile floor, 140

B

Backsplash, cleaning, 248–49
Backtracking, avoiding, 6–8, 43
Baseboard electric heaters, cleaning, 355
Baseboards
    stripping floor and, 157, 164, **164**
    wall cleaning and, 221
Bath mat, cleaning, 244
Bathroom cleaning, 60–61
    bath mat, 244
    bathtub, 50–51, 53–54, 243
    brass fixtures, 239–40
    cobwebs, 56
    countertops, 239
    dressing for, 49
    equipment and supplies, 48–50
    fingerprints, 56–57
    floor, 59–61, 142
    floor plan and, 49, **49**, 50
    grout, 236, 240–41, 241, 242
    hair spray, 245
    marble, 239
    medicine cabinet, 57
    middle of room, 55–57
    mildew, 235, 241–42
    mirrors, 56, 244–45
    nonslip strips, 242–43
    plants, 245–46
    preventive, 303–4
    second, 62
    setting up, 50

Bathroom cleaning (*Cont.*)
  shower
    curtains, 244
    doors and runners or tracks, 52–53, **53**,
      59, 231–33, **232**, 235–36, <u>236</u>
    fiberglass, 234
    hard-water spots, 235–36
    inside, 230–33, 310–11
    mildew, 235
    rinsing, 54, 232
    soap scum, 236
    walls, 51–52, **53**
  showerhead, 239, 379, **379**
  sink, 55, 57
  spare, 62
  spas and whirlpool baths, 243, 409
  starting point, 49, **49**
  toilet
    bowl rings, 237–38
    disinfecting, 238
    floor around, 59
    inside, 55
    maintenance cleaning, 395–97, **395**
    outside, 58
    rusty bowls, 238
    seats, 397, **397**
  towel racks, 56–57
Bathtub
  caulking, 310–11
  cleaning, 50–51, 53–54, 243
  unclogging drain of, 309–10, **309**
Batteries, cleaning and maintaining, 311–12,
  320, 401
BBB, 283
Beater head for vacuum cleaners, <u>100</u>
Bedding, cleaning, 312–14
Bedroom cleaning
  bedding, 312–14
  blankets, 312–13
  comforters, 314
  desk, 76
  dusting, 75–77
  mattresses, 364–65
  miniblinds, 76–77
  pillows, 312, 314
  telephone, 76
Bending in front of door, avoiding, 30
Better Business Bureau (BBB), 283
Bianchi, Keith, 401–3
Big Vac, 28, 98–101

Biodegradability of cleaning products, 425
Black heel marks on floor, cleaning, <u>167</u>
Blankets, cleaning, 312–13
Bleach, 17
  ammonia with chlorine, avoiding com-
    bining, 31, 267
  on carpet, 132
  Clorox, 17, 419–20
  environmental concerns, 419–20
  for mold, 60–61
  safety issues, 31, 267
  for shower cleaning, 231
Blenders, cleaning, 315
Blinds, cleaning, 76–77, 199–201, 365–66
Blood stains, 124, <u>133</u>
Blue Juice, 17
  in apron loop, 19, 35
  for brass fixtures, 239
  for computer monitor, 328
  environmental concerns and, 419
  for mirrors, 56
  for shower door, 59
  spray bottle for, 26
Body odor removal, 269
Bon Ami cleanser, 251–52
Bonnet method of carpet cleaning, 106–9
Books, cleaning, 315–16
Books, cleaning reference sources, 432
Bookshelves, cleaning, 73, 315–16
Borax, powdered, 420
Bottles
  spray, 26
  squirt, 27
Bounty paper towels, 421
Box fan, cleaning, 339
Brass, cleaning
  discoloration, 316–17
  film, 318
  fixtures, cleaning bathroom, 239–40
  maintenance cleaning, 316–18
  stains, 128
Breakage and professional cleaning services,
  287
Brick walls, cleaning, <u>217</u>, 249
Brite floor cleaner, 22
Broom, whisk, 29
Brushes
  ceiling, 18
  disinfecting, <u>427</u>
  floor scrub, 22

scrub, 156
soft-bristled, 18
stiff-bristled, 18
tile, 27
toilet, 27
wall, 18
Bucket, double, 21
Buffet, cleaning mirror-top, 74
Burglar alarm systems
  cleaning, 377–78
  professional cleaning services and, 285–86
Burned spots on carpet, 131–32
Burners, cleaning stove, <u>248</u>
Butcher block, cleaning, 251, 318–19

C

Cabinets, cleaning
  kitchen, 35–38, 249–50
  maintenance cleaning, 319
  medicine, 57
  wood, 249–50
Camcorders, cleaning, 401–2
Cameras, cleaning, 320
Candlesticks, cleaning, 266
Candle wax removal, 265–66
Can openers, cleaning, 42, 256–57, 320–21
Carbona fluid, 121
Carcinogens, 417
Carnauba wax, 22
Carpets, cleaning
  bonnet method, 106–9
  deep-cleaning, 104–6, 111–13
  do-nots regarding, <u>133</u>
  drying out after, 112–13
  dry powder, 105
  equipment and supplies, 105–9
  foam, 105
  maintenance cleaning, 106–9, 321–23
  professional, <u>66</u>, 134
  reference sources, 133
  rotary, 105
  spot-cleaning
    bleach spots, 132
    burned spots, 131–32
    chewing gum, 129–31
    fast treatment, 117–19
    fussy treatment, 119–29
    mildew, <u>130</u>
    solvent stains, 119–23

"spot" versus "stain" and, 115
  strategy, 116–17
  water-based stains, 123–29
steam, 104
tips, <u>133</u>
traffic areas, 109–15, <u>111</u>
vacuuming, 99, **99**
Carryall tray, 18
Cast-iron cooking utensils, cleaning, 323
Catch-up cleaning, 88
Cats. *See also* Pets
  litterboxes, 371
Caulking. *See also* Grout
  bathtub, 310–11
  shower, 233, 310–11
  windows, <u>67</u>, 410–11
Caulks, 311
CDs, cleaning, 325
Ceiling fan, cleaning, 208, 339–40
Ceilings, cleaning
  ammonia for, 203
  brush for, 18
  ceiling fans and, 208
  chair for, 208–9
  cleaning products for, 203–4
  drying, 205
  edges, 206
  equipment and supplies, 204
  furniture and, moving, 207
  ladder for, 208–9
  light fixtures and, 207–8
  maintenance cleaning, 403–4
  porous, 211–12
  reasons for, 203
  rinsing, 206
  scaffold plank for, 209–10, **209**
  Sh-Mop for, 204–5
  starting point, 204–5
  strategies, 205
  walls and, 202, 206, 219, 223–25
  work platform for, 209–11, **209**, **211**
Central air conditioners, cleaning, 358–59
Ceramic
  floor, cleaning, 143–44, 323
  pieces, cleaning, <u>263</u>
Cetaphil Lotion, 304
Chairs
  for ceiling cleaning, 208–9
  cleaning leather, 73
Chandeliers, cleaning, 260–61

Chewing gum, removing from carpet,
129–31
Chimneys, cleaning creosote buildup in, 345
Chlorine. *See* Bleach
Christmas trees, maintaining, 324
Cleaning lady, 271. *See also* Professional
cleaning services
Cleaning products. *See also specific types*
biodegradability of, 425
ceiling, 203–4
concentrates, 425–26
environmental concerns, 414–15, 425–26
floor, 22, 44–45, 145
labels on, 417
oven, 24, 89, 90, 422–23
powdered, 25, 420
wall, 215, 223
Clean surfaces, leaving alone, 9, 62
Clean Team
apron, 19, **19**
catalog, 429–30
leaving clean surfaces alone, 9
in magazine article, 4
questions about cleaning and, 4–5
rules
changing to heavy-duty cleaner or
tool, 10–11
keeping track of your time, 12
maintaining equipment and tools, 11
maximizing movement, 6–8
paying attention, 10–11
repetition for smoother moves, 11
rinsing once, 10
stopping when something is clean, 10
top-to-bottom strategy, 9
using both hands, 12
using right equipment and supplies,
8–9
working as a team, 12
Clervi Marble Co., 251
Clorox bleach, 17, 419–20
Closet
maintenance cleaning, 324
mildew in, cleaning, 267
Clothes dryers, 335–36
Cloths
cleaning, 20–21, **21**
dusting, managing, 66
furniture polishing, 22
Clutter, cleaning, 226–27

Coating, floor
finish versus, 135
polyurethane, 137–38, 152
varnish, 138
Cobwebs, cleaning
bathroom, 56
dusting, 68, 69
kitchen, 39
living room, 68, 69
Coffee grinders, cleaning, 325
Coffeemakers, cleaning, 324–25
Coloring agent for grout, 23
Combination solvents, 121
Comet cleanser, 234, 397, 420
Comforters, cleaning down, 314
Compact disc players, cleaning, 326–27
Companies, professional cleaning, 272. *See
also* Professional cleaning services
Computers, cleaning, 327–28
Concentrates, cleaning, 425–26
Concrete floor, cleaning, 146–47
Consumer Products Safety Commission
(CPSC), 417
Continental Manufacturing Company, 23
Convection oven, cleaning, 328–29
Cookware, cleaning, 323
Cooling systems, cleaning, 358–59
Copper, cleaning
maintenance, 316
stains, 128
Cord caddy, 22
Corian countertops, cleaning, 239
Cork tile floor, 140
Corners
stripping floors and, 164, **164**
wall cleaning and, 222
Couches, cleaning, 71–72
Countertops, cleaning
bathroom, 239
Corian, 239
grout on, 236
kitchen, 35–38
maintenance cleaning, 329
problems, 37–38
Red Juice for, 37–38
CPSC, 417
Crayon marks on walls, cleaning, **223**, 223
Creosote buildup in chimneys, cleaning,
345
Crystal display pieces, cleaning, 329–30

Cupboards, cleaning kitchen, 35–38
Curtains, cleaning, 72, 330

D

Daily cleaning, 226–27
Damp mopping, 176
Deep cleaning. *See also* Ceilings, cleaning;
  Floors, cleaning; Walls, cleaning;
  Windows, cleaning
  carpets, 104–6, 111–13
  catch-up cleaning, 88
  oven, 89–93, 90, 91, **92**
  refrigerator, 94–95, 95
  spring cleaning, 88, 227
Dehumidifiers, cleaning, 330
Desks, cleaning, 76, 269
Digestive stains, 123–24
Digital video disc players, cleaning,
  326–27
Dining room cleaning
  buffet, 74
  dusting, 74–75
  table, 74–75
Dinkel, Rudy, 370
Discoloration, brass, 316–17
Dishes, cleaning hard-water spots on, 256
Dish soap for window cleaning, 181–82
Dishwasher, cleaning, 255–56, 330–31
Disinfectants, 426–27, 427
Dogs. *See also* Pets
  dirt dragged in by, 267–68
  fleas and, 268
Doors
  bending in front of, avoiding, 30
  cleaning
    kitchen, 39
    louvered accordian, 266–67
    maintenance cleaning, 332–33
    shower, 52–53, **53**
    sliding, 333
  doorstops for, 333
  wall cleaning and, 221
Doorstops, installing, 333
Double bucket, 21
Double-hung windows, cleaning, 187–91,
  188, 189, 190
Down comforters, cleaning, 314
Downs, Lewis, 16–17
Dow oven cleaner, 90

Drains, cleaning and unclogging, 309–10,
  309, 333–35, **333**, 344, 391
Drapes, cleaning, 72, 330
Dried plants, cleaning, 262–63, 372
Drip trays, cleaning stove, 248
Dryers
  cleaning clothes, 335–36
  hair, 354–55
Drying
  blankets, 313
  carpets, 112–13
  ceiling, 205
Dry powder carpet cleaning, 105
Duster
  feather, 21–22, 66–68
  rabbit-ear, 25
Dusting
  bedrooms, 75–77
  cloths and, managing, 66
  cobwebs, 68, 69
  dining room, 74–75
  dressing for, 65
  dust mites and, 75
  equipment and supplies, 63–65
  family room, 77–78
  floor, 71
  floor plans and, 65, **65**, 68
  hallway, 75
  living room, 68–74
  overlooked areas in, 77
  preventive dust strategies, 66–67, 302–3,
    337
  starting point, 68
  strategies, 64
  tips, 66–67
  weekly, 257–58
Dust mites, 75
DVDs, cleaning, 325
Dye stains, cleaning, 128–29

E

Easy-Off oven cleaner spray, 24, 89, 90,
  422
Edges and ceiling cleaning, 206
Electrical maintenance, 337–38
Electric blankets, cleaning, 313
Electric heaters, cleaning, 355
Electric stoves, cleaning, 41
Electronic air filters, 357, 361

Electronics, cleaning, 338. *See also specific
        types*
Employment issues and professional cleaning
        surfaces, 273–74, 277–78
Emulsifiable wet stains, cleaning, 129
End tables, cleaning, 70–71, 73–74
Endust, <u>223</u>
Environmental concerns when cleaning, 416
    ammonia, 421–22
    biodegradability, 425
    bleach, 419–20
    Blue Juice, 419
    carcinogens, 417
    cleaning products, 414–15, 425–26
    Comet, 420
    concentrates, 425–26
    Consumer Products Safety Commission
        and, 417
    disinfectants, 426–27, <u>427</u>
    face mask, 415–16
    Federal Hazardous Substances Act and,
        417
    furniture polish, 424
    gloves, rubber, 416
    labels, 417
    Material Safety Data Sheet and, 417, <u>418</u>
    mutagens, 417
    Occupational Safety and Health
        Administration and, 417
    oven cleanser, 422–23
    paper towels, 420–21
    Red Juice, 417–19
    reference sources, 428
    teratogens, 417
    Tile Juice, 423–24
    water conservation, 424–25
Equipment and supplies. *See also specific types*
    acrylic floor finish, 16
    alcohol, 16–17
    ammonia, 17
    apron, cleaning, 18–19, **19**
    bathroom cleaning, 48–50
    bleach, 17
    Blue Juice, 17
    brushes, 17–18
    bucket, double, 21
    carpet cleaning, 105–9
    carrying tray, 18
    ceiling cleaning, 204
    cloths, 20–21, **21**

    dusting, 63–65
    extension cord and cord caddy, 22
    feather duster, 21–22
    floor cleaner and polish, 22
    floor scrub brush, 22
    Furniture Feeder, 22
    furniture polishing cloth, 22
    gloves, rubber, 26
    green scrub pad, 22–23
    grout-color agent, 23
    grout sealer, 23
    HEPA filter, 23
    kitchen cleaning, 33–35
    Kleenfast pad, 23
    liquid floor wax, 23
    maintaining, 11
    miscellaneous, 23
    mop, 23–24
    no-rinse stripper, 24
    no-wax finish, 24
    ordering, 429–30
    oven cleaner, 24
    plastic container, one-pint, 24
    powdered cleanser, 25
    for professional cleaning services, 289–90
    pumice stick, 25
    pump-spray furniture polish, 25
    pump-up pressure sprayer, 25
    rabbit-ear duster, 25
    razor-blade holder, 25
    Red Juice, 25–26
    scraper, 26
    spray bottle, 26
    squeegee, 26
    squeegee extension pole, 26
    squeegee scrub sleeve, 26–27
    squirt bottle, 27
    storing, 11
    stripping floor
        by hand, 154, 156–57
        by machine and wet-dry vac, 161–63
    switching to heavy-duty, 10–11
    tile brush, 27
    Tile Juice, 27
    toilet brush, 27
    toothbrush, 27
    traditional, 14–15
    using right, 8–9
    vacuum cleaners, 28
    variety of, 14

vinegar, white, 28
wall cleaning, 215–16
wax applicator, 28–29
waxing and sealing floor, 166–176
whisk broom, 29
white scrub pad, 29
window cleaning, 178–81, **179**
Ettore squeegee, 179
Exhaust fans, using and cleaning, 308, 340
Exhaust filter, cleaning, 248
Extension cord, 22
Extension pole, <u>189</u>, 192–93, <u>193</u>
Extraction (steam cleaning), 104

F

Fabric on furniture, cleaning, 348
Face mask, 415–16
Family room cleaning
    dusting, 77–78
    floor, 142
    stereo, 78
    television, 78
    VCR/DVD player, 78
Fans, cleaning, 208, 339–40
Faucets
    aerators on, 344
    brass, cleaning, 239–40
    maintenance cleaning
        aerators, 344
        bell faucet, **342**
        cartridge faucet, **343**
        ceramic disc faucet, **343**
        compression faucet, **342**
        washers, 340–44
        water shutoff for, 341, **341**
Fax machines, cleaning, 344
FDA, 421
Feather duster, 21–22, 66–68
Feces, stains from, 125
Federal Hazardous Substances Act, 417
Federal requirements for professional
        cleaning services, 276–77
Fiberglass cleaner, 234–35
Fiberglass shower, cleaning, 234–35
Film, cleaning brass, 318
Fingerprints, cleaning
    bathroom, 56–57
    kitchen, 35–38
    living room, 68

Red Juice for, 68
walls, 218
Finish, floor
    acrylic, 16, 137
    coating versus, 135
    emulsion, 136–37
    liquid, 136
    no-wax, 24, 44, 141–42
    paste wax, 136
    types of, 135–36
    wood, 147
Finishing person on cleaning team, 81
Fire extinguishers, cleaning, 344–45
Fireplaces, cleaning, 345
Fixtures. *See* Faucets; Light fixtures
Flagstone floor, cleaning, 144
Flat paint on walls, cleaning, 213
Fleas, removing, 268
Floor
    cleaning
        around toilet, 59
        bathroom, 59–61, 142
        black heel marks, <u>167</u>
        ceramic, 143–44, 323
        concrete, 146–47
        dusting, 71
        family room, 142
        flagstone, 144
        foyer, 143
        hair on, 59
        hallway, 143
        kitchen, 44–45, 140–42
        laundry room, 142
        living room, 71
        manufactured stone, 144
        marble, 144–46
        masonry, 144–47
        no-wax, 24, 141–42, <u>153</u>
        quarry tile, 143–44
        scrub brush for, 22
        skid marks on, <u>142</u>
        slate, 145, 389–90
        terra cotta, <u>146</u>
        terrazzo, 145
        vacuuming, 99, **99**
        vinyl (with nooks and crannies), 139,
            143
        wax, <u>149</u>
        wood, 147–48, <u>149</u>
    cleaning products, 22, 44–45, 145

Floor (*Cont.*)
  coating
    finish versus, 135
    polyurethane, 137–38, 152
    varnish, 138
  finish
    acrylic, 16, 137
    coating versus, 135
    emulsion, 136–37
    liquid, 136
    no-wax, 24, 44, 141–42
    paste wax, 136
    types of, 135–37
    wood, 147
  grout, 240–41, 240, 241
  life of, extending, 175
  mopping, wet versus damp, 176
  polisher, 22
  preventive cleaning, 301–2, **302**
  replacing, 152
  resilient
    asphalt tile, 140
    concept of, 138
    cork tile, 140
    linoleum sheet, 139
    polyurethane sheet, 139
    rubber tile and sheet, 139–40
    vinyl composition tile, 139
    vinyl sheet (inlaid and rotogravure),
      139
    vinyl tile, 139
  rewaxing, 174–75
  stripping
    baseboards and, 157, 164, **164**
    bathroom, 151
    corners and, 164, **164**
    hardwood, 151
    linoleum, 151
    no-wax, 153
    precautions, 150
    preparation of floor before, 154–76
    professional help with, 152
    replacing floor versus, 152
    Sh-Mop for, 163
    stripper for, choosing, 153
    test areas, 150, 156
    type of floor and strategy used, 149–50
    wax, 149
  water stain on, 148
  waxing and sealing

    cleanup after, 174
    coats, number of, 172
    condition of floor and, 167
    decisions about, 166
    equipment and supplies, 168
    maintenance cleaning, 175–76
    mystery globs, 172
    rewaxing, 174–75
    sealer for, 170
    setting up, 169–70, **169**
    starting point, 168–69
    strategies, 170–71
    traffic areas, 173
    wax applicator, using, 170–72
    wax buildup, 172–73
Floor plans
  bathroom, 49, **49**, 50
  dusting and, 65, **65**, 68
  kitchen, 34, **34**
Foam carpet cleaning, 105
Foam sealant, 410
Food and Drug Administration (FDA),
    421
Food processors, cleaning, 346
Fortified Floor Wax, 23, 135
Foyer floor, cleaning, 143
Freezers, cleaning, 305, 346–47
Freezing method for removing chewing
    gum, 129
French window panes, cleaning, 180, 180
Furnace, cleaning, 356–57
Furniture. *See also specific types*
  cleaning
    fabric, 348
    glass, 348
    grease stains, 350
    leather, 73, 348–50
    water-based stains, 350
    wax buildup, 264–65
    white rings, 261–62
    wicker, 268–69, 350–51
    wood, 351
  moving, 100–101, 207, 323
  polish, 25, 424
  polishing cloth, 22
  reaching under, caution about, 31
  surface protectors and, 347
  vacuuming, 99–101
Furniture Feeder, 22, 264, 319
Future floor finish, 135

G

Garbage disposers, cleaning, 352–54, **353**
Gas stoves, cleaning, 40–41
GFCI, 337–38, **337**
Glass. *See also* Windows, cleaning
  cleaning
    picture, 39, 68–70
    window, 39
  dropping, 31
  furniture, 348
Glazed tile floor, 144
Gloss paint on walls, cleaning, 213
Gloves, rubber, 26, 32, 91, 416
Goddard's paste wax, 424
Granite, cleaning, 251–52, 389
Grease stains, cleaning
  on carpet, 122–23
  on furniture, 350
  Red Juice for, <u>91</u>
  on stove, 91
  on wall, 216
Green scrub pad, 22–23
Gromm, Frank, 129
Ground-fault circuit interrupters (GFCI),
    337–38, **337**
Grout. *See also* Caulking
  in bathroom cleaning, 236, 240–41, <u>241</u>,
    <u>242</u>
  coloring agent, 23
  on countertops, 236
  floor, 240–41, <u>240</u>, <u>241</u>
  maintaining, 354
  sealer, 23
  in shower, 236
  urine stains in, <u>240</u>
  white film and, <u>241</u>
Gump's, 380
Gunk Remover, 122, 131, <u>223</u>

H

Hair dryers, cleaning, 354–55
Hair spray, cleaning, 245
Hale, Al, 255, 331, 376
Hallway cleaning
  dusting, 75
  floor, 143
Hands, using two, 12
Hand stripping floor
  applying stripper, 155–56, **155**

  baseboards and, 157
  cleaning sections of floor, 157
  dirt buildup after, 155–56, **155**
  dressing for, 154
  equipment and supplies for, 154, 156–57
  problem spots, 159
  removing last of stripper, 159–60, **160**
  scraper for, 156–57
  scrub brush for, 156
  scrub pads for, 156–57
  starting point, 154
  steel wool for, 156–57
  strategy, 155, **155**
  summary, 160
  wax removal, 158–59
Hardware, cleaning door, 332–33
Hard-water spots, cleaning
  dishes, 256
  kitchen, 250, 256
  shower, 235–36, <u>236</u>
  window, 194–95
Hardwood floor, stripping, 151
Heaters and heating systems, cleaning, 355–57
Heating, ventilation, and air-conditioning
    (HVAC) systems, 212, 356–57
Heat pumps, cleaning, 361
Heavy cleaning, 88. *See also* Deep cleaning
High-efficiency particulate air (HEPA) filter,
    23, <u>67</u>, 98, 309
High-Gloss Acrylic Floor Finish, 16, 135,
    137, 142
High-maintenance household items, 296–98
Hinges, cleaning door, 332
Home security issues and professional
    cleaning services, 284–86
Hot plates, cleaning, 362
Household employees for cleaning, 273–74,
    277–78. *See also* Professional
    cleaning services
Houseplants. *See* Plants
Howards Restor-A-Finish, 264, 319
Humidifiers, cleaning, 357, 362, **362**
HVAC systems, 212, 356–57
Hydrogen peroxide, 251–52, 427

I

Improvement in cleaning, recording, 83
Independent contractors for cleaning,
    273–74, 277–78

Indoor plants. *See* Plants
Insurance and professional cleaning services,
    286
Internal Revenue Service and professional
    cleaning services, 274–78
Invisible Shield liquid finish, 253
Irons, cleaning, 362–63
IRS and professional cleaning services,
    274–78
Ivory Liquid, 388

J

Jasco's Speedomatic stripper, 317
Johnson Wax Co., 24

K

Keyboard, cleaning computer, 327–28
Kirby vacuum cleaner, 97
Kitchen cleaning
    backsplash, 248–49
    blenders, 315
    brick wall, 249
    butcher's block, 251, 318–19
    cabinets, 35–38, 249–50
    can opener, 42, 256–57, 320–21
    cobwebs, 39
    coffee grinders, 325
    coffeemakers, 324–25
    cookware, 323
    countertops, 35–38
    cupboards, 35–38
    dishwasher, 255–56, 330–31
    doors, 39
    dressing for, 35
    equipment and supplies, 33–34
    exhaust filters, 248
    fingerprints, 35–38
    floor, 44–45, 140–42
    floor plan and, 34, **34**
    food processors, 346
    freezers, 305, 346–47
    garbage disposer, 352–54, **353**
    hard-water spots, 250, 256
    hot plates, 362
    microwave oven, 42, 365
    middle of room, 42, 254
    "miracle" mops and, 253
    mirrors, 39

mixers, 367
oven
    cleaning products, 24, 89, 90,
        422–23
    convection, 328–29
    deep cleaning, 89–93, 90, 91, **92**
    maintenance cleaning, 367–68
    microwave, 42, 365
    racks, 91
    self-cleaning, 90
    stainless steel hood on, 91
    toaster, 42, 394–95
picture glass, 39
preventive, 302
refrigerator
    coils, 347
    deep cleaning, 94–95, 95
    maintenance cleaning, 374–77, **374**
    outside, 39–40
    Red Juice for, 377
    shelves, 95
    sticker residue, 95
rice cookers, 387
rust, 253–54
salt and pepper shakers, 256
setting up for, 35
shelves
    glass, 250
    open, 39
Sh-Mop for, 44–45
sink, 43, 252–54, 384–85
spice grinders, 325
stains
    granite, 251–52
    porcelain, 252–53
    stainless steel, 253–54
starting point, 34, **34**
steamers, 387
stove
    burners, 248
    ceramic or black glass top, 391–92
    drip trays, 248
    electric, 41
    enamel top, 390–91
    front, 41–42
    gas, 40–41
    glass stove top, 247–48
    grease stains, 91
    hoods, 91, 392
    inside surface, 246–47

porcelain stove top, 247–48
top, 40–41, 247–48, 390–92
strategies, 246
summary of, 46–47
teakettle, 392
toaster, 42, 394–95
toaster oven, 42, 394–95
windows, 39
Kiwi Bois paste wax, 424
Kleenfast pads, 23
Knickknacks, cleaning, 70–71, 263

L

Labels on cleaning products, 417
Lacquer thinner, 129
Ladder
for ceiling cleaning, 208–9
for wall cleaning, 224
Lamp shades, cleaning, 263, 363–64
Language problems with professional
cleaning services, 292
Laundry
blankets, 312–13
clothes dryers, 335–36
down comforters, 314
floor in, cleaning, 142
irons and, cleaning, 362–63
pillows, 312, 314
washing machines, 404–6
Leaks, fixing
faucet, 340–44, **341**, **342**, **343**
toilet, 395–97, **395**
Leather furniture, cleaning, 73, 348–50
Liability insurance and professional cleaning
services, 286
Lightbulbs, preventive cleaning and, 304
Lighter fluid, 121–22
Light fixtures, cleaning, 207–8, 364
Limestone, cleaning, 389
Linoleum sheet floor, 139, 151
Lint screen on clothes dryer, cleaning, 336
Liquid cleaners, caution about, 32
Liquid floor wax, 23
Litter boxes, cleaning kitty, 371
Little Vac, 28, 101–3
Living room cleaning
bookshelves, 73
chairs, leather, 73
cobwebs, 68, 69

couches, 71–72
drapes, 72
dusting, 68–74
end tables, 70–71
fingerprints, 68
floor, 71
middle of room, 73
plants, 72
tables, 70–71, 73–74
wall marks, 70
window frames, 72
Longest cleaning job, 79–80
Looking up when cleaning, caution about,
30–31
Louvered accordian doors, cleaning, 266–67

M

Machine and wet-dry vac stripping floor
baseboards and, 164, **164**
corners and, 164, **164**
dressing for, 163
equipment and supplies, 161–63
picking up mess, 165, **165**
starting point, 163
stubborn spots, 165–66
Magazines, cleaning reference sources, 432
Maintenance cleaning. *See also specific areas
and items*
advantages of, 270, 299
carpets, 106–9, 321–23
caution about, 299
ceiling, 212
floor, waxed and sealed, 175–76
high-maintenance items and, 296–98
resources for, 295–96, 299–300
rules, 305–7
walls, 225, 403–4
Manufactured stone floor, cleaning, 144
Manufacturers's instructions, following, 299
Marble, cleaning
bar, 265
in bathroom, 239
Corian countertops, 239
floor, 144–46
maintenance cleaning, 389
Masonry floor, cleaning, 144–47
Material Safety Data Sheet (MSDS), 417,
418
Mattresses, cleaning, 364–65

McRoskey Airflex Mattress Co., 364–65
Medicine cabinet, cleaning, 57
Metallic stains, 128
Microwave ovens, cleaning, 42, 365
Mildew
    cleaning
        in bathroom, 235, 241–42
        bleach, 420
        books, 315–16
        on carpet, 130
        in closet, 266
    moisture issues and, 308–9
    preventing, 241–42, 267
    Tile Juice for, 235
Miniblinds, cleaning, 76–77, 199–201,
        365–66
"Miracle" mops, 253
Mirrors
    cleaning
        bathroom, 56, 244–45
        Blue Juice for, 56
        buffet, 74
        kitchen, 39
        living room, 68–70
    hanging, 32
    maintenance cleaning, 366–67
Mixers, cleaning handheld and standing, 367
Moisture issues, 308–9, 411
Mold, 60–61, 308–9
Molding and wall cleaning, 221
Monitor, cleaning computer, 328
Mop, 23–24
Mop-on No-Rinse Acrylic Stripper, 24
Mopping, wet versus damp, 176
Motivation for cleaning, 3–5
Mouse, cleaning computer, 328, **328**
Movement in cleaning, maximizing, 6–8,
        43
Mr. Muscle oven cleaner, 90
MSDS, 417, 418
Murphy's Oil Soap, 388
Mutagens, 417

N

National Association of Mirror
        Manufacturers, 366
National Christmas Tree Association, 324
Nickel-cadmium batteries, maintaining, 312
Nicotine on walls, cleaning, 217

Nonslip strips in bathroom, cleaning,
        242–43
No-rinse stripper, 24
No-wax floor, cleaning and stripping, 24,
        141–42, 153

O

Occupational Safety and Health
        Administration (OSHA), 417
Odor removal
    body, 269
    from dishwasher, 255
Oil-based solvents, 120–22
Oil paintings, cleaning, 264, 368–69
Old English furniture polish, 25, 70
Organization before cleaning, 228–29
Oscillating fan, cleaning, 339
OSHA, 417
Outdoors, vacuuming, 102–3
Oven cleanser, 24, 89, 90, 422–23
Ovens
    cleaning products for, 24, 89, 90, 422–23
    convection, 328–29
    deep cleaning, 89–93, 90, 91, **92**
    maintenance cleaning, 367–68
    microwave, 42, 365
    racks, 91
    self-cleaning, 90
    stainless steel hood on, 91
    toaster, 42, 394–95
Overloaded circuits, 338
Owner's manuals, following, 299

P

Paint
    flat, 213
    gloss, 213
    semigloss, 213
    splatters on window, cleaning, 193
Paintings, cleaning oil, 264, 368–69
Paper towels, 420–21
Patio tile floor, 144
Paver tile floor, 144
Pets. *See also* Cats; Dogs
    bathing, 370
    cleaning around, 369–71
    dishes, 370
    fleas, 268

grooming, 370, **370**
urine stains from, 125–26
vacuuming hair from, 103–4
Pewter, cleaning, 371
Phosphates, 423
Phosphoric acid, 423
pH scale, 385
Pianos, cleaning, 371–72
Pictures
cleaning
kitchen, 39
living room, 68–70
hanging, 32
Pigment stains, cleaning, 128–29
Pillows, cleaning, 312, 314
Plants, cleaning
artificial, 262, 372
in bathroom, 245–46
dried, 262–63, 372
in living room, 72
natural, 72, 245–46, 372–74
Plastic container, one-pint, 24
Plunger, using, 334
Polyurethane floor coating, 137–38, 152
Polyurethane sheet floor, 139
Porcelain sink, cleaning, 385
Porcelain stains, cleaning, 252–53
Porch, vacuuming, 102
Porous ceiling, 211–12
Portable electric fan heaters, cleaning, 355
Poultice, 251–52
Powdered cleansers, 25, 420
Practice and cleaning, 84
Preventive cleaning
bathroom, 303–4
dusting, 302–3
floors, 301–2, **302**
kitchen, 302
lightbulbs, 304
silver, 304
Professional cleaning services
boundary issues and, 289
breakage, 287
cancellations, 286–87
carpets, 66, 134
cleaning lady, 271
companies, 272
complaints about, 288–89
as employee, 273–74
employment issues and, 273–74, 277–78

equipment and supplies for, 289–90
federal requirements and, 276–77
home security issues and, 284–86
as independent contractor, 273–74,
277–78
insurance and, 286
Internal Revenue Service and, 274–78
language problems and, 292
lateness issues, 286–87
liability insurance and, 286
managing, 279
motivating, 280–82
problems with, 278–79
rates, 283–84
relationship with, 279–80, 288–89
scheduling, 286–87, 290
security alarms and, 285–86
selecting, 282–83
Social Security issues and, 274–78
special instructions for, 291
state requirements and, 277
tax issues and, 274–78
temporary, 271–72
terms of, 272–73
tipping, 291–92
training, 292
P-trap, 333, **333**, 344
Pumice stick, 25
Pump-spray furniture polish, 25
Pump-up pressure sprayer, 25

Q

Quarry tile floor, cleaning, 143–44
Questions about cleaning, answering, 3–5

R

Rabbit-ear duster, 25
Radiator, cleaning steam, 266
Radiator oil heaters, cleaning, 355
Rainbow vacuum cleaner, 97
Razor blade, 193, 265
Razor-blade holder, 25
Rechargeable batteries, maintaining, 312
Red Juice, 25–26
in apron loop, 11, 19, 35
for blood stains, 124
for brass fixtures, 239
for cabinets, 319

Red Juice (*Cont.*)
   for can openers, 42, 321
   for carpet spots, 112, 118, 133
   for ceiling fans, 208
   for chewing gum removal, 129, 131
   for countertops, 37–38
   for emulsifiable wet stains, 129
   environmental concerns, 417–19
   for feces stains, 125
   for fingerprints, 68
   for grease stains, <u>91</u>
   for kitchen countertops, 37–38
   for marble, 265
   for microwave oven, 365
   for oven deep cleaning, 90–91
   for pet stains and slobber, 371
   for pet urine stains, 125
   for refrigerator, 377
   for self-cleaning ovens, <u>90</u>
   for shower doors, 53
   for silver, 382
   for sinks
      bathroom, 57
      kitchen, 43
   for telephone, 393
   for toaster, 42, 395
   for toilet, 58
   for toilet seat, 397
   toothbrush for scrubbing with, 27
   for wall cleaning, 216
Red wine stains, cleaning, 126–28
Reference sources, cleaning
   books, 432
   carpet cleaning, 133
   environmental concerns, 428
   magazines, 432
   other, 433
   Web sites, 431–32
Refrigerators, cleaning
   coils, 347
   deep cleaning, 94–95, <u>95</u>
   maintenance cleaning, 374–77, **374**
   outside, 39–40
   Red Juice for, 377
   shelves, 95
   sticker residue, <u>95</u>
Remote controls, cleaning, 377
Repairs, minor, 269–70
Repetition for smoother moves, 11
Resilient floor

asphalt tile, 140
   concept of, 138
   cork tile, 140
   linoleum sheet, 139
   polyurethane sheet, 139
   rubber tile and sheet, 139–40
   vinyl composition tile, 139
   vinyl sheet
      inlaid, 139
      rotogravure, 139
   vinyl tile, 139
Resurfaced tubs, cleaning, 243
Rewaxing floor, 174–75
Rice cookers, cleaning, 387
Ring in toilet bowl, cleaning, 237–38
Rinsing
   bathtub, 54
   ceiling, 206
   once, 10
   shower, 54, 232
Rolltop desk, cleaning, 269
Rotary carpet cleaning, 105
Rubber gloves, 26, 32, 91, 416
Rubber tile and sheet floor, 139–40
Rubbing alcohol, 16, <u>133</u>
Rugs. *See* Carpets; Throw rugs
Rust, cleaning
   from stainless steel, 253–54
   from toilet bowl, 238
Rust-Oleum, 413

S

Safety issues when cleaning, 30–32, 267
Salt and pepper shakers, cleaning, 256
Scaffold plank for ceiling cleaning, 209–10,
   209
Sconces, cleaning brass, 317
Scotchguard surface protector, 348
Scraper
   general uses of, 26
   for stripping floor, 156–57
   technique, 38, **38**, 52–53, **53**
Screens, cleaning window, 198–99
Scrub brush, 156
Scrub pads
   green, 22–23
   Kleenfast, 23
   for stripping floor, 156–57
   white, 29

Sealants, grout, 23
Second bathroom, cleaning, 62
Security alarms, home
    cleaning, 377–78
    professional cleaning services and, 285–86
"See-through" process of cleaning, 10, 92
Self-cleaning ovens, 90
Semigloss paint on walls, cleaning, 213
Septic system, cleaning, 354, 378–79
Services, outside cleaning. *See* Professional
        cleaning services
Shades, cleaning lamp, 263, 363–64
Sh-Clean floor cleaner, 145
Shelves, cleaning
    book, 73
    glass, 250
    open, 39
    refrigerator, 95
Sh-Mop
    ceiling cleaning, 204–5
    general uses of, 24
    for kitchen cleaning, 44–45
    for stripping floor, 163
    for wall cleaning, 217, 217, 220–21
Shoe polish stains, 122
Shower
    caulking, 233, 310–11
    cleaning
        curtains, 244
        doors and runners or tracks, 52–53, **53**,
            59, 231–33, **232**, 235–36, 236
        fiberglass, 234
        hard-water spots, 235–36
        inside, 230–33, 310–11
        mildew, 235
        rinsing, 54, 232
        soap scum, 236
        walls, 51–52, **53**
    recaulking, 233
Showerhead, cleaning, 239, 379, **379**
Sh-Wipes, 205, 221
Silver, cleaning
    do-nots in, 381
    maintenance cleaning, 380–84
    ornate objects, 383
    polish for, 381
    preventive cleaning, 304, 383–84
    Red Juice for, 382
    treated cloth storage bag and, 380
Sink, cleaning

bathroom, 55, 57
kitchen, 43, 252–54, 384–85
maintenance cleaning, 384–85
porcelain, 385
stainless steel, 385
Skid marks on floor, cleaning, 142
Slate, cleaning, 145, 389–90
Sliding aluminum windows, cleaning,
        191–92
Sliding doors, cleaning, 333
Smoke detectors, cleaning, 385–86
Soap scum, cleaning, 31, 236
Social Security issues and professional
        cleaning services, 274–78
Soft-bristled brushes, 18
Solvent stains
    cleaning
        grease, 122–23
        shoe polish, 122
        tape residue, 123
    examples of, 120
    oil-based, 120–22
Soot on walls, cleaning, 217
Spare bathroom, cleaning, 62
Spas, cleaning, 243, 409
Speakers, cleaning sound, 386–87
Spice grinders, cleaning, 325
Spot-cleaning
    carpets
        bleach spots, 132
        burned spots, 131–32
        chewing gum, 129–31
        fast treatment, 117–19
        fussy treatment, 119–29
        mildew, 130
        solvent stains, 119–23
        "spot" versus "stain" and, 115
        strategy, 116–17
        water-based stains, 123–29
    walls, 216–18
Spots
    on carpet
        pretreating, 109
        Red Juice for, 112, 118, 133
        "stains" versus, 115
    floor
        black heel marks, 167
        skid marks, 142
    hard-water on window, 194–95
    on wall, 222

Spring cleaning, 87–88, 227
Squeegee
    Ettore, 179
    extension pole, 26
    general uses of, 26
    scrub sleeve, 26–27
    troubleshooting, 193–97
    for window cleaning, 179–80, **179**
Stainless steel sink, cleaning, 253–54, 385
Stains
    carpet, pretreating, 109
    dishwasher, 254–55
    granite, 251–52
    porcelain, 252–53
    solvent
        examples of, 120
        grease, 122–23, 216, 350
        oil-based, 120–22
        shoe polish, 122
        tape residue, 123
        "spot" versus, 115
    stainless steel, 253–54
    wall, 216, 222
    water-based
        blood, 124, <u>133</u>
        brass, 128
        copper, 128
        digestive, 123–24
        dye or pigment, 128–29
        emulsifiable, 129
        feces, 125
        on furniture, 350
        metallic, 128
        pet urine, 125–26
        red wine, 126–28
        tannin, 126, <u>127</u>
    water on floor, <u>148</u>
Stairs, vacuuming, 101
Stairwell work platform, 211, **211**
State requirements for professional cleaning
        services, 277
Steam cleaning carpets, 104
Steamers, cleaning, 387
Steam radiator, cleaning, <u>266</u>
Steel wool, 156–57
Stereo, cleaning, 78
Sticker residue, cleaning, <u>95</u>
Stiff-bristled brushes, 18
Stone building materials, cleaning, 387–90.
        See also specific types

Storage areas, cleaning, 390
Storage bags, 19
Stoves, cleaning
    burners, <u>248</u>
    ceramic or black glass top, 391–92
    drip trays, <u>248</u>
    electric, 41
    enamel top, 390–91
    front, 41–42
    gas, 40–41
    glass stove top, 247–48
    grease stains, <u>91</u>
    hoods, <u>91</u>, 392
    inside surface, 246–47
    porcelain stove top, 247–48
    top, 40–41, 247–48, 390–92
Streaks, cleaning window and mirror, <u>195</u>,
        244–45
Stripper solution
    applying, 155–56, **155**
    choosing, 153
    no-rinse, 24
    removing last of, 159–60, **160**
Stripping floor. *See also* Hand stripping
        floor; Machine and wet-dry vac
        stripping floor
    baseboards and, 157, 164, **164**
    bathroom, 151
    corners and, 164, **164**
    hardwood, 151
    linoleum, 151
    no-wax, <u>153</u>
    precautions, 150
    preparation of floor for
        by hand, 154–61
        by machine and wet-dry vac, 161–76
    professional help for, 152
    replacing floor versus, <u>152</u>
    Sh-Mop for, 163
    stripper for, choosing, 153
    test areas, 150, <u>156</u>
    type of floor and, 149–50
    wax, 149
    waxing and sealing floor after
        cleanup after, 174
        coats, number of, 172
        condition of floor and, 167
        decisions about, 166
        equipment and supplies, 168
        maintenance cleaning, 175–76

mystery globs, 172
rewaxing, 174–75
sealer for, 169
setting up, 169–70, **169**
starting point, 168–69
strategies, 170–71
traffic areas and, 173
wax applicator, using, 170–72
Supplies. *See* Equipment and supplies
Surface protector pads, 368–69, **368**
Surface protectors for furniture, 347
Surge protector, computer, 327

T

Tables, cleaning
dining room, 74–75
end, 70–71, 73–74
living room, 70–71, 73–74
Tannin stains, cleaning, 125, 127
Tape residue, removing, 123
TASCAM RC rubber cleaner, 17
Tax issues and professional cleaning services,
274–78
Teakettles, cleaning, 392
Team cleaning, 12, 79–80, **80**, 81–83
Teenagers and cleaning, 82–83
Telephone answering machines, cleaning, 393
Telephones, cleaning, 76, 392–93
Televisions, cleaning, 78, 393
Temporary professional cleaning service,
271–72
Teratogens, 417
Termites, removing, 394
Terra cotta floor, cleaning, 146
Terrazzo floor, cleaning, 145
Test areas for stripping floor, 150, 156
Thermostats, cleaning, 394
3M's Safest Stripper, 317
Three-member cleaning teams, 82
Throw rugs, vacuuming, 101
Tile brush, 27
Tile Juice
for bathtub cleaning, 53
environmental concerns, 423–24
for fiberglass, 234–35
general uses of, 27
for mildew, 235
recommendation of, 4
for shower walls, 51–52

Tipping professional cleaning services,
291–92
Toaster ovens, cleaning, 42, 394–95
Toasters, cleaning, 42, 394–95
Toilet, cleaning
bowl rings, 237–38
disinfecting, 238
floor around, 59
inside, 55
maintenance cleaning, 395–97, **395**
outside, 58
rusty bowls, 238
seats, 397, **397**
Toilet brush, 27
Tools. *See* Equipment and supplies
Toothbrush, 27
Top-to-bottom cleaning strategy, 9, 102,
220, 224–25
Towel racks, cleaning, 56–57
Traffic areas
cleaning carpet, 109–15, 111
waxing and sealing floor and, 173
Training professional cleaning services, 292
Trash compactors, cleaning, 397–98
Tray, carryall, 18
Troubleshooting
spray cleaner, 197–98
squeegee, 193–97
team cleaning, 81
Tub. *See* Bathtub
TV, cleaning, 78, 393

U

Urethane floor coating. *See* Polyurethane
floor coating
Urine stains, cleaning
in grout, 240
pet, 125–26
Uruburu, Tony, 365

V

Vacation maintenance checklist, 398
Vacuum cleaners, 28, 96–98
amps for, 96–97
beater head for, 100
Big Vac, 28, 98–101
canister, standard, 28
changing bags on, 66

Vacuum cleaners (*Cont.*)
    Little Vac, 28, 101–3
    maintenance cleaning, 399–401, **400**
    upright, 28
Vacuuming
    with Big Vac, 28, 98–101
    carpets, 99, **99**
    floors, 99, **99**
    furniture, 99–101
    with Little Vac, 28, 101–3
    as longest cleaning job, 79
    outdoors, 102–3
    pet hair, 103–4
    porch, 102
    screens on window, 198
    stairs, 101
    throw rugs, 101
    weekly, 257–60
Valuable Leisure Time (VLT), 10, 15
Varathane floor coating. *See* Polyurethane
    floor coating
Varnish floor coating, 138
Vase, cleaning, 263–64
VCR/DVD player, cleaning, 78
VCRs, cleaning, 401
Vent duct on clothes dryer, cleaning, 336
Vent fans, cleaning, 340
Vertical blinds, 201
Video camcorders, cleaning, 401–2
Video cassette recorders (VCRs), cleaning,
    401
Videotapes, cleaning, 402–3
Vinegar, white, 28, 128
Vinyl composition tile floor, 139
Vinyl sheet (inlaid and rotogravure), 139
Vinyl tile floor, 139, 143
VLT, 10, 15

W

Wallpaper, cleaning, 216, 403
Walls, cleaning
    baseboards and, 221
    brick, <u>217</u>, 249
    brush for, 18
    ceilings and, 202, 206, 219, 223–25
    cleaning products for, 215, 223
    corners and, 222
    crayon marks, **223**, <u>223</u>
    equipment and supplies, 215–16

    fingerprints, 218
    flat paints, 213
    gloss paints, 213
    grease stains, 216
    ladder for, 224
    living room, 70
    maintenance cleaning, 225, 403–4
    marks on, 70
    molding and, 221
    nicotine, 217
    nooks and crannies, 221–22
    preparation work for, 218–19
    Red Juice for, 216
    semigloss paints, 213
    Sh-Mop for, 217, <u>217</u>, 220–21
    shower, 51–52, **53**
    soot, <u>217</u>
    spot-cleaning, 216–18
    spots, 222
    stains, 222
    strategies, 220–22
    wallpaper, 216, 403
    window cleaning and, 221
    work platform for, 224
Washers on faucets, replacing worn, 340–44
Washing machines, cleaning, 404–6
Water-based stains, cleaning
    blood, 124, <u>133</u>
    brass, 128
    copper, 128
    digestive, 123–24
    dye or pigment, 128–29
    emulsifiable, 129
    feces, 125
    on floor, <u>148</u>
    on furniture, 350
    metallic, 128
    pet urine, 125–26
    red wine, 126–28
    tannin, 126, <u>127</u>
Water conservation, 424–25
Water heaters, cleaning, 332, 344, 406–8, **406**
Water pipes, cleaning and maintaining, 409
Water softeners, cleaning, 408–9
Water stain on floor, cleaning, <u>148</u>
Wax
    buildup, 172–73, 264–65
    liquid floor, 23
    removing, 158–59
Wax applicator, 28–29, 170–72

Wax floor, cleaning and stripping, <u>149</u>
Waxing and sealing floor
   cleanup after, 174
   coats, number of, 172
   condition of floor and, 167
   decision about, 166
   equipment and supplies, 168
   maintenance cleaning, 175–76
   mystery globs, 172
   rewaxing, 174–75
   sealer for, <u>169</u>
   setting up, 169–70, **169**
   starting point, 168–69
   strategies, 170–71
   traffic areas and, <u>173</u>
   wax applicator, using, 170–72
   wax buildup and, 172–73
WD-40, <u>223</u>, 397
Weather stripping around windows, 411, **411**
Web sites, cleaning reference sources, 431–32
Weekly cleaning, 226, 228–29. *See also specific areas and items*
Wet-dry vacuum, 165. *See also* Machine and wet-dry vac stripping floor
Wet mopping, <u>176</u>
Whirlpool baths, cleaning, 243, 409
Whisk broom, 29
White film in bathroom, cleaning, <u>241</u>
White rings on furniture, cleaning, 261–62
White scrub pad, 29, 38
White vinegar, 28, 128
Wicker furniture, cleaning, 268–69, 350–51
Window air conditioners, cleaning, 359–61
Windows
   caulking, <u>67</u>, 410–11
   cleaning
      ammonia for, 181–82
      attitude toward, common, 177–78
      cleaning solutions for, 181–82
      dish soap for, 181–82
      double-hung, 187–91, **188**, **189**, **190**
      dressing for, 181
      equipment and supplies, 178–81, **179**
      extension pole for, <u>189</u>, 192–93, <u>193</u>
      frames, 72, 187
      French panes, 180, <u>180</u>
      hard-water spots, 194–95
      kitchen, 39
      large, 187
      miniblinds and, 76–77, 199–201
      paint splatters, 193
      preparing window sills and, 181
      safety issues, 31
      screens and, 198–99
      sliding aluminum, 191–92
      spray cleaner troubleshooting, 197–98
      squeegee for, 179–80, **179**, 193–97
      starting point, 182–83
      streaks, <u>195</u>
      technique, 183–86, **185**
      window scrubber for, 180
   foam sealant for, 410
   maintenance cleaning, 409–12
   moisture issues and, 411
   wall cleaning and, 221
   weather stripping around, 411, **411**
Window scrubber, 180
Wood
   blinds, 201
   cabinets, 249–50
   floor
      cleaning, 147–48, <u>149</u>
      finishes, 147
   furniture, 351
Work platform
   for ceiling cleaning, 209–11, **209**, **211**
   for wall cleaning, 224
Wrought iron, cleaning and maintaining, 413

Y

Yearly cleaning, 88, 227

Z

Ziploc storage bags, 19